Constitutional Development in the USSR

A GUIDE TO THE SOVIET CONSTITUTIONS

ARYEH L. UNGER

Constitutional Development in the USSR

A GUIDE TO THE SOVIET CONSTITUTIONS

PICA PRESS

NEW YORK

Published in the United States of America in 1982
by Pica Press
Distributed by Universe Books
381 Park Avenue South, New York, N.Y. 10016

Printed in the United States of America

Library of Congress Cataloging in Publication Data

Unger, Aryeh L.
  Constitutional development in the USSR.

  Bibliography: p.
  Includes index.
  1. Soviet Union – Constitutional history. I. Title.
  LAW   342.47'029   81-12022
  ISBN 0-87663-732-2   344.70229   AACR2

Contents

Preface

This volume is designed to fill a gap in the textbook literature on Soviet government by enabling students to familiarize themselves with the contents of Soviet constitutions – aided, it is hoped, by commentary and annotation. It is an attempt to look at the political institutions and practices of the Soviet state through the prism of its own constitutional texts. The view thus obtained cannot reveal all facets of a multi-faceted reality; but I believe that it can reveal facets obscured by other prisms or 'models'.

The book contains the texts of all four Soviet constitutions. A chapter of commentary precedes each text and an overall assessment of Soviet constitutional development is offered in the concluding chapter.

The texts of the constitutions are presented in their original versions at time of adoption. Subsequent amendments are recorded in the notes on each text. The only amendments not fully recorded are those pertaining to the frequent and relatively inconsequential changes in the administrative-territorial divisions of the union republics and the structure of the all-union and union republic governments; in these cases only the final version of the relevant article is noted.

Although I have consulted other translations of Soviet constitutions, the translations in this book are my own and so is the responsibility for any errors or avoidable infelicities of language. I have naturally tried to adopt a consistent set of English equivalents, but exceptions had to be made where literal consistency might have obstructed understanding. Such adjustments will probably not be noticed by the reader who has only the English text before him. He may, however, be troubled by such apparent inconsistencies as 'deputy' and 'delegate' in the same article of the 1918 constitution, or 'nationwide vote (referendum)' and 'popular vote (referendum)' in different articles of the 1977 constitution – not to mention 'nationwide poll (referendum)' in the 1936 constitution. It should be stressed, therefore, that such variations are not due to unwarranted 'translator's licence' but reflect corresponding variations in the original. Apart from transforming the Russian present indicative tense into the English future imperative, I have generally endeavoured to adhere as closely as possible to the language of the original. In several cases this may have entailed some loss of readability; if so, my excuse is that I have sought to convey the original style without loss of precision.

Bibliographic references are confined in the main to works in English. Also, in order not to clutter up the annotations with further detail, I have not thought it necessary to provide citations to the official gazette and similar primary sources; readers wishing to consult the original will be able to trace it without difficulty from the date of enactment.

1980   ARYEH L. UNGER

Introduction

A constitution is fictitious when law and reality diverge; it is not fictitious when they coincide.

Lenin in 1909

I think that the Constitution of the USSR is the only thoroughly democratic Constitution in the world.

Stalin in 1936

We have not created the Constitution as a stage prop.

Brezhnev in 1977

When Aristotle enjoined students of politics to study constitutions he referred to 'an organization of offices in a state, by which the method of their distribution is fixed, the sovereign authority is determined, and the nature and end to be pursued by the association and all its members is prescribed'.[1] This might still serve as a good description of the contents of the formal 'documentary constitutions' of modern states. But it was not, of course, the sense in which Aristotle used the term. 'Constitution' (a translation of the Greek *politeia*) meant for Aristotle a system of social action and valuation 'directed to attaining a particular quality of life'; it embraced the reality of the political life of a state (city) and not merely the particular principles and legal rules abstracted from that reality and codified in a written document designated as 'the constitution'. Clearly, no political scientist setting out to study what we now call the 'political system' of a state can expect to find more than partial illumination from a study of such a document. The Soviet Union has enacted four constitutions – in 1918, 1924, 1936 and 1977. They will be analysed below against the background of Soviet political reality. But a book on the development of Soviet constitutions is assuredly not a book on the development of Soviet politics.

To acknowledge the limitations inherent in studying a political system through its constitutional texts is not to concede that such a study cannot yield valuable insights. Constitutions, it has been said, are 'power maps'.[2] And if political science may be defined as 'the study of the shaping and sharing of power',[3] then use of such a map should not be dismissed lightly. It may be argued that Soviet constitutions are incomplete, inaccurate and even deliberately misleading 'power maps'. This is certainly true, but it merely means that they require careful interpretation and must be used with due caution. When thus interpreted and used, Soviet constitutions can provide useful clues to the distribution of power in the system. Like other political elites, those of the Soviet Union came to realize that their rule required order and regularity and legitimacy, and that the formalization of public power in an authoritative legal document was an efficient means to these ends.

But Soviet constitutions are not only organizational charts of the power structure. They are also prescriptions for 'the nature of the end to be pursued by the association and all its members'. They are programmes for action; they elaborate the aims and purposes of the regime, they set out its agenda of perceived problems and projected solutions. 'This is our policy', said Lenin in 1921, 'and you will find it in our constitution.'[4] The statement was obviously less than the whole truth, but it reflected a view of the constitution as a document proclaiming general policy objectives. By contrast, Stalin drew a sharp distinction in 1936 between a programme and a constitution:

> Whereas a programme speaks of that which does not yet exist, of that which has yet to be achieved and won in the future, a constitution, on the contrary, must speak of that which already exists, of that which has already been achieved and won now, at the present time.

The new 1936 constitution, he insisted repeatedly, was 'the registration and legislative embodiment of that which has already been achieved and won'.[5] It was left to Brezhnev in 1977 to give a rather different and more accurate characterization of the nature of Soviet constitutions:

> Lenin and the Bolshevik Party believed that the constitution is not only a legal act but also a major political document. The Party regarded the constitution as a ratification of the gains of the revolution and also as a proclamation of the fundamental aims and objectives of building socialism.[6]

In regard to both the above aspects of what might be called their informative function, Soviet constitutions differ from those of other states in degree rather than in kind. No constitution provides a complete, accurate and up-to-date 'power map', if only because no single document can encompass the variety of 'actors' involved in the complex political process of a modern state; and most constitutions contain some declaratory statements which articulate the ethos of the national community and the goals prescribed for it by its leaders.

Where Soviet constitutions differ in kind from those of other states – more precisely, from those of constitutional democracies – is in relation to the essential purposes of constitutionalism, i.e. the effective control of the supreme power holders. Soviet constitutions are not designed to perform the crucial normative function of restraining the rulers and protecting the ruled, and such constitutional provisions as appear to place some limits upon the exercise of political power are either meaningless or inoperative. The basic reason for this is, of course, that the Soviet Union is a dictatorship. As such the notion of limited government could not be part of Soviet constitutionalism.

For many years the leaders of the Soviet Union openly identified the regime as a dictatorship – the 'dictatorship of the proletariat' or the 'dictatorship of the working class' (in Stalinist terminology the two were not identical). In 1961, the new Party Programme proclaimed that Soviet society had entered the stage of 'full-scale construction of communism', promising solemnly that 'the present generation of Soviet people shall live in communism'. One prominent feature of this new stage was the transformation of the dictatorship into a new type of state, the 'all-people's state' or 'state of the whole people'.

Even during the stage of self-professed dictatorship, however, Soviet spokesmen claimed that their government was far more democratic than that of any other previous or contemporary state. This claim did not contradict the designation of the Soviet state as a dictatorship, because in the official doctrine every state *qua* state was a class dictatorship. The various institutions and procedures upon which other states founded their claims to democracy were merely so many devices enabling the economically dominant class to exercise – and disguise – its dictatorial rule. The proletarian dictatorship was more democratic than, say, the 'bourgeois' dictatorship of contemporary liberal states because it was exercised by the great majority of the people and not by a small minority of 'exploiters'.

Thus the term 'dictatorship' took on a special meaning in Soviet parlance, and to say that Soviet spokesmen acknowledged the dictatorial character of their regime is not to imply that they accepted the same description when couched in the conventional language of political discourse. But Lenin, for one, had a very unambiguous conception of the universal nature of dictatorial government. 'Dictatorship', he declared, 'is rule based directly upon force and unrestricted by any laws.' This straightforward definition – in Lenin's words, 'this simple truth, a truth that is as plain as noonday to every class conscious worker' – applied fully to proletarian dictatorship: 'The revolutionary dictatorship of the proletariat is rule won and maintained by the use of violence by the proletariat against the bourgeoisie, rule that is unrestricted by any laws.'[7]

It will be obvious that the Soviet regime was from the very beginning a dictatorship of a very peculiar kind. Many states throughout history have been subject to some form of dictatorial rule, but it is doubtful whether their leaders enunciated the nature of their rule in such explicit fashion. Two peculiarities of the Soviet dictatorship, in particular, are relevant to a discussion of Soviet constitutional development and should therefore be briefly taken up. One relates primarily to political doctrine, though it has also had practical implications. The other relates primarily to political practice, though it has also become deeply embedded in doctrine.

The first peculiarity is that the Soviet dictatorship has been endowed – or perhaps we should say, burdened – with a doctrine that prescribes the abolition of state and law. The original Marxist teaching in this, as in other respects, is complex and not unambiguous, and has been diluted and adulterated by its Soviet interpreters in various ways at different times. But in 1917 when the Bolsheviks embarked upon the government of Russia they did so in the belief, derived from the writings of Marx and Engels and accepted as axiomatic, that state and law were repressive phenomena of the 'superstructure' of class society and would disappear or 'wither away' in direct proportion as the proletarian dictatorship evolved towards the classless communist society of the future. The founding fathers had not been very specific about the duration or nature of the withering away process, but Lenin and other Bolshevik leaders left no doubt that it would commence from the moment of proletarian victory in the revolution and would involve the direct participation of the broad masses in the administration of the state and the enforcement of 'revolutionary justice'. Some of the subsequent vicissitudes of this doctrine will be traced below. Here it will suffice to note that its immediate effect was to implant in the early Bolsheviks a profound ideological prejudice against state and law – not just against the state and law of 'bourgeois' society, but against state and law as institutions of any society, including socialist society.

The second peculiarity of the Soviet dictatorship relates to the role of the Communist party. Unlike earlier dictatorships, in which political power was exercised primarily through the apparatus of the state, the Soviet dictatorship may be regarded as the first party dictatorship of modern times. The Communist party is the ruling party of the Soviet Union not only in the sense that its leading organs establish the country's basic policies and that its 'representatives' occupy the highest offices of the state, but also in the sense that its own apparatus penetrates every sector of administration. At all levels and in all branches of government the organs of the party direct, supervise and not infrequently supplant those of the state. The real government of the Soviet Union is not the Council of Ministers but the Politburo of the party, and if the country may be said to have a legislature it is not the Supreme Soviet but the party's Central Committee. In the words of a recent article on 'ideological' questions:

It is the party, proceeding from Marxist-Leninist theory and taking

into account the totality of internal and external conditions, that
works out policy and organizes its practical application in all fields of
social life, by all state, economic and social organizations and by the
broad mass of the toilers.[8]

There is a clear link between these two peculiarities of the Soviet
dictatorship. Party rule, in the form outlined above, dates from the early
post-revolutionary years. While its emergence cannot be attributed to
ideological factors alone, it undoubtedly owed much to the fact that state
and law were ideologically discredited. To be sure, the exigencies of
government soon led the revolutionary regime to have recourse to both:
several months after taking power it began drafting a constitution that
formalized the new institutions of the state and explicitly identified itself
as its 'fundamental law'. But if at first there were some doubts as to the
party's precise role in the system it soon became clear that it was, as one
of the draftsmen of the first Soviet constitution put it, 'the judicial and
actual essence of our constitution'.[9] This central fact of Soviet government and 'constitutionalism' has not changed to this day, except that it is
now formally anchored in the constitutional text itself.

In July 1917 Lenin wrote with reference to Russia under the Provisional Government:

> Positively no steps can be taken towards a correct understanding of
> our tactical tasks in Russia today unless we concentrate above all on
> systematically and ruthlessly exposing constitutional illusions, rev-
> ealing all their roots and re-establishing a proper political perspec-
> tive.[10]

This book, needless to say, has set itself no 'tactical tasks'. Rather it seeks
to contribute to 'correct understanding' – by 'exposing constitutional
illusions', if necessary, and by 're-establishing a proper political perspective', if possible.

Notes

1 *The Politics of Aristotle,* translated with notes by E. Barker, Oxford, 1948, bk IV,
  ch. I, §10.
2 I.D. Duchacek, *Power Maps: Comparative Politics of Constitutions,* Santa Barbara,
  Calif., 1973.
3 H.D. Lasswell and A. Kaplan, *Power and Society,* New Haven, Conn., 1950, p.
  xiv.
4 V.I. Lenin, *Collected Works,* 45 vols, Moscow, 1960–70, vol. 32, p. 109.
5 J. Stalin, *Problems of Leninism*, Moscow, 1954, pp. 688, 696; see also pp. 689,
  698, 701.
6 L.I. Brezhnev, *On the Draft Constitution of the Union of Soviet Socialist Republics,*
  Moscow, 1977, p. 10.

7 V.I. Lenin, *Selected Works*, 2 vols, London, 1947, vol. II, p. 365. Lenin gave very similar definitions on several occasions.

8 *Pravda*, 13 July 1979.

9 G.S. Gurvich, *Osnovy Sovetskoi Konstitutsii*, Moscow, 1926, p. 88.

10 Lenin, *Coll. Works*, vol. 25, p. 194.

1

The RSFSR Constitution of 1918

Commentary on the Text

The 'Constitution (Fundamental Law) of the Russian Socialist Federated Soviet Republic' was adopted eight months after the October revolution on 10 July 1918. It was in many ways the most interesting of Soviet constitutions, for it still reflected the thrust of the revolution, its contempt for 'bourgeois', legalistic niceties, and its open adherence to the undiluted power of the 'formerly oppressed classes'. There were no concessions to the principle of political equality, to inherent freedoms protected by an independent judiciary (the constitution lacked any provision for judicial institutions), or to some form of separation of powers. Such guarantees and restraints, it was held, served bourgeois constitutions to camouflage the rule of the exploiting classes. The new regime spurned these devices; instead, it openly professed its dictatorial essence as well as its class character. The constitution was designed for 'the present transition period' during which classes would be abolished and conditions created for the complete disappearance of the state. It set about this task by establishing both undisguised class rule and 'a powerful All-Russian Soviet government' in the form of the 'dictatorship of the urban and rural proletariat and the poorest peasantry' [article 9].

On 28 January 1918 the Third All-Russian Congress of Soviets of Workers', Soldiers' and Peasants' Deputies adopted a resolution 'On the Federal Institutions of the Russian Republic', which in its final paragraph instructed the Central Executive Committee (CEC) of the Congress to prepare a draft of the 'fundamental principles of the constitution of the Russian Federal Republic' for submission to the next Congress of Soviets. The CEC took no immediate action, however, and it was only after the Fourth Congress of Soviets, which met in mid-March, and following a decision of the Central Committee (CC) of the Bolshevik party, that the CEC resolved on 1 April 1918 to form a constitutional commission. The commission was composed of fifteen members and included three representatives of two smaller parties, the Left Socialist Revolutionaries (recently resigned from a short-lived government coalition with the Bolsheviks) and the Maximalists, as well as two Left Communists. It was to be the last time that members of non-Bolshevik parties and of an overt opposition group within the Bolshevik party would participate in the work of a Soviet constitutional commission, and it deserves to be recorded for that fact alone. Only three of the top Bolshevik leaders served on the constitutional commission: Ya. M. Sverdlov, Party Secretary and CEC Chairman, who headed the commission, I.V. Stalin, who as Commissar of Nationalities was the only member of the Soviet Government on the commission and took a very active part in its work, and N.I. Bukharin, who was at that time a prominent spokesman of the Left Communist opposition.

The commission was expected to prepare a draft for adoption by the Fifth Congress of Soviets in July. At the end of June it became clear that its work would not be completed in time, and when the Bolshevik CC discussed the project on 26 June, several members, including Lenin, proposed that the subject of the constitution be dropped from the Congress agenda. However, on Sverdlov's insistence it was decided that work on those parts of the constitution which were already in an advanced state of preparation should be expedited, while the rest, which included provisions on the structure of the central state organs, would be completed at a later date. A draft reflecting this compromise was subsequently submitted by the constitutional commission to the CC and on 3 July a subcommittee of the latter, under Lenin's chairmanship, introduced last-minute changes and additions. On 10 July 1918 the Fifth Congress of Soviets, with hardly any discussion – only one delegate, a Maximalist, spoke from the floor – unanimously approved the revised draft, leaving the final editing to the CEC. The edited text was published on 19 July and went into effect on that date.

In the light of their open advocacy of dictatorship 'unrestricted by any laws' it is perhaps some cause for surprise that the Bolsheviks should have rushed to enshrine the new order in a 'fundamental law' so soon after taking power, particularly as the future of the regime seemed far from secure at the time. The main reason for what may well seem unwarranted haste in the pursuit of an unwanted objective must doubtless be sought in the fact that the forcible dispersal of the Constituent Assembly on 19 January 1918 made it politically expedient to carry through a task that should have belonged to the first (and last) national representative body of the republic. It was no accident that the decision to promulgate a constitution was adopted several days later in order, as one Bolshevik leader, G. Zinoviev, put it, 'to pass sentence on the Constituent Assembly'.

In his speech to the meeting of the CEC which resolved on the formation of the constitutional commission, Sverdlov explained the need for a constitution on the ground that the revolution had entered 'the stage of construction' in which the powers and functions of state organs would have to be clearly defined. It may be doubted whether these concerns were uppermost in the minds of the Bolshevik leaders. That Lenin did not have himself elected to the constitutional commission and generally took relatively little interest in its work may, considering his legal training and penchant for organizational matters, itself be taken as evidence that the Bolshevik leaders did not regard 'institution building' as a major objective of the exercise. To be sure, some of the other parties represented in the Congress of Soviets, and indeed some members of the Bolshevik faction, had hoped to use the occasion of constitution making in order to advance their own designs for the new state, particularly with a view to restricting the powers of the central government. But their proposals, some of them fairly radical, were rejected in the constitutional commission, and the final text merely encoded some of the more salient political practices and institutional relationships established since the revolution, without bestowing either notably greater precision or superior legal status upon any of them. The constitution, Lenin and other Bolshevik spokesmen were to affirm time and again, was the product of the practice of revolution, 'not the invention of a commission, nor the creation of lawyers'. Rather it embodied 'what experience has already given'; it 'recorded on paper what had actually been effected'.[1]

Such value as the Bolsheviks attached to the constitution as a 'record on paper' was largely proclamatory, reflecting the desire, characteristic of all new regimes but especially strong in one which viewed itself as the spearhead of an international movement, to mark the break with the past and present its credentials to the world at large. The adoption of a constitution was a great symbolic act, assured by its very nature of instant resonance at home and abroad. In the words of Yu. Steklov, a member of the constitutional commission, who introduced the draft to the Fifth Congress of Soviets, the constitution was of 'grandiose, colossal, world-historic significance', for unlike all previously known constitutions, including 'the most revolutionary' among them, it was not limited to one state or nation but was 'formulated . . . as the constitution of every nation where there is a proletariat and poorest peasantry'.[2]

The 'Declaration of the Rights of the Toiling and Exploited People' which formed Part One of the constitution was one of the revolutionary regime's earlier documents, issued as a deliberate counterpart to the 'Declaration of the Rights of Man and Citizen' of 1789, which similarly had been incorporated into the French Constitution of 1791. Drafted by Lenin for submission to the Constituent Assembly, it was first approved by the CEC on 16 January 1918 and then, after the Assembly rejected it, adopted in appropriately amended form by the Third Congress of Soviets later that month. On 3 July 1918 the CC subcommittee which examined the draft of the constitutional commission decided on the inclusion of the Declaration as an integral part of the constitution.[3]

The reproduction, word for word, of a document adopted by a different Congress for a different purpose gave rise to a number of textual anomalies. There were the various references to the Third Congress in a document adopted by the Fifth Congress. There were formulations relating to one-time events or measures, more appropriate to a resolution than to a constitution, such as the 'Congress . . . endorses unreservedly', or 'insists on' or 'welcomes' [articles 4–6]. There were repetitions and inconsistencies, such as the partly overlapping recitation of 'fundamental' aims [articles 3 & 9], or the provisions vesting power first in the 'toiling masses and their authorized representatives – the soviets' [article 7], and then in 'the entire working population of the country, united in urban and rural soviets' [article 10]. Finally, its title notwithstanding, Part One affirmed no rights, other than the general right of the 'toilers' to the government and wealth of the society, whereas a number of specific rights were listed in Part Two under the heading 'General Provisions of the Constitution of the RSFSR'.

But then the constitution was not intended to withstand close textual scrutiny, as its authors freely admitted. This was particularly true of Part One which in highly emotive but unmistakable terms established the identity of the regime and proclaimed a sweeping programme of political and socio-economic action. Four of the nine articles in Part One addressed themselves in the main to the enactments and policies of the Soviet regime in the first two months after the revolution [articles 3–6]; they therefore bore most clearly the imprint of a document intended originally for endorsement by the Constituent Assembly. However, the opening paragraph of one of these stated the 'fundamental aim' of the revolutionary regime [article 3], and this together with the constitutive and declaratory clauses contained in the remaining articles of Part One may be regarded as similar in form to the kind of statements often found in the constitutional preambles of other states.

Part Two, as already noted, included a list of specific rights as well as duties. The duties were two: to work, in accordance with the motto 'He who does not work, neither shall he eat' [article 18]; and to defend the 'socialist fatherland' [article 19]. But while the former was universal in that it applied to every 'citizen', the latter discriminated between the 'toilers' who were granted 'the honour of bearing arms', and the 'non-toiling elements', who were to perform 'other military duties'. The denotation of 'toilers', a word much beloved of Soviet rhetoric, has never been – and probably cannot be – satisfactorily specified. In the context of the constitution it seemed to refer to workers and to peasants not employing hired labour [cf. article 20], variously described as the 'poor peasantry' [articles 14 & 15] or the 'poorest' peasants [articles 9, 16 & 17]. (Current Soviet usage applies it to virtually the entire population, including non-manual groups.)

What is of interest, however, is not so much the precise denotation of these necessarily vague categories as the underlying principle of class discrimination openly, indeed proudly, displayed in the constitution. All states, in the official view, were class instruments, and the Soviet state was the instrument of the 'toiling classes'. The constitution, which inscribed the 'ruthless suppression' or 'crushing' of the former ruling class among the state's principal objectives [articles 3 & 9], could not posit the equality of groups or individuals as a general principle since this would be tantamount to a betrayal of the revolution or, at best, sheer hypocrisy.

This was also the attitude which informed the somewhat longer, but still modest, catalogue of rights, most of which were accorded, not without some inconsistency in formulation, to 'toilers' rather than to 'citizens'. The rights listed were: freedom of conscience – though freedom to propagate religious and anti-religious views was extended to every 'citizen' [article 13]; freedom of expression [article 14]; freedom of assembly – secured for the 'toilers' but also recognized as the right of 'citizens' [article 15]; freedom of association [article 16]; the right to education [article 17]; and the unique right, inserted on Lenin's proposal as one of the last-minute alterations, to full political equality for foreign residents of the RSFSR, provided they belonged to the category of 'toilers' (and also the granting of Russian citizenship to such foreigners 'without any troublesome formalities') [article 20]. Only two of the rights were not framed in class terms: the right to political asylum [article 21]; and, naturally enough, the right to freedom from discrimination on grounds of race or nationality [article 22].

When compared with other constitutions, including later Soviet ones, the list reveals several striking lacunae, most obviously in the realm of guarantees against arbitrary action by the state, such as inviolability of the person, the home and the privacy of postal communications. The omission of these and similar fundamental safeguards of individual rights was clearly not unwitting. In the state of the 'toilers', so ran the official rationalization at the time, the 'toilers' did not require – and the 'non-toiling elements' did not deserve – to be defended against the state. On the contrary, it was precisely through the state that their rights would be secured, would be turned into 'real' freedoms, as the constitution emphasized in each of the relevant provisions [articles 13–17]. In a sense, of course, this holds true of all states, even the ideal-type 'minimal state'. But the Soviet constitution, in a striking departure from accepted practice, went beyond the kind of rights provided by even the most welfare-oriented of modern states when it promised to transform the freedoms of expression, assembly and association into concrete reality, at least for the 'toilers', by placing at their disposal 'all technical and material resources' [article 14], 'premises', etc., [article 15], and granting them 'every assistance, material and otherwise' [article 16].

More important than the rights accorded to the 'toilers' was the power arrogated by the state to deprive individuals and groups of rights used 'to the detriment of the interests of the socialist revolution' [article 23]. It was this article, above all, which pointed up the character of constitutional rights as privileges granted by the state to some of its citizens, subject to good behaviour, rather than as inalienable freedoms recognized and protected by the state. It was also, as Lenin noted with barely concealed irony in December 1919, 'the article of the constitution that we observe most strictly and which shows that in all our activities we stick to the constitution'.[4]

Class discrimination was also introduced into the franchise. The active and passive voting right was confined to 'those earning their livelihood by productive and socially useful work' (and this, it may be observed, was a broader, if no less vague, category than 'toilers', since it included non-manual occupations, 'employees of all kinds' being specifically cited), 'persons engaged in domestic pursuits which enable the former to undertake productive work', soldiers and the disabled [article 64]. The constitution disenfranchised all those identified in revolutionary doctrine with the Tsarist regime, even if they came under one of the above categories. These so-called 'former people', also known as 'the deprived ones', were: employers of labour for profit, persons deriving income from capital, merchants, etc., clergy of all denominations, agents and employees of the Tsarist police, and members of the former royal house [article 65(a)–(e)]. Here, therefore, was a rather strict adumbration of the principle, enunciated in the preamble, that 'there can be no place for the exploiters in any organ of power' [article 7], denying them not only the right to be elected themselves but also to participate in the election of others. The application of some of these discriminatory criteria was bound to create difficulties in electoral practice but their general intent was clear enough.

It has been argued, not only by Soviet or Marxist commentators, that the conception of rights as linked to class and effected through the state was entirely derived from the Marxist teaching. The argument cannot be taken up here. But it should be noted that the 1903 Party Programme, co-authored by Lenin and not revised until 1919, contained an altogether non-discriminatory and far more comprehensive bill of rights, including not only the inviolability of the person, etc., but also freedom of travel, domicile and occupation, and even the right to strike and to legal redress against the state; the Programme also called for 'free elections by the entire people'.

The state structure elaborated in the constitution rested on the mass assemblies of the soviets (councils) which had sprung up in town and country since the February revolution. Modelled on the workers' soviets, which in the course of their brief appearance during the 1905 revolution had succeeded in winning the support of large sections of the urban proletariat, and presented as the Russian version of the Paris Commune, which Marx himself had acclaimed as 'the political form' of the proletarian dictatorship, the soviets were hallowed alike in revolutionary tradition and Marxist doctrine. In the interregnum of 'dual power' between February and October 1917 they had become effective foci of authority, rivalling and in many cases supplanting that of the

Provisional Government. The attitude of the Bolsheviks to the soviets had wavered in proportion to their strength in them. By October they had, however, secured a majority in the key soviets of Petrograd and Moscow as well as in several others. The October insurrection was launched under the slogan 'All power to the soviets!' and for some period of time the revolutionary regime was careful to invest its actions with the legitimacy of the soviets. In the circumstances, it was altogether natural that they should become the foundations of the new state structure.

The outline of that structure may be briefly described. It took the form of a pyramid which led from the local soviets (villages and towns) at the base, through the intermediate layers of the administrative-territorial divisions (rural district, county, province and – where applicable – region), up to the All-Russian Congress of Soviets at the summit. Depending on the size of the locality, town soviets numbered between fifty and 1000 deputies and village soviets between three and fifty [article 57]. Each local soviet elected a small executive committee accountable to it for the direction of local affairs, and sent delegates to a congress of soviets held at either one or two of the next higher levels of the administrative-territorial division within which it was located. The congress, for its part, elected an executive committee exercising authority on its behalf and accountable to it in the period between sessions of the congress [article 55]; it similarly sent delegates to the congress of a higher administrative-territorial division, and so on up to the All-Russian Congress of Soviets [article 53].

The latter body was to be convened not less than twice a year [article 26], but from the end of 1918 onwards met only at yearly intervals, and in December 1921 an amendment brought the constitution into line with current practice. The Congress elected the All-Russian Central Executive Committee (CEC) which was responsible to it and acted on its behalf in the interim between Congress sessions [articles 28–30]. The upper limit for the number of CEC members, fixed at 200 [article 28], was extended to 300 in 1920 and 386 in 1921. The constitution did not stipulate the frequency of CEC sessions, originally intended to be more or less continuous, and, with many of its members away on various war duties, the CEC did not meet for a period of some eighteen months between July 1918 and February 1920. In December that year, the Eighth Congress of Soviets set a minimum of one session for every two months, and one year later the Ninth Congress reduced this to three per year. The Government of the RSFSR, or Council of People's Commissars, was formed by the CEC and was responsible to it and to the Congress of Soviets [articles 35 & 46].

It will have been seen that the state pyramid was erected in the main through indirect elections. Representation was deliberately weighted in favour of the urban population at the ratio of one urban elector to five rural inhabitants [articles 25 & 53 (a), (b)]. This discriminatory arrangement was not explicit in the general class bias of the constitution, which had bracketed the 'poorest peasants' at least with the urban proletariat as the new ruling class, but was a continuation, in slightly amended form, of the different bases of representation used for elections to what had previously been two separate sets of assemblies – one for workers and soldiers, and the other for peasants. It was at times defended – by Steklov at the Fifth Congress of Soviets for instance – as entirely equitable because of the lower proportion of adults in the rural population. But there can be no question that it provided preferential representation for the urban workers and as such was but another expression of the Bolsheviks' long-standing distrust of the peasantry. Lenin, for one, admitted that 'the constitution recognizes the precedence of the proletariat in respect of the peasants', though he was careful to explain it as resulting from the proletariat's superior culture and organization and to promise that the inequality – in any case a matter of 'very small practical importance' – would be abolished as soon as possible.[5]

Thirteen articles of the constitution dealt with matters of electoral procedure [articles 66–78]. Except for one, which established the right of recall, long regarded as a basic requisite of proletarian democracy [article 78], all of these concerned details of the kind normally regulated in electoral laws rather than constitutions. There was no requirement that elections should be secret, nor any stipulation for the frequency of elections, nor, indeed, for any of the various devices regarding the apportionment of electoral mandates generally considered so crucial for the conduct of contested elections. Proposals for secret elections under a proportional list system had been considered in the constitutional commission and rejected as 'artificial, divorced from life and impractical'.[6] The constitution itself merely stated that elections were to be held 'according to established custom, on days fixed by local soviets' [article 66]. In practice, electoral procedures differed widely, particularly in the early years, except that open voting, by show of hands, was universally applied and overt pressures and abuses of different kinds were widespread.[7]

The principle which pervaded the entire governmental structure was the absolute unification of state power, both functionally and territorially. Soviet constitutional doctrine, invoking Marx's analysis of the Paris Commune, repudiated what it described as the wholly artificial separation of powers of 'bourgeois' constitutions. Whether regarded as a contrivance for the balancing of contending social forces, as in some Marxist writings, or for the limitation of state power *vis-à-vis* society, as in conventional constitutional theory, the separation of powers was manifestly incompatible with the express purposes of class rule effected through a dictatorial state. The soviets were consequently conceived not as 'talking shops', on the lines of the much-despised parliamentary bodies of liberal states, but as 'working organs' exercising both legislative and executive functions. The difference between the larger representative assemblies, the soviets and congresses of soviets, and their respective executive organs was hierarchical rather than functional, though the practical needs of government soon imposed a measure of functional differentiation.

The functional fusion was indicated in the constitutional definitions relating to the central state organs. 'Supreme power' was vested in both the All-Russian Congress of Soviets and – when the Congress was not in session – the CEC [article 12]. The Congress was further described as 'the highest authority' of the RSFSR [article 24], while the CEC was 'the highest legislative, executive and supervisory organ' [article 31]. Chapter 9, dealing jointly with the jurisdiction of both bodies, made no distinction in respect of their powers, except that the amendment of unspecified 'fundamental principles' of the constitution and the ratification of peace treaties was reserved for the Congress of Soviets [article 51], and that questions affecting the territorial integrity of the RSFSR and its foreign relations were only to be decided by the CEC when the Congress could not be convened [article 52].

The Council of People's Commissars was clearly conceived primarily as an executive organ with a structure similar to that of governments or cabinets in parliamentary regimes. The constitution entrusted the Council with 'the general direction of the affairs' of the state [article 37], empowering it *inter alia* to take 'all measures necessary for the proper and prompt dispatch of state affairs' [article 38], and establishing to this end eighteen people's commissariats more or less on the lines of the executive departments of other states [article 43]. But the Council of People's Commissars was also given broad legislative powers to issue 'decrees, regulations and instructions' [article 38] that in neither formal status nor material content differed from those of the CEC [cf. article 33]. That all its enactments (and decisions) had to be reported to the CEC and could be annulled by it [articles 39 & 40], and that those of 'major political importance' were subject to approval by the CEC (unless they were 'measures requiring immediate implementation') [article 41], reflected the hierarchical gradation of power rather than its functional division.

Attempts to translate the principle of collegiality, or 'collective leadership', to the highest echelons of state administration were evident in both the organization of the Council of People's Commissars and that of the individual commissariats. The constitution assigned no special powers to the Chairman of the Council; in fact, the only mention of the office was the obscure distinction drawn with regard to the appointment of the Council as a whole and the individual commissars, on the one hand, and the Chairman of the Council, on the other: while the Congress of Soviets and the CEC were empowered to appoint and dismiss the Council and the people's commissars, their jurisdiction apparently extended merely to the 'approval' of the appointment of the Chairman of the Council [article 49 (o)]. The individual commissariats were to be run by collegia. Formed in the early days of the revolution and composed of the people's commissar, his deputies and senior officials, the collegia had, in conformity with the collegiality principle, originally functioned as policy-making organs within the various commissariats. By the time of the adoption of the constitution, however, another principle, namely that of 'one-man management', had already begun to make large inroads into the practice of state and economic administration. The collegia were, therefore, designed by the constitution as advisory bodies with the right to appeal decisions of the commissar to the Council of People's Commissars and to the Presidium of the CEC [article 45].

The last-mentioned of these, the Presidium of the CEC, had been in existence since the beginning of the revolution. As the executive organ of the CEC it was one of the four key institutions at the centre of the state structure alongside the Congress, the CEC and the Council of Commissars. Its functions divided broadly into three: to coordinate the work of the CEC; to enact legislation and supervise administration in the interim between CEC sessions; and to act as the collective head of state. Yet, although the Presidium had figured prominently in the discussions of the constitutional commission, the final text of the constitution contained no more than a passing reference to it as an instance of appeal by the collegia. In March 1919, the Eighth Party Congress called on the forthcoming Seventh Congress of Soviets 'to formulate urgently the rights and duties of the Presidium' and specifically to demarcate its functions from those of the Council of Commissars. In December that year, the Seventh Congress of Soviets passed a decree which included the first attempt at a statutory definition of the Presidium's role, and in December 1920 this was supplemented by a further decree of the Eighth Congress of Soviets.

Both the conspicuous omission of the Presidium from the original text of the constitution and the loose formulations concerning the other central organs of government were no doubt due in part to the fact that the constitutional commission had been unable to complete its work. At the same time, they cannot be divorced from the attitude of indifference with which the Bolsheviks approached the task of delimiting power by means of legally-binding, and therefore necessarily precise, norms. It was, of course, an attitude that was perfectly consistent with the official doctrine of state and law; but it also exacerbated the confusion, friction and rivalry which inevitably attend the formation of a new power structure in the aftermath of revolution.

In contrast to the functional fusion of power, which was officially acknowledged, the territorial concentration of power was officially disclaimed – at least in the sense that self-government in local matters was widely asserted as an indispensable element of Soviet statehood. Relations between the centre and the localities were to be governed by the principle of 'democratic centralism', as originally evolved in relation to the organization of the Bolshevik party. Translated to the realm of the state and stripped of some of its rhetorical flourish 'democratic centralism' was said to combine centralized decision-making with democratic accountability and local autonomy. Its administrative expression was the so-called 'dual subordination' of every executive organ – to the body which had elected it and to the executive organ immediately above it in the administrative-territorial hierarchy.

It need hardly be emphasized that while centralism might conceivably be reconciled with democracy it was entirely incompatible with local autonomy. The administrative device of 'dual subordination' obscured this contradiction but could not resolve it. By coupling 'horizontal' with 'vertical' subordination it seemed to grant local authorities a measure of control over local affairs; by the same token, however, it ensured that no part of such control was truly autonomous. As the pattern of Soviet government established itself, charges of the degeneration of 'democratic centralism' into 'vertical', or 'authoritarian', or 'bureaucratic' centralism were made at Soviet and even party congresses. They formed a principal plank in the platform of one of the earliest intra-party opposition groups, the 'Democratic Centralists', and they have since continued to be voiced in one form or other whenever critical views could make themselves heard inside the Soviet Union.

The constitution made only little pretence at establishing any form of territorial division or even delegation of powers. Most striking in this regard was the absence of provisions to support the designation of the RSFSR as a federal state, a claim made in the title of the constitution and repeated in the text of Part One [articles 2 & 8]. One article of Part Two provided for regions with a 'distinct mode of living and national composition' to form 'autonomous regional unions' which would enter the RSFSR 'on a federal basis' [article 11]. But the constitution nowhere elaborated the nature of that federal basis, nor did it specify any other distinction between these 'autonomous' entities and other regional subdivisions of the republic.

While local government organization received considerable attention in the constitution, local government jurisdiction was treated most perfunctorily. Two articles affirmed that each local soviet or congress of soviets was 'the highest authority' in its territory [articles 56 and 60], but the spheres of local jurisdiction were only barely indicated in the constitution. A single article of Chapter 12, which ostensibly dealt with the subject, designated activities in which local government organs were competent to engage, and it was indicative of the order of priority favoured by the constitution – and of the practice of 'dual subordination' – that the first of the four activities listed enjoined the 'implementation of all instructions of the corresponding higher organs'; of the remaining three, only one – 'the adoption of all measures for the cultural and economic development of their territories' – pointed to the substantive concerns of local authorities envisaged by the constitution [article 61]. By contrast, the jurisdiction assigned to the two supreme central organs, the All-Russian Congress of Soviets and its CEC, was not only very comprehensive [article 49], but clearly intended to be illustrative rather than exhaustive, since it was supplemented by a blanket dispensation allowing these two organs 'to decide on any other matter which they deem within their jurisdiction' [article 50]. The lack of independence of local authorities was further evident in their limited budgetary powers, as estimates of revenues and expenditures were in each instance made subject to the approval of superior administrative agencies [article 86].

Its title notwithstanding, the constitution was unmistakably designed for a unitary state. Subsequent developments, such as the right granted by the Eighth Congress of Soviets in December 1920 to the provincial executive committees to suspend the execution of the regulations of individual commissariats ('in exceptional circumstances only' and under threat of 'collective legal responsibility'), and the identical right granted to county executive committees in respect of regulations issued by individual province departments, did little to alter the status of local authorities as administrative extensions of the central government.

A brief review of the 1918 constitution cannot hope to encompass the full diversity of actual power relationships that developed in the first years of the Soviet state. The constitution was never intended to provide effective constraints channelling the flow of public power into a preconceived mould. At best, it was considered as no more than a rough outline of some of the rules under which the new state would be administered. Moreover, it was always clear that even under optimal conditions such rules would have to be highly flexible in order to allow for changing needs and circumstances. In the event, of course, conditions were far from optimal. The revolutionary regime was compelled to engage in a desperate struggle for survival at the same time as it sought to press ahead with radical social change. In such a situation the institutionalization of power was scarcely to be confined by constitutional rules, but rather evolved by a kind of 'natural selection' in which the fittest survived and the weakest succumbed. Inevitably, too, such a competitive process in turn generated tensions which further obstructed the emergence of more or less stable interactions between the various institutions of government.

Of the central institutions provided under the constitution the Council of Commissars was far and away the one best equipped to wield the centralized powers to which all states tend to resort in times of emergency. A compact, permanently functioning body, composed of some of the top leaders of the Bolshevik party, including most notably

Lenin himself, and ruling directly over the executive machinery of the state, the Council possessed both a degree of authority and a capacity for action unmatched by any of the nominally superior state organs. In providing that measures of particular urgency could be taken on the sole authority of the Council, the constitution may be said to have anticipated this development.

But at different times very extensive powers were assigned to organs not even mentioned in the constitution. One such organ was the *Cheka*, the forerunner of the Soviet secret police establishment, which soon after its formation in December 1917 began to develop some of the features of the 'state-within-state' syndrome so often found in situations in which official terror is widely practised (in this case the development was fuelled by counter-revolutionary 'white terror'). Another was the Council of Workers' and Peasants' Defence, formed under Lenin's chairmanship in November 1918 to mobilize resources for the war effort. It was granted sweeping legislative and other powers, and at the height of the civil war seemed to overshadow the Council of Commissars in importance. In a different category, but similarly functioning outside the explicit sanction of the constitution, were the Committees of the Village Poor which in the second half of 1918 supplanted the rural soviets in all but name, and the Revolutionary Committees established in October 1919 to take control of territories directly affected by the war.

The displacement or disregard of constitutional arrangements did not proceed in linear fashion, nor was it accomplished without opposition; on the contrary, it was repeatedly challenged, and in some cases even reversed. The Ninth Congress of Soviets in December 1921 resolved to curb the arbitrary powers of the *Cheka* with a view to 'the strengthening of revolutionary legality'. Two months later, in February 1922, the *Cheka* was reorganized as the State Political Administration, the GPU, and placed under the Commissariat of Internal Affairs. (The Chairman of the *Cheka*, F. Dzerzhinsky, had earlier, in March 1919, been appointed Commissar of Internal Affairs.) The Council of Workers' and Peasants' Defence (renamed Council of Labour and Defence) was deprived of its extraordinary powers and reduced to the status of a commission of the Council of Commissars in December 1920. As the crisis of the civil war receded, measures were also taken to re-invigorate the CEC and its Presidium and, in particular, to strengthen their position *vis-à-vis* the Council of Commissars.

By this time, however, all major policy decisions were taken by the top party organs – the Central Committee, Politburo, Orgburo and Sec-retariat. The various attempts to define or re-define the jurisdictional boundaries of the central state institutions consequently had an air of unreality about them. One example may suffice to illustrate this. When the Seventh Congress of Soviets established the jurisdiction of the CEC Presidium in December 1919 it granted it powers to approve and suspend decrees of the Council of Commissars in the period between CEC sessions, and a year later the Eighth Congress of Soviets extended this to allow it to revoke the Council's decrees. The practical import of the Presidium's enhanced prerogatives was spelled out by N.N. Krestinsky, then Secretary of the Bolshevik party, when he declared that they concerned 'exclusively cases in which the CC of our party, which controls and directs the work of the central [state] organs, comes to the conclusion that this or that decree should, because of its importance, be approved by the CEC, but the CEC plenum cannot for technical reasons be convened'. Again: 'When it is necessary to annul or suspend this or that decree of the Council of Commissars then the CC effects this through the CEC Presidium.'[8] Official Soviet texts might affirm, as did a resolution of the Eighth Party Congress in 1919, that the party implemented its decisions 'within the framework of the Soviet constitution'. What this and similar statements meant must be understood in the light of Krestinsky's commentary. In practice, to be sure, even these formalities were not always observed. But even when they were observed they could hardly affect the distribution of power at the summit of the state pyramid.

Soviet spokesmen depicted the 'spontaneously discovered' framework of the soviets as the ideal vehicle of revolutionary democracy, designed not only to provide the widest possible representation for the 'toilers' but also to bring about their direct and continuous participation in government. Here, it was held, was the 'half-state' of socialism, devoid of the bureaucratic parasite, a true school for the masses and a stepping-stone to the complete self-administration which would eventually replace the state itself. If these were the authentic aspirations of the revolution it soon became clear that the facts of government in post-revolutionary Russia, more specifically, the facts of dictatorial government in the hands of a minority party, were rendering them altogether illusory. The mass assemblies of the soviets were too unwieldy, too inexperienced in the skills of government and, above all, politically too unpredictable to serve as effective and reliable instruments of the dictatorship. They could be little more than forums for the acclamation of policies handed down from above. Such participation in government as the soviets afforded to the mass of the people was that of 'transmission belts', to use Lenin's famous metaphor, operated by levers from within the power-house of the political system – the Bolshevik party.

Notes

1 V.I. Lenin, *Collected Works*, 45 vols, Moscow, 1960–70, vol. 28, pp. 36, 146, and vol. 30, pp. 30, 456.

2 An abridged English translation of Steklov's speech is in J. Bunyan, *Intervention, Civil War and Communism in Russia. April–December 1918. Documents and Materials,* Baltimore, 1936, pp. 501 ff.

3 Earlier, at its meeting of 17 May, the constitutional commission had decided to use the Declaration as 'the basis' for a 'Declaration of Rights and Duties of the Toilers' to be incorporated in the constitution.

4 Lenin, *Coll. Works,* vol. 30, p. 239.

5 ibid., vol. 29, pp. 184–5; also vol. 30, p. 456 and vol. 32, p. 108.

6 G.S. Gurvich, *Istoriya Sovetskoi Konstitutsii,* Moscow, 1923, pp. 62, 183 f.

7 Such figures on electoral participation as are available for the early years indicate that participation was generally low and varied greatly, from around 10 per cent in some provinces to around 50 per cent in others, with an average of over 20 per cent for the country as a whole. But participation increased continuously and in the mid-1920s began to exceed the 50 per cent mark in most areas.

8 *Devyaty S'ezd RKP (b), mart–aprel' 1920 goda. Protokoly,* Moscow, 1960, pp. 41–2.

The RSFSR Constitution of 1918

Constitution (Fundamental Law) of the Russian Socialist Federated Soviet Republic

[Adopted by the Fifth All-Russian Congress of Soviets on 10 July 1918][1]

The Declaration of the Rights of the Toiling and Exploited People, adopted by the Third All-Russian Congress of Soviets in January 1918, together with the Constitution of the Soviet Republic, adopted by the Fifth All-Russian Congress, shall constitute a single Fundamental Law of the Russian Socialist Federated Soviet Republic.

This Fundamental Law shall come into force upon its publication in final form in *Izvestiya Vserossiiskogo Tsentral'nogo Ispolnitel'nogo Komiteta Sovetov.*[2] It shall be republished by all local organs of Soviet power and shall be prominently displayed in all Soviet institutions.

The Fifth All-Russian Congress of Soviets instructs the People's Commissariat of Education to introduce in all schools and educational institutions without exception the study of the basic provisions of this Constitution, as well as their explanation and interpretation.

Part One Declaration of the Rights of the Toiling and Exploited People

Chapter One

Article 1 Russia is proclaimed a Republic of Soviets of Workers', Soldiers', and Peasants' Deputies. All power at the centre and in the localities shall be vested in these soviets.

Article 2 The Russian Soviet Republic is established on the basis of a free union of free nations, as a federation of Soviet national republics.

Chapter Two

Article 3   Its fundamental aim being the abolition of all exploitation of man by man, the complete elimination of the division of society into classes, the ruthless suppression of the exploiters, the establishment of the socialist organization of society and the victory of socialism in all countries, the Third All-Russian Congress of Soviets of Workers', Soldiers' and Peasants' Deputies further decrees:

(a)   In effecting the socialization of land, private ownership of land is abolished and all land is declared the property of the people and is turned over to the toilers without compensation on the basis of equal rights to its use.

(b)   All nationally important forests, minerals and waters, as well as all livestock and farm implements, model estates, and agricultural enterprises, are declared national property.

(c)   As a first step toward the complete transfer of factories, plants, mines, railroads, and other means of production and transportation to the ownership of the Soviet Republic of Workers and Peasants, and in order to ensure the power of the toilers over the exploiters, the Congress endorses the Soviet laws on workers' control and the Supreme Council of National Economy.

(d)   The Third All-Russian Congress of Soviets considers the Soviet law repudiating the debts contracted by the governments of the Tsar, the landlords and the bourgeoisie to be a first blow to international banking and finance capital, and expresses its confidence that the Soviet Government will firmly follow this course until the complete victory of the international workers' revolt against the yoke of capital.

(e)   The transfer of all banks to the ownership of the Workers' and Peasants' State is endorsed as one of the conditions for the emancipation of the toiling masses from the yoke of capital.

(f)   With the aim of destroying the parasitic strata of society and of organizing the economic life of the country, universal labour duty is introduced.

(g)   In the interest of ensuring complete supremacy of power for the toiling masses and of eliminating any possibility for the restoration of the power of the exploiters, the Congress decrees the arming of the toilers, the formation of the Socialist Red Army of Workers and Peasants and the complete disarming of the propertied classes.

Chapter Three

Article 4   Expressing its inflexible resolve to wrest mankind from the claws of capitalism and imperialism, which during this most criminal of all wars have drenched the world with blood, the Third All-Russian Congress of Soviets endorses unreservedly the policy of the Soviet Government in repudiating secret treaties, in organizing the most extensive fraternization among the workers and peasants of the belligerent armies, and in its efforts to bring about at all costs, by revolutionary means, a democratic peace of toilers without annexation and indemnities, on the basis of the free self-determination of nations.

Article 5   With the same aim in view the Third All-Russian Congress of Soviets insists on a complete break with the barbarous politics of bourgeois civilization which built the prosperity of the exploiters in a few chosen nations upon the enslavement of hundreds of millions of the toiling population in Asia, in colonies in general, and in small countries.

Article 6   The Third All-Russian Congress of Soviets welcomes the policy of the Council of People's Commissars in granting complete independence to Finland, in commencing the withdrawal of troops from Persia, and in proclaiming the right of self-determination for Armenia.

Chapter Four

Article 7   The Third All-Russian Congress of Soviets of Workers', Soldiers', and Peasants' Deputies believes that at the present moment of the decisive struggle of the proletariat against its exploiters there can be no place for the exploiters in any organ of power. Power must belong wholly and exclusively to the toiling masses and their authorized representatives – the soviets of workers', soldiers', and peasants' deputies.

Article 8   At the same time, desiring to create a really free and voluntary, and consequently all the more complete and lasting, union of the toiling classes of all nations in Russia, the Third Congress of Soviets confines itself to establishing the fundamental principles of the federation of the Soviet Republics of Russia, leaving it to the workers and peasants of each nation to decide independently at their own plenipotentiary Soviet congresses whether, and on what conditions, they wish to take part in the federal government and in other federal Soviet institutions.

Part Two   General Provisions of the Constitution of the Russian Socialist Federated Soviet Republic

Chapter Five

Article 9   The fundamental aim of the Constitution of the Russian

Socialist Federated Soviet Republic, designed for the present transition period, is to establish a dictatorship of the urban and rural proletariat and the poorest peasantry in the form of a powerful All-Russian Soviet government with a view to crushing completely the bourgeoisie, abolishing the exploitation of man by man, and establishing socialism, under which there will be no division into classes and no state power.

Article 10 The Russian Republic is a free socialist society of all the toilers of Russia. All power within the Russian Socialist Federated Soviet Republic shall belong to the entire working population of the country, united in urban and rural soviets.

Article 11 Soviets of regions with a distinct mode of living and national composition may unite in autonomous regional unions, at the head of which, as at the head of all other regional unions which may be formed, shall stand the regional congresses of soviets and their executive organs.

These autonomous regional unions shall enter the Russian Socialist Federated Soviet Republic on a federal basis.

Article 12 Supreme power in the Russian Socialist Federated Soviet Republic shall belong to the All-Russian Congress of Soviets and, in the interim between congresses, to the All-Russian Central Executive Committee of Soviets.

Article 13 In order to ensure for the toilers real freedom of conscience, the church shall be separated from the state, and the school from the church, and freedom of religious and anti-religious propaganda shall be recognized as the right of every citizen.

Article 14 In order to ensure for the toilers real freedom of expression of opinion, the Russian Socialist Federated Soviet Republic, abolishing the dependence of the press on capital, shall turn over to the working class and the poor peasantry all technical and material resources necessary for the publication of newspapers, pamphlets, books, and all other printed matter, and guarantee their free circulation throughout the country.

Article 15 In order to ensure for the toilers real freedom of assembly, the Russian Socialist Federated Soviet Republic, recognizing the right of the citizens of the Soviet Republic freely to organize assemblies, meetings, processions, etc., shall place at the disposal of the working class and the poor peasantry all premises suitable for public gatherings, together with furnishing, lighting, and heating.

Article 16 In order to ensure for the toilers real freedom of association, the Russian Socialist Federated Soviet Republic, having broken the economic and political power of the propertied classes and having thereby removed all obstacles which hitherto, in bourgeois society, prevented the workers and peasants from enjoying freedom of organization and action, shall render to the workers and poorest peasants every assistance, material and otherwise, in uniting and organizing.

Article 17   In order to ensure for the toilers real access to knowledge, the Russian Socialist Federated Soviet Republic shall undertake to provide for the workers and poorest peasants a complete, comprehensive, and free education.

Article 18   The Russian Socialist Federated Soviet Republic shall regard work as the duty of all citizens of the Republic and shall proclaim the slogan: 'He who does not work, neither shall he eat.'

Article 19   In order to protect in every possible way the gains of the Great Worker-Peasant Revolution, the Russian Socialist Federated Soviet Republic shall consider it the duty of all citizens of the Republic to defend the socialist fatherland and shall establish universal military service. The honour of bearing arms in defence of the revolution shall be granted only to the toilers; non-toiling elements shall have to perform other military duties.

Article 20   Acting on the principle of the solidarity of the toilers of all nations, the Russian Socialist Federated Soviet Republic shall grant all political rights enjoyed by Russian citizens to foreigners resident within the territory of the Russian Republic for purposes of employment and belonging to the working class or to the peasantry not employing hired labour. Local soviets shall be authorized to confer upon such foreigners, without any troublesome formalities, the rights of Russian citizenship.

Article 21   The Russian Socialist Federated Soviet Republic shall grant the right of asylum to all foreigners persecuted for political and religious offences.

Article 22   The Russian Socialist Federated Soviet Republic, recognizing the equality of rights of all citizens, irrespective of race or nationality, declares it contrary to the fundamental laws of the Republic to institute or tolerate any privileges or advantages based upon such grounds, or to repress national minorities, or to limit their equality of rights in any way.

Article 23   Guided by the interests of the working class as a whole, the Russian Socialist Federated Soviet Republic shall deprive individuals and groups of rights used to the detriment of the interests of the socialist revolution.

Part Three   The Structure of Soviet Power

A. The Organization of Central Power

Chapter Six The All-Russian Congress of Soviets of Workers', Peasants', Cossacks' and Red Army Deputies

Article 24   The All-Russian Congress of Soviets shall be the highest authority in the Russian Socialist Federated Soviet Republic.

Article 25   The All-Russian Congress of Soviets shall consist of representatives of urban soviets on the basis of one deputy for every 25,000 electors, and of representatives of province[3] congresses of soviets on the basis of one deputy for every 125,000 inhabitants.

> Note 1: In the event that the province congress of soviets does not precede the All-Russian Congress of Soviets, delegates to the latter shall be sent directly by county congresses of soviets.
>
> Note 2: In the event that the regional congress of soviets immediately precedes the All-Russian Congress of Soviets, delegates to the latter may be sent by the regional congress of soviets.

Article 26   The All-Russian Congress of Soviets shall be convened at least twice a year[4] by the All-Russian Central Executive Committee of Soviets.

Article 27   An Extraordinary All-Russian Congress shall be convened by the All-Russian Central Executive Committee of Soviets, either at its own initiative or upon the demand of the soviets of localities comprising not less than one-third of the total population of the Republic.

Article 28   The All-Russian Congress of Soviets shall elect an All-Russian Central Executive Committee of Soviets of not more than 200 members.

Article 29   The All-Russian Central Executive Committee of Soviets shall be responsible in all matters to the All-Russian Congress of Soviets.

Article 30   In the interim between congresses the All-Russian Central Executive Committee of Soviets shall be the highest authority of the Republic.

Chapter Seven The All-Russian Central Executive Committee of Soviets

Article 31   The All-Russian Central Executive Committee of Soviets shall be the highest legislative, executive, and supervisory organ of the Russian Socialist Federated Soviet Republic.

Article 32   The All-Russian Central Executive Committee of Soviets shall direct in a general way the activities of the Workers' and Peasants' Government and of all Soviet organs in the country. It shall unify and coordinate legislative and administrative work and supervise the implementation of the Soviet Constitution, the decisions of the All-Russian Congresses of Soviets and the central organs of Soviet power.

Article 33   The All-Russian Central Executive Committee of Soviets shall examine and approve draft decrees and other proposals submitted by the Council of People's Commissars or by individual departments, and shall also issue its own decrees and regulations.

Article 34   The All-Russian Central Executive Committee of Soviets shall convene the All-Russian Congress of Soviets, to which it shall submit an account of its activities, together with reports on general policy and specific questions.

Article 35   The All-Russian Central Executive Committee of Soviets shall form the Council of People's Commissars for the general direction of the affairs of the Russian Socialist Federated Soviet Republic, and departments (people's commissariats) for the direction of the different branches of administration.

Article 36   Members of the All-Russian Central Executive Committee of Soviets shall either work in the departments (people's commissariats) or carry out special assignments of the All-Russian Central Executive Committee of Soviets.

Chapter Eight The Council of People's Commissars

Article 37   The Council of People's Commissars shall be entrusted with the general direction of the affairs of the Russian Socialist Federated Soviet Republic.

Article 38   In the execution of this task the Council of People's Commissars shall issue decrees, regulations and instructions, and undertake all measures necessary for the proper and prompt dispatch of state affairs.

Article 39   The Council of People's Commissars shall immediately notify the All-Russian Central Executive Committee of Soviets of all its orders and decisions.

Article 40   The All-Russian Central Executive Committee of Soviets shall have the right to annul or suspend any order or decision of the Council of People's Commissars.

Article 41   All orders and decisions of the Council of People's Commissars of major political importance shall be submitted to the All-Russian

Central Executive Committee of Soviets for examination and approval.
   Note: Measures requiring immediate implementation may be put into
      effect directly by the Council of People's Commissars.

Article 42   Members of the Council of People's Commissars shall be in charge of the individual people's commissariats.

Article 43   Seventeen [Eighteen][5] People's Commissariats shall be formed, as follows: (a) Foreign Affairs; (b) War; (c) Naval Affairs; (d) Internal Affairs; (e) Justice; (f) Labour; (g) Social Security; (h) Education; (i) Posts and Telegraphs; (j) Nationality Affairs; (k) Finance; (l) Transport; (m) Agriculture; (n) Trade and Industry; (o) Food Supplies; (p) State Control; (q) Supreme Council of National Economy; (r) Public Health.

Article 44   Attached to each people's commissar, and under his chairmanship, a collegium shall be formed, the members of which shall be approved by the Council of People's Commissars.

Article 45   The people's commissar shall have the right to decide personally all matters under the jurisdiction of his commissariat but shall inform the collegium of his decisions. In the event that the collegium disagrees with any of the decisions of the people's commissar it may, without suspending the execution of the decision, appeal to the Council of People's Commissars or the Presidium of the All-Russian Central Executive Committee of Soviets.
   Individual members of the collegium shall have the same right of appeal.

Article 46   The Council of People's Commissars shall be responsible in all matters to the All-Russian Congress of Soviets and the All-Russian Central Executive Committee of Soviets.

Article 47   The people's commissars and the collegia of the people's commissariats shall be responsible in all matters to the Council of People's Commissars and the All-Russian Central Executive Committee of Soviets.

Article 48   The title of 'people's commissar' shall belong exclusively to members of the Council of People's Commissars, in charge of the general affairs of the Russian Socialist Federated Soviet Republic, and may not be conferred upon any other representative of Soviet power either in the centre or in the localities.

Chapter Nine   The Jurisdiction of the All-Russian Congress of Soviets and the All-Russian Central Executive Committee of Soviets

Article 49   The All-Russian Congress of Soviets and the All-Russian

Central Executive Committee of Soviets shall have jurisdiction over all matters of general state importance, namely:

(a) The approval and amendment of the Constitution of the Russian Socialist Federated Soviet Republic.

(b) The general direction of the entire foreign and domestic policy of the Russian Socialist Federated Soviet Republic.

(c) The establishment and modification of frontiers, as well as the alienation of parts of the territory of the Russian Socialist Federated Soviet Republic or of the rights belonging to it.

(d) The establishment of the boundaries and the competencies of the regional unions of soviets included in the Russian Socialist Federated Soviet Republic, and the settlement of disputes between them.

(e) The admission into the Russian Socialist Federated Soviet Republic of new members of the Soviet Republic and the recognition of the secession of different parts from the Russian Federation.

(f) The general administrative division of the territory of the Russian Socialist Federated Soviet Republic and the approval of regional unions.

(g) The establishment and modification of the system of weights, measures, and currency within the territory of the Russian Socialist Federated Soviet Republic.

(h) Relations with foreign powers, declaration of war and conclusion of peace.

(i) The concluding of loans, customs and trade treaties, and financial agreements.

(j) The establishment of the fundamentals and the general plan for the entire national economy and its different branches in the territory of the Russian Socialist Federated Soviet Republic.

(k) The approval of the budget of the Russian Socialist Federated Soviet Republic.

(l) The establishment of state taxes and duties.

(m) The establishment of the fundamentals of organization of the armed forces of the Russian Socialist Federated Soviet Republic.

(n) General state legislation, judicial organization and procedure, civil and criminal legislation, etc.

(o) The appointment and dismissal both of individual members of the Council of People's Commissars and of the Council of People's Commissars as a whole, as well as the approval of the appointment of the Chairman of the Council of People's Commissars.

(p) The issuing of general orders concerning the acquisition and loss of the rights of Russian citizenship and the rights of foreigners within the territory of the Republic.

(q) The right of granting complete or partial amnesty.

Article 50   In addition to the above matters the All-Russian Congress of Soviets and the All-Russian Central Executive Committee of Soviets may decide on any other matter which they deem within their jurisdiction.

Article 51   The following shall be within the exclusive jurisdiction of the All-Russian Congress of Soviets:
   (a)   The establishment and amendment of the fundamental principles of the Soviet Constitution.
   (b)   The ratification of peace treaties.

Article 52   Decisions on matters indicated in sections (c) and (h) of article 49 shall be taken by the All-Russian Central Executive Committee of Soviets only when the All-Russian Congress of Soviets cannot be convened.

B. The Organization of Soviet Power in the Localities

Chapter Ten The Congresses of Soviets

Article 53   Congresses of soviets shall be composed as follows:
   (a)   Regional congresses – of representatives of town soviets in the proportion of one deputy for every 5000 electors, and of county congresses of soviets in the proportion of one deputy for every 25,000 inhabitants, with not more than 500 delegates for the entire region; or of representatives of provincial congresses of soviets, elected on the same basis, if such congresses immediately precede the regional congress of soviets.
   (b)   Province congresses – of representatives of town soviets in the proportion of one deputy for every 2000 electors, and of rural district congresses of soviets in the proportion of one deputy for every 10,000 inhabitants, with not more than 300 deputies for the entire province; if the county congress of soviets immediately precedes the province congress, elections shall be held on the same basis, not by the rural district but by the county congress of soviets.
   (c)   County congresses – of representatives of village soviets in the proportion of one deputy for every 1000 inhabitants, with not more than 300 deputies for the entire county.
   (d)   Rural district congresses – of representatives of all the village soviets of the rural district in the proportion of one deputy for every ten members of the soviet.
      Note 1: The soviets of towns with a population not exceeding 10,000 persons shall be represented in the county congresses of soviets; village soviets of localities numbering

less than 1000 inhabitants shall combine in electing deputies to the county congress of soviets.

Note 2: Village soviets numbering less than ten members shall send one representative to the rural district congress of soviets.

Article 54 Congresses of Soviets shall be convened by the corresponding territorial executive organs of Soviet power (executive committees) at the discretion of the latter or upon the demand of local soviets comprising not less than one-third of the entire population of the given territory, but in any case not less than twice a year in the region, once every three months in the province and the county, and once every month in the rural district.[6]

Article 55 Each congress of soviets (region, province, county, rural district) shall elect its own executive organ (executive committee), the membership of which shall not exceed: (a) in the region and province – twenty-five[7] (b) in the county – twenty (c) in the rural district – ten. The executive committee shall be responsible in all matters to the congress of soviets which elected it.

Article 56 Within the limits of its jurisdiction the congress of soviets (region, province, county, rural district) shall be the highest authority of the given territory; in the interim between congresses this authority shall be vested in the executive committee.

Chapter Eleven The Soviets of Deputies

Article 57 Soviets of deputies shall be formed as follows:

(a) In towns – one deputy for every 1000 inhabitants, the total to be not less than fifty and not more than 1000 members.

(b) In rural localities (villages, hamlets, stanitsas, townships, towns with less than 10,000 inhabitants, auls, khutors,[8] etc.) – one deputy for every 100 inhabitants, the total to be not less than three and not more than fifty members. The term of office of the deputies shall be three months.

Note: In rural localities where it is considered possible, matters of administration shall be directly decided by the general assembly of electors of the given locality.

Article 58 For the conduct of current work the soviet of deputies shall elect from its members an executive body (executive committee), numbering not more than five in villages, and in towns in the proportion of one for every fifty members, but not less than three and not more than fifteen (in Petersburg and Moscow not more than forty). The executive committee shall be responsible in all matters to the soviet which elected it.

Article 59   The soviet of deputies shall be convened by the executive committee, at the initiative of the latter or upon the demand of not less than half of the members of the soviet, at least once a week in towns and twice a week in villages.

Article 60   Within the limits of its jurisdiction the soviet or, in the case envisaged in the note to article 57, the general assembly of electors shall be the highest authority in the given locality.

Chapter Twelve The Jurisdiction of Local Organs of Soviet Power

Article 61   The regional, provincial, county and rural district organs of Soviet power, and also the soviets of deputies, shall have the following functions:

    (a) the implementation of all instructions of the corresponding higher organs of Soviet power;

    (b) the adoption of all measures for the cultural and economic development of their territories;

    (c) the settlement of all questions of purely local importance (for the given territory);

    (d) the coordination of all soviet activity within their territories.

Article 62   The congresses of soviets and their executive committees shall have the right of control over the activities of the local soviets (i.e. congresses of regions shall have the right of control over all soviets of the region, those of provinces over all soviets of the province, with the exception of town soviets not forming parts of county congresses, etc.); congresses of regions and provinces shall, in addition, have the right to annul decisions of the soviets in their respective areas, provided they notify the central Soviet government in the most important instances.

Article 63   To enable the organs of Soviet power to perform the tasks entrusted to them, appropriate departments in charge of executives shall be formed in every soviet (town and village) and every executive committee (region, province, county and rural district).

Part Four   Active and Passive Electoral Rights

Chapter Thirteen

Article 64   The right to elect and be elected to the soviets shall belong, irrespective of religion, nationality, domicile, etc., to the following citizens of the Russian Socialist Federated Soviet Republic, of both sexes,

who have reached the age of eighteen on election day:
- (a) all those earning their livelihood by productive and socially useful work, and also persons engaged in domestic pursuits which enable the former to undertake productive work, such as, workers and employees of all kinds and categories engaged in industry, trade, agriculture, etc., peasants and Cossack farmers not employing hired labour for profit;
- (b) soldiers of the Soviet army and navy;
- (c) citizens coming under the categories specified in sections (a) and (b) of the present article who have in any degree lost their capacity for work.
    - Note 1: Local soviets may, with the approval of the central government, lower the age limit established by the present article.
    - Note 2: Of foreign residents, those mentioned in article 20 (Part Two, Chapter Five) shall also enjoy active and passive electoral rights.

Article 65   The right to vote or be elected shall be denied to the following, even if they come under one of the above-mentioned categories:
- (a) persons employing hired labour for profit;
- (b) persons living on unearned income, such as interest on capital, revenue from enterprises, income from property, etc.;
- (c) private traders and commercial middle-men;
- (d) monks and clergymen of all religious denominations;
- (e) employees and agents of the former police, of the special gendarme corps and secret service, as well as members of the former ruling dynasty of Russia;
- (f) persons declared, under established procedure, insane or mentally deficient, and also persons under guardianship;
- (g) persons convicted of mercenary or infamous crimes and sentenced to a term set by law or by the judgement of a court.

Chapter Fourteen Electoral Procedure

Article 66   Elections shall be conducted according to established custom, on days fixed by local soviets.

Article 67   Elections shall be conducted in the presence of an electoral commission and a representative of the local soviet.

Article 68   In cases where the presence of a representative of the soviet is technically impossible his place shall be taken by the chairman of the electoral commission, and, in his absence, by the chairman of the electoral assembly.

Article 69   A record of the proceedings and the results of the election shall be drawn up and signed by the members of the electoral commission and the representative of the soviet.

Article 70   Details of the electoral procedure, as well as the participation of trade unions and other workers' organizations in elections, shall be determined by the local soviets in accordance with instructions of the All-Russian Central Executive Committee of Soviets.

Chapter Fifteen The Verification and Annulment of Elections and Recall of Deputies

Article 71   All materials relating to the conduct of elections shall be forwarded to the appropriate soviet.

Article 72   The soviet shall appoint a credentials commission to verify the elections.

Article 73   The credentials commission shall report its findings to the soviet.

Article 74   The soviet shall decide disputed election results.

Article 75   In the case of the non-confirmation of any candidate the soviet shall call new elections.

Article 76   In the event that the election as a whole was carried out contrary to law, the question of annulling the election shall be decided by the next higher organ of Soviet power.

Article 77   The All-Russian Central Executive Committee of Soviets shall be the final court of appeal in matters of soviet elections.

Article 78   Electors shall have the right to recall at any time the deputy they have sent to the soviet and to hold new elections in accordance with the general statute.

Part Five   Budgetary Law

Chapter Sixteen

Article 79   The financial policy of the Russian Socialist Federated Soviet Republic during the present transition period of the dictatorship of toilers shall have as its fundamental aim the expropriation of the bourgeoisie and the creation of conditions for the general equality of citizens of the Republic in the production and distribution of wealth. With this in view it shall aim to place at the disposal of the organs of Soviet power, without regard for the rights of private property, all resources needed to meet the local and general state requirements of the Soviet Republic.

Article 80   The state revenues and expenditures of the Russian Socialist Federated Soviet Republic shall be combined in the general state budget.

Article 81   The All-Russian Congress of Soviets, or the All-Russian Central Executive Committee of Soviets, shall determine which revenues and duties shall accrue to the general state budget and which revenues and duties shall go to the local soviets, and shall also establish the limits of taxation.

Article 82   The soviets shall levy taxes and duties exclusively for local needs. General state requirements shall be met by allocations from the state treasury.

Article 83   No expenditure may be made from the funds of the state treasury unless provided for in the state budget or authorized by special order of the central government.

Article 84   To meet general state requirements the necessary credits from the state treasury shall be placed at the disposal of local soviets by the appropriate people's commissariats.

Article 85   All credits granted to the soviets out of the state treasury, as well as credits approved for local needs, shall be disbursed strictly within the limits of the estimates, by paragraphs and clauses, and may not be diverted to any other purpose without a special order of the All-Russian Central Executive Committee of Soviets and the Council of People's Commissars.

Article 86   Local soviets shall draw up semi-annual and annual estimates of revenues and expenditures. The estimates of village and rural district soviets, and town soviets participating in county congresses of soviets, as well as the estimates of county organs of Soviet power, shall be approved by the respective provincial and regional congresses or by their executive committees; the estimates of town, province and regional organs of Soviet power shall be approved by the All-Russian Central Executive Committee of Soviets and the Council of People's Commissars.

Article 87   In the event of the need for expenditure not provided for in the estimates, or insufficiently provided for, the soviets shall apply to the appropriate people's commissariats for supplementary credits.

Article 88   In the event that local resources prove inadequate to meet local needs, subsidies or loans from the state treasury to the local soviets to cover urgent expenditures shall be authorized by the All-Russian Central Executive Committee of Soviets and the Council of People's Commissars.

Part Six The Arms and Flag of the Russian Socialist Federated Soviet Republic

Chapter Seventeen

Article 89   The arms of the Russian Socialist Federated Soviet Republic shall consist of a golden sickle and hammer, crossed, with handles pointing downward, against a red background in the rays of the sun, and surrounded by a wreath of ears of grain with the inscriptions:

    (a) 'Russian Socialist Federated Soviet Republic', and

    (b) 'Proletarians of All Countries, Unite!'

Article 90   The commercial, naval[9] and military flag of the Russian Socialist Federated Soviet Republic shall consist of red (scarlet) material, with the letters in gold 'RSFSR' or the inscription 'Russian Socialist Federated Soviet Republic' in the upper left corner near the staff.

Notes

1 The constitution was completely revised on 11 May 1925, but had then already been superseded as the fundamental law of the Soviet state by the 1924 constitution of the USSR. In the years in which the 1918 constitution of the RSFSR remained in force, various enactments were passed which materially affected its provisions without resulting in formal constitutional amendment. The most important of these were briefly reviewed in the preceding chapter. Several new legal norms were, however, explicitly identified by the legislator as constitutional amendments, and these are noted below under the appropriate articles of the constitution. In none of these cases did the amending enactment specify the new version of the article concerned.

    Soviet nomenclature for official enactments has been unsystematic and thus confusing, especially during the early years. The enactments mentioned in the 1918 constitution have here been translated as follows: *dekret* – decree, *postanovlenie* – order (except when referring to acts of congresses of soviets, when it has been rendered as 'decision') *rasporyazhenie* – regulation, *instruksiya* – instruction, *polozhenie* – statute.

2 Daily newspaper; official organ of the Soviets.

3 The administrative-territorial subdivisions existing at the time have here been translated as follows: *oblast'* – region, *gubernya* – province, *uezd* – county, *volost* – rural district.

4 Amended by the Ninth Congress of Soviets on 28 December 1921 to once a year.

5 Error in the original text as published on 19 July 1918. The draft constitution submitted to the Fifth Congress of Soviets and published on 5 July 1918 contained the correct number.

6 An amendment of the Ninth Congress of Soviets of 28 December 1921 empowered provincial and county executive committees to convene extraordinary congresses of counties and rural districts, respectively, and the CEC Presidium to convene extraordinary congresses of autonomous republics, reg-

ions and provinces, and reduced the minimum frequency of congresses from rural district level upward to once a year. (Earlier, on 9 December 1919, the Seventh Congress of Soviets had already reduced the minimum frequency of regional, provincial and county congresses to twice a year, and that of rural district congresses to once every three months.)

7 An amendment of the Ninth Congress of Soviets of 28 December 1921, referring to article 57 [sic!] empowered provincial congresses to appoint members to their executive committees in excess of the norm fixed by the constitution.

8 Stanitsa, aul and khutor are designations of various types of rural settlements in different regions of the country.

9 An amendment adopted by the CEC on 29 September 1920 slightly modified the specifications for the commercial and naval flags.

2

The USSR Constitution of 1924

Commentary on the Text

By the end of the civil war the recovery of the greater part of the Tsarist heritage had been completed. With the exception of Poland, Finland, the Baltic states and Bessarabia, local Bolshevik parties aided by the Red Army had succeeded in establishing Soviet rule in most of the territories of the former Empire. The specific form of association with Moscow was largely governed by momentary considerations of political expediency and varied from one case to another. Some of the minority territories were formally independent 'Soviet republics' bound to the RSFSR by treaties of alliance, others were incorporated in the RSFSR as 'autonomous republics' or 'autonomous regions'. It was not till the adoption of the second Soviet constitution in 1923-4 that a more or less uniform, if flexible, pattern of quasi-federal relations between the constituent parts of the Soviet state was established.

Resolutions calling for the union of the several Soviet republics were passed by various party and state bodies from 1921 onwards. In that year, too, delegates from the non-Russian minority republics began to take part in the sessions of the All-Russian Congress of Soviets and were included in its Central Executive Committee (CEC). Beginning in August 1922, with the formation by the party Central Committee (CC) of a special commission headed by Stalin, central party organs discussed and formulated specific proposals for the constitutional framework of a federal state. In December 1922 the 10th All-Russian Congress of Soviets transformed itself into the First Congress of the Union of Socialist Soviet Republics, representing the four republics concerned at the time: the RSFSR, Ukraine, Belorussia, and Transcaucasia. (The latter was a recently formed union of Georgia, Armenia and Azerbaidzhan.) The Congress on 30 December adopted a treaty for the union of the several republics which was to serve as a basis for the future constitution. The first constitution of the union was promulgated by CEC decree on 6 July 1923. It came into force immediately but was submitted for 'final ratification' to the Second Congress of Soviets which with two minor amendments promulgated the constitution on 31 January 1924.

As the avowed object of the constitution was to provide a federal structure for a multi-national state it may be appropriate to review briefly the Bolshevik attitude to the national problem in general and the federal

solution in particular. In the long years of waiting for power the Bolsheviks had sufficient opportunity both to acquaint themselves with the
national question in Russia and to define their own attitudes and
policies. In this, as in many other matters, Bolshevik opinion at the time
was far from united, but if the views of Lenin and some of his closest
associates may be taken as representative of the party then there can be
no doubt of the Bolsheviks' uncompromising support for the rights of
Russia's national minorities. Recognition of the 'right to self-
determination for all nations forming part of the state' was included in
the first Party Programme of 1903, and in Lenin's subsequent interpretation this meant 'the right to secede and form a separate state'.[1] It may
be added that in purely tactical terms the Bolshevik position had much to
recommend it since it was likely to win friends for the party among the
country's minority nationalities and thus to open a second, national,
front against the Tsarist regime, in addition to that on which the class
war was being waged.

Self-determination and its corollary, secession, were of course difficult
to reconcile with 'the unity of proletarians of all nations' and 'the fusion
of all nations into a higher unity' which were respectively the basic
premise and ultimate goal of the Marxist international credo. But, as
Lenin repeatedly pointed out, recognition of the right to secession did
not entail approval of separatism, any more than recognition of the right
to divorce entailed approval of the destruction of family ties. On the
contrary, the freedom to separate was an essential requisite for a successful union of nations just as it was essential for a successful marriage. 'If
we demand freedom of secession . . .', declared Lenin in 1916, 'we do so
not because *we favour secession*, but *only* because we are for *free, voluntary*
association and merging as distinct from forcible association. That is the
only reason!'[2] Indeed, it was Lenin's firm conviction that the surest way
to maintain the integrity of post-revolutionary, socialist Russia was to
grant the right to separation. He believed, with some naivety perhaps,
but also with considerable ardour, that what was needed to transform
the Tsarist 'prison of nationalities' into a voluntary community of nations
was to open the prison gates. In short, while the Bolsheviks preached the
principle of self-determination to the point of secession they did so on
the assumption that in a socialist Russia it would not be widely practised.

Moreover, even as an abstract principle the right to separation was, for
all the prominence it was given in Bolshevik doctrine, unmistakably
subordinated to the class struggle. The first concern of the proletariat
was 'the self-determination not of peoples and nations but of the proletariat within each nation'. The party, Lenin asserted, must 'assess any
national demand, any national aspiration, *from the angle* of the workers'
class struggle'.[3] The right to self-determination was relative and condi-
tional; it would not be allowed to jeopardize the revolutionary interests
of the proletariat.

As to the structure of the multinational state under socialism, the Bolsheviks pronounced themselves unreservedly against a federal state. In their view, historical development led everywhere towards large territorial entities and the economic programme of socialism in particular required centralized control and administration. Federalism was a 'petty-bourgeois principle' retarding even capitalist, not to mention socialist, development. In 1913 Lenin declared:

> Marxists will never, under any circumstances, advocate either the federal principle or decentralization. The great centralized state is a tremendous historical step forward . . . and only *via* such a state (*inseparably* connected with capitalism) can there be any road to socialism.[4]

These views were reiterated in one form or another right up to the October revolution. Stalin, who had become the party's principal spokesman on nationality questions, affirmed in March 1917 that

> in order to convert Russia into a federation it would be necessary *to break* the already existing economic and political ties connecting the regions with one another, which would be absolutely unwise and reactionary.[5]

To the Bolsheviks there was nothing incompatible between their repeatedly stressed concern for the rights of the small nationalities and their unconcealed preference for large multinational states, on the one hand, and their outright rejection of federalism as a method capable of accommodating the diverse interests of different nationalities within a single state system, on the other. The unitary state, in the Bolshevik view, was an economic necessity; its patent advantages would induce the minority nationalities to join such a state voluntarily. If there were a few nationalities unwilling or unable to fit themselves into the larger framework, their self-determination would be realized through secession. For all others – Stalin estimated them at nine-tenths in the case of Russia – their specific national interests would be assured through a measure of autonomy within the unitary state. But it would be an autonomy granted by the centre, rather than arrived at by 'agreement between two partners' which Lenin regarded as the characteristic of federations. And it would be limited to '*purely* local (regional, national, etc.) questions' and thus remain fully consonant with '*centralism* in serious, important and fundamental matters'.[6]

With the onset of the revolution these views were substantially modified. The strength of the centrifugal forces unleashed by the breakdown of the old order severely tested Bolshevik tolerance to secession, and a federal, or rather quasi-federal, solution seemed to offer itself to the Bolshevik leaders as a means of containing the growing movement of separation from Russia. Already the Declaration of the Rights of the

Toiling and Exploited People of January 1918 proclaimed the new state 'a federation of national Soviet republics', and this designation was incorporated in the title of the constitution of July 1918. However, the concession to federalism, so far merely declaratory and bereft of any institutional backing in the operative clauses of the constitution, was depicted as a temporary device destined to pave the way for the creation of a unitary state in the future. Nor, apparently, was federalism regarded as incompatible with centralism. In March 1918 Lenin declared that 'within limits that are rational from an economic point of view' federation could under certain conditions be beneficial and was 'in no way in contradiction to democratic centralism.' These conditions existed in the case of Russia: 'The example of the Russian Soviet Republic shows us particularly clearly that federation, which we are introducing . . . is now the surest step towards the most lasting union of the various nationalities of Russia into a single, democratic, centralized Soviet state.'[7] Stalin, now People's Commissar of Nationalities, similarly stated in April 1918 that 'federalism in Russia is destined to serve as a means of transition – transition to the *socialist* unitarism of the future'.[8] This was also the formula adopted in the second Party Programme of December 1919 where Soviet federalism was described as 'one of the transitional forms to complete unity'.

To be sure, the meaning of federalism in Bolshevik pronouncements at the time was less than self-evident. Some of the ambiguity with which the concept was being handled came to the fore in the discussions that attended the drafting of the constitution. The first proposals prepared by Stalin's commission envisaged the 'federal' solution in the shape of the incorporation of the minority republics as autonomous units of the RSFSR. Stalin – and he was by no means alone among the Bolshevik leaders in this regard – entertained few illusions about either the desirability or the feasibility of maintaining what he clearly regarded as the fiction of differentiated status for the various national sub-units of the Soviet state. 'In your theses', he wrote to Lenin in 1921, 'you draw a distinction between Bashkir and Ukrainian types of national union, but in fact there is no such difference, or it is so small as to equal zero.' But the so-called 'autonomization' plan of his commission encountered sharp opposition, not only from several of the non-Russian Communist party organizations, particularly in Georgia,[9] but also from Lenin, who insisted most adamantly on the association of formally equal states that was finally adopted. That the niceties of equality among the republics were observed in the constitutional text was, of course, due in no small measure to the Soviet leaders' awareness of the crucial role of the Communist party in underpinning whatever form the state structure might take. It was the party which flexed the real sinews of power in the Soviet system, and the party was and remained highly centralized.

The federal features of the 1924 constitution (and indeed those of the two subsequent constitutions) will be seen in correct perspective if it is realized that the conversion to federalism did not involve abandonment of any of the tenets of the original doctrine namely, centralism, territorial autonomy and the right to secession. Instead, the federal form was superimposed upon these three long-standing commitments. And though it was always clear that unchallenged primacy was accorded to centralism, in theory as well as in practice, it may be doubted whether it would have been possible to run them in harness for any length of time without the overriding and unifying authority of the single party directed from a single centre.

Before passing on to a discussion of the contents of the constitution itself it is worth pointing out that there is some doubt whether Lenin would have given his blessing to the document in the form in which it was eventually enacted ten days after his death. The details of the constitutional provisions were worked out at a time when Lenin's illness had already removed him from active participation in the affairs of state. It was precisely at this time that, in the words of one eminent scholar of the subject,

> Lenin went through a reappraisal of Soviet nationality policy which bore all the marks of a true intellectual crisis. It is likely that had he not suffered a nearly fatal stroke in March 1923 the final structure of the Soviet Union would have been quite different from that which Stalin ultimately gave it.[10]

Lenin's second thoughts appear to have been prompted in particular by the Georgian question and the way it had been handled by Stalin and by two other Bolshevik leaders, Ordzhonikidze and Dzerzhinsky – both, like Stalin, of non-Russian origin. In any event, from his sick-bed Lenin dictated a series of memoranda which displayed profound concern over the fate of the minority nationalities in the face of continued manifestations of 'Great Russian chauvinism', not least because of the negative effect which even 'the slightest crudity or injustice towards our own non-Russian nationalities' would have on the awakening colonial peoples. Among his operative remedies was a proposal to extend the powers of republican governments, leaving only foreign and military affairs in the exclusive jurisdiction of the union government. Characteristically, any resultant problems of coordination between the centre and the republics could, in Lenin's view, 'be compensated sufficiently by Party authority, if it is exercised with sufficient prudence and impartiality'.[11]

The contents of the 1924 constitution reveal its origin as a covenant between formally sovereign states. The operative articles, grouped in Part Two (headed 'Treaty'), deal with the structure and institutions of the newly established union. Other matters, notably those relating to the rights and duties of citizens, were not made part of the federal constitution, but were left instead to be regulated by the constitutions of the member republics (on the model of the RSFSR constitution of 1918).

The institutions formed under the 1924 constitution followed the familiar pyramid model of its predecessor, with few major changes beyond those arising from the new federal structure. The CEC was transformed into a bi-cameral assembly: a Union Council, elected from among delegates to the Congress of Soviets (now the All-Union Congress) on the basis of population, and a Council of Nationalities, composed of five representatives from each union and autonomous republic and one representative from each autonomous region [articles 13–15]. The concurrence of both chambers was required for all acts of the CEC and fairly elaborate (and, in practice, quite superfluous) procedures were laid down for the resolution of disagreements between the two chambers [articles 22–4]. The constitution recognized the Presidium of the CEC as the 'highest legislative, executive and administrative organ of power' of the USSR. It was to be elected by the CEC at a joint sitting of the two chambers (voting separately), and to act on behalf of the CEC in the intervals between CEC sessions [articles 26 & 29]. (It will be recalled that the 1918 constitution of the RSFSR, while mentioning the Presidium, did not define its powers.) The central government was reorganized into a federal organ. The Council of Commissars now consisted of two categories of commissariats: all-union commissariats functioning at the level of the central government only ('with plenipotentiaries in the union republics') and responsible for both the direction and execution of policy in their respective fields; and unified, or as they were subsequently named, union-republic, commissariats which functioned in their respective fields through parallel commissariats in the governments of the member republics and were responsible for the implementation of policies devised at the centre [articles 50–4]. A third category of commissariats existed at the republic level only. (Exclusive administrative jurisdiction assigned to the republics under the 1924 constitution embraced agriculture, education, internal affairs, justice, public health and social security [cf. articles 67–8]. This two-fold division of government departments – all-union and unified at the centre, unified and republican in the constituent republics – had been in existence for some time prior to the adoption of the 1924 constitution and had proved its value in regulating the administrative relations between the RSFSR and the autonomous republics and, indeed, the 'independent' republics which subsequently joined the union.

Unlike its predecessor, the 1924 constitution provided for judicial institutions in the form of the Supreme Court of the Union and the Procuracy (Public Prosecutor's Office), thus reflecting a new-found, though as yet embattled, deference to the role of law in the proletarian state. The 'retreat', as Lenin called it, of the New Economic Policy launched in 1921 required a rather firmer foundation of legal norms and procedures than that created in the period of 'war communism' with its fundamentalist vision of the 'withering away' of state and law.

The Supreme Court was attached to the CEC, which meant in practice its Presidium. Aside from limited original jurisdiction – mainly disputes between member republics and charges brought against high officials – the Supreme Court was conceived primarily as a kind of constitutional tribunal empowered 'to render opinions' at the request of the CEC on the constitutionality of acts of the supreme organs of the member republics. (The 1923 Statute on the Supreme Court of the USSR did not limit this form of 'judicial review' to the acts of union republics but extended it also to those of the USSR Council of Commissars.) The Supreme Court of the USSR could also examine decisions of the supreme courts of the union republics for incompatibility with all-union legislation and infringement of the 'interests of other republics' [article 43]. As originally constituted the Supreme Court was not placed at the summit of an integrated court system. Only some ten years later, following enactments of 13 September 1933 and 10 July 1934 was the Supreme Court empowered to issue directives and judicial interpretations binding on all Soviet courts and also to review decisions of republican courts on its own initiative.

The procuracy is a unique Russian institution with antecedents dating back to the time of Peter the Great. It was traditionally charged not only with representation of the state in judicial proceedings but also – until 1864 – with supervision over the legality of the activities of all state organs (as the 'eye of the Tsar'), and it was restored in this dual capacity by statutes of 23 May 1922. A curious omission of the constitutional text [article 46] is the absence of any reference to the procuracy's distinctive role as guardian of legality (except in connection with the secret police – see p. 52 below). Yet this role had figured prominently in the discussions leading up to the re-introduction of the procuracy and had also been explicitly formulated in the May 1922 statutes. Only in 1935, following further statutory changes in the powers of the procuracy, was an appropriate amendment inserted in the constitution. It is of some interest, too, that Lenin, much perturbed at the time by the absence of a stable legal order ('Undoubtedly we are living amidst an ocean of illegality . . .'[12]), had pressed for a strong and highly centralized procuracy which would be directly subordinate to the top party organs. In the event, the procuracy was first (under the May 1922 statutes) placed in the Commissariat of Justice, and then (under the 1924 constitution) attached to the Supreme Court [article 46]. Moreover, the constitution did not endow the federal procuracy with supervisory powers over republican procuracies, which remained parts of their respective Commissariats of Justice. A fully centralized procuracy was only created in the 1930s. By a series of enactments, beginning with a decree of 20 June 1933, republican procuracies were progressively subordinated to the federal procuracy while the latter was detached from the Supreme Court and made directly responsible to the CEC, its Presidium and the Council of Commissars.

A special chapter of the constitution was devoted to the state security services, reflecting the importance which they had attained in the affairs of the country. As already noted in the previous chapter, the original political police, the dreaded *Cheka*, was established in December 1917, two months after the October revolution, as a Commission attached to the Council of Commissars, but received no mention in the RSFSR constitution of 1918. An attempt to curb its powers was made in February 1922 when the *Cheka* was reorganized as the State Political Administration, or GPU, and placed under the Commissariat for Internal Affairs. Under the new Constitution the GPU, now renamed OGPU, was given the form of a unified administrative organ attached to the Councils of Commissars at the centre and in the republics [article 61]. A provision by which the procuracy was charged with the supervision of the legality of OGPU actions [article 63], while indicative of the distrust in which the state security agencies were held at the time, remained wholly ineffective in practice. A further attempt to strengthen the supervisory powers of the procuracy under the decree of 20 June 1933, mentioned earlier, and the reintegration of the OGPU into a newly-formed Commissariat of Internal Affairs (NKVD) by the decree of 10 July 1934 similarly failed to place restraints upon the arbitrary exercise of police powers.

The division of powers between the union and its constituent republics was heavily weighted in favour of the former. The powers of the union were enumerated and those of the republics were residual [articles 1 & 3]. The all-important powers of budgetary control and economic planning and direction for the USSR as a whole were so broadly framed, as was the establishment of 'fundamental legislation', 'general principles' and 'general measures' for a variety of matters which did not fall within the exclusive competence of the union, that the residual jurisdiction of the republics was, in fact, severely circumscribed [article 1]. The constitution did not provide for appeal by republican authorities against acts of the all-union CEC and its Presidium, while both these supreme central organs were given all-embracing powers to revoke any acts of the republican authorities, including legislative acts of republican Congresses [articles 20 & 31]. (The all-union Presidium was empowered to suspend acts of republican Congresses, subject to CEC approval [article 32].) The republics could only protest decrees and orders of the all-union Council of Commissars to the CEC Presidium, without suspending their execution; regulations of individual union commissariats could be suspended by republican CECs or their Presidia in cases of 'manifest conflict' with the constitution or other union or republican legislation [articles 42 & 59].

The formation of a bi-cameral CEC was a concession to accepted notions on the structure of federal legislatures; the Bolsheviks had earlier been strenuously opposed to second chambers as typical institutions of 'class society'. Representation in the Council of Nationalities, not only of the four member republics but also of the autonomous republics and regions located within the federating units and not formally partners to the union, was a tribute to the Bolshevik doctrine of territorial autonomy and was designed to stress the character of the USSR as a 'union of nationalities' rather than of states. It also had the effect of giving numerical preponderance in the Council of Nationalities to the RSFSR, which contained the majority of the autonomous territories, and it had for that reason been opposed by representatives of the non-Russian republics in the discussions attending the adoption of the constitution.[13] Whatever the efficacy of these arrangements for the representation of the constituent republics and national minorities – in practice it was never to be tested by disagreements either within the Council of Nationalities or between it and the Union Council – it must be remembered that the CEC was merely one of the 'supreme organs of power' of the union. Neither the Congress of Soviets, which was formally superior to the CEC, nor the CEC Presidium, which wielded the powers of the CEC for most of the time, were bi-cameral bodies. (A Ukrainian suggestion for a bi-cameral Presidium was rejected on the grounds that it would unduly complicate the work of that organ.)

Amendment of the constitution was with one exception extremely simple and the concern of union organs only. Article 2 reserved the right of amendment of 'fundamental principles' to the all-union Congress, without either defining such principles or identifying the organ or organs competent to amend other, i.e. non-fundamental, principles. In fact, various types of normative acts entailing amendments of the constitution came into force by way of orders and decrees passed by other central organs, and all of these acts, including the most trivial ones, such as the re-naming of government agencies, were indiscriminately submitted to the all-union Congress of Soviets for subsequent ratification. The one exception in which the constitution provided for a limitation on the union's amending power relates to the right of secession: the provision guaranteeing each republic 'the right of free secession' [article 4], was not to be modified without the consent of all member republics [article 6].

The unconditional right of separation from the union, also stressed in the declaratory preamble which makes up the first part of the constitution, is indeed the only one of the provisions which radically departs from the general tenor of centralism. No other federal constitution of modern times – and among them there are many in which the rights of the constituent units are far more firmly anchored than is the case in the 1924 Soviet constitution – contains a similar provision. That a far-reaching deviation from accepted federal practice, tending almost to confederation, should have found its way into the otherwise predominantly centralist Soviet constitution can probably be explained, in part at least, by the long-standing commitment to the all-or-nothing doctrine of the right of secession dating from before the Bolsheviks' adoption of the federal compromise. In part, no doubt, it helped to camouflage the elements of centralism built into the less obtrusive clauses of the constitution, or at least to reconcile possible opposition to these clauses among present and prospective partners to the union. Soviet spokesmen, then as now, regard the right of secession as the very hallmark of what they describe as the 'sovereignty' of the member republics. But it was a right granted in the knowledge that it would not have to be honoured. This much had been made abundantly clear both in the words of the Soviet leaders, and in their forcible reintegration of the borderlands of the former Empire. Both left no doubt that, in so far as Soviet arms permitted, self-determination would have to recede before the class interests of the revolution as conceived in Moscow. The constitutional provision for the right to secession had, as one Soviet legal theorist put it at the time, 'merely declaratory and not legislative character'.[14]

The question as to whether the 1924 Soviet constitution conformed to the 'essential' characteristics of federal constitutions need not occupy us here. It clearly did not if federalism is understood as a division of powers which leaves the organs of the central government and those of the constituent units independent of each other in some spheres. Yet this must not be taken to imply that Soviet federalism did not help to serve the needs for which it, like other federal solutions, was designed, namely to create 'unity in diversity' by facilitating the association of different communities in a larger political entity. The dignity of 'sovereign' status, together with the symbols and accessories that went with it, such as national flags, constitutions, organs of government and representation in the central legislature, undoubtedly played some part in placating national aspirations and inducing the national minorities to operate the political system. The fact that the federal framework has been considerably extended since 1924 is evidence that the Soviet leadership has found it a useful device. Under the 1924 constitution three more union republics were added – Uzbekistan and Turkmenistan in 1925 and Tadzhikistan in 1929 – and since 1936 their number has risen further to the present total of fifteen.

Moreover, while Moscow was not prepared to grant meaningful political self-determination to the minority nationalities, it did allow, and in the early years actively encouraged, a considerable measure of indigenous cultural development in matters such as national language, arts and traditions. The political limits of such development were necessarily narrow; they were officially expressed in Stalin's famous formula: 'proletarian in content and national in form'.[15] And even the 'national form' was variously interpreted as fostering 'local nationalism' and therefore incompatible with 'international proletarian culture' or 'Soviet patriotism'. Yet it is probable that the readiness of the Soviet leaders to pour the 'proletarian content' of their policies into 'national form' did make these policies more palatable to the minority nationalities. It should be added that the concessions to national culture, though territorially bound, were not necessarily related to the formal constitutional status of the national territory as either union republic, autonomous republic or autonomous region.

In the period of some thirteen years in which the 1924 constitution remained in force the Soviet Union was transformed into a full-blown totalitarian system. All constitutional restraints, including the feeble safeguards for the rights of the federating units, were inevitably swept away in the process. The transfer of power from the larger deliberative assemblies to the smaller executive organs was completed and a thoroughly centralized administrative structure evolved. The all-union Congress of Soviets became progressively larger and more unwieldy – numbering eventually some 2500 delegates – as its sessions became both less frequent and less regular – from yearly intervals until 1927 to two-yearly intervals until 1931 and a final interval of four years between 1931 and 1935. (The last Congress under the 1924 constitution was an Extraordinary Congress convened in November and December 1936 for the specific purpose of adopting a new constitution.) Since the average duration of a Congress session was about one week it is clear that for all practical purposes the Congress was unable to function effectively as 'the supreme organ of power' in the USSR, as defined in the constitution [article 8]. The CEC underwent a similar process. Its membership increased from over 500 members at the time of the adoption of the constitution to around 750 in the mid-1930s. The constitutional requirement for three annual sessions of the CEC [article 21] was modified in 1931 to a minimum of three sessions in the intervals between sessions of the Congress. In fact, the number of CEC sessions decreased from an average of twice yearly until 1933 to once yearly in the following years. CEC sessions were not, however, convened at regular intervals and there were years in which it did not meet at all. The duration of a CEC session was only slightly longer than that of a Congress, lasting on the average some nine days, no more than was necessary to hear and approve reports on measures taken by the Presidium and the Council of Commissars. Both the Congress of Soviets and its CEC contained considerable numbers of rank-and-file workers and peasants elected in order to enhance the socially representative character of these organs rather than improve their effectiveness as legislative institutions.

The smaller and permanently functioning Presidium of the CEC and the Council of Commissars were composed of full-time politicians and administrators. Between them they shared such powers and functions as Soviet political practice assigned to the top organs of the state. Soviet constitutional theorists have had some difficulty in defining the roles of the Presidium and the Council of Commissars *via-à-vis* each other. But since both drew their authority from the instructions of the Communist party, and ultimately from Stalin, such problems as might have arisen from the overlapping competencies could generally be avoided.

There can be no doubt that it was the Council of Commissars which came to occupy the more important position in the Soviet structure, especially since the late 1920s when the scope of Soviet public administration increased by leaps and bounds. The main impetus for this came with the launching of the first Five-Year Plan which brought both an immediate increase in the administrative activity of the state and a further centralization of the administrative apparatus. Huge bureaucracies were created in the form of new or greatly expanded economic commissariats and planning and coordinating bodies with similar status and powers. With minor exceptions all of these were part of the central machinery operated from Moscow as either all-union or unified commissariats. Inevitably, this very considerable accretion in the administrative activity of the union altered decisively the division of powers and functions between the union and the member republics established under the original terms of the 1924 constitution.

From time to time the constitution was amended with a view to accommodating some of these developments. In so far as this was done, it may be said that the great changes which the country underwent during this period did not pass without rippling the surface of the constitutional scene to some extent. Yet this could not prevent the constitution becoming more and more remote from Soviet reality. Neither Stalin's growing personal power, nor that of the terror apparatus, nor any of the manifold repercussions of forced collectivization and industrialization, left any but the faintest traces in the formal constitutional framework. Clearly, as in the case of all complex, large-scale organizations, some of the activities of the Soviet state were governed by fairly uniform, stable and predictable rules. But the boundaries of such activities were flexible and ill-defined. What is more, they enclosed a comparatively insignificant area of Soviet public life. The crucial, complementary realms of political power and individual freedom remained far beyond the purview of Soviet 'constitutionalism'.

Notes

1 V.I. Lenin, *Collected Works*, 45 vols, Moscow, 1960–70, vol. 19, p. 243.
2 ibid., vol. 23, p. 67 (emphasis in the original).
3 ibid., vol. 20, p. 411 (emphasis in the original).
4 ibid., p. 46 (emphasis in the original).
5 J.V. Stalin, *Works*, 13 vols, Moscow, 1952–5, vol. 3, p. 28 (emphasis in the original).
6 Lenin, *Coll. Works*, vol. 20, p. 47 (emphasis in the original).
7 ibid., vol. 27, p. 207.

8 Stalin, *Works*, vol. 4, p. 75 (emphasis in the original).

9 At a later stage the Georgian party was to raise the further objection that their republic was expected to join the union indirectly via the Transcaucasian Federation (together with Armenia and Azerbaidzhan) and not directly as a full-fledged partner on a par with Belorussia and the Ukraine. The Georgian question became a most acrimonious issue between Moscow and the Georgian party and at one time led to the wholesale resignation of the Georgian Central Committee. It was also largely responsible for the rift that developed between Stalin and Lenin in the last months of the latter's life.

10 R. Pipes, *The Formation of the Soviet Union,* rev. edn, Cambridge, Mass., 1964, p. 276.

11 Lenin, *Coll. Works,* vol. 36, pp. 610–11.

12 ibid., vol. 33, pp. 365–6.

13 Amongst others, the Ukrainian Communist leader Rakovsky, himself of Bulgarian origin and previously known as a staunch 'centralist', noted that the RSFSR was accorded three times as many representatives in the Council as all other republics put together. His proposal that the representation of any one republic should not be allowed to exceed two-fifths of the total was dismissed by Stalin as 'administrative fetishism'.

14 S. Dranitsyn, *Konstitutsiya SSSR i RSFSR,* 2nd edn, Leningrad, 1924, p. 85.

15 J. Stalin, *Marxism and the National and Colonial Question*, London, 1942, p. 210. See also p. 260 where 'proletarian' is replaced by 'socialist'.

The USSR Constitution of 1924

Constitution (Fundamental Law) of The Union of Soviet Socialist Republics

[Adopted by the Central Executive Committee of the USSR on 6 July 1923 and ratified by the Second All-Union Congress of Soviets on 31 January 1924][1]

Part One   Declaration on the Formation of the Union of Soviet Socialist Republics

Since the formation of the Soviet republics, the states of the world have become divided into two camps – the camp of capitalism and the camp of socialism.

There, in the camp of capitalism, national hatred and inequality, colonial slavery and chauvinism, national oppression and massacres, imperialist brutalities and wars prevail.

Here, in the camp of socialism, mutual trust and peace, national freedom and equality, peaceful coexistence and fraternal cooperation of peoples are to be found.

The efforts of the capitalist world, in the course of decades, to solve the question of nationalities by combining the free development of peoples with the exploitation of man by man have been of no avail. On the contrary, the web of national contradictions is becoming ever more entangled, threatening the very existence of capitalism itself. The bourgeoisie has proved powerless to bring about cooperation among peoples.

Only in the camp of the soviets, only in the conditions of the pro-letarian dictatorship rallying the majority of the population, has it become possible to destroy national oppression root and branch, to create an atmosphere of mutual trust and to lay the foundations for the fraternal cooperation of peoples.

Only owing to these circumstances has it been possible for the Soviet republics to repel the external as well as the internal attacks of world im-perialism. Only owing to these conditions were they able to end the civil war successfully, to secure their existence and to pass to the tasks of peaceful economic construction.

But the years of war did not pass without leaving their mark. The devastated fields and idle factories, the breakdown of productive forces and the depletion of economic resources – this legacy of the war renders inadequate the isolated efforts of individual republics toward economic reconstruction. The revival of the economy proved impossible as long as the separate republics maintained a divided existence.

On the other hand, the instability of the international situation and the danger of new attacks make the formation of the Soviet republics into a common front against capitalist encirclement inevitable.

Finally, the very structure of Soviet power, which is international in its class character, propels the toiling masses of the Soviet republics along the path of unification into one socialist family.

All these circumstances imperatively demand the unification of the Soviet republics into one union state, capable of ensuring external security, internal economic prosperity and the free national development of peoples.

The will of the peoples of the Soviet republics, unanimously proclaimed at their recent congresses of soviets in the decision to form the 'Union of Soviet Socialist Republics', is a sure guarantee that this Union is a voluntary association of peoples with equal rights, that each republic is assured of the right of free secession from the Union, that admission to this Union is open to all socialist Soviet republics, those existing now as well as those arising in the future, that the new Union state is a fitting consummation of the principles of peaceful coexistence and fraternal cooperation of peoples established in October 1917, that it is a firm bulwark against world capitalism and a decisive step toward the union of the toilers of all countries into one World Soviet Socialist Republic.

Part Two   Treaty on the Formation of the Union of Soviet Socialist Republics

The Russian Socialist Federated Soviet Republic (RSFSR), the Ukrainian Socialist Soviet Republic (USSR), the Belorussian Socialist Soviet Republic (BSSR), and the Transcaucasian Socialist Federated Soviet Republic (TSFSR: the Soviet Socialist Republic of Azerbaidzhan, the Soviet Socialist Republic of Georgia, and the Soviet Socialist Republic of Armenia) hereby unite into one union state – THE UNION OF SOVIET SOCIALIST REPUBLICS.[2]

Chapter One The Jurisdiction of the Supreme Organs of Government of the Union of Soviet Socialist Republics

Article 1   The jurisdiction of the Union of Soviet Socialist Republics, as embodied in its supreme organs, shall include:

   (a) representation of the Union in international affairs, the conduct of all diplomatic relations and the conclusion of political and other treaties with foreign states;

   (b) modification of the frontiers of the Union and the regulation of questions concerning the modification of boundaries between the union republics;

   (c) conclusion of treaties on the admission of new republics into the Union;

   (d) declaration of war and conclusion of peace;

   (e) concluding foreign and domestic loans by the Union of Soviet Socialist Republics and authorizing foreign and domestic loans by the union republics;

   (f) ratification of international treaties;

   (g) direction of foreign trade, and establishment of a system of internal trade;[3]

   (h) establishment of the fundamentals and general plan for the entire national economy of the Union; determination of the branches of industry and individual industrial enterprises that are of all-union importance; and the conclusion of concession agreements, on behalf of both the Union as a whole and the union republics;

   (i) direction of transport, posts and telegraphs;[4]

   (j) organization and direction of the Armed Forces of the Union of Soviet Socialist Republics;

   (k) approval of a single state budget[5] for the Union of Soviet Socialist Republics, incorporating the budgets of the union republics; establishment of all-union taxes and revenues, and also deductions therefrom and additions thereto for the budgets of the union republics; authorization of supplementary taxes and duties for the budgets of the union republics;

   (l) establishment of a single currency and credit system;

  (m) establishment of general principles governing the distribution and use of land, and the exploitation of minerals, forests and waters throughout the territory of the Union of Soviet Socialist Republics;

   (n) all-union legislation on migration from one republic to another, and establishment of a migration fund;

   (o) establishment of the fundamentals of judicial organization and procedure and also of civil and criminal legislation of the Union;

   (p) enactment of fundamental laws on labour;

(q) establishment of the general principles of public education;

(r) adoption of general measures for the protection of public health;

(s) establishment of a system of weights and measures;

(t) organization of all-union statistics;

(u) fundamental legislation on union citizenship and the rights of foreigners;

(v) the right of amnesty throughout the territory of the Union;

(w) the right to annul decisions of the congresses of soviets and central executive committees of the union republics which are in violation of this Constitution;

(x) settlement of disputed matters arising between the union republics.

Article 2   The approval and amendment of the fundamental principles of this Constitution shall be in the exclusive jurisdiction of the Congress of Soviets of the Union of Soviet Socialist Republics.

Chapter Two The Sovereign Rights of the Union Republics and Union Citizenship

Article 3   The sovereignty of the union republics shall only be restricted within the limits specified in this Constitution and solely in matters assigned to the competence of the Union. Except as so restricted, each union republic shall exercise its state power independently. The Union of Soviet Socialist Republics shall protect the sovereign rights of the union republics.

Article 4   Every union republic shall retain the right of free secession from the Union.

Article 5   The union republics shall amend their constitutions in conformity with this Constitution.

Article 6   The territory of union republics may not be modified without their consent, and amendment, limitation or repeal of article 4 shall require the consent of all republics constituting the Union of Soviet Socialist Republics.

Article 7   A single union citizenship shall be established for the citizens of the union republics.

Chapter Three The Congress of Soviets of the Union of Soviet Socialist Republics

Article 8   The supreme organ of power of the Union of Soviet Socialist Republics shall be the Congress of Soviets and, in the interim between congresses, the Central Executive Committee of the Union of Soviet Socialist Republics, consisting of the Union Council and the Council of Nationalities.

Article 9 The Congress of Soviets of the Union of Soviet Socialist Republics shall consist of the representatives of the soviets of towns and urban settlements in the proportion of one deputy for every 25,000 electors, and of representatives of province congresses of soviets[6] in the proportion of one deputy for every 125,000 inhabitants.

Article 10 The delegates to the Congress of Soviets of the Union of Soviet Socialist Republics shall be elected at the provincial congresses of soviets. In republics not divided into provinces,[7] the delegates shall be elected directly at the congress of soviets of the respective republic.

Article 11 Regular sessions of the Congress of Soviets of the Union of Soviet Socialist Republics shall be convened by the Central Executive Committee of the Union of Soviet Socialist Republics once a year;[8] extraordinary sessions shall be convened by the Central Executive Committee of the Union of Soviet Socialist Republics either on its own initiative or on the demand of the Union Council or the Council of Nationalities or of any two union republics.

Article 12 In extraordinary circumstances preventing the convening of the Congress of Soviets on the appointed date, the Central Executive Committee of the Union of Soviet Socialist Republics shall have the right to postpone the convening of the Congress.

Chapter Four The Central Executive Committee of the Union of Soviet Socialist Republics

Article 13 The Central Executive Committee of the Union of Soviet Socialist Republics shall consist of the Union Council and the Council of Nationalities.

Article 14 The Congress of Soviets of the Union of Soviet Socialist Republics shall elect the Union Council, which shall consist of 414 members, from among the representatives of the union republics in proportion to the population of each republic.[9]

Article 15 The Council of Nationalities shall be formed of the representatives of the union and autonomous soviet socialist republics on the basis of five representatives from each; and of representatives of the autonomous regions of the RSFSR[10] on the basis of one representative from each. The composition of the Council of Nationalities as a whole shall be approved by the Congress of Soviets of the Union of Soviet Socialist Republics.

> Note: The Autonomous Republics of Adzharia and Abkhazia and the Autonomous Region of South Ossetia shall send one representative each to the Council of Nationalities.[11]

Article 16 The Union Council and the Council of Nationalities shall examine all decrees, codes and orders submitted to them by the Presidium of the Central Executive Committee and the Council of People's Commissars of the Union, by individual people's commissariats of the Union, or by the central executive committees of the union republics, and also those enacted upon the initiative of the Union Council or the Council of Nationalities.

Article 17   The Central Executive Committee of the Union of Soviet Socialist Republics shall issue codes, decrees, orders and regulations, coordinate the legislative and executive activity of the Union of Soviet Socialist Republics, and define the sphere of activity of the Presidium of the Central Executive Committee and the Council of People's Commissars of the Union of Soviet Socialist Republics.

Article 18   All decrees and orders defining general norms of the political and economic life of the Union of Soviet Socialist Republics and also those introducing fundamental changes in the existing practices of state organs of the Union of Soviet Socialist Republics, must obligatorily be submitted for examination and approval to the Central Executive Committee of the Union of Soviet Socialist Republics.

Article 19   All decrees, orders and regulations issued by the Central Executive Committee shall take immediate effect throughout the territory of the Union of SSR.

Article 20   The Central Executive Committee of the Union of Soviet Socialist Republics shall have the right to suspend or annul all decrees, orders and regulations of the Presidium of the Central Executive Committee of the Union of Soviet Socialist Republics, and also of the congresses of soviets and of the central executive committees of the union republics, and of other organs of power within the territory of the Union of SSR.

Article 21   Regular sessions of the Central Executive Committee of the Union of Soviet Socialist Republics shall be convened by the Presidium of the Central Executive Committee three times a year.[12] Extraordinary sessions shall be convened by order of the Presidium of the Central Executive Committee of the Union of Soviet Socialist Republics at the demand of the Presidium of the Union Council, or the Presidium of the Council of Nationalities, and also at the demand of the central executive committee of one of the union republics.

Article 22   Legislative drafts submitted for examination by the Central Executive Committee of the Union of Soviet Socialist Republics shall become laws only after their adoption by both the Union Council and the Council of Nationalities, and shall be published in the name of the Central Executive Committee of the Union of Soviet Socialist Republics.

Article 23   In case of disagreement between the Union Council and the Council of Nationalities, the matter shall be referred to a conciliation commission formed by these two organs.

Article 24   If no agreement is reached in the conciliation commission, the matter shall be referred to a joint sitting of the Union Council and the Council of Nationalities; in the event that no majority vote of the Union Council or the Council of Nationalities is obtained the matter may be referred, at the demand of either of these organs, for decision to a regular or extraordinary Congress of the Union of Soviet Socialist Republics.

Article 25   The Union Council and the Council of Nationalities shall each elect a presidium composed of seven members[13] to prepare and direct their sessions.

Article 26   In the interim between sessions of the Central Executive Committee of the Union of Soviet Socialist Republics, the highest organ of state power shall be the Presidium of the Central Executive Committee of the Union of Soviet Socialist Republics; the Presidium shall be formed by the Central Executive Committee and comprise 21 members,[14] including the full membership of the Presidia of the Union Council and the Council of Nationalities.

For the formation of the Presidium of the Central Executive Committee and the Council of People's Commissars of the Union of Soviet Socialist Republics (articles 26 & 37 of this Constitution) a joint sitting of the Union Council and the Council of Nationalities shall be held. Voting at the joint sitting of the Union Council and the Council of Nationalities shall be conducted separately by the Union Council and the Council of Nationalities.

Article 27   The Central Executive Committee shall, in accordance with the number of union republics, elect four[15] chairmen of the Central Executive Committee of the Union of Soviet Socialist Republics from among the members of the Presidium of the Central Executive Committee of the Union of Soviet Socialist Republics.

Article 28   The Central Executive Committee of the Union of Soviet Socialist Republics shall be responsible to the Congress of Soviets of the Union of Soviet Socialist Republics.

Chapter Five The Presidium of the Central Executive Committee of the Union of Soviet Socialist Republics

Article 29   In the interim between sessions of the Central Executive Committee of the Union of Soviet Socialist Republics, the Presidium of the Central Executive Committee of the Union of Soviet Socialist Republics shall be the highest legislative, executive and administrative organ of power of the Union of Soviet Socialist Republics.

Article 30   The Presidium of the Central Executive Committee of the Union of Soviet Socialist Republics shall supervise the application of the Constitution of the Union of Soviet Socialist Republics and the execution of all decisions of the Congress of Soviets and the Central Executive Committee of the Union of Soviet Socialist Republics by all organs of government.

Article 31   The Presidium of the Central Executive Committee of the Union of Soviet Socialist Republics shall have the power to suspend and annul the orders of the Council of People's Commissars and the individual people's commissariats of the Union of Soviet Socialist Republics, and also of the central executive committees and the councils of people's commissars of the union republics.

Article 32   The Presidium of the Central Executive Committee of the Union of Soviet Socialist Republics shall have the power to suspend the decisions of the congresses of soviets of the union republics, but shall subsequently submit such decisions for examination and approval to the Central Executive Committee of the Union of Soviet Socialist Republics.

Article 33   The Presidium of the Central Executive Committee of the Union of Soviet Socialist Republics shall issue decrees, orders and regulations and shall examine and approve the drafts of decrees and orders submitted by the Council of People's Commissars, the individual departments of the Union of Soviet Socialist Republics, or the central executive committees of the union republics, their presidia and other organs of government.

Article 34   The decrees and orders of the Central Executive Committee, its Presidium, and the Council of People's Commissars of the Union of Soviet Socialist Republics shall be printed in all languages in general use in the union republics (Russian, Ukrainian, Belorussian, Georgian, Armenian, Turko-Tatar).[16]

Article 35   The Presidium of the Central Executive Committee of the Union of Soviet Socialist Republics shall decide on matters concerning the mutual relations between the Council of People's Commissars of the Union of Soviet Socialist Republics and the people's commissariats of the Union of Soviet Socialist Republics, on the one hand, and the central executive committees of the union republics and their presidia, on the other hand.

Article 36   The Presidium of the Central Executive Committee of the Union of Soviet Socialist Republics shall be responsible to the Central Executive Committee of the Union of Soviet Socialist Republics.

Chapter Six The Council of People's Commissars of the Union of Soviet Socialist Republics

Article 37   The Council of People's Commissars of the Union of Soviet Socialist Republics shall be the executive and administrative organ of the Central Executive Committee of the Union of Soviet Socialist Republics and shall be formed by the Central Executive Committee of the Union of Soviet Socialist Republics comprising:

> Chairman of the Council of People's Commissars of the Union of Soviet Socialist Republics;
> Deputy Chairmen;
> People's Commissar of Foreign Affairs;
> People's Commissar of War and Naval Affairs;
> People's Commissar of Foreign Trade;
> People's Commissar of Transport;
> People's Commissar of Posts and Telegraphs;
> People's Commissar of Workers' and Peasants' Inspection;
> Chairman of the Supreme Council of National Economy;
> People's Commissar of Labour;
> People's Commissar of Food Supplies;
> People's Commissar of Finance.[17]

Article 38   The Council of People's Commissars of the Union of Soviet Socialist Republics, within the powers conferred upon it by the Central Executive Committee of the Union of Soviet Socialist Republics and on the basis of the Statute of the Council of People's Commissars of the Union of Soviet Socialist Republics, shall issue decrees and orders with effect throughout the territory of the Union of Soviet Socialist Republics.

Article 39   The Council of People's Commissars of the Union of Soviet Socialist Republics shall examine decrees and orders submitted to it by the individual people's commissariats of the Union of Soviet Socialist Republics or by the central executive committees of the union republics and their presidia.[18]

Article 40   The Council of People's Commissars of the Union of Soviet Socialist Republics shall be responsible to the Central Executive Committee of the Union of Soviet Socialist Republics and to its Presidium in regard to all of its activities.

Article 41   The orders and regulations of the Council of People's Commissars of the Union of Soviet Socialist Republics may be suspended or annulled by the Central Executive Committee of the Union of Soviet Socialist Republics or its Presidium.[19]

Article 42   The central executive committees of the union republics and their presidia may protest against the decrees and orders of the Council of People's Commissars of the Union of Soviet Socialist Republics to the Presidium of the Central Executive Committee of the Union of Soviet Socialist Republics, without suspending the implementation of such decrees and orders.

Chapter Seven The Supreme Court of the Union of Soviet Socialist Republics[20]

Article 43   With the aim of strengthening socialist legality within the territory of the Union of Soviet Socialist Republics, a Supreme Court shall be established and attached to the Central Executive Committee of the Union of Soviet Socialist Republics, with competence:

(a)   to give guiding explanations on questions of all-union legislation to the supreme courts of the union republics;

(b)   to review, at the request of the Procurator of the Supreme Court of the Union of Soviet Socialist Republics, the orders, decisions and judgments of the supreme courts of the union republics and, in the event of their violating all-union legislation or infringing the interests of other republics, to protest against them to the Central Executive Committee of the Union of Soviet Socialist Republics;[21]

(c)   to render opinions at the request of the Central Executive Committee of the Union of Soviet Socialist Republics, on the constitutionality of any orders issued by the union republics;

(d)   to resolve legal disputes between the union republics;

(e)   to examine charges against high officials of the Union for offences related to the discharge of their duties.

Article 44   The Supreme Court of the Union of Soviet Socialist Republics shall function comprising: (a) the plenary session of the Supreme Court of the Union of Soviet Socialist Republics; (b) Civil and Criminal Divisions of the Supreme Court of the Union of Soviet Socialist Republics; (c) Military and Military Transport Divisions.[22]

Article 45   In plenary session the Supreme Court of the Union of Soviet Socialist Republics shall consist of eleven members,[23] including the Chairman and his deputy, the four chairmen[24] of the plenary sessions of the supreme courts of the union republics, and one representative of the Unified State Political Administration of the Union of Soviet Socialist Republics. The Chairman, his deputy and the other five members[25] shall be appointed by the Presidium of the Central Executive Committee of the Union of Soviet Socialist Republics.[26]

Article 46   The Procurator of the Supreme Court of the Union of Soviet Socialist Republics and his deputy shall be appointed by the Presidium of the Central Executive Committee of the Union of Soviet Socialist

Republics. The duties of the Procurator of the Supreme Court of the Union of Soviet Socialist Republics shall include rendering opinions on all questions within the jurisdiction of the Supreme Court of the Union of Soviet Socialist Republics, conducting the prosecution at its sessions, and, in the event of his disagreeing with the decisions of the plenary session of the Supreme Court of the Union of Soviet Socialist Republics, lodging protests to the Presidium of the Central Executive Committee of the Union of Soviet Socialist Republics.[27]

Article 47   The right to submit matters specified in article 43 for examination by the plenary session of the Supreme Court of the Union of Soviet Socialist Republics shall belong exclusively to the Central Executive Committee of the Union of Soviet Socialist Republics, its Presidium, the Procurator of the Supreme Court of the Union of Soviet Socialist Republics, the procurators of the union republics and the Unified State Political Administration of the Union of Soviet Socialist Republics.

Article 48   The plenary sessions of the Supreme Court of the Union shall form special judicial divisions for the examination of:
   (a) criminal and civil cases of exceptional importance affecting two or more union republics;
   (b) personal charges against members of the Central Executive Committee and the Council of People's Commissars of the Union of Soviet Socialist Republics.
   Examination of these cases by the Supreme Court of the Union of Soviet Socialist Republics shall take place exclusively upon a special order issued for each case by the Central Executive Committee of the Union or its Presidium.

Chapter Eight The People's Commissariats of the Union of Soviet Socialist Republics

Article 49   For the immediate direction of the individual branches of state administration within the jurisdiction of the Council of People's Commissars of the Union of Soviet Socialist Republics, ten people's commissariats[28], specified in article 37 of this constitution, shall be formed, and shall function on the basis of statutes on people's commissariats approved by the Central Executive Committee of the Union of Soviet Socialist Republics.

Article 50   The people's commissariats of the Union of Soviet Socialist Republics shall be divided into:
   (a) all-union people's commissariats for the entire Union of Soviet Socialist Republics, and
   (b) unified people's commissariats of the Union of Soviet Socialist Republics.

Article 51   The all-union people's commissariats of the Union of Soviet Socialist Republics shall be the following:

Foreign Affairs; War and Naval Affairs; Foreign Trade; Transport; Posts and Telegraphs.[29]

Article 52   The unified people's commissariats of the Union of Soviet Socialist Republics shall be the following:

Supreme Council of National Economy; Food Supplies; Labour; Finance; Workers' and Peasants' Inspection.[30]

Article 53   The all-union people's commissariats of the Union of Soviet Socialist Republics shall have plenipotentiaries,[31] directly subordinated to them, in the union republics.

Article 54   The organs exercising the functions of the unified people's commissariats of the Union of Soviet Socialist Republics in the territories of the union republics shall be the identically named people's commissariats of these republics.

Article 55   The people's commissariats of the Union of Soviet Socialist Republics shall be headed by members of the Council of People's Commissars – the people's commissars of the Union of Soviet Socialist Republics.

Article 56   Attached to each people's commissar and under his chairmanship a collegium shall be formed, the members of which shall be appointed by the Council of People's Commissars of the Union of Soviet Socialist Republics.[32]

Article 57   The people's commissar shall have the right to personally decide all questions under the jurisdiction of his commissariat but shall inform the collegium of his decisions. In the event that the collegium, or its individual members, disagree with any of the decisions of the people's commissar they may, without suspending the execution of the decision, appeal to the Council of People's Commissars of the Union of Soviet Socialist Republics.[33]

Article 58   The regulations of individual commissariats of the Union of Soviet Socialist Republics may be annulled by the Presidium of the Central Executive Committee or by the Council of People's Commissars of the Union of Soviet Socialist Republics.

Article 59   The regulations of the people's commissariats of the Union of Soviet Socialist Republics may be suspended by the central executive committees or the presidia of the central executive committees of the union republics, whenever such regulations are in manifest conflict with the Constitution of the Union, with union legislation or with the legislation of the respective union republic. The central executive committees or the presidia of the central executive committees shall immediately communicate such suspension of regulations to the Council of People's Commissars of the Union of Soviet Socialist Republics and to the people's commissar concerned.

Article 60   The people's commissars of the Union of Soviet Socialist Republics shall be responsible to the Council of People's Commissars, to the Central Executive Committee of the Union of Soviet Socialist Republics and to its Presidium.

Chapter Nine The Unified State Political Administration[34]

Article 61   With the aim of unifying the revolutionary efforts of the union republics in the struggle against political and economic counter-revolution, espionage and brigandage, a Unified State Political Administration (OGPU) shall be created and attached to the Council of People's Commissars of the Union. The Chairman of this Administration shall join the Council of People's Commissars of the Union with the right of an advisory vote.

Article 62   The Unified State Political Administration of the Union of Soviet Socialist Republics shall direct the activities of the local organs of the State Political Administration (GPU) through its plenipotentiaries in the councils of people's commissars of the union republics, acting on the basis of a special statute approved by legislation.

Article 63   Supervision over the legality of the acts of the Unified State Political Administration of the Union of Soviet Socialist Republics shall be exercised by the Procurator of the Supreme Court of the Union of Soviet Socialist Republics on the basis of a special order of the Central Executive Committee of the Union of Soviet Socialist Republics.

Chapter Ten The Union Republics

Article 64   Within the territory of each union republic the supreme organ of power shall be the congress of soviets of the republic and, during the intervals between congresses, its central executive committee.

Article 65   The mutual relations between the supreme organs of power of the union republics and the supreme organs of power of the Union of Soviet Socialist Republics shall be established by this Constitution.

Article 66   The central executive committees of the union republics shall elect from among their members the presidia, which in the interim between central executive committee sessions shall constitute the highest organs of power.

Article 67   The central executive committees of the union republics shall form their executive organs, the councils of people's commissars, comprising the following:

Chairman of the Council of People's Commissars; Deputy Chairmen; Chairman of the Supreme Council of National Economy; People's Commissar of Agriculture; People's Commissar of Finance; People's Commissar of Food Supplies; People's Commissar of Labour; People's Commissar of Internal Affairs; People's Commissar of Justice; People's Commissar of Workers' and Peasants' Inspection; People's Commissar of Education; People's Commissar of Public Health; People's Commissar of Social Security; and also, with the right of an advisory or deciding vote, according to the decisions of the central executive committees of the union republics, plenipotentiaries of the People's Commissariats of Foreign Affairs, War and Naval Affairs, Foreign Trade, Transport, and Posts and Telegraphs.[35]

Article 68   The Supreme Council of National Economy and the People's Commissariats of Food Supplies, Finance, Labour, and Workers' and Peasants' Inspection of each union republic, while subordinate to the central executive committee and council of people's commissars of their union republic, shall execute the directives of the corresponding people's commissariat of the Union of Soviet Socialist Republics.[36]

Article 69   The right of amnesty, as well as the right of pardon and rehabilitation of citizens condemned by the judicial or administrative organs of the union republics, shall belong to the central executive committees of these republics.

Chapter Eleven The Arms, Flag and Capital of the Union of Soviet Socialist Republics

Article 70   The state arms of the Union of Soviet Socialist Republics shall consist of a sickle and hammer against a globe depicted in the rays of the sun and framed by ears of grain with the inscription, in the six languages mentioned in article 34[37]: 'Proletarians of All Countries, Unite!' At the top of the arms shall be a five-pointed star.

Article 71   The state flag of the Union of Soviet Socialist Republics shall consist of red or scarlet cloth with a golden sickle and hammer depicted in the upper corner near the staff, and a five-pointed red star bordered in gold above them. The ratio of width to length shall be 1:2.

Article 72   The city of Moscow shall be the capital of the Union of Soviet Socialist Republics.

Notes

1 Amendments are given below in these notes, under the appropriate articles of the constitution and according to the date of enactment of the amending legislation by the Congress of Soviets. In all cases formal amendment followed the implementation of measures first authorized by other Soviet organs. Where appropriate, for greater clarity, the changed wording is placed in italics. For the translation of the designation of official enactments see above p. 40, n. 1.

2 Amended on 20 May 1925 to include Turkmenistan and Uzbekistan, and again on 17 March 1931 to include Tadzhikistan. In the latter case an identical amendment had earlier been enacted by the all-union CEC on 5 December 1929.

3 Amended on 17 March 1931 to 'system of *supplies and* internal trade'.

4 Amended on 5 February 1935 to 'direction of transport and communications'.

5 Amended on 17 March 1931 to 'approval of *a single financial plan and* a single state budget'.

6 Amended on 26 April 1927 to 'representatives of province *and area* congresses of soviets' and on 17 March 1931 to 'representatives of *village soviets'*. These amendments followed a series of reforms which eventually resulted in three categories of administrative–territorial (non-national) subdivisions: territory (*krai*) – in the RSFSR alone, region (*oblast'*), and district (*raion*).

7 Amended on 26 April 1927 to 'elected at the province *and area* congresses of soviets. In republics not divided into provinces *or areas* the delegates'. The article was revised on 17 March 1931:

Article 10   The delegates to the Congress of Soviets of the Union of Soviet Socialist Republics shall be elected as follows:

    (a)   directly at the congress of soviets of the union republics which are not divided into territories or regions;

    (b)   at the congresses of soviets of territories and regions in those union republics that are divided into territories and regions;

    (c)   at the Congresses of Soviets of the Soviet Socialist Republics of Azerbaidzhan, Georgia and Armenia, and at the congresses of the autonomous republics and autonomous regions, both those which form parts of territories and regions and those which do not.

8 Amended on 26 April 1927 to 'once every two years'.

9 Amended on 20 May 1925 to 'shall consist of representatives of union republics in proportion to the population of each and in such number as shall be determined by the Congress of Soviets of the USSR'.

10 The words 'of the RSFSR' were deleted by amendment of 20 May 1925.

11 The entire Note was deleted by amendment of 20 May 1925.

12 Amended on 17 March 1931 to 'not less than three times in the period between regular sessions of the Congress of Soviets of the USSR'.

13 Amended on 20 May 1925 to 'nine members'.

14 Amended on 20 May 1925 to '27 members'.

15 An amendment of 20 May 1925 replaced 'four' by 'the'.

16 Amended on 17 May 1931 to include Tadzhik. The revised version of this article listed the various languages as 'Russian, Ukrainian, Belorussian, Georgian, Armenian, Azerbaidzhani, Uzbek, Turkmen and Tadzhik (Farsi)'.

17 The organization of the Council of Commissars underwent repeated changes. In its final version, as amended on 5 February 1935, the article provided for the following:

Chairman of the Council of People's Commissars of the Union of Soviet Socialist Republics and of the Council of Labour and Defence; Deputy Chairmen; Chairman of the State Planning Commission; People's Commissar of Foreign Affairs; People's Commissar of Defence of the USSR; People's Commissar of Internal Affairs; People's Commissar of Foreign Trade; People's Commissar of Heavy Industry; People's Commissar of Timber Industry; People's Commissar of Light Industry; People's Commissar of Food Industry; People's Commissar of Internal Trade; People's Commissar of Agriculture; People's Commissar of Grain and Livestock State Farms; People's Commissar of Transport; People's Commissar of Water Transport; People's Commissar of Communications; People's Commissar of Finance.

18 An amendment of 5 February 1935 added the following paragraph to this article:

The Commission of Soviet Control attached to the Council of People's Commissars of the Union of Soviet Socialist Republics, through its representatives at the centre and in the republics, shall exercise systematic control over the implementation of all Government decisions.

19 Note that the enactments of the Council of Commissars are here designated 'orders and regulations' rather than 'decrees and orders', as elsewhere in the text (e.g., article 42). See also the amended article 46(a) below n. 27.

20 The heading was amended on 5 February 1935 to 'The Supreme Court and the Procuracy'.

21 The section was revised on 5 February 1935:

(b) to review and annul the orders, decisions and judgments of the supreme courts of the union republics in the event of their violating all-union legislation or infringing the interests of other republics.

22 Amended on 26 April 1927 to '(c) Military Division'. An amendment of 17 March 1931 added: '(d) Division for Transport Affairs'. Finally, the entire article was revised on 5 February 1935:

Article 44 The Supreme Court of the Union of Soviet Socialist Republics shall function comprising: (a) the plenary session; (b) Judicial Supervision Division; (c) Civil and Criminal Divisions; (d) Military Division; (e) Division for Transport Affairs; (f) Water Transport Division; (g) Special Division.

23 Amended on 20 May 1925 to 'fifteen members'.

24 Amended on 20 May 1925 to 'the chairmen'.

25 Amended on 20 May 1925 to 'seven members'.

26 The entire article was revised on 17 March 1931:

Article 45 The plenary session of the Supreme Court of the Union of Soviet Socialist Republics shall be composed as follows: the Chairman of the Supreme Court, his deputy, the chairmen of the plenary sessions of the supreme courts of the union republics, the chairmen of the Divisions of the Supreme Court of the Union of Soviet Socialist Republics, and four members appointed by the Presidium of the Central Executive Committee of the USSR and including one representative of the Unified State Political Administration of the Union of Soviet Socialist Republics.

An amendment of 5 February 1935 replaced 'representative of the Unified State Political Administration' by 'representative of the People's Commissariat of Internal Affairs'.

27 The article was revised on 5 February 1935:

Article 46   The Procurator of the Union of Soviet Socialist Republics shall be charged with

(a) supervising the orders and regulations of the departments of the Union of Soviet Socialist Republics, the union republics, and the lower organs of power, to ensure conformity with the Constitution of the Union of Soviet Socialist Republics and the orders and regulations of the Government of the Union of Soviet Socialist Republics;

(b) observing the correct and uniform application of laws by judicial institutions;

(c) instituting criminal proceedings and conducting the prosecution in all courts throughout the territory of the Union of Soviet Socialist Republics;

(d) supervising, on the basis of a special statute, the legality and propriety of acts of the People's Commissariat of Internal Affairs;

(e) general direction of the activity of the procurators of the union republics:

(f) protesting the decisions of the Supreme Court of the Union of Soviet Socialist Republics to the Presidium of the Central Executive Committee of the Union of Soviet Socialist Republics in the event that he disagrees with such decisions.

The Procurator of the Union of Soviet Socialist Republics shall be appointed by the Central Executive Committee of the Union of Soviet Socialist Republics; the Deputy Procurators shall be approved by the Presidium of the Central Executive Committee of the Union of Soviet Socialist Republics.

The Procurator of the Union of Soviet Socialist Republics shall be responsible to the Council of People's Commissars of the Union of Soviet Socialist Republics, the Central Executive Committee of the Union of Soviet Socialist Republics, and its Presidium.

28 Amended on 5 February 1935 to 'fifteen people's commissariats'.

29 This article was repeatedly amended following the frequent changes in the organization of the Council of Commissars. The final version, as revised on 5 February 1935, provided for the following twelve all-union commissariats: 'Foreign Affairs; Defence of the USSR; Internal Affairs; Foreign Trade; Heavy Industry; Timber Industry; Light Industry; Food Industry; Grain and Livestock State Farms; Transport; Water Transport; Communications'.

30 This article was repeatedly amended following the frequent changes in the organization of the Council of Commissars. The final version, as revised on 5 February 1935, provided for the following three unified commissariats: 'Agriculture; Internal Trade; Finance'.

31 Amended on 5 February 1935 to 'plenipotentiaries *or other organs*'.

32 The article was revised on 5 February 1935:

Article 56   Attached to each people's commissariat a council shall be organized; representatives of local organs and enterprises shall comprise not less than half its members.

33 The article was repealed on 5 February 1935.

34 Following the reintegration of the secret police apparatus into the reconstituted Commissariat of Internal Affairs, in July 1934, all three articles of this chapter were repealed on 5 February 1935.

35 The organization of the councils of commissars of the republics underwent repeated changes. In its final version, as revised on 5 February 1935, this article read:

Article 67   The central executive committee of the union republics shall form their executive organs, the councils of people's commissars, comprising the following:

Chairman of the Council of People's Commissars; Deputy Chairmen; Chairman of the State Planning Commission; People's Commissar of Agriculture; People's Commissar of Finance; People's Commissar of Local Industry; People's Commissar of Municipal Economy; People's Commissar of Internal Trade; People's Commissar of Justice; People's Commissar of Education; People's Commissar of Public Health; People's Commissar of Social Security; and also, with the right of an advisory or deciding vote according to the decisions of the central executive committees of the union republics, the plenipotentiaries of the People's Commissariats of Foreign Affairs, Defence, Foreign Trade, Heavy Industry, Timber Industry, Light Industry, Food Industry, Grain and Livestock State Farms, Water Transport, and Communications.

In all union republics, except the Russian Socialist Federated Soviet Republic, the Council of People's Commissars shall include a People's Commissar of Internal Affairs; the Council of People's Commissars of the Russian Socialist Federated Soviet Republic shall include a plenipotentiary of the People's Commissariat of Internal Affairs of the Union of Soviet Socialist Republics.

36 This article was repeatedly amended following various administrative changes. The final version, as revised on 5 February 1935, amended 'the Supreme Council of National Economy . . ., while subordinate' to 'the People's Commissariats of Agriculture, Internal Trade and Finance, while subordinate'.

37 Amended on 17 March 1931 to 'in the languages in general use in the union republics'.

3

The USSR Constitution of 1936

Commentary on the Text

The constitution of 1936 marked a notable break in Soviet constitutional law. That Stalin's 'revolution from above', launched at the end of the 1920s, and the mass terror which followed, first bringing the 'class war' to the countryside, and then directing its fury against the urban elites and leading cadres of the party, should have coincided roughly with the partial restoration of traditional patterns of authority and legal stability (in ordinary civil and criminal law cases) is but one of the many paradoxes of Soviet political history. This aspect of the 'Great Retreat'[1] from the aspirations of the revolution was also reflected in the 1936 constitution. It was a much more conservative document than its predecessors, more akin in both style and content to the 'bourgeois' constitutions so much despised in the early years. Lacking an inspirational preamble of the kind contained in the 1918 and 1924 constitutions, it was designed, as Stalin put it, to deal 'in simple and concise terms, almost in the style of minutes, with the facts of the victory of socialism in the USSR . . . with the facts of the victory in the USSR of full and thoroughly consistent democracy'.[2] As an essential part of this dual victory of socialism and democracy the constitution guaranteed the right to personal property alongside a greatly expanded list of other civil rights and freedoms, abolished all forms of class discrimination, established universal, direct and secret elections and, without renouncing its time-honoured opposition to the principle, separated the powers – or as official commentators continued to insist, the 'functions' – of the several state organs rather more precisely than had hitherto been the case.

The constitution, known for many years as the 'Stalin constitution', remained in force for slightly over four decades, by far the longest period for any constitution in Soviet history. If there is a single 'fundamental law' by which the structures and processes of the contemporary Soviet system may be assessed, and constitutional myth separated from political reality, it is still the constitution which Stalin enacted in December 1936 and which survived his death by nearly a quarter of a century.

The circumstances in which the constitution came into being are worth recalling. Characteristically, the formal initiative originated with the Communist party. On 1 February 1935 a plenum of the Central Committee (CC), on a motion by Stalin, instructed the Chairman of the Council of Commissars, V.M. Molotov, to present a proposal at the forthcoming Seventh Congress of Soviets 'on the need to introduce certain amendments into the constitution of the USSR'. They were to be directed towards: a) 'further democratization' of the election system by introducing universal and equal suffrage and substituting direct for indirect elections, and b) 'rendering more precise the socio-economic basis of the constitution in the sense of bringing the constitution into conformity with the present correlation of class forces in the USSR'. On 6 February 1935 the Seventh Congress of Soviets adopted the CC proposal to the letter and in addition directed its Central Executive Committee (CEC) to elect a constitutional commission for the purpose of preparing a 'revised text of the constitution' for approval by the CEC. The commission was formed on the following day and had thirty-one members with Stalin as chairman.

By the time the commission completed its work in the spring of 1936 it was clear that an entirely new constitution was about to be promulgated. On 17 May 1936 it was announced that the commission had reviewed a draft constitution consisting of thirteen chapters. On 1 June a CC plenum approved the draft 'in the main' and called for the convocation of an Extraordinary Congress of Soviets. The CEC Presidium on 11 June similarly approved the draft constitution and summoned the Congress for 25 November 1936. More surprisingly, the CEC also ordered that the draft be submitted for 'nationwide discussion'. This was an entirely unprecedented procedure; the only similar example of public participation in legislation occurred in the same month in connection with a reform of family law aimed at restricting abortions and lowering the divorce rate.

In the months that followed the 'nationwide discussion' proceeded at full steam. Tens of millions of people[3] were said to have participated in a campaign which long after Stalin's demise was still described as 'a massive demonstration of general approval' and a 'remarkable school of the political upbringing of the people'. When the Eighth Extraordinary Congress of Soviets met on 25 November, with a draft constitution as the only item on the agenda, Stalin personally introduced it as an 'historical document', the international significance of which could 'hardly be exaggerated' even though its domestic significance was 'still greater'.[4] On 5 December 1936 the Congress unanimously approved the final text of the constitution with forty-eight alterations, most of them relatively inconsequential.[5]

Such in brief was the history of the promulgation of the 1936 constitution. It only remains to be added that its principal draftsman was Bukharin who less than two years later, in the last of the notorious show trials of the 1930s, was condemned to death for a variety of highly treasonable acts, including espionage, terrorism and conspiracy to dismember the USSR. It is a telling reflection on the surrealist character of Stalinist constitution making that the work of a man convicted of such grave crimes against the state became the supreme law of the land.[6]

Among the reasons that led to the enactment of the constitution the desire to set the country on a course of stability, following the upheavals of collectivization and forced industrialization, undoubtedly loomed large. But Stalin, for one, may well have pursued additional objectives. Certainly, he had no intention of making fundamental changes in the political system. In his speech on the draft constitution, he went out of his way to emphasize that he regarded it as a 'merit' of the new constitution that it preserved 'the regime of the dictatorship of the working class just as it also preserves unchanged the present leading position of the Communist Party of the USSR'.[7]

Stalin explained that the constitution came about because of the need to provide 'legislative embodiment' for the changes which the country had undergone since 1924. Foremost amongst these, as befits a Marxist interpretation, was the change in the economic base of Soviet society. Collectivization and the rapid growth of state-owned industry had brought 'the complete victory of the socialist system in all spheres of the national economy' and, in the process, had eliminated 'the exploitation of man by man'. Such a profound transformation necessarily produced important consequences for the class structure. Instead of 'antagonistic classes', Soviet society was now composed of two 'friendly classes', the working class and the peasantry, and one 'stratum', the intelligentsia, 'bound by its very roots' to the two classes. Each of these was 'an entirely new' social formation 'the like of which you will not find in any other country on earth', or 'the like of which the history of mankind has never known before'. Finally, the changes in the economic base and the class structure, together with 'the actual practice of mutual aid', the development of national cultures and other unspecified causes had brought about a 'radical change' in the relations of Soviet nationalities, one to another – 'their feeling of mutual distrust has disappeared [and] a feeling of mutual friendship has developed'.

This picture of class and national harmony or, to use a formulation that was soon to gain official currency, of 'the moral-political unity of Soviet society', served as the theoretical underpinning of the constitution, in Stalin's words, 'the only thoroughly democratic constitution in the world'. Though the working class, as the 'leading' or 'most advanced' class of society, continued to exercise its dictatorship – the term 'proletariat' was considered by Stalin as inappropriate to conditions of socialism – it now shared power with the whole of the peasantry ('it is these classes, the two labouring classes, that are in power') and also the intelligentsia, which had become an 'equal member of Soviet society'. At the same time, the very concept of dictatorship, defined by Lenin as 'rule based directly upon force and unrestricted by any laws', was transformed into the comparatively anaemic 'state guidance of society' by a

Stalin who insisted that 'we need stability of laws now more than ever'.

The actual course of events was to provide ample proof, if such was still needed, that Stalin's notion of the dictatorship was anything but anaemic. But even without the benefit of hindsight it seems clear that while Stalin's account might have served to rationalize certain features of the new constitution, such as the abolition of class discrimination, it could hardly be taken as representative of his own beliefs, still less of the true state of Soviet society. Only one year before it was formally decided to revise the constitution Stalin had coupled similar, if less sweeping, claims about the extent of Soviet economic accomplishments with the warning that 'the development of people's minds lags behind their economic position', and had scathingly referred to party members who 'dropped into a state of moon-calf ecstasy in the expectation that soon there will be no classes and therefore no class struggle'. Such people, in Stalin's view, were guilty of a 'confusion of mind' which threatened to leave the party 'demobilized and disarmed'. The national question, too, was still then plagued by survivals of capitalism; in fact, such survivals were 'much more tenacious in the sphere of the national problem . . . because they are able to disguise themselves well in national costume'.[8] On 29 June 1936, just as the public discussions of the constitution were getting underway, a top secret CC circular called for the renewal of 'revolutionary vigilance', declaring that the 'inalienable quality' of every Bolshevik was the ability 'to recognize an enemy of the party no matter how well he may be masked'; and some three months after the adoption of the constitution, at the February-March plenum of the CC which set the stage for the final stage of the terror, Stalin once more argued that the class struggle intensified as Soviet socialism grew stronger, a thesis he had first advanced publicly four years earlier, in January 1933.[9]

The clue to the appearance of the 1936 constitution probably lies as much in the manner of its making as in its contents. The first point to be noted in this regard is the escalation which the entire enterprise under-went from February 1935 when it was resolved to introduce 'certain amendments' into the existing constitution until December 1936 when, following several months of 'nationwide discussion', Stalin presented an 'historical document' of immeasurable national and international importance to an Extraordinary Congress of Soviets. Stalin complained at the time that some foreign critics had 'thought it best simply to hush up the draft constitution, and to pretend that there is no such draft and never has been'.[10] Yet even such sympathetic commentators as the veteran British socialist leaders, Beatrice and Sidney Webb, who could certainly not be faulted for undue neglect of the formal aspects of Soviet politics, when writing of the 'sensation' which Molotov's proposal had caused at the Seventh Congress of Soviets, believed that what was involved was a reform of the electoral system with which 'the evolution of Soviet democracy would be completed'.[11]

Stalin's grievance did, however, point to what most observers regarded as one of the main objectives of the exercise, namely its propaganda impact at home and abroad. Several reasons may be advanced to explain the regime's need for an impressive propaganda success at this particular time. In the international arena, the growing threat of Nazi Germany impelled the Soviet Union to seek closer links with the Western democracies. Soviet entry into the League of Nations, the 'Popular Front' tactics of foreign Communist parties and the general toning down of the class war theme in ideological pronouncements by the Communist International (Comintern) were all evidence of this re-orientation in Soviet foreign policy. Both the new constitution, by intimating a desire to break with the past and open a new phase in Soviet political development, and the unusual publicity in the form of the 'nationwide discussion' which attended its promulgation, by demonstrating the democratic legitimacy of the regime, could manifestly enhance the Soviet Union's credentials as a suitable partner in a broad democratic alliance. At home, forced collectivization and industrialization had left a residue of exhaustion and even disaffection among broad sections of the population, including the party itself. Here too, the constitution could be expected to silence the doubters and hearten the faithful. By giving 'legislative embodiment' to Soviet accomplishments it seemed to confirm that the travails and sacrifices of the past had not been in vain. In Stalin's words: 'After the path of struggle and privation that has been traversed it gives pleasure and happiness to have our constitution, which treats of the fruit of our victories.'

Finally, the coincidence in time between the adoption of the constitution and the terror of the so-called Great Purge is too striking to go unmentioned. Both the show trials of Bolshevik leaders which began in 1935 and the mass arrests and executions which reached their climax in 1937 could, of course, be expected to derogate from the constitution's positive effect on public opinion. By the same token, however, the constitution and the fanfare of publicity which surrounded it could be expected to blunt the Great Purge's negative effect on public opinion. If such was the strategy it may well have been partly responsible for the remarkably restrained reaction of world opinion to the horrors of the period. By lulling some of the terror's future victims into a false sense of security it may even have contained opposition inside the Soviet Union.[12] In any event, whether or not the enactment of the 1936 constitution was deliberately designed to camouflage the preparation and execution of the Great Purge, it remains incontestable that this, 'the only thoroughly democratic constitution in the world', proved a cruelly deceptive opening to one of the darkest chapters in Soviet history.

The socio-political order

The text of the constitution opened with a separate chapter entitled 'The Social Structure'. The chapter specifically provided that 'legislative embodiment' of the principal socio-economic changes which according to Stalin rendered the promulgation of a new constitution timely and appropriate. The definition of the USSR as 'a socialist state of workers and peasants' [article 1] reflected Stalin's two principal theses: that socialism had been established in the country and that Soviet society now consisted of two 'friendly classes'. The word 'socialism' had, of course, formed part of the official designation of the Soviet state from the very beginning and had also figured in the rhetoric of both the 1918 and 1924 constitutions. Indeed, article 10 of the 1918 constitution explicitly defined the new republic as 'a free socialist society of all the toilers of Russia'; however, it was quite clear that 'socialist' here was employed as a category of aspiration rather than of achievement.

The constitutional formulation of the 'class' basis of the state had always been less than satisfactory. The 1918 constitution proclaimed a 'Republic of Soviets of Workers', Soldiers' and Peasants' Deputies' in article 1 and 'a dictatorship of the urban and rural proletariat and the poorest peasantry' in article 9, while the 1924 text, designed to establish 'a voluntary union of peoples', contented itself with a vague reference to 'Soviet power which is international in its class character'. The 1936 definition of 'a state of workers and peasants' seemed clear enough, since these were now the two officially recognized 'classes' of Soviet society; though it must be noted that official doctrine continued to stress the historic role of the workers as the 'leading' or 'most advanced' class of Soviet society, rightfully exercising what was henceforth known as the 'dictatorship of the working class' (rather than the 'proletariat'). The omission of the intelligentsia from article 1 was explained by Stalin on the grounds that it had 'never been a class and never can be a class – it was and remains a stratum, which recruits its members from among the classes of society'.[13] An element of confusion was introduced into the official class definition of the USSR in 1961 when the new Party Programme announced the arrival of the 'all-people's state, an organ expressing the interests and the will of the people as a whole'. As the constitutional definition was not revised until 1977 the two most authoritative definitions of the Soviet state remained at variance with one another for fifteen years.

Notwithstanding the heading, 'The Social Structure', the next two articles dealt with matters belonging to the political structure of the USSR: the soviets, now called 'soviets of toilers' deputies', were 'the political foundation of the state' [article 2], with 'all power' vested in the 'toilers of town and country' as represented by the soviets [article 3].

The main features of the prevailing system of 'socialist ownership' – state ownership and cooperative–collective farm ownership – were delineated in articles 4–8. Alongside this 'predominant form of economy', article 9 allowed for 'small-scale private economy' of peasants and artisans provided it was based on personal labour and excluded exploitation. Article 10 affirmed the right to 'personal' ownership in the form of savings, a dwelling house, subsidiary husbandry and articles of domestic and personal use. The right to inherit such property, not included in the first draft of this article, was only added in the final version; the significance of this addition must not, however, be over-rated, for the right of inheritance, abolished in 1918 in the first flush of the revolution, had been progressively restored from 1922 onward. Article 11 provided for what may be described as the dynamic counter-part to 'socialist ownership', namely, centralized state planning of the economy. Finally, article 12 reiterated the duty to work in terms familiar from the RSFSR constitution [1918 – article 18], adding only the principle of distribution applicable to the stage of socialism: 'From each according to his ability, to each according to his work.' To sum up this chapter: while most of its provisions made their first appearance in formal con-stitutional law, none introduced substantive changes in the material law of the country.

The structure of the Union

In February 1935, when the decision to revise the 1924 constitution was formally adopted, there were seven union republics in the USSR. Although the original decisions of the CC and the Seventh Congress of Soviets contained no intimation that it was proposed to expand the federal framework such expansion was, in fact, a prominent feature of the constitutional text adopted nearly two years later. The Trans-caucasian Federation was dissolved and its three constituent republics, Georgia, Armenia and Azerbaidzhan, joined the union directly, while the Kazakh and Kirghiz Autonomous Republics were raised to the rank of full union republics. As a result the number of union republics in the USSR rose to eleven. In 1940 five more union republics were added in the following order: the Karelo-Finnish Union Republic, consisting of the territory of the former Karelian Autonomous Republic (which had been part of the RSFSR) and additional territory acquired as the result of the war with Finland, the Moldavian Union Republic, consisting of the Moldavian Autonomous Republic (which had been part of the Ukraine), along with additional territories ceded by Romania, and the formerly independent Baltic states, Latvia, Lithuania and Estonia. In 1956 the Karelo-Finnish Union Republic reverted to the status of autonomous republic and was re-absorbed in the RSFSR. The number of union republics was thus brought down to fifteen and has remained unchanged since then.

In his speech to the Eighth Congress of Soviets Stalin took the opportunity to lay down three conditions which the territory of a national minority should satisfy to gain union republic status: (1) the territory in question must be a borderland, since otherwise it could not 'logically and actually' secede from the union and the right of secession would become a 'meaningless scrap of paper'; (2) the titular nationality must constitute 'a more or less compact majority' within the territory; and (3) the total population inhabiting the territory must not be 'too small . . . say, not less but more than one million', because otherwise it would be unable 'to maintain its existence as an independent state . . . [and] the imperialist beasts of prey would soon lay hands on it'.

These conditions, however plausible and convenient they may have seemed at the time, were quickly ignored in practice. The Karelo-Finnish Union Republic, when formed four years later, contained a population considerably below the required minimum of one million; nor did the (nominally) titular nationalities – the Finnish population had almost totally evacuated the areas occupied in the 1939–40 war – constitute anything like a 'compact majority' of the republic's inhabitants. Similarly, although population shifts have long since caused the Kirghiz and Kazakhs to become minorities in their respective republics, this had no effect on the status of their national territories as union republics. (In the case of Kazakhstan, it is the Russians who for the past twenty years, at least, have constituted a clear plurality of the republic's population.[14]) The geographic condition, to be sure, has been consistently applied and the borders of union republics are all contiguous with those of the USSR. Stalin's emphasis on the 'logical and actual' possibility of secession will be placed in correct perspective, however, if it is noted that in several cases the secession of a union republic would cause the break-up of the territorial continuity of the USSR. Thus the secession of Kazakhstan would separate the four other Central Asian republics (Turkmenistan, Uzbekistan, Tadzhikistan and Kirghizia) from the rest of the union; similarly, the secession of the Ukraine would leave Moldavia without a common border with other parts of the USSR, and in the case of secession by Lithuania a portion of the RSFSR itself, the East Prussian territory annexed after World War II, now Kaliningrad region, would be cut off from the USSR. (It is, of course, even now separated from the rest of the union republic of which it forms an administrative part.)

The right of secession was guaranteed in article 17 to each union republic in terms identical to those of article 4 of the 1924 constitution, and remained equally devoid of real content. It may be noted that while the 1924 constitution had entrenched the right to secession in a special provision requiring the consent of all union republics to the amendment of article 4 [1924 – article 6] the 1936 constitution did not thus single out its own secession clause, but subjected it instead to the general amendment procedure which applied to all other articles of the constitution. Like its predecessor, the 1936 constitution did not provide for procedural machinery by means of which a formal demand for secession by a union republic could be processed, and while national resentment manifested itself in various forms at different times it was never allowed to develop to the point where a demand for secession would be addressed to, not to mention considered by, any of the formal organs of state authority. The attitude of the authorities is perhaps best exemplified by the reply of a senior investigator in the 1961 trial of a group of Ukrainian nationalists charged with an attempt to 'sever' the Ukraine from the USSR: 'Lukyanko, you are a literate man, so why pretend to be a simple-minded dolt. You understand perfectly well that article 17 of the Constitution only exists for [the delusion of] the outside world.'[15] In the circumstances, Stalin's assumption, made at the time of the constitution's adoption, namely, 'that there is not a single Republic that would want to secede,'[16] proved entirely realistic, and it only remained for Soviet constitutional lawyers to argue that 'the right to self-determination consists both of the right to secede and the right not to secede', and that 'experience in building the world's first multinational socialist state . . . has shown that where nations have the right to self-determination, including the right to secession, they will freely associate'.[17]

The provision of the 1924 constitution requiring the consent of a union republic to any change in its territory was retained in the 1936 constitution [article 18; 1924 – article 6]. It was never more than a mere formality; the organs of the union republics consented to territorial changes in the same way as they consented to other initiatives of the centre, i.e. instantly and unanimously. Even so, the formalities were not always observed. In 1940 the areas to be added to the Ukraine and those to be transferred from it to the newly-formed Moldavian Union Republic were designated in two all-union laws which left the state organs of the two republics to submit proposals for the 'precise borders' between them. Similarly, the northern part of the Karelian Isthmus, which had been incorporated in the Karelo-Finnish Union Republic in 1940, was transferred to the jurisdiction of the RSFSR in 1947, together with other areas ceded by Finland after World War II, without the consent of the Karelo-Finnish Union Republic. In subsequent territorial changes the formal consent of the republics concerned appears to have been obtained. The constitution did not specify the procedure to be followed in such cases, and in practice it has varied from the simple declaration by union republic representatives given at meetings of all-union organs (as in the case of border adjustments with Iran in 1954 which affected the territories of Azerbaidzhan and Turkmenistan) to the adoption of formal decisions by the appropriate union republic organs (as in the case of the transfer of the Crimea from the jurisdiction of the RSFSR to that of the Ukraine earlier in the same year).

More important than the particular procedure adopted was the almost total absence of public information, not to say, public participation. The transformation of the Karelo-Finnish Union Republic into an autonomous republic in 1956 is a case in point. It was enacted by means of an all-union law of 16 July 1956 purportedly 'taking account of the wishes of the toilers of the Karelo-Finnish Republic'. Appropriate legislation was said to have been passed earlier by the state organs of the two republics concerned – the Karelo-Finnish Union Republic on 24 April and the RSFSR on 14 June 1956. Yet the first public announcement of what was after all an unprecedented and ostensibly significant demotion of a national territory from the status of 'sovereign' republic came with the publication of the all-union law on 17 July 1956. The lack of publicity was all the more striking as the central press had carried various news items of comparatively minor administrative changes during the preceding weeks, and *Pravda*, for one, had found space on 3 May 1956 to inform its readers of the session of a committee convened in far-off Lhasa to prepare the formation of the Tibetan Autonomous Republic in China.

The division of powers between the union and its constituent republics established in article 14 was broadly similar to that of the 1924 constitution. Once again the powers of the union were enumerated and those of the republics left in residual form, and, once again, the enumerated powers of the union were very comprehensive indeed, including economic planning and budgetary control [article 14 (j), (k)], and the determination of 'fundamentals' or 'basic principles' in such matters as land tenure and the exploitation of natural resources, education and public health, and labour legislation [article 14 (q), (r), (t)]. Several provisions clearly pointed to a continuation of the centralizing trend. Legislation concerning the judicial system, judicial procedure and criminal and civil codes was brought under the exclusive jurisdiction of the union [article 14 (u)], whereas under the previous constitution the union had merely been empowered to establish the 'fundamentals' of legislation in these areas [1924 – article 1(o)]. Although work on the drafting of all-union civil and criminal codes was taken in hand almost immediately, only one law, 'On Court Organization of the USSR and of Union and Autonomous Republics' of 16 August 1938, was enacted on the basis of the enlarged powers granted to the union. In 1957 an amendment once more confined the union to the legislation of basic principles, thus restoring the position originally established under the terms of the 1924 constitution. A further addition to the enumerated powers of the union was the requirement for union confirmation of the formation of autonomous republics and administrative-territorial subdivisions within the union republics [article 14(f)]. The practical importance of this provision, extended further by a 1947 amendment to include autonomous regions, should not be exaggerated, since tight administrative control from the centre had always been a prominent feature of the Soviet system, but it is indicative of the direction in which Soviet federalism was moving at the time. Indeed, not only did the constitution require union approval for the establishment of new territorial subdivisions, it also anchored the existing ones in the text of the constitution itself by specifying the administrative-territorial composition of each union republic [articles 22–9]. In his speech on the draft constitution Stalin justified this on the grounds of much-needed stability: it would restrain those 'who are always ready and eager to go on tirelessly recarving the territories and regions and thus cause confusion and uncertainty in our work'.[18] In the event, the recarving of territories went on much as before, the only change being a continuous flow of constitutional amendments from this source. In 1957 the union republics were given jurisdiction over the division of their territories into administrative units and the requirement of union confirmation was limited to the creation of new autonomous regions; at the same time, the constitutional provisions enumerating the administrative units were amended or repealed as appropriate.

So far, as has been seen, the changes in the distribution of powers between the union and the union republics introduced by the 1936 constitution tended to favour the former, though in some cases post-Stalin amendments later moderated the original intent. However, on 1 February 1944 two constitutional provisions were enacted which extended the formal powers of the union republics by awarding them the right to enter into direct relations and conclude treaties with foreign states as well as to maintain their own military forces [articles 18(a), 18(b) & 60]. To be sure, the constitution reserved to the union the right to establish 'the general procedure' governing the foreign relations of union republics [article 14 (a)], and also the 'guiding fundamentals' of the organization of union republic military formations [article 14(g)]. Still, the rights granted to the union republics in foreign affairs and defence, even in this limited form, were radical deviations from the general centralist trend of the constitution.

This was particularly true of the attempt to endow the union republics with a formal international personality and treaty-making capacity. In the negotiations leading up to the 1924 constitution a similar proposal by Ukrainian delegates had been promptly dismissed as 'unacceptable, since we are actually forming a single union state which will appear before the outside world as an integral whole'.[19] The retreat from this position in 1944 was officially justified by V. M. Molotov, then Commissar of Foreign Affairs, as reflecting 'a great broadening in the range of activity of the union republics which has become possible as a result of their political, economic and cultural growth'. In fact, of course, the attempt to enhance the international status of the union republics cannot be attributed to sudden recognition of the general development of the union republics, five of which had joined the USSR less than four years earlier and had moreover been under German occupation for most of this period. Instead, it should be seen primarily as a step calculated to secure greater representation for the USSR in the future United Nations Organization. Two union republics, the Ukraine and Belorussia, did subsequently join the UN and its special organizations. But neither they, nor any of the other union republics entered into diplomatic relations with foreign states, including the so-called 'fraternal states of the socialist camp'. Soviet authors, concerned to stress the status of the union republics as 'international subjects', adduce the obligations of several union republics (mainly the Ukraine and Belorussia) as signatories to international conventions and their participation in international conferences and cultural exchange programmes, as evidence of union republic transactions in the international arena.

The provision for military formations in the republics also aimed at strengthening the claim to international recognition of their 'sovereignty'. It was clearly not intended that the unified command structure of the Soviet armed forces be weakened in the midst of war. Some national military forces, units recruited wholly or mainly from particular nationalities, not organizationally autonomous formations, formed part of the Red Army in the 1920s and 1930s, and were reconstituted during World War II. (In 1939, at the 18th Congress of the party, Defence Commissar Marshal K. E. Voroshilov declared that their existence 'contradicted the fundamentals of the Stalin constitution and the principles of the extra-territorial recruitment of our army'.)

The right of the union republics to enact their own constitutions, implied in the 1924 constitution [1924–article 5], was explicitly granted in article 16 of the 1936 constitution and has frequently been cited in Soviet writings as one of the hallmarks of union republic sovereignty. Of the two requirements attached to a union republic constitution, namely, that it should 'take into account the specific features' of each republic and at the same time be in 'full conformity with the constitution of the USSR', only the latter has been observed in practice. Union republic constitutions were either enacted in the wake of the promulgation of the 1936 USSR constitution or immediately following the formation or incorporation of a new union republic and were almost literal copies of the USSR constitution. The 'specific features', which in view of the differences in size, geography, culture and general socio-political development of the union republics might have been reflected in their respective constitutions, were comparatively few. Perhaps the most noteworthy in this connection were the provisions which declared the language of the titular nationality as the 'state language' in the Transcaucasian republics (first in the Georgian constitution and subsequently in those of Armenia and Azerbaidzhan) but not in any of the other union republic constitutions, as well as the somewhat more elaborate provisions concerning equal rights for women which distinguished the constitutions of the five Central Asian republics. For the rest, the constitutions deviated from each other mainly in regard to matters of administrative-territorial division. (Some union republics contained national territories, others did not; some were subdivided into regions, in others the largest local unit was the district.)

Other features of the relationship between the USSR and its component republics will be discussed below. For the moment it will suffice to note that while the 1936 constitution did not formulate the powers of the all-union organs of government as sweepingly as did its predecessor, it did leave the absolute superiority of all-union law over the law of the member republics intact.

Before leaving the subject of federalism it will be appropriate to say something about the subordinate national territories. The constitution recognized three categories of national-territorial entity below the level of union republic. These were, in ascending order of status, the national area, autonomous region and autonomous socialist soviet republic (ASSR).[20] The national areas, first established for smaller nationality groups in the northern part of the RSFSR in 1925, were subordinated to the administrative-territorial subdivisions (territory and region) of the republic. The 1936 constitution awarded them representation in the USSR Council of Nationalities[21] but otherwise left their status unchanged. The autonomous regions and autonomous republics, which already enjoyed such representation under the terms of the 1924 constitution, were now listed by name in the articles setting out the composition of the relevant union republics [articles 22–7]. The position of autonomous regions was in all respects similar to that of other regions, except that they were to be governed under a 'Statute on the Autonomous Region'.[22] The autonomous republics were always regarded in Soviet constitutional theory as 'state' entities. Their right to their 'own' constitutions as well as to governmental organs paralleling those of the union republics was established in the 1936 constitution [articles 89–93]. But it was clear from the USSR constitution that the constitutions of the autonomous republics were subject to confirmation by the union republics [article 60(b)], and from those of the union republics and the autonomous republics themselves that their government organs lacked any independent legislative or administrative authority.

Neither the USSR constitution nor those of the union republics guaranteed the territorial integrity of the autonomous republic. (Article 60(b) assigned the determination of the boundaries of an autonomous republic to the supreme organ of the union republic concerned.) True, the constitutions of the autonomous republics asserted that their territories could not be altered without their consent and Soviet jurists have claimed that 'the existence of an autonomous republic as a state formation naturally presupposes its existence in a defined territory not subject to change without its consent'.[23] But this did not prevent the dissolution of several autonomous republics and the mass deportation of the titular nationality groups during World War II. The Volga Germans, the Crimean Tatars, the Chechens and Ingushi, the Balkars and Kalmyks were all exiled from their autonomous republics (as were the Karachai from their autonomous region) and their identities expunged from the register of Soviet nationalities. The Volga German, Chechen-Ingush and Kalmyk ASSRs were abolished; the Crimean ASSR was transformed into an administrative region, first of the RSFSR and then (in 1954) of the Ukraine; the Kabardino-Balkar ASSR was simply renamed the Kabardino ASSR. The deportation of the Volga Germans was justified in 1941 as a preventive measure made necessary by the alleged presence among them of 'thousands and tens of thousands of saboteurs and spies'; the dissolution of the Crimean and Chechen-Ingush ASSRs was announced in 1946, some two years after the event, as punishment for war-time collaboration with the German invaders. In other cases no official acknowledgements were made; the names of the autonomous republics simply disappeared from the text of the constitution or reappeared in altered form.

In Khrushchev's famous 'secret speech' to the 20th Congress of the CPSU, in 1956, the war-time deportations were cited as a 'monstrous' example of Stalin's repressive policies, and one year later all the above-mentioned nationalities, except the Volga Germans and the Crimean Tatars, were officially rehabilitated and subsequently restored to their former territories and constitutional status. The rehabilitation of the Volga Germans was delayed until 1964 and that of the Crimean Tatars until 1967 and neither people has been allowed to return to its home territory. The decrees exonerating the two nationalities noted that their former territories had since been settled and called upon the authorities in their present locations to assist them in 'developing economic and cultural life in accordance with national interests and traits', and in so doing left no doubt that they were expected to remain in the areas to which they had been 're-settled' by Stalin.[24]

The framework of government

The 1936 constitution brought about major changes in the formal framework of Soviet government. Before reviewing these, however, the fact that the constitution broke its predecessors' silence on the Communist party should be noted. The party was mentioned twice, in articles 126 and 141, both times alongside other 'social organizations'. Article 141 merely listed the party (together with trade unions, cooperatives, youth organizations and cultural societies) among the 'social organizations and societies of toilers' entitled to nominate candidates for elections to the soviets. By contrast, the party was singled out in article 126 which dealt with the rights of Soviet citizens to unite in 'social organizations'. After mentioning the various organizations that served 'to develop the organizational initiative and political activity of the masses of the people', article 126 went on to affirm that 'the most active and conscious citizens from the ranks of the working class and other strata of toilers shall unite in the All-Union Communist Party (Bolsheviks), which is the vanguard of the toilers in their struggle to strengthen and develop the socialist system and the leading core of all organizations of the toilers, both social and state'.

It will be seen that the party, which had always insisted on describing itself as 'proletarian', was here also acknowledged to contain other, i.e. non-proletarian, 'strata of the toilers'. A particularly striking innovation was the expression 'vanguard of the toilers' in place of the time-honoured 'vanguard of the proletariat'. The new formulation was in keeping with the constitution's general class neutrality, and also signalled a shift in the party's actual recruitment policy. Before the 1936 constitution (more precisely, until January 1933, when recruitment was stopped only to be resumed in November 1936) fairly intensive, though only partially successful, efforts had been made to raise the number of the party's working class recruits. In the years following the adoption of the 1936 constitution, however, the bulk of new members was drawn from the ranks of the Soviet intelligentsia.[25] The Party Rules adopted by the 18th Party Congress in 1939 gave formal expression to this development by abolishing the discriminatory entrance conditions which had since 1919 favoured the manual classes generally and the working class in particular. Yet the Rules continued to define the party as the 'vanguard of the working class'. Once again, therefore, we find – as in the case of the social definition of the Soviet state mentioned above – that official class designations were at variance with one another: 'vanguard of the toilers' in the 1936 constitution, 'vanguard of the working class' in the 1939 Party Rules.

In 1952 the 19th Party Congress adopted new Rules and this time the party was defined as 'a voluntary militant union of like-thinking Communists, organized from among people of the working class, toiling peasantry and labouring intelligentsia'. This definition was more in line with article 126 of the constitution – as well as with the actual membership composition of the party – but by dropping the traditional 'vanguard' claim it also deviated from it in a manner that seemed to reflect the party's eclipse in the last years of Stalin's rule. In August 1953, i.e. five months after Stalin's death, article 126 was amended. Amongst other things the new version adapted the constitutional definition of the party's class composition to that of the Party Rules by explicitly mentioning the 'toiling peasantry and labouring intelligentsia'. The designation 'vanguard of the toilers' was, however, retained. Nor was it altered when the Party Programme and Party Rules of 1961 introduced the party's new status as 'vanguard of the Soviet people' or 'vanguard of the whole people'. True, the distinction between Soviet 'people' and Soviet 'toilers' was a semantic one, which makes the ideological fanfare that presented the innovation as a major advance on the road to communism all the more difficult to take seriously.

The changes in the structure of Soviet government introduced by the 1936 constitution reflected the substitution of direct for indirect elections, already envisaged in the original CC resolution of 1 February 1935. The reform of the electoral system broke the continuity of the pyramid of soviets and thus dismantled one of the principal pillars of 'council democracy'. The congresses of soviets were replaced by separate tiers of soviets elected directly for each national and administrative unit – from the Supreme Soviet of the USSR [article 30], via the supreme soviets of the national 'state' entities, the union and autonomous republics [articles 57 & 89], down to the 'soviets of toilers' deputies' in the regions and localities [article 94]. Since the abolition of the congresses of soviets entailed the abolition of their central executive committees, the organs of government at the all-union, union republic and autonomous republic levels henceforth numbered three: supreme soviet, presidium of the supreme soviet and council of ministers.[26]

The theory of the constitution continued to subscribe to the fusion rather than the separation of powers, but this was no longer held to be incompatible with 'limiting the jurisdiction of authority as between separate organs'.[27] Thus, just as the adoption of direct elections to all 'representative' institutions of the state, including the supreme soviets, undermined the claim that the soviets were 'the political foundation of the USSR' [article 2] in anything but a purely metaphorical way, so the distribution of powers between the several organs of government brought the constitution considerably closer to officially disavowed notions of 'bourgeois parliamentarism'. One aspect of this was the somewhat artificial and not entirely consistent distinction which the constitution attempted to draw between the elected soviets as 'organs of state power' and the executive bodies as 'organs of state administration'.

The Supreme Soviet of the USSR inherited the place of the all-union Congress of Soviets and its CEC and was accordingly declared 'the highest organ of state power of the USSR' [article 30]. Yet its role was also presented as similar to that of legislatures in parliamentary systems; in fact, Soviet commentators repeatedly referred to it as 'the people's parliament' or 'the Soviet parliament'.[28] The constitution, in a notable departure from previous theory and practice, ostensibly attempted to vest legislative monopoly in the Supreme Soviet: 'The legislative power of the USSR shall be exercised exclusively by the Supreme Soviet of the

USSR' [article 32]. According to Stalin this provision followed from the need for legal stability mentioned earlier:

> It is time we put an end to a situation in which not one but a number of bodies legislate. Such a situation runs counter to the principle that laws should be stable . . . Legislative power in the USSR must be exercised only by one body, the Supreme Soviet of the USSR.[29]

Moreover, the constitution also precluded the Supreme Soviet, its designation as 'the highest organ of state power' notwithstanding, from infringing upon matters assigned to the competencies of the Presidium, the Council of Ministers and individual ministries. These organs were responsible and/or accountable to the Supreme Soviet but their powers derived from and were protected by the constitution. The authority granted to the Supreme Soviet in article 31 to exercise 'all rights' vested in the union by virtue of article 14 was limited to matters that did not fall within the constitutional competencies of the above-mentioned organs. Neither of the two previous constitutions imposed such a limitation on the Congress of Soviets or the CEC.

The above must not be taken to mean that anything like a clear-cut separation of legislative and executive powers was attempted, still less that such a separation was achieved in practice, only that in this respect, too, the constitution blurred the distinction between 'council democracy' and 'bourgeois parliamentarism'. Whereas the two previous constitutions had explicitly affirmed the fusion of legislative and executive powers in the highest organs of state power [1918 – article 31; 1924 – articles 17 & 29], official commentators regarded it as one of the main virtues of the 1936 constitution that it purportedly provided 'distinct limitation of jurisdiction with complete supremacy of legislative authority'.[30] It is difficult to see how this formula differed from that applicable to parliamentary regimes generally.

Because the Supreme Soviet of the USSR replaced both the all-union Congress of Soviets and the all-union CEC it cannot easily be compared to either of them. It was designed as the highest organ of the Soviet governmental structure and thus came to occupy the status formerly held by the Congress of Soviets. But other than that it is probably best considered as the successor to the CEC.

Like the CEC, the USSR Supreme Soviet was constituted as a bicameral body with one of the chambers, now named Council of the Union, representing the electorate as a whole on the basis of one deputy for 300,000 of population [article 34], and the other, as before, known as the Council of Nationalities, representing the various nationality units on a differentiated scale [article 35]. Suggestions apparently made during the drafting of the constitution that the nationality chamber be abolished were rejected by Stalin on the ground that

the nationalities of the USSR have *their particular, specific* interests . . .
Can these interests be ignored? No, they cannot. Do we need a special
supreme body to reflect precisely these specific interests? Unquestionably, we do. There can be no doubt that without such a body it
would be impossible to administer a multinational state like the
USSR.[31]

The constitution preserved the formal equality of the two chambers
[articles 37–9] and devised equally elaborate and superfluous procedures
for the reconciliation of differences between them [article 47]. Concern
for the equality of the two chambers induced Stalin to support a proposal
stipulating an equal number of deputies in both chambers: 'In my opinion, it has definite advantages, for it emphasizes the equality of the
chambers.'[32] In the event, the proposal was not adopted – a rare case of
disregard of the Leader's publicly expressed 'opinion' – presumably
because it was difficult to reconcile with fixed norms of representation
for both chambers. Instead, the basis of representation in the Council of
Nationalities was greatly enlarged in the final version of the constitutional text, with the result that the two chambers became, in fact, equal in
size. In the first Supreme Soviet, elected in 1937, the number of deputies
was 569 in the Council of Nationalities and 574 in the Council of the
Union. In subsequent years the latter chamber grew more rapidly and by
1962 there were only 652 deputies in the Council of Nationalities as
against 791 in the Council of the Union. A 1966 constitutional amendment restored the numerical balance by raising the representation of the
union republics from twenty-five to thirty-two, and from then on until
1979 (when elections were held under the 1977 constitution) there were
750 deputies in the Council of Nationalities and 767 in the Council of the
Union.[33]

The total number of deputies could not, of course, be laid down by the
constitution since the size of the Council of the Union would vary with
the size of the population, but it followed from the representation norms
adopted that the Supreme Soviet would be a comparatively numerous
body. As is evident from the figures quoted above it was approximately
twice as large as the CEC, growing from 1143 deputies in 1937 to 1517
between 1966 and 1979. The social composition of the two bodies was
very similar; the Supreme Soviet was also to be a socially 'representative'
assembly rather than one made up predominantly of professional politicians. The figures have fluctuated over the years and a detailed breakdown such as is prominently published in Soviet election returns, much
in the way in which the results of contested elections are published in
democratic regimes, cannot be attempted here. Suffice it to say that the
Supreme Soviet, while in no sense a mirror image of Soviet society,
typically contained a substantial proportion of workers and collective
farmers (up to about 50 per cent); but these figures must be treated with

caution for official statistics did not always distinguish between social origin and actual occupation. Among the non-manual groups, party and state officials provided by far the largest single contingent, supplemented by military officers, economic managers, scientists, writers and other white-collar occupations. The share of women rose continuously – from around 16 per cent in 1937 to around 30 per cent in recent years.

Elections to the Supreme Soviet were to be held every four years [article 36] and except during World War II this requirement was generally observed. The constitution stipulated two annual sessions, to be convened either by the Presidium of the Supreme Soviet, which could also call extraordinary sessions, or by one of the union republics, none of which has ever exercised this right [article 46]. Until 1941, two and in one case three sessions were held each year. Four sessions took place during the war years and a total of ten sessions in the period 1946–54. Since then the prescribed two annual sessions have been the rule, albeit with some exceptions. Sessions of the Supreme Soviet are even shorter than those of the CEC, usually lasting between two and four days and only rarely exceeding a week.

These facts must be borne in mind when considering the various constitutional provisions relating to the Supreme Soviet's powers and procedures. The ostensible legislative monopoly, the responsibility and accountability of the Council of Ministers [article 65], the formation of commissions of investigation and inspection with the right to call for documents [article 51], and, equally, the care with which the constitution regulated such matters as the majority needed for the adoption of laws [article 39], the settlement of disputes between the two chambers [article 47], the immunity of deputies [article 52] and their right to question ministers [article 71] – all these and other provisions concerned with various organizational details [articles 41–5 & 53–6] are misleading if they give the impression that the Supreme Soviet was intended to function in a manner similar, or even comparable to, that of democratically elected legislatures. Its membership no less than the infrequency and brief duration of its sessions clearly indicate that the Supreme Soviet was not equipped to debate public policy, to supervise the executive or to legislate laws. These activities were carried on by other organs. The men and women, the party officials and government administrators no less than the miners and milkmaids, who gathered in Moscow for several days each year, were required to acclaim measures decided elsewhere and in most cases, indeed, already implemented. This they did with unfailing alacrity. The voluminous reports of Supreme Soviet proceedings over the past forty years do not record a single instance of a negative or abstaining vote, or of an exchange of views that bore the remotest resemblance to genuine debate. From time to time mild criticism concerning the implementation of policies or the allocation of resources might be aired and occasionally a deputy would put a question from the floor. But such interventions were few and far between; moreover, they were often instantly recognizable as inspired or, in Soviet parlance, 'prepared' from above.

As part of a campaign for the restoration of 'Soviet democracy' in the post-Stalin period various measures were taken to reinvigorate the system of soviets (see p. 110). In regard to the USSR Supreme Soviet by far the most notable of these was the proliferation and activation of its standing commissions. The constitution only empowered the Supreme Soviet to elect a credentials commission [article 50] and to appoint *ad hoc* investigatory or inspection commissions 'on any matter' [article 51]. But by 1938 the Supreme Soviet had established three standing commissions (in addition to the credentials commission) to deal with legislative proposals, budget (later planning and budget) and foreign affairs. In 1957 an economic commission was formed in the Council of Nationalities, as part of an attempt – also reflected in other areas – to enlarge the rights of the union republics. It was abolished in 1966 and at the same time six new so-called 'branch' commissions were formed in each of the chambers for agriculture, industry, construction, trade and public services, education and health and social welfare. Since then the number of standing commissions increased further to a total of sixteen in each chamber.

That the standing commissions constituted the core of the Supreme Soviet is evident from their composition. While turnover in the Supreme Soviet was generally fairly high, with approximately two-thirds of deputies serving one term only, members of the standing commissions were disproportionately drawn from among the party and state officials who made up the stable pool of 'permanent' deputies, i.e. those elected twice or more.[34]

Under a 1967 Statute on the Standing Commissions of the Council of the Union and the Council of Nationalities the commissions were to be 'coordinated' by the Supreme Soviet Presidium and to perform two main functions: the preparation of legislative drafts for the consideration of the full sessions of their respective chambers, and the scrutiny of government departments. Their activity probably helped to turn the Supreme Soviet into a functionally more meaningful institution. But its immediate impact was technical rather than political: the improvement of legislative bills, often with the help of outside experts, and the exposure of bureaucratic shortcomings in the executive machinery. Certainly, it cannot be said to have markedly strengthened the position of the Supreme Soviet in relation to other central organs, or to have enhanced its 'democratic' credentials as an arena for the articulation and reconciliation of conflicting interests. Indeed, there is some evidence that the Supreme Soviet's limited potential for autonomous activity actually declined since the dismissal of Khrushchev in 1964.[35]

The Presidium of the Supreme Soviet may be considered as the direct descendant of the CEC Presidium. Originally it had thirty-seven members, elected, according to article 48, at a joint sitting of the two chambers of the Supreme Soviet (though no longer voting separately [1924 – article 26]). Its size and composition were altered several times up to 1966 when its membership was again fixed at thirty-seven: a chairman, fifteen deputy chairmen, a secretary and twenty members. The change between the draft and final versions of article 48 is noteworthy, for it discloses another rare case in which a proposal enjoying Stalin's approval was not fully implemented. The draft provided for only four deputy chairmen. In his report to the Congress of Soviets Stalin supported an alteration that would increase the number of deputy chairmen 'to eleven, one from each union republic', because this 'would enhance the prestige of the Presidium'.[36] The number of deputy chairmen was indeed raised to eleven in the final version, but the stipulation about 'one from each republic' was omitted, only to be inserted some twenty years later by an amendment of 25 February 1958. The reason for the omission in 1936 was never explained. It is all the more curious as the custom, already established under the previous constitution, of electing deputies from the union republics to the posts of deputy chairmen was continued. In practice, the posts were reserved for the chairmen of the supreme soviets of the republics.

Another 'constitutional convention' applied to article 48, but one which deviated from previous practice, was the disqualification from membership in the Presidium of government ministers, chairmen and deputy chairmen from both chambers [cf. 1924 – article 26]. The argument was that membership overlap would impair accountability (shades of the separation of powers?) of the Council of Ministers to the Presidium, in the first case, and of the Presidium to the Supreme Soviet, in the second.

Aside from representatives of the union republics the Presidium generally contained several members of the top party leadership, a number of regional party leaders and one or two representatives each from the armed forces, the mass social organizations, science and culture, as well as several workers and collective farmers. Thus, for example, the last Presidium elected under the 1936 constitution in 1974 included Brezhnev himself, the party leaders of the four largest union republics (Shcherbitskii – Ukraine, Kunaev – Kazakhstan, Rashidov – Uzbekistan, Masherov – Belorussia, all of whom were also members or candidate members of the Politburo), five regional party leaders, one local state official, an economic manager and an astronaut (both women), a scientist, a poet, a collective farmer and four workers.

The Secretary of the Presidium, though an elected deputy, in practice functioned as an administrative official with appropriately extended tenure. The present Secretary, M.P. Georgadze, was first elected to the post in 1957, having previously served as a regional party functionary.

The post of Chairman of the Presidium was in the past occupied by respected national figures who were no longer considered serious contenders for political power: M.I. Kalinin (1919–46), N.M. Shvernik (1946–53) and Marshal K.E. Voroshilov (1953–60). With the first election of Brezhnev in 1960, followed by that of Mikoyan in 1964, Podgorny in 1965, and Brezhnev again in 1977 (this time as General Secretary of the CPSU) the office came to be held by active and ambitious politicians who sought to use it in order to advance their policies and careers. The constitution, in keeping with the tradition of a 'collective presidency' of the state, did not endow the office of Chairman with distinct powers of its own. A suggestion made during the preparation of the constitution for a popularly elected Chairman of the Presidium was not adopted because, in Stalin's words, 'it runs counter to the tradition of our constitution. According to the system of our constitution there must not be an individual president in the USSR, elected by the whole population on a par with the Supreme Soviet, and able to put himself in opposition to the Supreme Soviet'.[37] In Soviet conditions this argument, like so many others of Stalin's constitutional reflections, had an unmistakable aura of unreality about it. But if the underlying intention was to prevent the office falling into the hands of a powerful party leader it has clearly been thwarted since, most conspicuously by Brezhnev's accession in 1977.

When compared with the position occupied by the CEC Presidium under the 1924 constitution there can be little doubt that the design of the 1936 constitution was to downgrade the Presidium of the Supreme Soviet. The reason for this is not entirely clear but may have been connected with the public relations objective of the constitution. Unlike the Supreme Soviet (as parliament) and the Council of Ministers (as government) the Presidium was a thoroughly unfamiliar institution, difficult to fit into Western conceptions concerning the organization of democratic government. This was particularly true of its previous incarnation as 'the highest legislative, executive and administrative organ of power' [1924 – article 29]. It was hardly the result of oversight that the 1936 constitution omitted this or any other definition of the new Supreme Soviet Presidium. The latter was treated alongside the Supreme Soviet in a chapter entitled 'The Highest Organs of State Power' and Soviet commentators often referred to it as 'the permanently functioning highest organ of power', but the constitutional text itself made no such claim.

The competence of the Presidium was detailed in article 49. Most of the powers listed in the fourteen (eventually eighteen) sections of this article were of the kind typically exercised by heads of state in parliamentary regimes. The less conventional powers, those that had given substance to its predecessor's formal status as 'highest organ of power' were either reduced or abolished altogether. Thus the general power of the CEC Presidium to revoke acts of the all-union government and of the governments of the union republics was modified in the case of the Supreme Soviet Presidium to apply only in the event that such acts 'do not conform to the law' [article 49(e); 1924 – article 31]. Unlike its predecessor, the Supreme Soviet Presidium was not empowered 'to supervise the execution of all decisions' of the USSR Supreme Soviet [cf. 1924 – article 30], to suspend the decisions of the supreme soviets of the union republics [cf. 1924 – article 32], to 'examine and approve' the drafts of decrees and regulations of the all-union Council of Ministers [cf. 1924 – article 33], nor to 'decide on matters concerning the mutal relations' between the USSR Council of Ministers and the governments of the union republics, on the one hand, and the supreme soviets of the union republics and their presidia, on the other [cf. 1924 – article 35].

Admittedly, the constitutional status of the Presidium was left ambiguous, and in the post-Stalin years this was to cause some argument among academic jurists. One school of thought saw the Presidium as an institution separate from, though accountable to, the Supreme Soviet and endowed with its own distinct competence. Another regarded it essentially as the executive committee of the Supreme Soviet, much as the CEC Presidium had been in relation to its own parent body; it assumed that the Presidium acted as the Supreme Soviet's agent and as such was vested with the full plenitude of the latter's powers. Leaving aside the question of the extent of the Supreme Soviet's own powers – itself a debatable issue in light of the restrictive clause of article 31 – both arguments had merit. On the one hand, the constitution did not endow the Presidium with general authority to act as agent of the Supreme Soviet in the interim between its sessions; but rather, the powers which the Presidium was to exercise in place of the Supreme Soviet were specifically designated and confined to the appointment and dismissal of individual ministers of the all-union government (subject to subsequent confirmation by the Supreme Soviet), to the proclamation of a state of war [article 49(f) and (j)] and to the withdrawal of immunity from Supreme Soviet deputies [article 52]. On the other hand, the constitution not only delegated these Supreme Soviet powers to the Presidium, but also made the all-union government responsible and accountable to the Presidium when the Supreme Soviet itself was not in session [article 65] (This last provision was not included in the draft version.)

Both the (intended) demotion of the new Presidium and the (intentional?) ambiguity of its status under the 1936 constitution are best illustrated in respect of its legislative competence. The avowed intent of the constitution was to withdraw the power to legislate by decree, power the Presidium's predecessor had exercised under the 1924 constitution. Stalin's above-quoted argument for the legislative monopoly of the Supreme Soviet was expressly directed against a proposal that the Presidium be granted the right to issue 'provisional acts of legislation'. The constitution empowered the Presidium to issue what were now called

'edicts' but made it appear that these were to be confined to the elucida-
tion of existing laws. This, at least, was the implication of the provision
that the Presidium shall 'interpret the laws of the USSR currently in
force, and issue edicts' [article 49(b)], though it should be added that the
draft version of this clause had 'issuing corresponding edicts' instead of
'and issue edicts' and was therefore less obscure on this point. Ten years
later a 1947 amendment split the two parts of this clause into two
separate sections of article 49 and thus unequivocally divorced the function (interpretation of laws) from the form (edicts). Henceforth, therefore, the Presidium enjoyed the unqualified right to 'issue edicts'.

Actually the authority to issue edicts (or decrees – the latter term
continued to be applied to some of the Presidium's acts) was from the
beginning invoked to cover a broad range of purposes. The largest
number of edicts were those issued in pursuance of the Presidium's
executive functions, such as the awarding of orders and titles, the
appointment of ministers, etc. Interpretative edicts, in the narrow sense
of authoritative rulings clarifying the meaning of legislative acts, were
comparatively few and substantively similar, though superior, to the
'guiding explanations' issued by the Supreme Court of the USSR.
(Soviet doctrine, denying the existence of 'judge-made law' in the USSR,
has insisted on a somewhat artificial distinction between the 'interpretation' of laws, the prerogative of the Supreme Soviet Presidium, and the
'application' of laws entrusted to an 'independent' judiciary.) A third
and more numerous category of edicts comprised normative acts which
in Western terminology would be described as subordinate or delegated
legislation designed to elaborate and implement statutes passed by the
legislature. Soviet commentators have referred in this context to the
'concretizing' function of Presidium edicts and have, reasonably
enough, subsumed it under the interpretation of laws. In practice, such
edicts on occasion exceeded the limits or even contradicted the contents
of the legislative acts they purported to 'concretize'. But in principle, the
existence of this sub-legislative function – also assigned to the Council of
Ministers [articles 66–7] did not transgress the legislative monopoly of
the Supreme Soviet and, in the broad sense of the interpretation of laws,
could be regarded as being sanctioned by the constitution.

Far more problematic were the many edicts that could only be
regarded as straightforward legislative acts, supplementing and amending the law of the country on matters substantively indistinguishable
from those legislated by the Supreme Soviet. They included major
changes in the criminal law involving the imposition of the death penalty. That these edicts were customarily submitted to the Supreme
Soviet for ratification, often after a considerable interval in time, and that
after ratification – a foregone conclusion in every case – they attained the
formal status of law, does not alter the fact that they constituted a clear
breach of the provision that 'the legislative power of the USSR shall be

exercised exclusively by the Supreme Soviet of the USSR' [article 32]. Not even the most generous interpretation of the power to 'issue edicts' could force this legislation under the umbrella of the constitution. Indeed, early Soviet commentators under Stalin insisted that an edict 'can be issued only on the basis of a statute, and must neither contradict it nor deviate from it'.[38]

Although the original legislation of the Supreme Soviet increased somewhat in the post-Stalin period the great bulk of its laws continued to emerge in the first instance in the form of Presidium edicts. Only the budget and, since the 1950s, the annual economic plan as well as a few major pieces of legislation were generally submitted directly to the Supreme Soviet. Even allowing for the speed and facility with which the Supreme Soviet regularly dispatched its legislative business, the infrequency and brevity of its sessions hardly enabled it to cope with the vast amount of legislation required for the running of a modern state. A permanently functioning legislative organ was a manifest necessity. The Presidium, its dubious constitutional authority notwithstanding, could fill this role better than any other state organ. Of course, it could do so only in a formal capacity. It, too, only met in full session at fairly rare intervals – for the past ten years approximately every two or three months. The policy decisions which led to new legislation, whether of Supreme Soviet laws or of Presidium edicts, emerged from the central organs of the party and the executive departments of the Council of Ministers. The actual drafting was also, in most cases, performed by these organs.

Even constitutional amendments were frequently implemented first by way of Presidium edicts, contrary to the provision which required that the constitution 'shall be amended only by decision of the Supreme Soviet' and, moreover, stipulated a two-thirds majority in each of the chambers [article 146]. Thus, for example, the minimum age for the exercise of the passive electoral right for deputies to the Supreme Soviet was raised from 18 to 23 by edict of 10 October 1945 while the appropriate amendment of article 135 of the constitution was enacted five months later on 14 March 1946 by a Supreme Soviet elected on the basis of the new age limit. Exactly the same procedure was followed in 1966 when the number of representatives from the union republics in the Supreme Soviet was increased from twenty-five to thirty-two. This measure altering the ratios of representation in the nationality chamber was enacted by Presidium edict on 19 March, while article 35 of the constitution was amended by a newly elected Supreme Soviet on 3 August. The frequent reorganizations of government departments were regularly carried out under the authority of edicts with subsequent ratification and constitutional amendment by the Supreme Soviet.

The controversy of the Presidium's constitutional status, mentioned earlier, also turned on its usurpation of the Supreme Soviet's legislative prerogative. The position of the critics was clear enough: the Presidium was acting outside its constitutional authority and it was necessary

> either to renounce the practice of issuing 'legislative edicts' and to enact all laws and all changes in laws only during sessions of the Supreme Soviet, or to secure, through legislation, the right of the Presidium to enact such edicts *expressis verbis*, within the established limits.[39]

The defenders of the orthodox position often argued in highly legalistic terms, looking for support to the posited Supreme Soviet – Presidium agency relationship. That the Presidium was similarly 'representative' in its social composition was taken as additional legitimation for its 'little Supreme Soviet' role.[40] Above all, it was argued, much of current legislation was urgent and could not be delayed until the next session of the Supreme Soviet. But the force of this argument lay in need rather than in law. Moreover, it ignored both the many legislative edicts which patently involved no urgency at all and those issued only a few days before or after Supreme Soviet sessions, as if in deliberate defiance of the Supreme Soviet's legislative authority.

Nearly everything said above in respect of the all-union Supreme Soviet and its Presidium applies *mutatis mutandis* to the parallel organs of the union republics. The main difference lay in the structure and size of the republican organs. All the supreme soviets of the union republics, including those containing autonomous republics in their territories, were unicameral bodies. Their size varied with the number of inhabitants – from around 900 deputies in the RSFSR (one deputy for 150,000 of population) to less than 200 in Estonia (one deputy for every 10,000 of population). The presidia in these two republics numbered thirty-three and eleven members respectively. While the powers of the supreme soviets of the union republics were enumerated in the all-union constitution [article 60], those of their presidia were left to be specified in the republican constitutions, and these followed the all-union model almost to the letter.

The competencies of the USSR Council of Ministers were basically unaffected by the 1936 constitution. Nevertheless, the constitution seemed to come closer to acknowledging the real position of the Council as it had evolved over the preceding years of Soviet rule. It was no longer the organ of another state institution – 'the executive and administrative organ' of the CEC [1924 – article 37] – but a separate governmental institution, in fact, 'the highest executive and administrative organ of state power' of the USSR [article 64], vested by the constitution with its own distinct sphere of competence [article 68]. Under the previous constitution the 'orders and regulations' of the government could be annulled or suspended by the CEC or the CEC Presidium [1924 – article

41]. The 1936 constitution, by contrast, did not explicitly grant this right to the Supreme Soviet or its Presidium, though Soviet authors have inferred it from the hierarchical superiority of these two organs. Instead, as already mentioned, article 49(e) merely authorized the Supreme Soviet Presidium to annul those acts of the Council of Ministers that did not conform to the law.

To be sure, in deference to some of the proprieties of legislative supremacy, the Council of Ministers was now held to issue its 'decrees and regulations on the basis and in execution of the laws currently in force' [article 66].[41] Since the Presidium itself was entrusted with the interpretation of laws it could therefore be said that its powers to set aside the acts of the Council of Ministers remained substantially unchanged. But the issue was an academic one. No case of Presidium annulment of a Council decree was ever known, and this despite the fact that many decrees had no basis in existing law but like the edicts of the Presidium created new law. The clear stipulation of article 66 in regard to the decrees and regulations of the Council of Ministers was no more able to prevent encroachment upon the legislative prerogative of the Supreme Soviet than the ambiguous language of article 49(b) in regard to the edicts of the Presidium. The decrees issued by the Council of Ministers were virtually unlimited as to subject matter and, since they greatly outnumbered both laws and edicts, constituted in effect the principal source of Soviet law. The great majority of decrees were never published and some – usually the more important among them – were published jointly with the CC of the CPSU, a body with no formal constitutional standing at all.[42] Under Stalin even constitutional rights were not immune to amendment by decree: the restriction of the right to free secondary and higher education was imposed by decree of 2 October 1940 and formal amendment of article 121 of the constitution only followed six years later on 25 February 1947.

The constitution also strengthened the position of the USSR Council of Ministers in relation to the organs of the union republics. As before, the decrees and regulations of the central government were declared binding for the entire territory of the USSR [article 67; 1924 – article 38]. But the 1936 constitution withdrew the right of union republic organs to protest these acts to the USSR Presidium [1924 – article 42], except under article 49(e), at the same time as it empowered the USSR Council of Ministers to suspend the decrees and regulations of the republican governments in matters that fell within the jurisdiction of the USSR [article 69]. Similarly withdrawn was the right, granted to republican CECs and their presidia under the previous constitution, to suspend enactments of individual commissariats when such enactments were in 'manifest conflict' with all-union or union republic law [1924 – article 59].

The Council of Ministers was to be formed by the Supreme Soviet and was declared 'responsible and accountable' to it and, in the interim between its sessions, to the Supreme Soviet Presidium [articles 56 & 65; cf. 1924 – articles 37 & 40]. The formation of the Council, like all Supreme Soviet business, was a highly efficient, closely synchronized routine. It was performed by each newly elected Supreme Soviet at a joint sitting of both chambers and consisted of two stages: on the first day the Supreme Soviet would adopt a motion, proposed 'in the name of the Central Committee of the CPSU', to appoint Deputy X as Chairman of the Council of Ministers and 'request him to submit proposals' for the composition of the government; on the following day a list of ministers 'endorsed by the Central Committee of the CPSU and the party group of the USSR Supreme Soviet' would be duly presented and voted into office.

Inasmuch as the constitution authorized the Supreme Soviet to set up commissions of investigation and inspection and required government ministers to reply to deputies' inquiries [articles 51 & 71] it also established some of the instruments by which accountability of the government could be implemented. By contrast, the constitution conspicuously omitted to provide the means for the enforcement of governmental responsibility. The power to dismiss the government, the accepted sanction of parliamentary regimes, was missing from this as from both the previous constitutions. There was apparently a point beyond which the reality of one-party government could no longer be reconciled with the fiction of 'complete supremacy of legislative authority'. In any event, the makers of the constitution did not think it necessary to envisage a situation in which the government no longer enjoyed the confidence of the Supreme Soviet, not to mention the possible consequence of such an eventuality, namely, dissolution of the legislature and new elections. (Dissolution and elections were, however, provided for under article 47 when the two chambers of the Supreme Soviet could not settle their differences, an eventuality that was, needless to say, no less improbable than that the Supreme Soviet would pass a vote of no-confidence in the Council of Ministers.)

Between sessions of the Supreme Soviet and, subject to its approval, individual ministers could be dismissed by the Supreme Soviet Presidium on the recommendation of the Chairman of the Council [article 49(f)]. This power was frequently – though again only nominally – exercised by the Presidium. That it did not cover the dismissal (or resignation) of the Chairman of the Council was to prove no obstacle in practice. The last such case, the ousting of Khrushchev from both his party and state posts, took place at a CC plenum on 14 October 1964. The Presidium of the Supreme Soviet on 15 October accepted Khrushchev's resignation as Chairman of the Council of Ministers – 'for reasons of advanced age and deteriorating health' – and appointed Kosygin in his place; two months later, on 9 December, the Supreme Soviet confirmed the change. The two preceding replacements, that of Malenkov by

Bulganin in 1955 and of Bulganin by Khrushchev in 1958, were carried out by the Supreme Soviet itself. The major reshuffle that followed Stalin's death involving the posts of both Chairman of the Council of Ministers and Chairman of the Supreme Soviet Presidium was announced as the decision of a joint meeting of the CC of the CPSU, the Council of Ministers and the Presidium of the Supreme Soviet on 7 March 1953 and ratified by the Supreme Soviet one week later on 15 March.

The recommendation of the Chairman of the Council for the appointment and dismissal of ministers – not stipulated in the two previous constitutions – was the only provision that established the Chairman's superior status *vis-à-vis* other members of the government. As in most regimes, the extent of the Chairman's actual influence on the composition of his government depended on the realities of power rather than the formalities of law. All the incumbents of this office – Lenin (1917–24), Rykov (1924–30), Molotov (1930–41), Stalin (1941–53), Malenkov (1953–5), Bulganin (1955–8), Khrushchev (1958–64), Kosygin (1964–80) – were full members of the party Politburo (Presidium), but only Lenin, Stalin and Khrushchev were simultaneously the top leaders of the Communist party.[43]

Neither the structure nor the size of the Council of Ministers were significantly affected by the 1936 constitution, but in the years that followed the Council was subjected to an almost continuous procession of major or minor administrative reforms in which new ministries or similar agencies were added, and old ones merged or divided or otherwise restructured and/or renamed. Since the composition of the Council was again specified in the constitution [articles 70, 77 & 78] these changes necessitated frequent constitutional amendments.

The details of the many reorganizations cannot be pursued here. Their cumulative effect was to increase the size of the Council from twenty-four members in 1936 to 105 in 1976. Undoubtedly, the main impetus for this enormous expansion came from the need to administer an increasingly complex and yet highly centralized command economy. Two attempts to check the proliferation of central ministries – in 1953, immediately following Stalin's death, and again in 1957 – proved of little avail in the long run. The latter attempt involved a broader reform aimed at decentralizing the administration of Soviet industry. As part of this reform most of the industrial ministries were abolished and their executive functions transferred to 105 regional economic councils. (These are the Councils of National Economy mentioned in the amended article 82 and the new articles 88a and 88b). Planning and coordination, as well as research and development, were entrusted to newly formed state committees in the central government. Even under Khrushchev these reforms were considerably watered down. The regional economic councils were progressively reduced in number and given correspondingly larger territorial jurisdictions – for example, the four Central Asian republics constituted one economic region – and many of the former industrial ministries gradually re-emerged in the guise of state committees and other agencies of the central government. In 1965 Khrushchev's successors completed this process. The economic councils were disbanded and responsibility for some economic decisions devolved to individual enterprises or associations of enterprises. At the centre the state committees continued to function alongside a ministerial structure restored on the traditional pattern; in 1965 alone the number of central ministries rose from twelve to forty-eight.

Some of these changes naturally affected the distribution of competencies between the union and republican governments. The regional economic councils were initially subordinated to the republican governments; a significant, if transient, accretion of power for the republics was thus one aspect of the Khrushchev reform. Other steps that had the effect of strengthening the rights of the union republics were taken at the same time. Of those directly related to the Council of Ministers and reflected in amendments of the constitution, albeit again temporarily, the abolition of two central ministries, Justice in 1956 and Internal Affairs in 1960, and the transfer of their functions to republican ministries, should be noted here. Both ministries were later re-established: the Ministry of Internal Affairs in 1966 (until 1968 under the name of Ministry for the Preservation of Public Order) and the Ministry of Justice in 1970. A further, more pronouncedly centralist measure was the formation of a USSR Ministry of Education in 1966; education, other than higher and specialized, had always been a preserve of republican governments. (All three ministries were given the status of what in the awkward nomenclature of the 1936 constitution were designated 'union-republic' ministries – previously: 'unified' ministries – i.e. ministries functioning in both the all-union and the republican governments.) More permanent, but more symbolic than real in its value, was a 1957 amendment to article 70 under which the chairmen of the republican councils of ministers became *ex officio* members of the USSR Council of Ministers.

The composition and structure of the Council of Ministers at any one time was certainly not free from political considerations. Its position at the pinnacle of the executive machinery rendered it a tempting power base in the various leadership struggles. Yet, it would probably not be wrong to say that the Council functioned essentially as the administrative arm of the party leadership. Most of its members were administrators and technical specialists, rather than politicians, and it is doubtful whether they met in plenary session more often than three or four times annually. The Council was, in any case, far too large to act as an effective policy-making organ.

The task of coordinating the activities of the various government

agencies fell to a smaller body – the Presidium of the Council of Ministers. The existence of the Presidium only became known after Stalin's
death. For some time previous to that two smaller organs appear to have
functioned within the Council of Ministers. The announcement of the
various changes instituted in the days following Stalin's death notified
the Soviet public that it had been decided 'to recognize the necessity of
having in the USSR Council of Ministers, instead of two bodies – the
Presidium and the Bureau of the Presidium – one body, the Presidium',
composed of the Chairman and First Deputy Chairmen of the Council.
Soviet authors later claimed that other members of the Council of Ministers were also included in the Presidium, but such appointments were
never made public. Nor was the official recognition of the Presidium's
existence followed by an appropriate amendment of the constitution.

The provisions on the councils of ministers of the union republics –
now grouped under a separate heading (chapter VI) – generally paralleled
those on the all-union government. One notable exception to this was the
absence of provisions specifying the areas of competence of the republican
governments; these were stated in almost identical manner in the constitution of each union republic. Until amended in 1947, the 1936 constitution
followed the practice of its predecessors in listing the composition of
republican governments [article 83; 1924 – article 67]. The list reveals a
continued centralizing trend. Agriculture and Internal Affairs had already
been removed from the exclusive jurisdiction of republican governments
by amendments of the 1924 constitution; the 1936 constitution transformed Justice and Public Health from republic into union-republic ministries.

Local government was not covered in the 1924 constitution. The 1936
constitution devoted a short chapter of eight articles to the subject (chapter
VIII) confining itself largely to structural aspects. Apart from changes in
nomenclature, instituted by administrative-territorial reforms in the
1920s, it reflected the replacement of the congresses of soviets by directly
elected soviets. A uniform term of two years was established for all local
soviets [article 95].

The scope of local government responsibilities was indicated in very
general terms, and again – as in the 1918 constitution – no attempt was
made to provide for an autonomous jurisdiction [article 97; 1918 – article
61]. In the official doctrine of democratic centralism, local self-
administration continued to mean that popularly elected organs represented the single, indivisible authority of the state in a particular
locality. The principle of 'dual subordination' according to which executive committees were 'directly accountable' both to the soviets which
elected them and to superior executive committees, was explicitly
affirmed in article 101. That this included the right of higher organs to set
aside the decisions and regulations of lower ones was stated only in

regard to the right of the republican councils of ministers [article 82]. But the constitutions of the union republics generalized this for all tiers of local government: higher soviets were empowered to annul the acts of lower ones; higher executive committees were empowered to suspend the acts of lower soviets and to annul the acts of lower executive committees.[44]

As already noted in discussing the 1918 constitution, such powers as were not arrogated by the party passed quickly from the soviets and congresses of soviets to their executive organs. The frequency of the sessions of directly elected village and town soviets may be taken as an indication of the extent to which the mass assemblies were allowed to atrophy: under the 1918 constitution soviets were to be convened once weekly in towns and twice weekly in villages [1918 – article 59]; the revised RSFSR constitution of 1925 omitted to stipulate the frequency of sessions, while the 1937 constitution of the RSFSR (like that of other union republics) was content with six annual sessions for both village and town soviets. In practice, the sessions of soviets – often convened at less frequent intervals – were almost entirely dominated by the executive committees. In some cases, members of the executive committees were not even elected deputies.

In the 1950s the post-Stalin leadership embarked on a campaign for the revival of 'Soviet democracy' with local soviets as a primary target. At the 20th Party Congress in 1956, Khrushchev, stressing the need to strengthen the ties between the soviets and their electors, called on the soviets 'to observe strictly all the provisions laid down in the constitution', and the then Chairman of the Supreme Soviet Presidium, Voroshilov, specifically criticized the failure of the soviets to exercise effective control over their executive organs. Less than one year later, on 22 January 1957, the CC of the CPSU issued a decree 'On Improving the Work of the Soviets of Toilers' Deputies and Strengthening their Ties with the Masses'. This castigated virtually every aspect of the local soviets' activity: the work of the soviets suffered from 'serious defects', deputies were 'not exercising to a sufficient degree the rights granted to them by the constitution', and executive committees and officials failed to report to their soviets whose sessions were 'confined to discussing trivial matters . . . in a formal way, sometimes only for outward approval of draft decisions prepared by the executive committees'. Even the party came in for criticism. Local party organizations were guilty of undue 'interference' in administrative matters, neglecting that 'most important instruction' of the Eighth Party Congress, namely that 'the functions of party collectives must not under any circumstances be confounded with the functions of state organs such as the soviets'. The decree called for sessions of soviets that would be conducted 'not for show, or for the trivial or ceremonial approval of proposed legislation, but for business-like discussion', and instructed party and state organs to implement 'as soon as possible practical measures to extend the rights of the soviets'.

That improvement was slow to materialize may be seen from the fact that very similar strictures continued to be voiced by individual Soviet leaders in subsequent years, and that the CC published two further decrees with substantially the same message on 8 March 1967 and 16 November 1972. Nevertheless, both under Khrushchev and under his successors the goal of turning the local soviets into somewhat more effective organs of government was pursued by a variety of measures, the more important of which were eventually incorporated in a series of legislative enactments on village, district and town soviets.[45]). These enactments, together with a Law on the Status of Deputies of Soviets of Toilers' Deputies of 20 September 1972, considerably extended the competencies of local government organs, strengthened their budgetary rights, defined the exclusive powers of the soviets as distinct from those of their executive committees, and enhanced the role of the individual deputy. While these must certainly be seen as important changes, it should be stressed that the real powers of the local soviets always fell short of their legal rights. Moreover, as Soviet commentators were careful to point out, the new legislation embodied the decentralization of power, not a grant of local autonomy.[46]

Probably, the single most tangible effect of the attempts to revive 'Soviet democracy' was to increase the number of Soviet citizens directly involved in local government affairs. The number of deputies alone rose from 1.5 million in 1957 to 2.2 million in 1977, and to the latter figure must be added some 30 million 'activists' in standing commissions of the local soviets, comrades' courts, people's guards, street and house committees, and similar more or less voluntary bodies. By drawing a substantial proportion of the adult population into the various fields of local administration, the post-Stalin reforms thus strengthened the soviets' traditional role as 'transmission belts' between the political leadership and the mass of the Soviet people.

The 'further democratization' of the electoral system, it will be recalled, was one of the two original objectives of constitutional reform. It was apparently assumed at the time that contested elections were intended – perhaps because the notion of democratization by way of uncontested elections still seemed outlandish to a generation comparatively innocent of the manipulative techniques of 20th century dictatorships. Stalin, in March 1936, in a celebrated interview with the American journalist, Roy Howard, added the weight of his own authority to these expectations, when he said: 'You think there will be no election contests; but there will be and I foresee very lively election campaigns.' If this was good public relations it was certainly bad forecasting. Since 1937, when the first elections under the 1936 constitution were held, close on 30 million candidates 'ran' for elections to soviets at all levels; every one of them, so far as is known, had the track to himself.

The eleventh chapter of the constitution contained impeccable guarantees for electoral rectitude, and these were translated into detailed legislation regulating every aspect of the electoral process from the registration of voters to the counting of ballots. Article 134 declared that elections shall be universal, equal, direct and secret. Each of these attributes, elaborated in articles 135–40, constituted an innovation in Soviet electoral law.

As part of the constitution's disavowal of class discrimination, article 135 granted the active and passive electoral right to every citizen aged 18 irrespective, amongst other things, of 'social origin, property status and past activities'. The franchise was thus extended to the surviving remnants of 'former people', but withdrawn from resident aliens [cf. 1918 – articles 64–5]. Of Soviet citizens, only the insane and, until 1958, those deprived of the right to vote by sentence of a court remained disqualified. In 1946 the minimum age for deputies to the USSR Supreme Soviets was raised to 23 and in 1947 that for deputies to the supreme soviets of the union and autonomous republics was raised to 21; earlier, Soviet writers had presented the uniform qualifying age limit of 18 as a particularly praiseworthy feature of Soviet democracy.

It is safe to say that no other constitutional right was as widely exercised as the right to vote. Except for the first elections in 1937, when 96.79 per cent of eligible voters went to the polls, overall participation at national and local elections never fell below 99 per cent; at the last elections held under the 1936 constitution, the local elections of 1977, a turn-out of 99.98 per cent was recorded. The mechanism by which these remarkable results were achieved at every election – indeed, with a few minor exceptions, in every polling precinct – cannot here be described. Suffice it to say that it featured a combination of meticulous organization and persistent exhortation.

Though official spokesmen used to deny the existence of discrimination among the enfranchised population, such had been both the intent and effect of the representation ratio of one urban voter to five rural inhabitants adopted for elections to the congresses of soviets under the previous two constitutions [1918 – articles 25 & 53; 1924 – article 9]. The 1936 constitution provided that 'all citizens shall participate in elections on an equal basis' [article 136] and thus abolished the advantage which urban voters enjoyed under the previous arrangements. The electoral rights of women [article 137] and soldiers [article 138] had already been established under the first constitution [1918 – article 64].

As noted above, the introduction of direct elections [article 139] severed the links between the various tiers of the pyramid of soviets. It also attested to the regime's greater confidence in its ability to control the composition of the higher 'representative' organs. Hitherto, the successive stages of indirect elections by comparatively small and hence easily controllable assemblies could be relied upon to help screen the delegates and weed out those unsuitable for election to the next higher layer of congresses. Henceforward, the direct election of deputies to all soviets, including the Supreme Soviet of the USSR, involved mass electorates at the grass roots of Soviet society.

The secrecy rule [article 140] was consistently violated in practice. Although polling stations were equipped with voting cabins or similar facilities, their use was discouraged by a voting procedure which did not require voters to mark the name of the candidate of their choice, but to delete the names of the candidates they did not wish to vote for. Since the ballot paper contained the name of one candidate only, a voter who entered the cabin exposed himself to the suspicion that he intended to cross out the name of the official candidate. Under the circumstances, it is not surprising that most voters preferred to conduct the entire exercise in full view of the election officials.

It is difficult to estimate the extent to which these arrangements contributed to the near-unanimous support for the regime displayed at every Soviet election. In 1937, in the first elections under the 1936 constitution, 98.61 per cent of eligible voters voted for official candidates to the Council of the Union of the USSR Supreme Soviet; in the last elections of 1974, the figure was 99.79 per cent. Yet on both occasions some voters did avail themselves of the right to a secret ballot, and of these a small, if declining, number registered a negative vote – 632,808 in 1937 and 332,664 in 1974. Nor was it entirely unknown for candidates to fail in obtaining the required absolute majority of votes. Such cases, to be sure, were very rare; moreover, they occurred exclusively in local elections and then almost entirely in small rural constituencies numbering a few dozen voters or so. In 1939, when the first local elections under the 1936 constitution were held, altogether 125 candidates out of a total of 1.3 million failed to get elected; in 1977 the equivalent figures were 61 out of 2.2 million.

With the result of the election preordained in all but a handful of cases, competition, if any, could only take place at the stage of candidate nomination. Article 141 secured the right of nomination to 'Communist party organizations, trade unions, cooperatives, youth organizations, and cultural societies'; electoral law extended it to 'general meetings' at places of work and in army units, and in practice nomination was generally consummated, at least formally, at such meetings. Individuals were not allowed the right of nomination, though it is a reasonable assumption that they canvassed behind the scenes on their own behalf or on the behalf of others. Even more than in most electoral systems, this crucial aspect of the nomination process remained hidden from public view.

What is certain is that the selection of candidates was carefully controlled, even monopolized, by the Communist party. Control was patently necessary, if only to ensure that the correct number of candidates emerged from the multitude of nomination meetings. But it was necessary, too, in order to achieve the correct 'mix' of deputies. The composition of soviets, following any one election, revealed a remarkable uniformity in regard to a number of socio-political variables, notably party membership, age, sex, and class origin, such as could only be explained by the fact that party organizations throughout the Soviet Union selected candidates according to centrally determined norms. Above all, of course, party control was necessary in order to prevent the nomination of undesirable candidates. As one Soviet author put it: 'Party study of the working and political qualities of candidates is a specific guarantee against any kind of accident which might take place were the candidates to be nominated spontaneously.'[47]

The institution of recall, long regarded as a principal feature of 'council democracy' [1918 – article 78], was established in article 142, but it was not until the late 1950s, following the party leaders' call for the reactivation of the soviets, that implementing legislation was brought in. Under the Law on the Procedure for the Recall of Deputies to the Supreme Soviet of the USSR of 30 October 1959, the right to initiate recall was given to the same organizations that enjoyed the right of nomination, which meant in practice the organizations of the Communist party. As at elections, an absolute majority of votes of the electors of a given constituency was required for the recall of a deputy. Unlike elections, however, recall proceedings were to be conducted by open vote at 'meetings of electors'. Compared to the 1920s and early 1930s, when thousands of deputies were recalled from local soviets in periodic campaigns, use of the recall procedure was minimal in the post-1936 period. Among deputies of supreme soviets only isolated cases occurred over the years; the absolute number of deputies recalled from local soviets was somewhat larger but proportionately equally insignificant – perhaps a hundred or so, or 0.005 per cent, in any one year. Apart from involving a fairly cumbersome procedure, recall reflected on the party's candidate selection; it was usually simpler to induce a deputy to tender his resignation.

It is perhaps difficult to see what possible purpose Soviet 'elections without choice'[48] could be expected to achieve. Very obviously they did not enable voters to express preferences among different platforms and candidates. But this does not mean that they should be dismissed as witless parodies of pluralist democracy. For Soviet citizens, participation in a political ritual on a basis of equality may well have served the function of integrating them into the broader community and identifying them with its institutions and symbols. In some instances, the encounter with candidates and election agitators provided voters with the opportunity to vent grievances on a variety of private or local concerns – a leaking roof, an unpaved road, inadequate shopping facilities, etc. – and even to 'bargain' their votes in return for the promise of redress.

To the extent that the elections performed these functions and afforded these opportunities they could be regarded as a legitimating and socializing device. Certainly, the fact that over 99 per cent of the adult population turned out on election day to cast their votes for official candidates was claimed as evidence of popular support for the regime – though, of course, one may doubt whether, in the absence of choice, Soviet election returns could reasonably be claimed as evidence for anything other than the system's mobilizational capacity.[49] But then the election itself was, in any case, less important than the campaign which preceded it. For some six to eight weeks in three out of every four years, national and local election campaigns provided the occasions for massive propaganda exercises, extolling the virtues and successes of the regime and calling on the people for a new burst of enthusiasm in the performance of the numerous tasks of 'socialist construction'. In a very important sense, election day in the Soviet Union was merely a pretext for the election campaign.

The rights and duties of the individual

Until 1936, the constitutional rules governing relations between the individual and the state had been confined to the constitutions of the several union republics, on the model of the first RSFSR constitution of 1918. The original directives for the revision of the 1924 constitution did not indicate that this practice was to be abandoned. When the draft of the 1936 constitution was published the inclusion of an elaborate bill of rights in chapter X was therefore regarded as one of its most surprising and, indeed, most important innovations. Certainly, it was the one feature of the text most likely to win good will for the regime at home and abroad, even though Soviet practices at the time and, for that matter, the language of some of the relevant provisions, might have been expected to cause most observers to view the constitutional promises with some scepticism.

Chapter X contained altogether sixteen articles of which twelve dealt with the rights of the Soviet citizen and four with his duties.[50] The coupling of rights and duties, a somewhat unusual, though by no means unique, feature of Soviet (and later Communist) constitutions, was rooted in an official doctrine which posited the fundamental conformity of interests between individual and state (under socialism) and oriented itself towards a future conflict-less society in which distinctions between rights and duties would be altogether obliterated. The 1936 text may be said to have 'legislated' the first step in this direction when it referred to work both as a duty [article 12] and a right [article 118].[51] The unity of rights and duties, in any case, was viewed as an integral element of the concept of membership in socialist society. Other societies apportioned 'rights for the bourgeoisie, duties for the toilers'. In Soviet society, by contrast,

> there are no rights without duties, just as there are no duties without rights . . . Being complete masters of their country, the working people have themselves established the rights and duties of Soviet citizens. Each one of these duties fully accords with the vital interests of the working people. In the USSR there is no conflict between the interests of the working people and those of the state. The interests of both coincide completely.[52]

Two articles provided for entirely new constitutional duties: article 130, which stipulated a general frame for the social behaviour of the Soviet citizen, obliging him not only to observe the constitution and laws of the country but also 'to maintain labour discipline, to be honestly concerned with his social duties, and to respect the rules of socialist community life'; and article 131, which was specifically concerned with the preservation and strengthening of socialist ownership ('sacred and inviolable') and – in the idiom of the time – branded offenders as 'enemies of the people'. The duties of military service and defence, elaborated in two articles (and typically embellished by the adjectives 'honourable' and 'sacred'), had already figured in the 1918 constitution [articles 132–3; 1918 – article 19].

Of the rights listed in chapter X, several had counterparts in the 1918 constitution of the RSFSR. This applied to the freedoms of expression and assembly [article 125; 1918 – articles 14–15]; freedom of association [article 126; 1918 – article 16]; the right to education [article 121; 1918 – article 17]; freedom of conscience [article 124; 1918 – article 13]; the right of political asylum [article 129; 1918 – article 21]; and guarantees of non-discrimination on grounds of nationality or race [article 123; 1918 – article 22].

Apart from the fact that the above rights were now extended to all citizens irrespective of social origin or occupation – in keeping with the official disavowal of class bias – several changes deserve to be briefly noted. The right to education was stated in much more specific and concrete terms. The right of asylum was no longer granted to persons persecuted for 'religious offences' but, in addition to political refugees (also covered in the 1918 constitution), now embraced persons persecuted for their scientific activities – this evidently with a view to events in Nazi Germany.[53] Freedom of conscience was stated more restrictively, with freedom of anti-religious propaganda 'balanced' by freedom of worship rather than, as in 1918, by freedom of religious propaganda. (This asymmetry had already been introduced into the republican constitutions in 1929.) Finally, the political rights were reformulated.

Whereas the 1918 constitution had placed the freedoms of expression and assembly in two separate articles, the 1936 constitution joined them in a single article but detailed their several components rather more systematically – the former as freedom of speech and of the press, the latter as freedom to assemble and meet, and freedom for street processions and demonstrations. As in the 1918 text, the effective exercise of these freedoms was to be 'ensured' by providing 'the toilers and their organizations' (note: 'toilers' and not 'citizens') with the necessary 'material' conditions, without which, as Stalin emphasized, 'all these liberties may be merely a hollow sound for the working class'.[54] The article establishing the right of association was more elaborate than its 1918 counterpart, enumerating the types of organizations which Soviet citizens could join, but was otherwise mainly remarkable for its mention of the Communist party (see p. 92).

A distinctive feature of the last-mentioned two articles was that each was prefaced by a proviso which significantly limited its application. The language of the provisos differed somewhat but the substantive intent was identical: 'In conformity with the interest of the toilers, and in order to strengthen the socialist system . . .' [article 125]; 'In conformity with the interests of the toilers, and in order to develop the organizational initiative and political activity of the masses of the people . . .' [article 126]. Some commentators held that these formulas should be interpreted as declaratory preambles which merely affirmed that the subsequently enumerated rights served the interests of the toilers, the strengthening of socialism and the development of mass activism. In the 1960s several Soviet dissidents were to argue this in their writings and, indeed, before Soviet courts.[55] But such was never the official Soviet interpretation. Referring to article 125, one of the earliest, and for many years most authoritative, commentaries on the constitution, declared:

> In our state, naturally, there is and can be no place for freedom of speech, press and so on for the foes of socialism. Every sort of attempt on their part to utilize, to the detriment of the state – that is to say, to the detriment of all toilers – these freedoms granted to the toilers must be classified as a counterrevolutionary crime . . . Freedom of speech, of the press, of assembly, of street parades and of demonstrations are the property of all the citizens in the USSR, fully guaranteed by the state upon the single condition that they be utilized in accord with the interests of the toilers and to the end of strengthening the socialist order.[56]

Needless to add, since it was the political authorities, i.e. the leadership of the Communist party, who remained the sole arbiters of the interests of the toilers, this 'single condition' provided ample constitutional legitimation for the virtual denial of freedom. In 1852 Karl Marx wrote of the French constitution of the time that 'each paragraph of the Constitution contains its own antithesis, its own Upper and Lower House, namely, liberty in the general phrase, abrogation of liberty in the marginal note'.[57] The observation could not have been more apt if it had been addressed to articles 125–6 of the 1936 USSR constitution, except that here the limiting clause was set out in the 'Upper House'.

The novel rights established by chapter x divided into two categories: personal or civil liberties and positive socio-economic rights. The first category consisted of two articles granting, respectively, inviolability of the person [article 127] and inviolability of the home and private correspondence [article 128]. These were conventional guarantees framed in conventional language; there was nothing to distinguish them from similar provisions in 'bourgeois' constitutions. The first, the Soviet guarantee of *habeas corpus*, was formulated as a general and unqualified statement: 'No one may be subjected to arrest except by court decree or the sanction of a procurator.' By contrast, the second merely promised that 'inviolability of the citizens' homes and secrecy of correspondence shall be protected by law'. Clearly, the nature and extent of the protection offered would depend on the law; it was not ascertainable by reference to the constitutional clause alone. But this way of framing a fundamental right is by no means unusual. The constitutions of many other states, including those in which the respect of the authorities for individual rights is far less suspect than was the case in Stalin's Russia, formulate their guarantees in a manner that reduces the constitutional clause to a general declaration of intent.[58]

If the two civil liberty articles assimilated the Soviet bill of rights to accepted notions of constitutionalism, the five socio-economic rights provided in articles 118–22 set it off rather more sharply from most other contemporary constitutions. The rights to work [article 118], rest and leisure [article 119], social security for the aged, the sick and the incapacitated [article 120], education [article 121], equality of status and welfare benefits for women [article 122], were in fact the special pride of the constitution makers. With the exception of the right to education all of these made their first appearance in a Soviet constitution. The granting of these rights, it was claimed, had been made possible by the advance of socialism and particularly by the industrialization of the first two five-year plans which had laid the necessary material basis. In the official doctrine, economic security constituted the essential prerequisite for the enjoyment of all other rights and freedoms. As Stalin put it in the above-mentioned interview with Roy Howard:

> Real liberty exists only where exploitation has been abolished . . . where there is no unemployment and poverty, where man is not haunted by fear that tomorrow he may lose his job, home or bread. Only in such a society is real – and not paper – personal, and every other kind of liberty, possible.

This order of priority was also reflected in the arrangement of the articles: the chapter opened with an enumeration of the socio-economic rights, headed by the right to work – 'the foundation whereon the Soviet citizen's rights and freedoms rest'.[59]

The constitution was not content with the simple affirmation of the socio-economic rights. Instead, as in the case of the political rights of expression and assembly of article 125, each affirmation of a socio-economic right was accompanied by a clause which purportedly 'ensured' its realization in practice. Unlike article 125, however, these 'enabling' clauses contained not only general programmatic statements ('the provision of an extensive network of sanatoria', etc.) but also prescriptions for fairly specific benefits, such as a seven-hour working day ('for the overwhelming majority of workers'), annual paid vacations, free medical services, free education, and equal pay for women. Only the right to work was entirely 'ensured' by a declaration of faith: 'the socialist organization of the national economy, the steady growth of the productive forces of soviet society, the elimination of the possibility of economic crises, and the liquidation of unemployment'.

A detailed review of the extent to which the various rights granted in the constitution were actually observed in practice cannot be attempted here. Observance was at all times at the mercy of the political authorities but as a general rule it improved markedly in the post-Stalin years. The only right of which this cannot be said was freedom of conscience. Always construed narrowly as freedom from religious compulsion, it has remained uniformly restricted under Stalin and since. Stalin, in fact, found it expedient to make some concessions to the religious sensibilities of the population during World War II, while his successors, especially Khrushchev, pursued the regime's struggle against the 'residues of religious belief' with renewed vigour. Only freedom of anti-religious propaganda ever enjoyed reality in the Soviet Union; its corollary, freedom of religious worship, remained subject to an array of administrative restrictions as well as periodic campaigns of particularly intensive harassment.

The provisions for the inviolability of the person, sanctity of the home and privacy of correspondence were introduced into constitutional law at a time when 'socialist legality' became the watchword of the regime. Whatever mutations the concept was to undergo in later Soviet interpretations, at the time it certainly did not mean the rule of law. As far as the personal security of Soviet citizens was concerned the law in force was in any case vague and flexible. 'Wherever the law is, crime can be found', was how Solzhenitsyn summed up the notorious article 58 of the RSFSR Criminal Code.[60] Under Stalin the literal application of this line of reasoning gave rise to what one Western scholar aptly characterized as the 'jurisprudence of terror'.[61] Nor did the authorities hesitate to go outside their own law: extra-legal terror joined legal terror in an 'unholy alliance' that brought immeasurable suffering to millions of Soviet citizens. Stalin's successors put an end to the arbitrary and massive repressions and, by employing the police powers more discriminately, provided a modicum of legal security for Soviet citizens – or at least the 'silent majority' among them. Unquestionably this was the single most important change in the life of the Soviet Union since the late 1920s (see also pp. 129 ff.).

Few states can boast of their credentials in the field of race or nationality relations. The fragility of Soviet constitutional guarantees was shockingly demonstrated by the wholesale deportations of nationalities during World War II.[62] Since then policies of Russification in general and anti-semitism in particular have continued to blemish the Soviet record. Other forms of discrimination should also be mentioned in this context. We have already noted that religious believers suffered disadvantages. We should now add that all religions were not treated alike. The dominant religions, most notably the Orthodox Church, but also Islam and Roman Catholicism, were generally treated more leniently than the smaller denominations, such as Judaism, Baptism and Buddhism, while the full brunt of persecution was reserved for a number of small sects not officially recognized – Jehova's Witnesses, Seventh Day Adventists, dissident Baptists, and others. Soviet practice has also discriminated on the grounds of political affiliation, granting members of the Communist party important material and non-material privileges. In particular, the preferential access of party members to most professional appointments, and their exclusive access to all senior posts, have long been facts of Soviet life. The constitution did not, of course, explicitly sanction such discrimination. But it did divide Soviet citizens into two categories: 'the masses of the people', who could join the various social organizations (trade unions, cooperative societies, etc.); and 'the most active and conscious citizens', who could enter the ranks of the 'vanguard of the toilers', i.e. the Communist party [article 126].

As already noted, the rights of expression, assembly and association were formulated in a manner which left little doubt that they were intended to be exercised at the regime's discretion. In 1918, one of the foremost European revolutionary Marxists, Rosa Luxemburg, criticized what she called the 'Lenin-Trotsky theory of the dictatorship' by writing: 'Freedom only for the supporters of the government . . . is no freedom at all. Freedom is always and exclusively freedom for the one who thinks differently.'[63] In 1967, the year of the 50th anniversary of the Bolshevik revolution, the Soviet dissident Vladimir Bukovsky, on trial for organizing a demonstration in protest against recent legislation restricting the right of expression, echoed these sentiments in his final address to the court:

What is the use of freedom to demonstrate 'for' if we can't demonstrate 'against'? . . . We know that freedom of speech and of the press is, in the first place, freedom to criticize. No one has ever been forbidden to praise the Government.[64]

Bukovsky was sentenced to three years in a labour camp. Under Stalin the sentence would unquestionably have been very much harsher. But apart from that, the line that led from the 'Lenin-Trotsky theory of the dictatorship' to Brezhnev-Kosygin practice remained unbroken: freedom in the Soviet Union was still freedom 'for', not 'against'.

The socio-economic provisions on the whole fared very much better than the other constitutional rights. They contained no formal limitations on the political freedom of action of the Soviet rulers, and they were generally in tune with the policy objectives of the Soviet regime. To be sure, the fact that they were anchored in the constitution did not mean that they could not be ignored or restricted at will. We have already noted that tuition fees were introduced in 1940 for secondary and higher education notwithstanding the constitutional provision for free education at all levels. In the same year, too, the seven-hour working day was raised to eight hours for all but the most arduous occupations.[65] And the right to material security – guaranteed to 'citizens' but 'ensured' amongst other things, by social insurance for 'workers and employees' – did not really become general until 1965 when collective farmers were incorporated into the state pension scheme. Nevertheless, while the socio-economic rights were clearly not immune to policy change, the regime endeavoured fairly consistently to improve and expand its services for the population. The Soviet standard of living still falls considerably short of that of the advanced Western nations, but especially in education and health progress has undoubtedly been impressive. Unlike other fundamental rights, those providing for the material welfare of Soviet citizens could at no time be regarded as entirely devoid of substance.

The legal system

In contrast to most other legal systems, the role of Soviet courts in protecting the constitutional rights of the citizen has always been minimal. Only in recent years did the crucial problem of the legal enforceability of rights begin to receive due attention in the writings of Soviet jurists. Until then, most commentators contented themselves with some perfunctory references to political, economic and juridical guarantees, invariably listed in that order and unmistakably emphasizing the 'material' guarantees said to inhere in the Soviet political and economic system. That the 'most substantial guarantee of the fundamental rights of citizens is Soviet power itself' was the basic premise of all legal commentary.[66] For many years, indeed, the prevalent view was that the provisions of the constitution merely enunciated general principles, not directly enforceable legal norms. The applicability of these principles as subjective rights, it was held, depended on their 'concretization' in specific sub-constitutional law. This view, too, has increasingly been challenged of late. The point to be stressed, however, is that in Soviet practice neither legislative nor – with some exceptions – administrative acts were subject to judicial review. The opportunities of Soviet citizens to seek redress in the courts for violations of their constitutional rights, even those 'concretized' in ordinary legislation, were thus exceedingly limited.

Judicial review of legislation was precluded by virtue of the doctrine of the fusion of powers. Control by the courts over the acts of the legislature would have amounted to a limitation on 'the will of the sovereign people' as embodied in the highest organs of state power and was therefore entirely unacceptable. It will be recalled that, under the previous constitution, the USSR Supreme Court could 'render opinions' on the constitutional validity of acts of union republic organs [1924 – article 43(c)]. Some rudimentary foundation for judicial review – albeit of republican and not all-union legislation – had therefore been laid. The 1936 constitution excluded even this limited form of judicial intervention, and in the article specifying the jurisdiction of the union blandly assigned control of constitutionality to the 'highest organ' of power and state administration [article 14(d)] – and this without indicating anywhere which of these organs was to exercise such control, again in contrast to the 1924 constitution which had entrusted it to the CEC Presidium [1924 – article 30].

Judicial review of administrative acts, unlike that of legislation, was not incompatible with official doctrine on state and law. In the early post-revolutionary period the regime even considered establishing a separate system of administrative courts for this purpose. The project was then laid aside as impractical and untimely. In later years, however, the need to protect the individual against the state, not only through administrative courts but also through regular courts, came to be rejected on principle. It was held to contradict the collectivist ethos of Soviet society, and, in any case, there could be no conflict of interest between the toilers and their state and hence no need for independent supervision of state officials, at least not by the judiciary. That Engels had criticized the new Draft Programme of the German Social Democratic Party in 1875 because it ignored 'the first condition of all freedom: that all functionaries should be responsible for all their official actions to every citizen before the ordinary courts according to common [general] law', and, Lenin, in his comments on the Draft Programme of the Russian Social Democratic Party in 1895, had demanded 'for every citizen . . . the right to prosecute any official' (a demand subsequently incorporated as paragraph 10 of the 1903 Programme),[67] did not prevent later Soviet spokesmen from repudiating the entire notion of judicial control over the administration.

This basically negative attitude notwithstanding, a number of reviewable administrative actions were established under various laws. Some covered matters of considerable importance for Soviet citizens – primarily, civil suits for damages arising from wrongful official acts, disputes concerning housing orders, dismissal from work and administrative fines; others related to issues such as errors in electoral rolls and the collection of taxes, which in Soviet conditions were almost entirely irrelevant. Because authorization for judicial control was dispersed in various enactments and because legal commentators in the Soviet Union (as elsewhere) argued about the definition of administrative law, the categories of reviewable cases listed in Soviet texts differ somewhat. But the precise boundaries of judicial review are not our concern.[68] It will be sufficient to note, first, that Soviet courts had no general mandate to control administrative legality, and, second, that the individual enactments providing for such control in specific cases did not, except in the case of the right to work, relate to any of the fundamental rights granted in the constitution. In the absence of the 'extraordinary remedies' provided in common law systems, there was therefore no way in which an individual could invoke judicial protection for his constitutional rights – to obtain a court order, for example, restraining an administrative agency from infringing his right of expression, or compelling it to take positive action in order to secure his right to an old-age pension.

This is not to say that other means of redress were not available. Soviet citizens could complain to the administrative agency concerned, or, more effectively, to the procuracy (see p. 126); and they could seek the intervention of the press or of various state and social organs, including those of the party. The regime generally encouraged aggrieved citizens to utilize these mechanisms to combat administrative abuse and illegality. What it did not permit them to do, except in the relatively few cases enumerated in separate laws, was to enforce their rights in a judicial proceeding.

It should be added that in the post-Stalin period calls for a broader and even general judicial review of administration began to appear in Soviet legal writings. The calls have so far remained unanswered. Nevertheless, the fact that Soviet jurists proposed legislation allowing a court 'to declare void any acts of administrative organs which violate the rights and legal interests of citizens' and granting 'to every Soviet citizen the right to go to court in case of the violation of any (but particularly constitutional) rights and legal interests by administrative organs and officials',[69] must be seen as a significant change from the days when such proposals would have been regarded as expressions of distrust in the 'material' guarantees of Soviet power.

Whereas the 1918 constitution did not mention the courts (the first) Soviet courts had been established by decree of 22 November 1917), and the 1924 constitution dealt exclusively (though in some detail) with the Supreme Court of the USSR, the 1936 constitution outlined the foundations of the entire court system. Aside from listing the various courts, from the people's courts at the base to the USSR Supreme Court at the top, chapter IX of the constitution affirmed the basic organizational and procedural features of the Soviet judiciary.

Two of these features may be noted at the outset. First, all courts were elected: regional and higher courts – indirectly, by their respective soviets (or supreme soviets) for a term of five years [articles 105–8], people's courts – directly, by the citizens of the districts for a term of three years [article 109]. The provision for direct elections of people's courts was an innovation of the 1936 constitution but was not implemented until 1948–9. Ten years later, following the enactment of the 1958 Fundamentals of Legislation on Court Organization, the term of the people's courts was extended to five years. Second, court cases were tried with the participation of lay judges known as 'people's assessors' [article 103]. The institution of collegial trial, by one judge and two people's assessors, dated back to the earliest days of the revolution. The assessors enjoyed the same rights as the judge in deciding questions of law and of fact, in questioning witnesses and litigants, and in all other matters pertaining to the conduct of the trial. But they participated only in courts of first instance. The language of article 103 – 'In all courts cases shall be heard with the participation of people's assessors' – was therefore misleading. Neither the constitution itself nor the subsequent Law on Court Organization of 1938 distinguished between judges and assessors in regard to mode of election or term of office. But the above-mentioned Fundamentals of 1958 provided for open elections by 'general meetings' at places of work or residence for assessors to people's courts and reduced their term of office to two years.

The court structure as set out in the constitution was exceedingly simple. The Supreme Court of the USSR and the unnamed 'special courts of the USSR' were the only federal courts [articles 102 & 105]. All other courts made up a single hierarchy headed by the supreme courts of the union republics. (This also applied to the supreme courts of the autonomous republics; they were 'supreme' in name only.) The special courts of the USSR consisted of military tribunals, and railway and waterway transport courts. Military tribunals tried not only members of the armed forces but also civilians charged with particularly dangerous crimes against the state such as treason, espionage and terrorism; in 1958 their jurisdiction over civilians was limited to cases of espionage. The transport courts dealt with criminal cases related to the operation of their respective transport systems; they were abolished in 1957.

The constitution stipulated neither the composition nor the jurisdiction of the various courts. But article 104 declared the USSR Supreme Court to be 'the highest judicial organ' and charged it with 'supervision over the judicial activity of all judicial organs of the USSR and the union republics'. 'Supervision' here referred above all to an extraordinary review procedure, outside the ordinary appeal channel, by means of which a sentence that had entered into force could be protested to a higher court by the procurator or the chairman of the court. It will be seen that this method of review which, unlike ordinary appeal procedure, was not available to the defendant in a criminal trial or parties to a civil suit (except by petition to the procurator or the higher court), provided a convenient means of control over lower courts. As the USSR Supreme Court was thus able to review 'by way of supervision' the decisions of all Soviet courts, including the supreme courts of the union republics, it was in effect placed at the summit of a unitary court system. By amendment of 1957 the chairmen of the Supreme Courts of the union republics became *ex officio* members of the USSR Supreme Court.

In addition to sitting as a court of original jurisdiction in particularly important cases and as a court of appeal in cases brought up from 'the special courts of the USSR', the USSR Supreme Court also exercised administrative supervisory powers over all other courts, especially between 1956 and 1970 when there was no Ministry of Justice in the central government, and issued judicial interpretations in the form of 'guiding explanations' binding upon all Soviet courts.

Several articles of chapter IX may be regarded as guarantees of 'due process'. Thus article 102 introduced the list of courts with the declaration: 'Justice in the USSR shall be administered by . . .' It will be noted, however, that the article did not, as in the case of the legislative monopoly stipulated under article 32, affirm that justice shall be 'exclusively' administered by the courts. In any event, the article referred only to the regular courts, ignoring the realm of 'administrative justice', dispensed by extra-judicial agencies. Probably the best known of these at the time was the Special Board of the security services established by decree of 10 July 1934 with powers to exile, banish and sentence to deprivation of freedom in a labour camp for a term of up to five years persons 'deemed to be socially dangerous'. It was abolished several months after Stalin's death, in September 1953, but until then constituted a most fearsome weapon in the Stalinist armoury of terror.[70]

Of the other 'due process' provisions, those concerning the language of court proceedings [article 110] were taken over from existing codes of civil and criminal procedure. Insofar as can be judged, they seem to have been generally applied in judicial practice. The same cannot, however, be said of the new provisions for open trial and the right of the accused to defence [article 111]. These were violated in countless political cases, not only those 'tried' in administrative proceedings but also those brought before the courts. The notorious *lex Kirov* of 1 December 1934, enacted in connection with the assassination of the Leningrad party leader, Kirov, under circumstances still unclear to this day, and directed against 'terrorist acts' (including participation in 'terrorist organizations'), expressly denied the right to defence counsel. The law was repealed on 19 April 1956.

The principle of judicial independence formulated in article 112 was new to Soviet law; previous Soviet doctrine had denounced it as a 'bourgeois' principle. It was, of course, entirely incompatible with proletarian, or any other, dictatorship, and, even after it had been enshrined in the constitution, it was not interpreted as precluding subordination to the political authorities. As one Soviet lawyer, writing in 1938, candidly put it: 'The demand that the judiciary remain outside politics is nowhere and under no circumstances realized'.[71] The constitution itself, as noted above, provided under article 49(b) for the 'interpretation of laws' by a non-judicial organ, the Supreme Soviet Presidium. But far more important were the instructions of other political authorities, particularly the Communist party. These instructions related not only to general judicial policy but also to specific cases currently before the courts. On some occasions, attempts by local party officials to influence a particular judicial decision would be condemned in official pronouncements. On others, however, that is whenever such attempts had the sanction of higher authority, they would be openly pursued, often through press campaigns in which the accused was presumed guilty well in advance of the court's verdict.

Soviet spokesmen recognized that independence for the courts presupposed also a degree of personal independence for judges, and purported to see guarantees of the latter in the fact that, unlike other officials, judges were elected and could only be removed by recall of their electors or by sentence of a court (on a criminal charge instituted with the sanction of the Supreme Soviet Presidium, in the case of federal judges, and the presidia of union republic supreme soviets, in the case of all other judges). But, whatever virtues may be claimed for a judiciary elected for a limited term in other countries, independence of the institutions forming and articulating 'public opinion', such as political parties, interest groups and communication media, is not one of them. Certainly in the conditions of the Soviet Union it could only mean subordination to the Communist party, which controlled the election and recall of judges with the same ease and success as it controlled those of the deputies to the soviets.

The development of the procuracy was briefly sketched in chapter 2. A 1935 amendment to the 1924 constitution embodied the newly-expanded function of the procuracy, as detailed in a number of enactments passed from 1933 onwards. A further decree of 20 July 1936 separated the local procurators from the republican Commissariats of

Justice and placed them under the exclusive control of the Procurator of the USSR. Henceforth, in line with Lenin's wishes of 1922, the procuracy was the only state organ exempted from the principle of 'dual subordina- tion'. Organizationally the local procurators remained agencies of their respective republics, but they were appointed or, in the case of lower procurators, confirmed by the USSR Procurator [articles 115–16], and the constitution explicitly instructed them to 'exercise their functions inde- pendently of any local organs whatsoever' [article 117]. The Procurator of the USSR, renamed 'Procurator General of the USSR' in 1946, was appointed by the Supreme Soviet for the unusually long term of seven years [article 114], and was no longer, as under the 1935 amendment of the previous constitution, responsible to the USSR Council of Ministers. It was now possible to view the procuracy as 'in an important sense . . . a fourth branch of government in the Soviet system, independent of the executive, legislative and judicial branches'.[72]

Until 1955, when a new Statute on Procuracy Supervision in the USSR was enacted, the procuracy's detailed powers were elaborated in legisla- tion issued prior to the adoption of the 1936 constitution. The latter, unlike its predecessor (as amended in 1935), was content to set out the basic function of the Procurator General in a single clause of article 113: 'Supreme supervision over the strict execution of the laws by all People's Commissariats and their subordinate institutions, as well as by indi- vidual officials and citizens of the USSR, shall be vested in the Procurator of the USSR.' But this exclusive concentration on the procuracy's func- tion as guardian of legality – in sharp contrast to the original text of the 1924 constitution which had omitted it altogether – covered what was, after all, the most distinctive feature of the Soviet procuracy.

In Soviet practice, procuracy supervision extended to both judicial and administrative action and generally meant the right to file protests: procurators were not empowered to annul the acts of the organs subject to their supervision, only to protest them, on the grounds of illegality, to higher courts or administrative agencies. The right to supervision over judicial legality was not explicitly stated in article 113. But it had been included in the amended article 46(b) of the 1924 constitution and was re-affirmed in even stronger terms in the 1955 statute. It will be readily apparent that its dual responsibility, for both the conduct of criminal prosecutions and the observance of judicial legality, involved the procu- racy in some role conflict. Even in non-political cases, this was not always resolved in favour of legality: Soviet procurators were less likely to protest legally flawed convictions than acquittals. A similar conflict inhered in the fact that procurators were also responsible for the pre-trial investigation of criminal cases.

For the Soviet citizen the procuracy constituted his principal defence against violations of the law by administrative officials. The procedure for lodging complaints with a procurator was comparatively simple, although the procurator could not order the appropriate remedy directly. He had only to set the remedial machinery in motion, and, once he had taken up a complaint, redress was almost automatic. Most procurators' protests related to violations of labour law and the illegal imposition of administrative fines, and the cases in which administrative authorities refused to comply with these protests were extremely rare: according to one prominent Soviet scholar 96 per cent of initial protests were successful.

Under Stalin, the procuracy allowed, indeed actively participated in, countless illegalities. The notorious show trials staged in the late 1930s with the Procurator of the USSR, A.A. Vyshinsky, in the star role, were merely the best-known examples of the procuracy's collusion in the 'jurisprudence of terror'. In the changed climate of the post-Stalin era procurators generally discharged their duties as guardians of legality far more scrupulously. But this must not be taken to mean that they were able – or, in so far as is known, willing – to oppose illegality sanctioned by official policy.

While the procuracy has come to perform an increasingly important function in ensuring the uniform enforcement of the law and has undoubtedly provided Soviet citizens with an accessible and efficient means of redress in many cases of administrative illegality, it has at no time posed a challenge to the power of the central leadership. In this connection, it will be noted that article 113 stopped short of extending the procuracy's right of administrative supervision to 'the highest executive and administrative organ of state power', i.e., the USSR Council of Ministers. Nor has the procuracy exercised supervisory powers over the CPSU. The 1955 statute listed 'co-operative and other social organizations' among the institutions subject to procuracy supervision, but it was never suggested that 'social organizations', in this context at least, embraced the organizations of the Communist party.

In recent years, several western observers have compared the role of the Soviet procuracy to that of the Scandinavian ombudsman and similar institutions elsewhere. Some similarities may indeed be found. Before these are carried too far, however, it is well to remember essential differences. The procuracy, in the words of one western authority,

> is neither prepared nor designed – by law, by Party decision or by its own principles of structure and responsibility – to defend the citizen against the State and Government, even in cases of clear violation of explicit laws or civil rights. As part of the state apparatus, it constitutes an instrument of the regime, not of justice.[73]

In the decade that followed Stalin's death the regime embarked on an extensive programme of legal reforms. Of these, the recodification of the criminal law was particularly relevant to the legal security of Soviet citizens and several of the more important innovations should be briefly mentioned.

It may be regarded as an indication of the new spirit of the law that the 1958 all-union Fundamentals of Criminal Legislation listed the protection of 'the person and rights of citizens' among the tasks of Soviet criminal law for the first time. (Previous law, e.g. the 1926 RSFSR Code of Criminal Law, had defined the tasks of criminal legislation exclusively in terms of 'the protection of the socialist state of workers and peasants and the legal order established therein'.) In conformity with this new spirit the scope of the criminal law was confined to punishment for acts prescribed by law at the time of their commission, and the notorious doctrine of analogy, according to which acts not expressly defined in the law could be punished under laws proscribing 'analogous' acts, was expunged from the legal system. Similarly repudiated were the unusually broad interpretations of complicity and collective responsibility as well as reliance on the special evidential force of confessions in cases of what used to be known as 'counter-revolutionary crimes' but were now designated 'especially dangerous crimes against the state'. Laws establishing the punishability of an act or providing increased punishments were denied retroactive force and penal sanctions generally became more lenient. (The maximum term of imprisonment was reduced from 25 to 15 years). The new codes unequivocally affirmed the monopoly of the courts over the administration of justice ('Justice in criminal cases shall be administered solely by a court') and incorporated procedural guarantees amounting to a recognition of the principle of the presumption of innocence.[74] Detention and investigation by the security services were also placed under the supervision of the procuracy and subjected to the same rules that applied to ordinary police and other agencies of enquiry.

The effect of these and many other changes was to render the law and its enforcement both more humane and less arbitrary. This development must undoubtedly be attributed to the determination of the post-Stalin leaders to create a rather more predictable legal order. But in important respects it represented the culmination of a turn in legal doctrine originally signalled by Stalin's insistence on 'the stability of laws' in his speech on the 1936 draft constitution. The implementation of the reforms may only have been possible after Stalin's death, but some of the underlying principles had been debated in Soviet legal circles long before. Thus, a distinguished Soviet legal reformer, N.S. Strogovich, argued, as early as 1940, that 'in Soviet criminal procedure the presumption of innocence is one of the guiding procedural principles'. This view was by no means representative at the time, but in a more limited version, namely that the burden of proof could not be shifted to the defence, it increasingly gained ground in Soviet legal thinking and was articulated in several rulings of the USSR Supreme Court. The doctrine of analogy had already been excluded from several all-union codes drafted, but not enacted, in the years before and after World War II.

To point out that these ideas originated under Stalin is to indicate the limits of the reforms. Certainly, they were not intended, any more than the constitution itself, to alter the fundamental subordination of the legal system to considerations of social and political expediency. If at first some doubt remained on this score it was dispelled almost as soon as the ink had dried on the new legislation.

The re-establishment in 1959 of the comrades' courts, a vintage Soviet institution which had been allowed to atrophy under Stalin, marked a clear, if comparatively innocuous, breach of the recently re-affirmed judicial monopoly of the courts. The comrades' courts were lay tribunals elected by open ballot for a two-year term at 'general meetings' of collectives in enterprises and housing units. Statutes on comrades' courts were enacted in 1961, and after several amendments completely revised in 1977. The jurisdiction of the comrades' courts came to encompass not only various infractions of 'the rules of socialist community life', such as damage to public amenities, neglect of family responsibilities, drunkenness, quarrels among neighbours, violations of labour discipline and – in the original version – 'other [unspecified] anti-social acts not entailing criminal responsibility', but also minor civil suits (subject to the consent of the parties), petty theft, petty hooliganism, petty speculation and other 'criminal acts committed for the first time unless they represent a great social danger'.

In keeping with their status as social organs, the comrades' courts were said to apply 'measures of social pressure' and not criminal punishments, though the former concept was broad enough to include the imposition of fines and recommendations for demotion and – in some cases – even dismissal from work, alongside such moral sanctions as a 'comradely warning' or a 'social reprimand'. The statutes referred to 'members of the comrades' court' rather than to 'judges', and to 'the person brought before the comrades' court' rather than to the 'accused' (but in the 1977 version to the 'guilty person' rather than, as before, the 'offender'). However, these terminological distinctions could not obscure the fact that the comrades' courts dispensed a type of 'popular justice' free from the procedural restraints under which the ordinary courts were required to conduct their proceedings. That this opened the way to a variety of abuses was frequently criticized in the Soviet press. The 1977 revision of the statutes, presumably in response to these criticisms, provided for tighter procedural guarantees, including the right to appeal to the appropriate trade union committee or executive committee of the local soviet. While the new statutes introduced greater formality and regularity into the proceedings of the comrades' courts, they also reaffirmed the regime's commitment to a system under which both minor crimes and non-crimes could be tried by non-courts in violation of the principles enunciated in the 1958 Fundamentals.

A rather more serious violation of these principles were the 'anti-parasite' edicts introduced in the various republics between 1957 and 1961. Under this legislation a new non-crime of parasitism was established and applied to persons who derived unearned income from a variety of 'anti-social acts which enable them to lead a parasitic way of life'. The law distinguished between two categories of parasites: those who did not work at all and those who worked 'only for the sake of appearances'. Both categories were subject to punishment ('measures of social influence') by exile ('resettlement') to designated localities for a term of two to five years. Jurisdiction over the first category lay exclusively with the people's courts, but since the prescribed sanction was not considered a criminal penalty, persons charged with parasitism were deprived of the normal protection granted under general criminal procedure. Thus, there was no right of appeal (though the procurator could file a protest) and the rights to be defended by counsel and to summon witnesses were at the discretion of the court. A particularly objectionable feature of the legislation was that the second category of parasites, i.e. those who worked 'only for the sake of appearances', could be tried either by the courts or by 'collectives' in enterprises, institutions, collective farms, etc. The 'social sentence' of these collectives was not subject to judicial review and came into effect upon approval by the district or city soviet executive committee.

With some notable exceptions the anti-parasite legislation appears to have been invoked largely to combat social deviance rather than political dissent.[75] But the broad definition of the offence, the severity of the sanctions, the absence of procedural guarantees and the intrusion of 'popular justice' clearly posed formidable threats to legal security. From the beginning anti-parasite law attracted considerable criticism in Soviet legal writings, and in the years following Khrushchev's fall it was greatly whittled down. Amendments of 1965, amongst other major revisions, abolished the concurrent jurisdiction of the work collectives, and further enactments of 1970 and 1975 incorporated parasitism in the criminal codes as an ordinary crime subject to the rules of criminal procedure. What was left of the original anti-parasite edifice was a single, if ominously vague, reference to a 'parasitic way of life' as a criminal offence punishable, like begging and vagrancy with which it was bracketed, by deprivation of freedom for a period of up to one year.

Another retrograde development was the enactment in 1961-2 of a series of edicts introducing new crimes and harsher punishments. Coming, as they did, shortly after the promulgation of the new criminal codes, the edicts threw the fragility of the codes into particularly sharp relief. Especially serious was the extension of capital punishment to a wide variety of crimes, including economic crimes not involving violence – this despite the fact that the 1958 Fundamentals of Criminal Legislation (and the republican criminal codes) had described the death penalty as 'an exceptional measure of punishment, pending its complete abolition'. Moreover, in at least one case (and very probably in several others) the death penalty was applied retroactively. In this case, which involved charges of speculation in foreign currency, a special (unpublished) edict of the Supreme Soviet Presidium appears to have authorized the retroactive application of the law 'as an exception'.[76] But this attempt to provide a flimsy cover of formal legality could not conceal the fact that the political authorities, the courts and the procuracy, all collaborated to subvert the integrity of the legal process. Only several months earlier the new RSFSR Criminal Code had affirmed: 'The criminality and punishability of an act shall be determined by the law prevailing at the time of the commission of that act . . . A law establishing the punishability of an act or increasing a punishment shall not have retroactive effect.'

Finally, and most importantly, the violation of the legal codes was the norm in 'anti-Soviet' cases, whether of religious believers, non-conformist intellectuals, spokesmen for various nationality groups or other critics of the regime. Such abuses were too numerous and varied to be recounted here. Suffice it to say that in none of the cases brought to trial were the guarantees of procedural due process allowed to obstruct the course of political 'justice'. Nor was the persecution of dissent in its manifold manifestations confined to the courts. The tolerance threshold of the authorities was considerably higher than it had been under Stalin and the scale and methods of extra-legal repression differed accordingly, but the tradition of official lawlessness endured. In place of Stalin's massive and largely arbitrary terror came a series of more selective and limited reprisals, carefully graded from intimidation, to dismissal from work or withdrawal of 'privileges' such as travel abroad, to enforced psychiatric confinement – a particularly pernicious form of punishment in which a diagnosis of 'incipient schizophrenia' could be derived from symptoms of 'reformist delusions'.[77]

But the authorities failed in their efforts to crush political dissent by these measures, and this failure alone may be regarded as testimony that respect for the law had struck some roots – however tender and precarious – in the public life of post-Stalin Russia. It is therefore altogether appropriate that we should conclude our discussion of the 1936 constitution by taking account of the remarkable phenomenon known loosely as the Soviet dissident movement.

The movement emerged in the 1960s, in the years immediately following the promulgation of the new legal codes, and although it never numbered more than a few thousand members, at best, it managed to assert itself in ways that would have been unthinkable twenty, or even ten, years earlier – to issue protests, to organize demonstrations, to publish underground literature, to maintain contacts with sympathizers at home and abroad, and to defend its members in Soviet courts. One of the most salient aspects of dissident activity was precisely the attempt to enforce observance of individual rights by reliance on the provisions of the constitution and the law. It was the specific concern of the Action Group for the Defence of Human Rights founded in 1969, the Human Rights Committee founded in 1970 and the Helsinki 'watch groups' which monitored Soviet compliance with the Final Act of the 35-nation European Conference on Security and Cooperation held in Helsinki in 1975. But it was also a common concern of the dissident movement as a whole, cutting across the particular interests of its various components. Many of the protests, both public and private, were addressed to the Soviet leadership and focused on the need to respect the laws of the country. In the court room, political defendants also fought tenaciously and often skilfully, if generally unsuccessfully, to take full advantage of the protection afforded by the law. By their actions the dissidents undoubtedly both reflected and enhanced greater awareness in Soviet society of the state's duty to observe its own laws. Henceforth the contest between the regime and those Soviet citizens who sought to affirm their constitutional rights was to be governed by new rules. The rules as applied remained manifestly unfair. But they did seem to impose some constraints on the regime and to open some options to a minority of determined and courageous citizens. They allowed some contest, however unequal, to take place.

Notes

1 N.S. Timasheff, *The Great Retreat*, New York, 1946.

2 J.V. Stalin, *Problems of Leninism*, Moscow, 1954, p. 711.

3 Official figures have been inconsistent, varying from 36 million to 50 million. One recent article even gave the figure of 75 million or 80 per cent of the adult population, which is exactly the proportion said to have participated in the discussions of the 1977 draft constitution (see p. 178). The article, which is based on archival sources, also offers some interesting items of information on the preparatory stages of the drafting process. (V.V. Kabanov, 'Iz istorii sozdaniya Konstitutsii SSSR 1936 goda', *Istoriya SSSR*, 1976, no. 6, pp. 116–27.)

4 Stalin, *Problems of Leninism*, p. 712.

5 The changes are recorded in the notes to the text of the constitution under the appropriate articles; for the more substantive changes see articles 8, 10, 14(f), 35, 40, 48, 65, 76, 77 and 80.

6 Bukharin who, it will be recalled, had also participated in the drafting of the 1918 constitution, was both secretary of the 1936 constitutional commission and chairman of its legal sub-commission. Privately he claimed to have written the constitution 'from first word to last' with only a little help from K. Radek, but this is regarded by his biographer as an exaggeration. (S.E. Cohen, *Bukharin and the Bolshevik Revolution*, London, 1974, pp. 356–7.) Radek, who chaired another constitutional sub-commission, was also a victim of the show

trials of the 1930s, as was another sub-commission chairman, V. Ya. Chubar.

7 Stalin, *Problems of Leninism*, p. 699.

8 ibid., pp. 630–2, 639–40.

9 ibid., p. 538; R. Conquest, *The Great Terror*, London, 1968, pp. 101, 196.

10 Stalin, *Problems of Leninism*, p. 693.

11 S. and E. Webb, *Soviet Communism: A New Civilization*, two vols, London, 1936, I, 84–5.

12 Bukharin, for one, seemed to believe that 'in this constitution the people will have more room. They can no longer be pushed around'. (B. Nicolaevsky, *Power and the Soviet Elite*, London, 1966, p. 22.)

13 Stalin, *Problems of Leninism*, p. 702.

14 But the latest (1979) census figures show that the relative share of both nationalities has been increasing since 1959. Thus Kazakhs made up 30 per cent of the population of Kazakhstan in 1959 and 36 per cent in 1979; comparable figures for Kirghiz in Kirghizia were 40.5 and 47.9 per cent. During the same period the share of Russians in the two republics declined from 42.7 to 40.8 per cent in Kazakhstan and from 30.2 to 25.9 per cent in Kirghizia.

15 M. Browne, ed., *Ferment in the Ukraine*, London, 1971, p. 51.

16 Stalin, *Problems of Leninism*, p. 704.

17 V.M. Chkhikvadze et al., *The Soviet State and Law*, Moscow, 1969, pp. 90–1.

18 Stalin, *Problems of Leninism*, pp. 705–6.

19 A. Denisov and M. Kirichenko, *Soviet State Law*, Moscow, 1960, p. 75.

20 There were in 1936 altogether eleven national areas (all in the RSFSR), nine autonomous regions and twenty-two autonomous republics. Since then their number has fallen to ten, eight, and twenty respectively.

21 In the final version of the text; the draft of article 35 did not provide for the representation of national areas. (See note 43, p. 162, n. 34.)

22 Provisions to that effect were included in the constitutions of the four union republics concerned. In so far as could be ascertained, however, such statutes were never issued. The same applies to the 'Statute on National Areas' provided by the constitution of the RSFSR.

23 A.Y. Vyshinsky, ed., *The Law of the Soviet State*, New York, 1948, p. 301.

24 In his speech to the 20th Congress Khrushchev conspicuously refrained from mentioning the Volga Germans and Crimean Tatars. Instead, he referred to the Ukrainians as potential victims: 'The Ukrainians avoided meeting this fate only because there were too many of them and there was no place to which to deport them. Otherwise he [Stalin] would have deported them also (Laughter and animation in the hall.)' (*The Anti-Stalin Campaign and International Communism*, edited by the Russian Institute, Columbia University, New York, 1956, p.57.) Since the early 1970s over 30,000 ethnic Germans were granted permission to emigrate to West Germany. The struggle of the Tatars to return to the Crimea has attracted worldwide attention, not least through the efforts of the famous Soviet dissident, General P.G. Grigorenko.

25 Precise figures on the social composition of post-1936 recruits are not available, but in the years 1936–41 members of white-collar occupations are estimated to have constituted around 70 per cent of new recruits. (See Aryeh L. Unger, 'Stalin's Renewal of the Leading Stratum: A Note on the Great Purge', *Soviet Studies*, 1968, no. 3, pp. 321–30.)

26 The title 'minister' only replaced that of 'people's commissar' in 1946 but for

the sake of convenience will be used throughout the following discussion. The official explanation of the change in terminology was that it 'reflects the increased role of the Soviet state, the increased range of competence and responsibility that the constitution of the USSR places upon the central organs and upon the persons who head the individual branches of state administration'.

27 Vyshinsky, *Law of the Soviet State*, p. 318.
28 See, e.g., M. Saifulin, ed., *The Soviet Parliament*, Moscow, 1967.
29 Stalin, *Problems of Leninism*, p. 708.
30 Vyshinsky, *Law of the Soviet State*, pp. 321–2.
31 Stalin, *Problems of Leninism*, p. 707 (emphasis in the original).
32 ibid., p. 708.
33 It will be noted that the size of the Council of the Union was reduced at the same time as that of the Council of Nationalities was raised. With a continuously growing population this clearly could not be accomplished without enlarging the size of electoral districts; whereas up to 1962 the average size of electoral districts had been below the constitutional norm of 300,000, it began to exceed the latter from 1966 onward – around 303,000 in 1966, 315,000 in 1970 and 327,000 in 1974.
34 D. Richard Little, 'Soviet Parliamentary Committees after Khrushchev: Obstacles and Opportunities', *Soviet Studies*, 1972, no. 1, pp. 41–60.
35 S. White, 'Communist Systems and the "Iron Law of Pluralism"', *British Journal of Political Science*, 1978, no. 1, pp. 101–17.
36 Stalin, *Problems of Leninism*, p. 709.
37 ibid., p. 708.
38 Vyshinsky, *Law of the Soviet State*, p. 341; see also V. Karpinsky, *The Social and State Structure of the USSR*, Moscow, 1951, p. 119.
39 Quoted from A.V. Mitskevitch, *Akty vysshikh organov sovetskogo gosudarstva*, Moscow, 1967, p. 102, in D. Richard Little, 'Legislative Authority in the Soviet Political System', *Slavic Review*, 1971, no. 1, pp. 71–2.
40 'Thus, by its representative character, its social and national composition, the Presidium is, as it were, a small replica of the Supreme Soviet, a collective capable of discharging the complex functions of the supreme organ of state power.' (Saifulin, *Soviet Parliament*, p. 78.)
41 Soviet authors have had difficulty in agreeing on clear and uniform criteria for distinguishing between decrees and regulations. The common denominator of the various definitions offered in the literature appears to be that decrees are normative acts, i.e. behavioural rules of general application and general legal force issued by the Council as a whole or its Presidium, whereas regulations 'as a rule' lack the quality of a legal norm and are issued by the Chairman of the Council or one of his deputies.
42 Because of the many unpublished decrees, the various problems concerning the definition of normative acts and the fact that many laws were either ratified edicts or budgetary and planning acts, precise figures are difficult to come by and must, moreover, be handled with great care. One Western scholar estimated a total of some 200 laws, 10,000 edicts and 57,400 decrees (over 80 per cent unpublished) for the period of 1945-65. (D.A. Loeber, 'Legal Rules "For Internal Use Only"', *International and Comparative Law Quarterly*, 1970, January, pp. 75–7.) These figures would be greatly reduced and their ratios altered if

only normative acts in the strict sense were considered.

43 In contrast to his predecessors, the present holder, N.A. Tikhonov, was a Politburo member of relatively junior standing when he succeeded to the post of Chairman of the Council of Ministers on 23 October 1980; he joined the Politburo as a candidate member in November 1978 and was promoted to full membership in November 1979.

44 Constitution of the RSFSR, articles 90–1. An English translation is in H.J. Berman and J.B. Quigley Jr, eds, *Basic Laws of the Soviet State*, Cambridge, Mass., 1969, pp. 29–57.

45 These enactments were initially issued as all-union legislation, in fact, as edicts of the Supreme Soviet Presidium – an edict on village soviets of 8 April 1968 and two edicts on town and district soviets of 19 March 1971 – and accompanied by decrees of the USSR Council of Ministers enlarging the financial powers of the local government units. Simultaneously, the Presidium issued 'model statutes' which provided a strict frame for the laws subsequently adopted by the union republics. The legality of this procedure was later questioned by some Soviet jurists on the grounds that the constitution did not place the legislation of such 'fundamentals' within the jurisdiction of the union.

   Similar legislation for the soviets of superior administrative–territorial units was projected by Brezhnev at the 25th Party Congress in 1976 and enacted by the Supreme Soviet on 25 June 1980 in the form of an all-union law.

46 Something like a grant of local autonomy was intimated in the 1961 Party Programme: 'The rights of the local soviets of toilers' deputies (local self-administration) will be extended. Local soviets will make the final decisions on all matters of local significance.'

47 Yu. Shabanov, *Partiinoe rukovodstvo sovetami trudyashchikhsya*, Minsk, 1969, pp. 42–3, quoted in R.J. Hill, 'The CPSU in a Soviet Election Campaign', *Soviet Studies*, 1976, no. 4, p. 595.

48 This is the title of a recent book edited by G. Hermet, R. Rose and A. Rouquié (London, 1978). See in particular A. Pravda, 'Elections in Communist Party States', pp. 169–95, for a review of what the author calls 'plebiscitary elections', of the Soviet type, and 'limited choice elections', practised in several other Communist states.

49 Even this claim is questionable. Western studies have shown that electoral participation, particularly in the towns, has in recent years been considerably lower than claimed by the official returns. (T.H. Friedgut, *Political Participation in the USSR*, Princeton, N.J., 1979, pp. 116 ff; V. Zaslavsky and R.J. Brym, 'The Functions of Elections in the USSR', *Soviet Studies*, 1978, no. 3, pp. 362–71.)

50 Several rights and one duty were included in other parts of the text. As has been seen, the right to personal property was granted in chapter I and work declared to be 'a duty and matter of honour'; electoral rights were set out in chapter XI and a number of 'due process' rights were guaranteed in chapter IX (see p. 125).

51 This is not to suggest, of course, that the Soviet constitution of 1936 was the only modern constitution which decreed this particular fusion – similar provisions may be found in the constitutions of Weimar Germany, the Fourth French Republic, and post-war Japan and Italy, among others; nor is it to ignore the fact that the realities of Soviet life transmuted other ostensible rights

into virtual duties – the right to vote, for example, or the right to join a trade union.

52 Karpinsky, *The Social and State Structure of the USSR*, pp. 190–2. The Rules of the First International drafted by Marx in 1864 similarly acknowledged *'no rights without duties, no duties without rights'*. (K. Marx, *On the First International*, edited and translated by S.K. Padover, New York, 1973, p. 14 (emphasis in the original).)

53 'The USSR, granting the right of asylum to persons of the capitalist world active in science, defends human culture from fascist fanaticism, and saves those living forces which can serve the toiling masses, from being physically exterminated by the moribund class.' (Vyshinsky, *Law of the Soviet State*, p. 636.)

54 Stalin, *Problems of Leninism*, p. 692.

55 V. Chalidze, *To Defend these Rights: Human Rights and the Soviet Union*, New York, 1974, pp. 68–9.

56 Vyshinsky, *Law of the Soviet State*, p. 617.

57 K. Marx and F. Engels, *Selected Works*, 2 vols, Moscow, 1951, I, 259.

58 For example, the West German constitution treats these rights as follows:

> *Article 10*   Secrecy of mail and secrecy of posts and telecommunications are inviolable. Restrictions may be ordered only pursuant to a law.
>
> *Article 13*   (1) The home is inviolable.
> (2) Searches may be ordered only by a judge or, in the event of danger in delay, by other organs as provided by law and may be carried out only in the form prescribed by law.

Constitutions of Modern States. Selected Texts, edited with an Introduction, Commentaries and Notes by L. Wolf-Phillips, London, 1968, pp. 28–9. See generally K.C. Wheare, *Modern Constitutions*, rev. edn, London, 1964, pp. 55 ff.)

59 Vyshinsky, *Law of the Soviet State*, p. 563. Soviet spokesmen have generally regarded the right to work as the most important of the rights granted in the constitution 'because it constitutes a necessary guarantee for the very physical existence of man'. At a time of widespread unemployment in the West, emphasis on work as constitutional right was, of course, particularly effective in propaganda terms.

60 A.I. Solzhenitsyn, *The Gulag Archipelago: 1918–1956. An Experiment in Literary Investigation*, parts I–II, New York, 1974, p. 67.

61 R. Sharlet, 'Stalinism and Soviet Legal Culture', in R.C. Tucker, ed., *Stalinism: Essays in Historical Analysis*, New York, 1977, p. 163.

62 To the nationalities mentioned above in connection with the break-up of national territories (p. 92), should be added the Meskhetians and several other Turkicized ethnic groups, whose deportation in November 1944, from an area of Georgia along the Turkish frontier, did not become known to the outside world until 1968.

63 R. Luxemburg, *The Russian Revolution and Leninism or Marxism?* Ann Arbor, 1961, p. 69.

64 P. Litvinov, *Demonstration in Pushkin Square*, London, 1969, pp. 87, 93.

65 In both cases formal constitutional amendment followed six years later; the two amendments were repealed in 1956 and 1960, respectively.

66 Denisov and Kirichenko, *Soviet State Law*, p. 321.

67 K. Marx and F. Engels, *Correspondence: 1846–1895*, London, 1934, p. 336; Lenin, *Coll. Works*, vol. 2, p. 97.

68 The interested reader is referred to the following discussions of this specialized topic: R.J. Osborn, 'Citizen versus Administration in the USSR', *Soviet
Studies*, 1965, no. 2, pp. 226–37; G. Ginsburgs, 'Judicial Controls over
Administrative Acts in the Soviet Union – The Current Scene', *Osteuropa – Recht*,
1968, no. 1, pp. 1–33; G.B. Smith, 'Judicial Review of Administrative Activity
in the Soviet Union', ibid., 1978, no. 4, pp. 296–307; D.D. Barry, 'Administrative Justice and Judicial Review in Soviet Administrative Law', in D.D. Barry,
G. Ginsburgs and P.B. Maggs, eds., *Soviet Law after Stalin* (*Law in Eastern
Europe*, vol. 20, part II) Alphen aan den Rijn, 1978, pp. 241–69.

69 Quoted from P.E. Nedbailo and V.M. Gorsheneva, eds., *Yuridicheskaya i
protsessual'naya forma*, Moscow, 1976, p. 127, in Barry, 'Administrative Justice',
p. 253.

70 It should be stressed that the Special Board, when established in 1934, was
merely the latest link in a long chain of extra-judicial agencies. Indeed, its
powers were limited by comparison to those of its immediate predecessor, the
Judicial Collegium of the OGPU. The abolition of the latter organ was accompanied by the transfer of jurisdiction over political crimes to the military
tribunals, leaving only a comparatively limited sphere of 'administrative justice' to the security services. At the time, therefore, it was seen as an attempt to
curb the arbitrary powers of the terror apparatus.

71 Quoted in J. Towster, *Political Power in the USSR: 1917–1947*, New York, 1948,
p. 304.

72 H.J. Berman, *Justice in the USSR*, Cambridge, Mass., rev. edn, 1966, p. 246.

73 L. Boim, 'Ombudsmanship in the Soviet Union', *American Journal of Comparative Law*, 1974, no. 3, p. 511.

74 The applicability of the presumption of innocence to Soviet law has been
debated by legal scholars both inside and outside the Soviet Union. (The
phrase itself was not used in the codes.) The view taken here is that of H.J.
Berman, *Soviet Criminal Law and Procedure. The RSFSR Codes*, 2nd edn Cambridge, Mass., 1972, pp. 59–62. For a different view see G.P. Fletcher, 'The
Presumption of Innocence in the Soviet Union', and the reply by H.J. Berman
and J.B. Quigley, Jr in *UCLA Law Review*, June 1968, pp. 1203–39.

75 Two well-known political 'parasites' tried under this legislation were the poet
Iosif Brodsky and the historian Andrei Amalrik. For the Brodsky case see S.
Kucherov, *The Organs of Soviet Administration of Justice*, Leiden, 1970, pp.
212–34. Amalrik's trial and exile are recounted in his own book, *Involuntary
Journey to Siberia*, London, 1970.

76 Berman, *Justice in the USSR*, p. 36.

77 Both judicial and extra-judicial repression have been extensively documented
in the Soviet underground literature and in reports of recent Soviet émigrés.
See, for example, A. Brumberg, ed., *In Quest of Justice: Protest and Dissent in the
Soviet Union Today*, New York, 1970; P. Reddaway, ed., *Uncensored Russia:
Protest and Dissent in the Soviet Union*, New York, 1972; M. Hayward, ed., *On
Trial: The Soviet State versus 'Abram Tertz' and 'Nikolai Arzhak'*, New York, 1966;
V. Chalidze, *To Defend these Rights: Human Rights and the Soviet Union*, New
York, 1974; Z. and R. Medvedev, *A Question of Madness*, New York, 1971; S.
Bloch and P. Reddaway, *Russia's Political Hospitals*, London, 1977.

The USSR Constitution of 1936

Constitution (Fundamental Law) of the Union of Soviet Socialist Republics

[*Adopted at the Extraordinary Eighth Congress of Soviets of the USSR on 5 December 1936*][1]

Chapter I The Social Structure

Article 1   The Union of Soviet Socialist Republics is a socialist state of workers and peasants.

Article 2   The soviets of toilers' deputies, which arose and grew strong as a result of the overthrow of the power of the landlords and capitalists and the victory of the dictatorship of the proletariat, shall constitute the political foundation of the USSR.

Article 3   All power in the USSR shall belong to the toilers of town and country as represented by the soviets of the toilers' deputies.

Article 4   The socialist system of economy and the socialist ownership of the instruments and means of production established as a result of the liquidation of the capitalist system of economy, the elimination of private ownership of the instruments and means of production, and the abolition of exploitation of man by man, shall constitute the economic foundation of the USSR.

Article 5   Socialist ownership in the USSR shall have either the form of state ownership (the wealth of the whole people) or the form of cooperative–collective farm ownership (ownership of individual collective farms and ownership of cooperative associations).

Article 6   The land, its minerals, the waters, forests, plants, factories, mines, and quarries, rail, water and air transport, banks, means of communication, large state-organized agricultural enterprises (state farms, machine-tractor stations, etc.), as well as municipal enterprises[2] and the bulk of housing in towns and industrial sites, shall be in state ownership, that is, the wealth of the whole people.

Article 7   Social enterprises in collective farms and cooperative organizations, with their livestock and implements, the output produced by collective farms and cooperative organizations as well as their public buildings, shall constitute the social, socialist property of the collective farms and cooperative organizations.

Every collective farm household, in addition to its basic income from the social collective farm economy,[3] shall have for personal use a small plot of land attached to the house and, in personal ownership, subsidiary husbandry on the plot, a house, livestock and poultry, and minor agricultural implements – in accordance with the charter of the agricultural artel.

Article 8   The land occupied by collective farms shall be allotted to them free of charge[4] for use for an unlimited time, that is in perpetuity.

Article 9   Alongside the socialist system of economy, which shall be the predominant form of economy in the USSR, small-scale private economy of individual peasants and artisans based on their personal labour and precluding the exploitation of the labour of others, shall be permitted by law.

Article 10   The right of personal ownership by citizens of their income and savings from work, dwelling house and subsidiary household husbandry, articles of domestic and everyday use, articles of personal consumption and convenience, as well as the right to inherit the personal property of citizens,[5] shall be protected by law.

Article 11   The economic life of the USSR shall be determined and directed by the state national economic plan in the interests of increasing social wealth, steadily raising the material and cultural level of the toilers and strengthening the independence of the USSR and its defence capability.

Article 12   Work in the USSR shall be a duty and a matter of honour[6] for every able-bodied citizen, in accordance with the principle: 'He who does not work, neither shall he eat.'

In the USSR the principle of socialism shall be realized: 'From each according to his ability, to each according to his work.'

Chapter II The State Structure

Article 13   The Union of Soviet Socialist Republics shall be a union state, formed on the basis of the voluntary association of equal Soviet Socialist Republics:

the Russian Soviet Federated Socialist Republic,
the Ukrainian Soviet Socialist Republic,
the Belorussian Soviet Socialist Republic,
the Azerbaidzhan Soviet Socialist Republic,

the Georgian Soviet Socialist Republic,
the Armenian Soviet Socialist Republic,
the Turkmen Soviet Socialist Republic,
the Uzbek Soviet Socialist Republic,
the Tadzhik Soviet Socialist Republic,
the Kazakh Soviet Socialist Republic,
the Kirghiz Soviet Socialist Republic.[7]

Article 14 The jurisdiction of the Union of Soviet Socialist Republics, as embodied in its highest organs of power[8] and organs of state administration, shall include:

(a) representation of the Union in international relations, and conclusion and ratification of treaties with other states;[9]

(b) questions of war and peace;

(c) admission of new republics into the USSR;

(d) control over the implementation[10] of the Constitution of the USSR and ensuring the conformity of the Constitutions of the union republics with the Constitution of the USSR;

(e) approval of modifications of boundaries between union republics;

(f) approval of the formation of new territories and regions and also of new autonomous republics within the union republics;[11]

(g) organization of the defence of the USSR and the direction of all the armed forces of the USSR;[12]

(h) foreign trade on the basis of state monopoly;

(i) protection of state security;

(j) establishment of the national economic plans of the USSR;

(k) approval of a single state budget for the USSR and also of the taxes[13] and revenues which go to form the union, republican and local budgets;

(l) administration of the banks, industrial and agricultural institutions and enterprises, and also of trading enterprises of all-union importance;[14]

(m) administration of transport and communications;[15]

(n) direction of the monetary and credit system;

(o) organization of state insurance;[16]

(p) concluding and granting loans;

(q) establishment of the basic principles of land use as well as of the use of minerals, forests and waters;

(r) establishment of the basic principles in the spheres of education and public health;

(s) organization of a uniform system of national economic accounting;

(t) establishment of the fundamentals of labour legislation;

(u) legislation on judicial organization and procedure and of criminal and civil codes;[17]

(v) laws on union citizenship; laws on the rights of foreigners;[18]
(w) issuing all-union acts of amnesty.[19]

Article 15 The sovereignty of the union republics shall be restricted only within the limits specified in article 14 of the Constitution of the USSR. Outside these limits each union republic shall exercise state power independently. The USSR shall protect the sovereign rights of the union republics.

Article 16 Every union republic shall have its own Constitution which shall take into account the specific features of the republic and which shall be drawn up in full conformity with the Constitution of the USSR.

Article 17 Every union republic shall retain the right of free secession from the USSR.

Article 18 The territory of union republics may not be modified without their consent.

[Article 18a][20]

[Article 18b][21]

Article 19 The laws of the USSR shall have the same force in the territory of all union republics.

Article 20 In the event of a divergence between a law of a union republic and an all-union law, the all-union law shall prevail.

Article 21 A single union citizenship shall be established for citizens of the USSR.
Every citizen of a union republic shall be a citizen of the USSR.

Article 22 The Russian Soviet Federated Socialist Republic shall consist of the Azov-Black Sea, Far Eastern, West Siberian, Krasnoyarsk and North Caucasian territories; the Voronezh, East Siberian, Gorky, Western, Ivanovo, Kalinin, Kirov, Kuibyshev, Kursk, Leningrad, Moscow, Omsk, Orenburg, Saratov, Sverdlovsk, Northern, Stalingrad, Chelyabinsk and Yaroslavl regions; the Tatar, Bashkir, Daghestan, Buryat-Mongolian, Kabardino-Balkar, Kalmyk, Karelian, Komi, Crimean, Mari, Mordovian, Volga German, North Ossetian, Udmurt, Chechen-Ingush, Chuvash and Yakut autonomous soviet socialist republics; the Adygei, Jewish, Karachai, Oirot, Khakass and Cherkess autonomous regions.[22]

Article 23 The Ukrainian Soviet Socialist Republic shall consist of the Vinnitsa, Dnepropetrovsk, Donetsk, Kiev, Odessa, Kharkov and Chernigov regions and the Moldavian ASSR.[23]

Article 24 The Azerbaidzhan Soviet Socialist Republic shall include the Nakhichevan ASSR and the Nagorno-Karabakh autonomous region.

Article 25 The Georgian Soviet Socialist Republic shall include the Abkhaz ASSR, the Adzhar ASSR, and the South Ossetian autonomous region.[24]

Article 26 The Uzbek Soviet Socialist Republic shall include the Kara-Kalpak ASSR.[25]

Article 27 The Tadzhik Soviet Socialist Republic shall include the Gorno-Badakhshan autonomous region.[26]

Article 28 The Kazakh Soviet Socialist Republic shall consist of the Aktyubinsk, Alma-Ata, East Kazakhstan, West Kazakhstan, Karaganda, Kustanai, North Kazakhstan and South Kazakhstan regions.[27]

Article 29 The Armenian SSR, the Belorussian SSR, the Turkmen SSR and the Kirghiz SSR shall contain neither autonomous republics nor territories and regions.[28]

[**Article 29a**][29]

[**Article 29b**][30]

[**Article 29c**][31]

Chapter III The Highest Organs of State Power of the Union of Soviet Socialist Republics

Article 30 The Supreme Soviet of the USSR shall be the highest organ of state power of the USSR.

Article 31 The Supreme Soviet of the USSR shall exercise all rights vested in the Union of Soviet Socialist Republics in accordance with article 14 of the Constitution, insofar as they do not, by virtue of the Constitution, come within the competence of organs of the USSR which are accountable to the Supreme Soviet of the USSR: the Presidium of the Supreme Soviet of the USSR, the Council of People's Commissars of the USSR and the People's Commissariats of the USSR.[32]

Article 32 The legislative power of the USSR shall be exercised exclusively by the Supreme Soviet of the USSR.

Article 33 The Supreme Soviet of the USSR shall consist of two chambers: the Council of the Union and the Council of Nationalities.

Article 34 The Council of the Union shall be elected by citizens of the USSR by electoral districts[33] on the basis of one deputy per 300,000 of population.

Article 35 The Council of Nationalities shall be elected by citizens of the USSR by union and autonomous republics, autonomous regions and national areas on the basis of twenty-five deputies from each union republic, eleven deputies from each autonomous republic, five deputies from each autonomous region and one deputy from each national area.[34]

Article 36   The Supreme Soviet of the USSR shall be elected for a term of four years.

Article 37   The two chambers of the Supreme Soviet of the USSR, the Council of the Union and the Council of Nationalities, shall have equal rights.

Article 38   Legislative initiative shall belong in equal measure to the Council of the Union and the Council of Nationalities.

Article 39   A law shall be considered approved if adopted by both chambers of the Supreme Soviet of the USSR, by a simple majority[35] in each.

Article 40   Laws adopted by the Supreme Soviet of the USSR shall be published in the languages of the union republics[36] over the signatures of the chairman and the secretary of the Presidium of the Supreme Soviet of the USSR.

Article 41   Sessions of the Council of the Union and the Council of Nationalities shall begin and terminate simultaneously.

Article 42   The Council of the Union shall elect a chairman of the Council of the Union and two[37] deputy chairmen.

Article 43   The Council of Nationalities shall elect a chairman of the Council of Nationalities and two[38] deputy chairmen.

Article 44   The chairmen of the Council of the Union and of the Council of Nationalities shall direct the sittings of the respective chambers and have charge of their internal proceedings.

Article 45   Joint sittings of both chambers of the Supreme Soviet of the USSR shall be conducted alternately by the chairmen of the Council of the Union and the Council of Nationalities.

Article 46   Sessions of the Supreme Soviet of the USSR shall be convened by the Presidium of the Supreme Soviet of the USSR twice a year.

Extraordinary sessions shall be convened by the Presidium of the Supreme Soviet of the USSR at its discretion or upon the demand of one of the union republics.

Article 47   In the event of disagreement between the Council of the Union and the Council of Nationalities the matter shall be referred for settlement to a conciliation commission formed[39] on a parity basis. If the conciliation commission does not arrive at an agreed decision, or if its decision does not satisfy one of the chambers, the matter shall be considered for a second time by the chambers. Failing an agreed decision of the two chambers,[40] the Presidium of the Supreme Soviet of the USSR shall dissolve the Supreme Soviet of the USSR and call new elections.

Article 48 The Supreme Soviet of the USSR, at a joint sitting of both chambers, shall elect the Presidium of the Supreme Soviet of the USSR, consisting of the chairman of the Presidium of the Supreme Soviet of the USSR, eleven deputy chairmen, the secretary of the Presidium and twenty-four members of the Presidium.[41]

The Presidium of the Supreme Soviet of the USSR shall be accountable to the Supreme Soviet of the USSR for all its activity.

Article 49 The Presidium of the Supreme Soviet of the USSR shall:[42]
- (a) convene sessions of the Supreme Soviet of the USSR;
- (b) interpret the laws of the USSR currently in force, and issue edicts;[43]
- (c) dissolve the Supreme Soviet of the USSR on the basis of article 47 of the Constitution of the USSR and call new elections;
- (d) conduct a nationwide poll (referendum) at its own initiative or upon the demand of one of the union republics;
- (e) annul decrees and regulations of the Council of People's Commissars of the USSR and the Councils of People's Commissars of the union republics in the event that they do not conform to the law;
- (f) in the interim between sessions of the Supreme Soviet of the USSR, dismiss and appoint individual People's Commissars of the USSR upon the recommendation of the Chairman of the Council of People's Commissars of the USSR, with subsequent submission for approval by the Supreme Soviet of the USSR;
- (g) award orders and confer honorary titles[44] of the USSR;
- (h) exercise the right of pardon;
- (i) appoint and remove the high command of the armed forces of the USSR;
- (j) in the interim between sessions of the Supreme Soviet of the USSR, proclaim a state of war in the event of an armed attack on the USSR, or in the event of the need to fulfill international treaty obligations on mutual defence against aggression;[45]
- (k) proclaim general or partial mobilization;
- (l) ratify international treaties;
- (m) appoint and recall plenipotentiary representatives of the USSR to foreign states;
- (n) accept the credentials and letters of recall of[46] diplomatic representatives of foreign states accredited to it.

Article 50 The Council of the Union and the Council of Nationalities shall elect credentials commissions which shall verify the credentials of the deputies of each chamber.

Upon the representation of the credentials commission[47] the chambers shall decide either to recognize the credentials or to annul the election of individual deputies.

Article 51   The Supreme Soviet of the USSR, when it considers it necessary, shall appoint commissions of investigation and inspection on any matter.

All institutions and officials shall be obliged to comply with the demands of these commissions and to submit to them the necessary materials and documents.

Article 52   A deputy of the Supreme Soviet of the USSR may not be brought to judicial responsibility or arrested without the consent of the Supreme Soviet of the USSR, and, in the period when the Supreme Soviet of the USSR is not in session,[48] without the consent of the Presidium of the Supreme Soviet of the USSR.

Article 53   Upon expiry of the term of the Supreme Soviet of the USSR, or after the Supreme Soviet has been dissolved prior to the expiry of its term, the Presidium of the Supreme Soviet of the USSR shall retain its powers until the formation of a new Presidium of the Supreme Soviet of the USSR by the newly elected Supreme Soviet of the USSR.

Article 54   Upon expiry of the term of the Supreme Soviet of the USSR, or in the event of its dissolution prior to the expiry of its term, the Presidium of the Supreme Soviet of the USSR shall call new elections within a period not exceeding two months from the date of expiry of the term or the dissolution of the Supreme Soviet of the USSR.

Article 55   The newly elected Supreme Soviet of the USSR shall be convened by the outgoing Presidium of the Supreme Soviet of the USSR not later than one month[49] after the elections.

Article 56   The Supreme Soviet of the USSR, at a joint sitting of both chambers, shall form the Government of the USSR – The Council of People's Commissars[50] of the USSR.

Chapter IV The Highest Organs of State Power of the Union Republics

Article 57   The Supreme Soviet of a Union Republic shall be the highest organ of state power of the Union Republic.

Article 58   The Supreme Soviet of a Union Republic shall be elected by the citizens of the republic for a term of four years.

The norms of representation shall be established by the Constitutions of the union republics.

Article 59   The Supreme Soviet of a Union Republic shall be the sole legislative organ of the republic.

Article 60   The Supreme Soviet of a Union Republic shall:
- (a)   adopt the Constitution of the republic and amend it in conformity with article 16 of the Constitution of the USSR;
- (b)   approve the Constitutions of its autonomous republics and determine the boundaries of their territories;
- (c)   approve the national economic plan and the budget of the republic;
- (d)   exercise the right of amnesty and pardon of citizens sentenced by the judicial organs of the Union Republic.[51]

Article 61   The Supreme Soviet of a Union Republic shall elect the Presidium of the Supreme Soviet of the Union Republic consisting of the chairman of the Presidium of the Supreme Soviet of the Union Republic, deputy chairmen, the secretary of the Presidium[52] and members of the Presidium of the Supreme Soviet of the Union Republic.

The powers of the Presidium of the Supreme Soviet of a Union Republic shall be determined by the Constitution of the Union Republic.

Article 62   The Supreme Soviet of a Union Republic shall elect its chairman[53] and deputy chairmen to conduct its sittings.

Article 63   The Supreme Soviet of a Union Republic shall form the Government of the Union Republic – the Council of People's Commissars [54] of the Union Republic.

Chapter V The Organs of State Administration of the Union of Soviet Socialist Republics[55]

Article 64   The Council of People's Commissars of the USSR shall be the highest executive and administrative organ of state power of the Union of Soviet Socialist Republics.

Article 65   The Council of People's Commissars of the USSR shall be responsible and accountable to the Suprreme Soviet of the USSR and, in the interim between sessions of the Supreme Soviet, to the Presidium of the Supreme Soviet of the USSR.[56]

Article 66   The Council of People's Commissars of the USSR shall issue decrees and regulations on the basis and in execution of the laws currently in force and verify their execution.

Article 67   Decrees and regulations of the Council of People's Commissars of the USSR shall be binding throughout the territory of the USSR.

Article 68   The Council of People's Commissars of the USSR shall:
- (a) coordinate and direct the work of the all-union and union

republic People's Commissariats of the USSR and of other economic and cultural institutions subordinate to it;[57]

(b) take measures to carry out the national economic plan and the state budget and to strengthen the credit and monetary system;

(c) take measures to secure public order, to defend the interests of the state, and protect the rights of citizens;

(d) exercise general direction in the sphere of relations with foreign states;

(e) determine the annual contingent of citizens subject to call-up for active military service and direct the general construction of the armed forces of the country;

(f) form, when necessary, special committees and Chief Administrations attached to the Council of People's Commissars of the USSR for matters of economic, cultural and defence construction.[58]

Article 69   The Council of People's Commissars of the USSR shall have the right, in respect of branches of administration and economy that come within the competence of the USSR, to suspend decrees and regulations of the Councils of People's Commissars of the Union Republics and to annul orders and instructions of People's Commissars of the USSR.[59]

Article 70   The Council of People's Commissars of the USSR shall be formed by the Supreme Soviet of the USSR, and shall consist of:

Chairman of the Council of People's Commisars of the USSR;

Deputy Chairmen of the Council of People's Commissars of the USSR;

Chairman of the State Planning Commission of the USSR;

Chairman of the Commission of Soviet Control;

People's Commissars of the USSR;

Chairman of the Committee for Agricultural Procurements;

Chairman of the Committee for the Arts;

Chairman of the Committee for Higher Education.[60]

Article 71   The Government of the USSR or a People's Commissar of the USSR to whom an inquiry from a deputy of the Supreme Soviet of the USSR is addressed shall be obliged within not more than three days to give an oral or written reply in the respective chamber.

Article 72   The People's Commissars of the USSR shall direct the branches of state administration which come within the competence of the USSR.

Article 73   The People's Commissars of the USSR shall issue, within the limits of the competence of their respective People's Commissariats, orders and instructions on the basis and in execution of the laws currently in force and also of the decrees and regulations of the Council of People's Commissars of the USSR, and shall verify their execution.

Article 74 The People's Commissariats of the USSR shall be either all-union or union republic commissariats.

Article 75 The all-union People's Commissariats shall direct the branches of state administration entrusted to them throughout the territory of the USSR either directly or through organs appointed by them.

Article 76 The union republic People's Commissariats shall, as a rule, direct the branches of state administration entrusted to them through the identically named People's Commissariats of the union republics, and shall administer directly only a definite and limited number of enterprises according to a list approved by the Presidium of the Supreme Soviet of the USSR.[61]

Article 77 The following People's Commissariats shall be all-union People's Commissariats:
Defence;
Foreign Affairs;
Foreign Trade;
Transport;
Communications;
Water Transport;
Heavy Industry;
Defence Industry.[62]

Article 78 The following People's Commissariats shall be union-republic People's Commissariats:
Food Industry;
Light Industry;
Timber Industry;
Agriculture;
Grain and Livestock State Farms;
Finance;
Internal Trade;
Internal Affairs;
Justice;
Public Health.[63]

Chapter VI The Organs of State Administration of the Union Republics[64]

Article 79 The Council of People's Commissars of a Union Republic shall be the highest executive and administrative organ of state power of the Union Republic.

Article 80 The Council of People's Commissars of a Union Republic shall be responsible and accountable to the Supreme Soviet of the Union Republic and, in the interim between sessions of the Supreme Soviet of the Union Republic, to the Presidium of the Supreme Soviet of the Union Republic.[65]

Article 81 The Council of People's Commissars of a Union Republic shall issue decrees and regulations on the basis and in execution of the laws currently in force in the USSR and the Union Republic, and of decrees and regulations of the Council of People's Commissars of the USSR, and shall verify their execution.

Article 82 The Council of People's Commissars of a Union Republic shall have the right to suspend decrees and regulations of Councils of People's Commissars of autonomous republics and to annul decisions and regulations of executive committees of soviets of toilers' deputies of territories, regions and autonomous regions.[66]

Article 83 The Council of People's Commissars of a Union Republic shall be formed by the Supreme Soviet of the Union Republic and shall consist of:

Chairman of the Council of People's Commissars of the
  Union Republic;
Deputy Chairmen;
Chairman of the State Planning Commission;
People's Commissars of
  Food Industry;
  Light Industry;
  Timber Industry;
  Agriculture;
  Grain and Livestock State Farms;
  Finance;
  Internal Trade;
  Internal Affairs;
  Justice;
  Public Health;
  Education;
  Local Industry;
  Municipal Economy;
  Social Security;
  Plenipotentiary of the Committee for Procurements;
  Head of the Administration for the Arts;
  Plenipotentiaries of all-union People's Commissariats.[67]

Article 84 The People's Commissars of a Union Republic shall direct the branches of state administration that come within the competence of the Union Republic.

Article 85 The People's Commissars of a Union Republic shall issue, within the limits of the competence of the respective People's Commissariats, orders and instructions on the basis and in execution of the laws of the USSR and the Union Republic, of decrees and regulations of the Council of People's Commissars of both the USSR and the Union Republic, and of orders and instructions of the union republic People's Commissariats of the USSR.

Article 86 The People's Commissariats of a Union Republic shall be either union republic or republic commissariats.

Article 87 The union republic People's Commissariats shall direct the branches of state administration entrusted to them, and shall be subordinate both to the Council of People's Commissars of the Union Republic and to the corresponding union republic People's Commissariats of the USSR.

Article 88 The republic People's Commissariats shall direct the branches of state administration entrusted to them, and shall be directly subordinate to the Council of People's Commissars of the Union Republic.

[**Article 88a**][68]
[**Article 88b**][69]

Chapter VII The Highest Organs of State Power of the Autonomous Soviet Socialist Republics

Article 89 The Supreme Soviet of an ASSR shall be the highest organ of state power of the Autonomous Republic.

Article 90 The Supreme Soviet of an Autonomous Republic shall be elected by the citizens of the republic for a term of four years according to the norms of representation established by the Constitution of the Autonomous Republic.

Article 91 The Supreme Soviet of an Autonomous Republic shall be the sole legislative organ of the ASSR.

Article 92 Every Autonomous Republic shall have its own Constitution, which shall take into account the specific features of the Autonomous Republic and shall be drawn up in full conformity with the Constitution of the Union Republic.

Article 93 The Supreme Soviet of an Autonomous Republic shall elect the Presidium of the Supreme Soviet of the Autonomous Republic and form the Council of People's Commissars of the Autonomous Republic, in accordance with its Constitution.

Chapter VIII The Local Organs of State Power

Article 94   The soviets of toilers' deputies shall be the organs of state power in territories, regions, autonomous regions, areas, districts, towns and rural localities (stanitsas, villages, khutors, kishlaks, auls).[70]

Article 95   The soviets of toilers' deputies in territories, regions, autonomous regions, areas, districts, towns and rural localities (stanitsas, villages, khutors, kishlaks, auls) shall be elected by the toilers of the respective territories, regions, autonomous regions, areas, districts, towns and rural localities for a term of two years.

Article 96   The norms of representation for soviets of toilers' deputies shall be determined by the Constitutions of the union republics.

Article 97   The soviets of toilers' deputies shall direct the activities of the organs of administration subordinate to them; ensure the protection of state order, the observance of the laws, and protection of the rights of citizens; direct local economic and cultural construction, and establish the local budget.

Article 98   The soviets of toilers' deputies shall adopt decisions and issue regulations within the limits of the rights granted to them by the laws of the USSR and the Union Republic.

Article 99   The executive and administrative organs of the soviets of toilers' deputies of territories, regions, autonomous regions, areas, districts, towns and rural localities shall be the executive committees elected by them, consisting of a chairman, deputy chairmen, secretary[71] and members.

Article 100   The executive and administrative organs of rural soviets of toilers' deputies in small localities shall, in conformity with the Constitutions of the union republics, be the chairman, the deputy chairman and the secretary elected by them.[72]

Article 101   The executive organs of the soviets of toilers' deputies shall be directly accountable to both the soviets of toilers' deputies which elected them and to the executive organ of the superior soviet of toilers' deputies.

Chapter IX The Court and the Procuracy

Article 102   Justice in the USSR shall be administered by the Supreme Court of the USSR, the Supreme Courts of the union republics, the courts of territories and regions, the courts of the autonomous republics and autonomous regions, the courts of areas,[73] special courts of the USSR created by decree of the Supreme Soviet of the USSR, and the people's courts.

Article 103   In all courts, cases shall be heard with the participation of people's assessors, except in instances specially provided for by law.

Article 104   The Supreme Court of the USSR shall be the highest judicial organ. The Supreme Court of the USSR shall be charged with supervision over the judicial activity of all judicial organs of the USSR and the union republics.[74]

Article 105   The Supreme Court of the USSR and the special courts of the USSR shall be elected by the Supreme Soviet of the USSR for a term of five years.[75]

Article 106   The Supreme Courts of the union republics shall be elected by the Supreme Soviets of the union republics for a term of five years.

Article 107   The Supreme Courts of the autonomous republics shall be elected by the Supreme Soviets of the autonomous republics for a term of five years.

Article 108   The courts of territories and regions, autonomous regions and areas shall be elected by the territorial, regional or area[76] soviets of toilers' deputies or by the soviets of toilers' deputies of the autonomous regions for a term of five years.

Article 109   People's courts shall be elected by the citizens of the district on the basis of universal, direct and equal suffrage by secret ballot for a term of three years.[77]

Article 110   Court proceedings shall be conducted in the language of the union republic, autonomous republic or autonomous region, persons not knowing this language being ensured full familiarization with the materials of the case through an interpreter and also the right to speak in court in their native language.

Article 111   Examination of cases in all courts shall be open, in so far as exceptions are not provided for by law, with the accused being guaranteed the right to defence.

Article 112   Judges shall be independent and subordinate only to the law.

Article 113   Supreme supervision over the strict execution of the laws by all People's Commissariats and their subordinate institutions, as well as by individual officials and by citizens of the USSR, shall be vested in the Procurator of the USSR.[78]

Article 114   The Procurator of the USSR shall be appointed by the Supreme Soviet of the USSR for a term of seven years.

Article 115   Procurators of republics, territories and regions, and also procurators of autonomous republics and autonomous regions, shall be appointed by the Procurator of the USSR for a term of five years.

Article 116   Area, district and town procurators[79] shall be appointed for a term of five years by the procurators of union republics and confirmed by the Procurator of the USSR.

Article 117   The organs of the procuracy shall exercise their functions independently of any local organs whatsoever, being subordinate solely to the Procurator of the USSR.

Chapter X The Fundamental Rights and Duties of Citizens

Article 118   Citizens of the USSR shall have the right to work, that is, the right to guaranteed employment with payment for their work in conformity with its quantity and quality.

The right to work shall be ensured by the socialist organization of the national economy, the steady growth of the productive forces of Soviet society, the elimination of the possibility of economic crises, and the liquidation of unemployment.

Article 119   Citizens of the USSR shall have the right to rest and leisure.

The right to rest and leisure shall be ensured by the reduction of the working day to seven hours for the overwhelming majority of the workers,[80] the establishment of annual vacations with pay for workers and employees and the provision of an extensive network of sanatoria, rest homes and clubs for the use of the toilers.

Article 120   Citizens of the USSR shall have the right to material security in old age and also in the event of illness or loss of the capacity to work.

This right shall be ensured by the extensive development of social insurance for workers and employees at state expense, free medical aid for the toilers,[81] and the provision of an extensive network of health resorts for the use of the toilers.

Article 121   Citizens of the USSR shall have the right to education.

This right shall be ensured by universal and compulsory elementary education, by education, including higher education, being free of charge, by a system of state stipends for the overwhelming majority of students in higher schools, by instruction in schools in the native language, and by the organization of free production, technical and agronomic instruction for the toilers at plants, state farms, machine-tractor stations and collective farms.[82]

Article 122   Women in the USSR shall be granted equal rights with men in all spheres of economic, state, cultural and socio-political life.

The possibility of exercising these rights of women shall be ensured by granting women the right, equal to that of men, to work, payment for work, rest and leisure, social insurance and education, and by state protection of the interests of mother and child,[83] by granting vacations for women during pregnancy with retention of support and by an extensive network of maternity homes, nurseries and kindergartens.

Article 123 The equality of rights of citizens of the USSR, irrespective of their nationality or race, in all spheres of economic, state, cultural, social and political life, shall be an indefeasible law.

Any direct or indirect restriction of rights or, conversely, the establishment of direct or indirect privileges for citizens on account of their race or nationality, and equally any advocacy of racial or national exclusiveness or of hatred and contempt, shall be punishable by law.

Article 124 In order to ensure freedom of conscience to citizens, the church in the USSR shall be separated from the state, and the school from the church. Freedom of religious worship and freedom of antireligious propaganda shall be recognized for all citizens.

Article 125 In conformity with the interests of the toilers, and in order to strengthen the socialist system, citizens of the USSR shall be guaranteed by law:[84]

(a) freedom of assembly and meetings;
(b) freedom of the press;
(c) freedom of assembly and meetings;
(d) freedom of street processions and demonstrations.

These rights of citizens shall be ensured by placing at the disposal of the toilers and their organizations, printing presses, stocks of paper, public buildings, the streets, means of communication and other material conditions necessary for their exercise.

Article 126 In conformity with the interests of the toilers, and in order to develop the organizational initiative and political activity of the masses of the people, citizens of the USSR shall be ensured the right to unite in social organizations – trade unions, cooperative associations, youth organizations, sport and defence organizations, cultural, technical and scientific societies; and the most active and conscious citizens from the ranks of the working class and other strata of the toilers shall unite in the All-Union Communist Party (Bolsheviks), which is the vanguard of the toilers in their struggle to strengthen and develop the socialist system and the leading core of all organizations of the toilers, both social and state.[85]

Article 127 Citizens of the USSR shall be ensured inviolability of the person. No one may be subjected to arrest except by court decree or with the sanction of a procurator.

Article 128 The inviolability of citizens' homes and secrecy of correspondence shall be protected by law.

Article 129   The USSR shall grant the right of asylum to foreigners persecuted for defending the interests of the toilers, or for their scientific activities, or for their struggle for national liberation.

Article 130   Every citizen of the USSR shall be obliged to observe the Constitution of the Union of Soviet Socialist Republics, to carry out the laws, to maintain labour discipline, to be honestly concerned with his social duties, and to respect the rules of socialist community life.

Article 131   Every citizen of the USSR shall be obliged to preserve and strengthen social, socialist ownership as the sacred and inviolable foundation of the Soviet system, as the source of the wealth and might of the motherland, and as the source of the prosperous and cultured life of all the toilers.

Persons offending against social, socialist ownership shall be enemies of the people.

Article 132   Universal military duty shall be law. Military service in the Workers' and Peasants' Red Army[86] shall be the honourable duty of citizens of the USSR.

Article 133   Defence of the fatherland shall be the sacred duty of every citizen of the USSR. Treason to the motherland – violation of the oath of allegiance, desertion to the enemy, damaging the military power of the state, or espionage[87] – shall be punishable with all the severity of the law as the gravest malefaction.

Chapter XI The Electoral System

Article 134   Deputies to all soviets of toilers' deputies – the Supreme Soviet of the USSR, the Supreme Soviets of the union republics, the soviets of toilers' deputies of the territories and regions, the Supreme Soviets of the autonomous republics, the soviets of toilers' deputies of autonomous regions, areas, districts, towns and rural localities (stanitsas, villages, khutors, kishlaks, auls) – shall be elected by the electors on the basis of universal, equal and direct suffrage by secret ballot.

Article 135   Elections of deputies shall be universal: all citizens of the USSR who have reached the age of 18, irrespective of race and nationality, religious persuasion, educational qualification, domicile, social origin, property position and past activities, shall have the right to participate in the election of deputies and to be elected, with the exception of the insane and of persons convicted by a court of law to sentences that include deprivation of electoral rights.[88]

Article 136   Elections of deputies shall be equal: every citizen shall have one vote; all citizens shall participate in elections on an equal basis.[89]

Article 137   Women shall have the right to elect and be elected on equal terms with men.

Article 138   Citizens serving in the Red Army[90] shall have the right to elect and be elected on equal terms with all other citizens.

Article 139   Elections of deputies shall be direct: all soviets of toilers' deputies, from rural and town soviets of toilers' deputies up to the Supreme Soviet of the USSR, shall be directly elected by the citizens by means of direct elections.

Article 140   Voting at elections of deputies shall be secret.

Article 141   Candidates in elections shall be nominated by electoral districts.

The right to nominate candidates shall be ensured to social organizations and societies of toilers: Communist party organizations, trade unions, cooperatives, youth organizations, and cultural societies.

Article 142   Every deputy shall be obliged to report to the electors on his own work and on the work of the soviet of toilers' deputies, and may be recalled at any time, in the procedure established by law, upon the decision of a majority of the electors.

Chapter XII Arms, Flag, Capital

Article 143   The state arms of the Union of Soviet Socialist Republics shall consist of a sickle and hammer against a globe depicted in the rays of the sun and framed by ears of grain with the inscription in the languages of the union republics: 'Proletarians of All Countries, Unite!' At the top of the arms shall be a five-pointed star.

Article 144   The state flag of the Union of Soviet Socialist Republics shall consist of red cloth with a golden sickle and hammer depicted in the upper corner near the staff and a five-pointed red star bordered in gold above them. The ratio of width to length shall be 1:2.

Article 145   The city of Moscow shall be the capital of the Union of Soviet Socialist Republics.

Chapter XIII The Procedure for Amending the Constitution

Article 146   The Constitution of the USSR shall be amended only by decision of the Supreme Soviet of the USSR adopted by a majority of not less than two-thirds of the votes in each of its chambers.

Notes

1 The footnotes to the articles of the constitution include changes introduced in the draft by the Eighth Congress of Soviets, as well as subsequent amendments to the final text up to 1977. Where appropriate, for greater clarity, the changed wording is placed in italics. The dates refer in all cases to the formal enactment of the amending legislation by the Supreme Soviet.

The official enactments mentioned in the 1936 constitution have here been translated as follows: *zakon* – law, *ukaz* – edict, *postanovlenie* – decree, *rasporyazhenie* – regulation, *prikaz* – order, *instruktsiya* – instruction, *polozhenie* – statute. An admirably lucid attempt to sort out the 'extraordinarily confused and confusing' hierarchical relationships among the various enactments is W.E. Butler, 'Sources of Soviet Law', *Current Legal Problems*, 1975, no. 2, pp. 223–42.

2 Added to the draft: 'as well as municipal enterprises'.

3 Added to the draft: 'in addition to its basic income from the social collective farm economy'.

4 Added to the draft: 'free of charge'.

5 Added to the draft: 'as well as the right to inherit the personal property of citizens'.

6 Added to the draft: 'and a matter of honour'.

7 On 31 March 1940 the Karelo-Finnish SSR, and on 7 August 1940 the Moldavian, Lithuanian, Latvian and Estonian SSRs (in that order) were added to the list. By amendment of 25 February 1947 the republics were listed according to size of population, in descending order, as follows:

the Russian Soviet Federated Socialist Republic, the Ukrainian Soviet Socialist Republic, the Belorussian Soviet Socialist Republic, the Uzbek Soviet Socialist Republic, the Kazakh Soviet Socialist Republic, the Georgian Soviet Socialist Republic, the Azerbaidzhan Soviet Socialist Republic, the Lithuanian Soviet Socialist Republic, the Moldavian Soviet Socialist Republic, the Latvian Soviet Socialist Republic, the Kirghiz Soviet Socialist Republic, the Tadzhik Soviet Socialist Republic, the Armenian Soviet Socialist Republic, the Turkmen Soviet Socialist Republic, the Estonian Soviet Socialist Republic, the Karelo-Finnish Soviet Socialist Republic.

On 16 July 1956 the Karelo-Finnish SSR was deleted.

8 Amended on 25 February 1947 to '*state* power'.

9 An amendment of 1 February 1944 added 'establishment of the general procedure for the mututal relations of union republics with foreign states'. An amendment of 25 February 1947 inserted: 'ratification *and abrogation* of treaties'.

10 Amended on 25 February 1947 to 'control over the *observance*'.

11 This section was added to the draft.

An amendment of 25 February 1947 inserted 'new autonomous republics *and autonomous regions*'. On 11 February 1957 approval of the formation of new territories and regions was removed from union jurisdiction (see p.161, note 27). The final revised version of this section read:

> (f) approval of the formation of new autonomous republics and autonomous regions within the union republics.

12 An amendment of 1 February 1944 added: 'establishment of the guiding fundamentals of the organization of the military formations of the union republics'.

13 Amended on 25 February 1947 to: 'approval of a single state budget for the USSR *and of the report of its execution, and establishment* of the taxes'.

14 An amendment of 10 May 1957 replaced 'all-union importance' by 'all-union subordination', and added: 'and the general direction of industry and construction of union-republic subordination'.

15 An amendment of 11 February 1957 added: 'of all-union importance'.

16 Deleted from draft: 'insurance *of property*'.

17 An amendment of 11 February 1957 confined the union to the establishment of the 'fundamentals' of legislation and replaced 'codes' by 'legislation'. A further amendment of 11 July 1969 added 'and corrective labour legislation'. The revised version of this section read:

> (u) establishment of the fundamentals of legislation of judicial organization and judicial procedure, and the basic principles of civil, criminal and corrective labour legislation.

18 The word 'laws' in this section was replaced by 'legislation' on 25 February 1947.

19 By amendment of 25 February 1947 this section became section (y), and a new provision was substituted:

> (w) establishment of the fundamentals of legislation on marriage and family.

20 Added by amendment of 1 February 1944:

> **Article 18a** Every union republic shall have the right to enter into direct relations with foreign states, to conclude agreements with them, and to exchange diplomatic and consular representatives.

21 Added by amendment of 1 February 1944:

> **Article 18b** Every union republic shall have its own republican military formations.

22 This article was amended ten times following administrative-territorial changes, until an amendment of 11 February 1957 transferred approval of the formation of purely administrative territorial subvidisions from the jurisdiction of the union to that of the respective union republics (see p. 161, note 27). On the same day by a separate law, the administrative (non-autonomous) territories and regions were deleted from the article. A third law, also of 11 February 1957, further amended the article in partial rehabilitation of the nationalities exiled during World War II (see p. 92), as follows: the Kabardian ASSR was once more renamed Kabardino-Balkar ASSR, the Chechen-Ingush ASSR was added, the former Kalmyk ASSR re-appeared as an autonomous region, and the Cherkess autonomous region became the Karachai-Cherkess autonomous region. It will be recalled that these national units had earlier simply disappeared from the constitution without any public formal amendment; their re-emergence in the constitution followed edicts of the SS Presidium of 9 January 1957. By amendment of 25 December 1958 the Kalmyk autonomous region was once more listed as an ASSR and the Buryat-Mongolian ASSR was listed as the Buryat ASSR. By amendment of 8 December 1961 the Tuva autonomous region was listed as an ASSR. The final version of this article contained the autonomous republics and autonomous regions in the order listed in articles 85 and 87 of the 1977 constitution (see p. 249).

23 This article was amended nine times up to 1957 after administrative-territorial changes and the elevation of Moldavia to union republic status (see p. 159, note

7). As the Ukraine contained no other national territorial subdivisions, the article was repealed on 11 February 1957 (see below, note 27). In its final version (before repeal) the article read:

Article 23 The Ukrainian Soviet Socialist Republic shall consist of the Vinnitsa, Volhynian, Voroshilovgrad, Dnepropetrovsk, Drogobych, Zhitomir, Trans-Carpathian, Zaporozhye, Kiev, Kirovograd, Crimean, Lvov, Nikolayev, Odessa, Poltava, Rovno, Stalino, Sumi, Ternopol, Kharkov, Kherson, Khmelnitsky, Cherkassy, Chernigov and Chernovtsy regions.

24 Amended on 8 March 1952 to add, and on 26 April 1954 to delete, two administrative regions: Tbilisi and Kutaisi.

25 Amended twice to accommodate administrative-territorial changes up to 11 February 1957, when the nine then existing administrative regions were deleted (see below, note 27) and the article reverted to its original 1936 version.

26 Amended three times to accommodate administrative-territorial changes until 11 February 1957, when the then remaining Leninabad region was deleted (see below, note 27), and the article reverted to its original 1936 version.

27 Amended three times until 11 February 1957, when an entirely new provision was substituted:

Article 28 The resolution of matters concerning the regional and territorial administrative-territorial structure of the union republics shall come within the jurisdiction of the union republics.

28 Amended four times to accommodate first (on 15 January 1938) the creation of, and then changes in, the administrative regions of the Belorussian SSR, and also of the Turkmen and Kirghiz SSRs (see below, notes 29 & 30). On 11 February 1957 the article was repealed (see above, note 27). In its final version (before repeal) the article read:

Article 29 The Belorussian Soviet Socialist Republic shall consist of the Brest, Vitebsk, Gomel, Grodno, Minsk, Mogilev and Molodechno regions.

29 This article was added on 4 April 1940 and later amended three times to accommodate the creation of, and subsequent changes in, the administrative regions of the Turkmen SSR. On 11 February 1957 the article was repealed (see above, note 27). In its final version (before repeal) the article read:

Article 29a The Turkmen Soviet Socialist Republic shall consist of the Ashkhabad, Mary, Tashauz and Chardzhou regions.

30 This article was added on 4 April 1940 and subsequently amended twice to accommodate the creation of, and changes in, the administrative regions of the Kirghiz SSR. On 11 February 1957 the article was repealed (see above, note 27). In its final version (before repeal) the article read:

Article 29b The Kirghiz Soviet Socialist Republic shall consist of the Dzhalal-Abad, Issyk-Kul, Osh, Tyan-Shan and Frunze regions.

31 This article was added on 10 March 1951 following the creation of four administrative regions in the Lithuanian SSR:

Article 29c The Lithuanian Soviet Socialist Republic shall consist of the Vilnius, Kaunas, Klaipeda and Siauliai regions.

The four regions were abolished by edict of the SS Presidium of 28 May 1953, and the article was repealed on 26 April 1954.

32 An amendment of 25 February 1947 replaced the words 'People's Commissars' and 'People's Commissariats' and 'Ministers' and 'Ministries', respectively.

33 Added to the draft: 'by electoral districts'.

34 The draft version of this article provided for an indirectly elected Council of Nationalities with considerably lower representation for the union republics, autonomous republics and autonomous regions, and no representation at all for the national areas:

Article 35 The Council of Nationalities shall be composed of deputies chosen by the Supreme Soviets of the union and autonomous republics and the soviets of toilers' deputies of the autonomous regions on the basis of ten deputies from each union republic, five deputies from each autonomous republic and two deputies from each autonomous region.

By amendment of 3 August 1966 the number of deputies from each union republic was increased from twenty-five to thirty-two.

35 Amended on 25 February 1947 to 'a simple majority *of votes'*.

36 Added to the draft: 'in the languages of the union republics'.

37 Amended to 'four' on 17 June 1950.

38 Amended to 'four' on 17 June 1950.

39 Amended on 25 February 1947 to 'formed *by the chambers'*.

40 Amended on 25 February 1947 to 'of *both* chambers'.

41 The draft provided for four deputy chairmen and thirty-one members. On 7 August 1940 the number of deputy chairmen was amended to sixteen, and on 25 February 1958 to 'fifteen deputy chairmen – one from each union republic'. The number of other Presidium members was amended to fifteen on 25 February 1947, and to twenty on 3 August 1966.

42 An amendment of 15 January 1938 added the provision listed as section (r). On 25 February 1947 the article was amended as follows: section (b) was split into two; the words 'People's Commissars' in sections (e) and (f) were replaced by 'Ministers'; the words 'and medals of the USSR' were inserted in section (g); the words 'and abrogate' were inserted in section (l); and two new provisions, listed below as sections (h) and (k), were added. In its revised version the article read:

Article 49 The Presidium of the Supreme Soviet of the USSR shall:

(a)   convene sessions of the Supreme Soviet of the USSR;

(b)   issue edicts;

(c)   interpret the laws of the USSR currently in force;

(d)   dissolve the Supreme Soviet of the USSR on the basis of article 47 of the Constitution of the USSR and call new elections;

(e)   conduct a nationwide poll (referendum) at its own initiative or upon the demand of one of the union republics;

(f)   annul decrees and regulations of the Council of Ministers of the USSR and the Councils of Ministers of the union republics in the event that they do not conform to the law;

(g)   in the interim between sessions of the Supreme Soviet of the USSR, dismiss and appoint individual Ministers of the USSR upon the recommendation of the Chairman of the Council of Ministers of the USSR, with subsequent submission for approval by the Supreme Soviet of the USSR;

(h)   institute orders and medals of the USSR and establish honorary titles of the USSR;

(i)   award orders and medals of the USSR and confer honorary titles of the USSR;

(j)   exercise the right of pardon;

(k)   establish military ranks, diplomatic ranks, and other special ranks;

(l)   appoint and remove the high command of the armed forces of the USSR;

(m)   in the interim between sessions of the Supreme Soviet of the USSR, proclaim a state of war in the event of an armed attack on the USSR, or in the event of the need to fulfill international treaty obligations on mutual defence against aggression;

(n)   proclaim general or partial mobilization;

(o)   ratify and abrogate international treaties;

(p)   appoint and recall plenipotentiary representatives of the USSR to foreign states;

(q)   accept the credentials and letters of recall of diplomatic representatives of foreign states accredited to it;

(r)   proclaim martial law in individual localities or throughout the USSR in the interests of the defence of the USSR or in order to ensure public order and state security.

43 The words 'and issue edicts' replaced 'issuing corresponding edicts' in the draft.

44 Added to the draft: 'and confer honorary titles'.

45 Added to the draft: 'or in the event of the need to fulfill international treaty obligations on mutual defence against aggression'.

46 Added to the draft: 'the credentials and letters of recall of'.

47 Amended on 25 February 1947 to the plural 'commissions'.

48 Amended on 25 February 1947 to 'in the interim between sessions of the Supreme Soviet of the USSR'.

49 Amended on 25 February 1947 to 'three months'.

50 Amended on 25 February 1947 to 'Council of Ministers'.

51 On 1 February 1944 two sections were added to this article:

(e)   establish the representation of the union republic in international relations;

(f)   establish the procedure for the formation of republican military formations.

An amendment of 10 May 1957 added 'and form economic administrative districts' to section (c); on 19 December 1963 this was amended to 'economic districts of the republic'; on 2 October 1965 the added wording was deleted and the section reverted to its original version.

52 Added to the draft: 'the secretary of the Presidium'.

53 Amended on 25 February 1947 to 'elect the Chairman of the Supreme Soviet of the union republic'.

54 Amended on 25 February 1947 to 'Council of Ministers'.

55 The words 'People's Commissar' and 'People's Commissariat', which recur throughout this chapter were altered to 'Minister' and 'Ministry', respectively, by amendment of 25 February 1947.

56 Added to the draft: 'and in the interim between sessions of the Supreme Soviet, to the Presidium of the Supreme Soviet of the USSR'.

57 An amendment of 10 May 1957 deleted 'economic and cultural', and added 'and exercise direction over the Councils of National Economy of the economic administrative districts through the Councils of Ministers of the union republics'. This was amended on 22 December 1960 by the insertion of the words 'direction over *the republican Councils of National Economy and*'. A revised version of this section was enacted on 19 December 1963:

(a) coordinate and direct the work of the Supreme Council of National Economy of the USSR of the Council of Ministers of the USSR (VSNKh SSSR), all-union and union-republic Ministries of the USSR, State Committees of the Council of Ministers of the USSR and other institutions subordinate to it.

By amendment of 2 October 1965 the words 'Supreme Council of the National Economy of the USSR of the Council of Ministers of the USSR (VSNKh SSSR)' were deleted.

58 This section was added to the draft. It was amended on 19 December 1963 by the insertion of the words 'form *State Committees of the USSR, and also,* when necessary'.

59 An amendment of 10 May 1957 inserted the words '*and the Councils of National Economy of the economic administrative districts,* and to annul'. On 22 December 1960 a further amendment inserted '*republican Councils of National Economy* and the Councils of National Economy of the economic administrative districts'. By amendment of 19 December 1963 both the above insertions were deleted and the words 'and also acts of other institutions subordinate to it' were added at the end of the article.

60 This article was amended 27 times. With one exception, an amendment of 25 February 1957 which included a provision for the *ex officio* membership of the heads of the republican governments in the USSR Council of Ministers (see the last paragraph of article 70 below), all amendments reflected administrative changes in the central government. The final version of this article, following the last amendment of 29 October 1976, read:

Article 70 The Council of Ministers of the USSR shall be formed by the Supreme Soviet of the USSR, and shall consist of: Chairman of the Council of Ministers of the USSR; First Deputy Chairman of the Council of Ministers of the USSR; Deputy Chairmen of the Council of Ministers of the USSR; Ministers of the USSR; Chairman of the State Planning Committee of the Council of Ministers of the USSR; Chairman of the State Committee of the Council of Ministers of the USSR for Construction; Chairman of the State Committee of the Council of Ministers of the USSR for Material-Technical Supply; Chairman of the Committee of People's Control of the USSR; Chairman of the State Committee of the Council of Ministers of the USSR for Labour and Social Questions; Chairman of the State Committee of the Council of Ministers of the USSR for Science and Technology; Chairman of the State Committee of the Council of Ministers of the USSR for Inventions and Discoveries; Chairman of the State Committee of the Council of Ministers of the USSR for Prices; Chairman of the State Committee of the Council of Ministers of the USSR for Standards; Chairman of the State Committee of the Council of Ministers of the USSR for Professional-Technical Education; Chairman of the State Committee of the Council of Ministers of the USSR for Television and Radio; Chairman of the State Committee of the Council of Ministers of the USSR for Cinematography; Chairman of the State Committee of the Council of Ministers of the USSR for Publishing, Printing and the Book Trade; Chairman of the State Committee of the Council of Ministers of the USSR for Forestry; Chairman of the State Committee of the Council of Ministers of the USSR for Foreign Economic Relations; Chairman of the Committee of State Security attached to the Council of Ministers of the USSR; Chairman of the All-Union Association 'Soyuzsel'-khoztekhnika' [Agricultural Technology] of the Council of Ministers of the USSR; Chairman of the Board of the State Bank of the USSR; Head of the Central Statistical Administration attached to the Council of Ministers of the USSR.

The Chairman of the Councils of Ministers of the union republics shall be *ex officio* members of the Council of Ministers of the USSR.

61 Added to the draft: 'as a rule', in the first line of the article, and 'and shall administer directly only a definite and limited number of enterprises according to a list approved by the Presidium of the Supreme Soviet of the USSR.'

62 Added to the draft: 'Defence Industry'.
The article was amended 32 times as a result of administrative changes. In its final version, following the last amendment of 9 July 1975, the article read:
Article 77   The following Ministries shall be all-union Ministries:
Aviation Industry; Automobile Industry; Foreign Trade; Gas Industry; Civil Aviation; Machine-Building; Machine-Building for Livestock and Fodder Production; Machine-Building for Light and Food Industries and Household Instruments; Medical Industry; Maritime Fleet; Petroleum Industry; Defence Industry; General Machine-Building; Instrument-Making, Means of Automation and Control Systems; Industry for Means of Communications; Transport; Radio Industry; Medium Machine-Building; Machine-Tool and Instrument Industry; Construction, Road, and Municipal Machine-Building; Construction of Enterprises of the Petroleum and Gas Industry; Ship-Building Industry; Tractor and Agricultural Machine-Building; Transport Construction; Heavy and Transport Machine-Building; Chemical and Petroleum Machine-Building; Chemical Industry; Cellulose-Paper Industry; Electronics Industry; Electrical Engineering Industry; Power Machine-Building.

63 This article was amended 30 times as a result of administrative changes. In its final version, following the last amendment of 10 December 1970, the article read:
Article 78   The following Ministries shall be union-republic Ministries:
Internal Affairs; Higher and Secondary Specialized Education; Geology; Procurements; Public Health; Foreign Affairs; Culture; Light Industry; Timber and Wood-Processing Industry; Soil and Water Conservation; Assembly and Special Construction Works; Meat and Dairy Industry; Oil Refining and Petrochemical Industry; Defence; Food Industry; Industrial Construction; Industry of Construction Materials; Education; Fisheries; Communications; Rural Construction; Agriculture; Construction; Construction of Enterprises of Heavy Industry; Trade; Coal Industry; Finance; Non-ferrous Metallurgy; Ferrous Metallurgy; Power and Electrification; Justice.

64 The words 'People's Commissar' and 'People's Commissariat' which recur throughout the chapter were altered to 'Minister' and 'Ministry' respectively, by amendment of 25 February 1947.

65 Added to the draft: 'and, in the interim between sessions of the Supreme Soviet of the Union Republic, to the Presidium of the Supreme Soviet of the Union Republic'.

66 An amendment of 10 May 1957 added 'and also decrees and regulations of Councils of National Economy of economic administrative districts'; on 22 December 1960 this was extended by the insertion of 'decrees and regulations

of a *republican Council of National Economy and'*; on 19 December 1963 'administrative' was deleted from 'economic administrative districts'. By amendment of 2 October 1965 the references to the Councils of National Economy were deleted and the article reverted in substance to its original version.

67 This article was amended four times after administrative changes, until an amendment of 25 February 1947 abolished the enumeration of ministries. Three further amendments were necessitated by administrative changes relating to other agencies of the republican governments until 25 December 1958, when a revised final version was enacted – 'in connection with the broadening of the rights of union republics in the field of state and economic construction' – as follows:

Article 83   The Council of Ministers of a Union Republic shall be formed by the Supreme Soviet of the Union Republic, and shall consist of:

Chairman of the Council of Ministers of the Union Republic; Deputy Chairmen of the Council of Ministers; Chairmen of state committees and commissions, and heads of other departments of the Council of Ministers formed by the Supreme Soviet of the Union Republic in conformity with the Constitution of the Union Republic.

68 Added by amendment of 10 May 1957:

Article 88a   The Councils of National Economy of economic administrative areas shall direct the branches of economic activity entrusted to them and shall be directly subordinate to the Council of Ministers of the Union Republic.

The Councils of National Economy shall issue decrees and regulations within the limits of their competencies on the basis and in execution of the laws of the USSR and the Union Republic, and the decrees and regulations of the Council of Ministers of the USSR and the Council of Ministers of the Union Republic.

On 22 December 1960 the following was inserted as the second paragraph of this article:

In union republics in which republican Councils of National Economy are formed, the Councils of National Economy of economic administrative districts shall be subordinate in their activity to the Council of Ministers of the Union Republic as well as to the republican Council of National Economy.

On 19 December 1963 the article was repealed.

69 Added by amendment of 22 December 1960:

Article 88b   The republican Council of National Economy shall coordinate the economic activity of the Councils of National Economy of economic administrative districts, being directly subordinate to the Council of Ministers of the Union Republic.

The republican Council of National Economy shall issue decrees and regulations on the basis and in execution of the laws of the USSR and the Union Republic, and the decrees and regulations of the Council of Ministers of the USSR and the Council of Ministers of the Union Republic.

The republican Council of National Economy shall have the right to suspend the decrees and regulations of the Councils of National Economy of economic administrative districts.

On 19 December 1963 the article was repealed.

70 Stanitsa, khutor, kishlak and aul are designations of various types of rural settlements in different regions of the country.

71 Added to the draft: 'secretary'.

72 Added to the draft: 'and the secretary'. By amendment of 25 February 1947 the word 'rural' was deleted from the first line of the article and the last word 'them' was replaced by 'soviets of toilers' deputies'.

73 Added to the draft: 'the courts of areas'.

74 By amendment of 12 February 1957 the word 'all' was deleted from the second sentence of this article, and the words 'and the union republics' at the end of the article were replaced by 'and also the judicial organs of the union republics within the limits established by law'.

75 By amendment of 12 February 1957 the words 'and the special courts of the USSR' were deleted, and a second paragraph was added:

The chairmen of the Supreme Courts of the union republics shall be *ex officio* members of the Supreme Court of the USSR.

76 The words 'and areas' and 'or area' were added to the draft.

77 An amendment of 25 December 1958 extended the term of office of judges of people's courts to five years and added a new provision regarding the election of people's assessors. The revised article read:

Article 109   People's judges of district (town) people's courts shall be elected by citizens of the district (town) on the basis of universal, equal and direct suffrage by secret ballot for a term of five years.

People's assessors of district (town) people's courts shall be elected at general meetings of workers, employees and peasants at their place of work or residence, and of servicemen in military units, for a term of two years.

78 By amendment of 25 February 1947 the words 'People's Commissariats' and 'Procurator of the USSR' were replaced respectively by 'Ministries' and 'Procurator General of the USSR' (see also articles 114–17).

79 The draft referred to district procurators only, thus: 'District procurators shall be appointed'.

80 By amendment of 25 February 1947 the words 'the reduction of the working day to seven hours for the overwhelming majority of the workers' were replaced by 'the establishment of an eight-hour working day for workers and employees and the reduction of the working day to seven and six hours for a number of professions with arduous working conditions, and to four hours in shops with especially arduous working conditions'. (The eight-hour working day had in fact been introduced by edict of the SS Presidium of 26 June 1940.)

On 7 May 1960 the 'eight-hour working day' was again amended to a 'seven-hour working day', and the words 'seven and' were deleted from 'seven and six hours for a number of professions'.

81 Added to the draft: 'for the toilers'.

82 An amendment of 25 February 1947 reflected the limitation, first imposed on 2 October 1940 by decree of the Council of Ministers, of free education to elementary schools and of stipends for students in higher schools to 'excellent students'. The revised opening of the second paragraph of this article thus read: 'This right shall be ensured by universal and compulsory elementary education, by seven-year education being free of charge, by a system of state stipends for excellent students at higher schools.' On 14 July 1956, following the renewed abolition of secondary and higher school fees, this was amended as follows: 'This right shall be ensured by universal, compulsory seven-year education, by the extensive development of secondary education, by

education of all types, secondary as well as higher, being free of charge, by a system of state stipends for excellent students.' As part of the educational reforms of 1958 compulsory education was extended to eight years. Other aspects of the reforms were also reflected in the final version of the article as amended on 25 December 1958.

Article 121 Citizens of the USSR shall have the right to education.

This right shall be ensured by universal and compulsory eight-year education, by the extensive development of secondary general polytechnical education, professional-technical education, secondary specialized and higher education on the basis of linking study with life and with production, by the comprehensive development of evening and correspondence education, by all types of education being free of charge, by a system of state stipends, by instruction in schools in the native language, and by the organization of free production, technical and agronomic instruction for the toilers.

83 An amendment of 25 February 1947 inserted here 'state assistance to mothers with many children and to single mothers'.

84 Added to the draft: 'by law'.

85 The draft constitution had somewhat prematurely, as it turned out, altered the party's title to 'Communist Party of the USSR', although its official title at the time was as rendered in the final text. An amendment of 8 August 1953, enacted 'in connection with the change in the name of the party' (following the adoption of new Party Rules by the 19th Party Congress in 1952), apart from renaming the party, introduced three additional changes. As a result, the second part of this article now read: 'and the most active and conscious citizens from the ranks of the working class, *the toiling peasantry and the labouring intelligentsia* shall unite *voluntarily* in the *Communist Party of the Soviet Union,* which is the vanguard of the toilers in their struggle to *build a communist society* and the leading core of all organizations of the toilers, both social and state'.

86 On 25 February 1947 the words 'Workers' and Peasants' Red Army' were replaced by 'ranks of the Armed Forces of the USSR'.

87 Deleted from the draft: 'espionage *on behalf of a foreign state'*.

88 An amendment of 14 March 1946 inserted the word 'sex' after 'race and nationality', and added the following second paragraph:

Every citizen of the USSR who has reached the age of 23 may be elected a deputy to the Supreme Soviet of the USSR, irrespective of race and nationality, sex, religious confession, education qualification, social origin, property position and past activities.

This amendment was intended to take account of the higher age limit for deputies to the USSR Supreme Soviet introduced by edict of the Supreme Soviet Presidium on 10 October 1945. Exactly one year later a further Presidium edict raised the age limit for deputies to the Supreme Soviets of union and autonomous republics to 21. Subsequently an amendment of 25 February 1947 deleted the words 'and to be elected' from the first paragraph of this article.

An amendment of 25 December 1958 abolished the deprivation of electoral rights as a legal penalty and revised the last part of the first paragraph as follows: 'with the exception of persons certified as insane in the procedure established by law'.

89 The draft included the words 'irrespective of race and nationality, religious

confession, educational qualification, domicile, social origin, property position and past activities', which in the final text were transferred to article 135. The words 'every citizen shall have one vote, all citizens shall participate in elections on an equal basis' were added to the draft.

90 An amendment of 25 February 1947 replaced 'Red Army' by 'Armed Forces of the USSR'.

4

The USSR Constitution of 1977

Commentary on the Text

Probably the most interesting, if still puzzling, fact about the 1977 constitution of the USSR is its inordinately long period of gestation. The first intimation that constitutional reform was being contemplated came in the beginning of 1959. Until then Stalin's successors, although they had openly disassociated themselves from some of the more repressive and arbitrary features of Stalin's rule, had shown no signs that they planned to replace Stalin's constitution. The relatively frank, even critical, discussion of constitutional questions to be found in Soviet legal journals after the 20th Party Congress of 1956 still proceeded on the assumption that it was the observance of existing constitutional provisions, rather than the enactment of new ones, that was needed to ensure the return to 'Leninist norms' in general and to 'socialist legality' in particular. As one author put it,

> no matter what distortions of and departures from the Constitution of the USSR took place in practice, this does not affect its substance. The basic principles of the USSR Constitution . . . have stood the test of time and are as solid and stable as the socio-economic bases of the Soviet state.'[1]

At the 21st Party Congress, in January 1959, Khrushchev officially opened the stage for the 'full-scale construction of communism', and in a somewhat off-hand manner, reminiscent of the muted tones in which the Stalin constitution had been launched in February 1935, he took the opportunity to call for 'certain amendments and additions to the Constitution'. In its internal development the USSR had, according to Khrushchev, entered a 'new and momentous stage' in which the 'building of Communist society has become an immediate and practical task'. Its international situation, too, had been transformed beyond recognition as 'socialism has emerged from the framework of one country to become a mighty world system'. These were 'sweeping changes', and they required 'expression and legislative consolidation in the Constitution of the Soviet Union, the Fundamental Law of our land'.

Khrushchev's remarks on the constitution occupied no more than two short paragraphs in a speech extending to nearly a hundred pages in print, and although the Congress duly adopted an appropriate resolution, it was already fairly clear at the time that the quest for constitutional reform reflected Khrushchev's personal policy preference rather than that of the Soviet leadership as a whole. With one exception all of Khrushchev's colleagues in the leadership maintained a conspicuous silence on the subject in their speeches at the Congress. Voroshilov alone referred to it and even elaborated upon it as an 'urgent' need, but he occupied the then largely ceremonial post of Chairman of the Supreme Soviet Presidium and was soon to be exposed as a member of the 'anti-party group' which had tried to displace Khrushchev in June 1957. His support for Khrushchev in the matter of constitutional reform may have been no more than an attempt to curry favour in atonement for past sins – vainly as it turned out, for he was soon (in 1960) to be dismissed from his party and state posts.

Following the 21st Congress some discussion of constitutional reform took place in legal circles (see p. 219 ff.) but no steps were taken to translate Khrushchev's proposals into practice. The 22nd Party Congress was held in October 1961. Aside from renewing the de-Stalinization campaign, and extending it to those of Stalin's former collaborators who had in the meantime incurred Khrushchev's disfavour, the Congress was mainly engaged in adopting the new Party Rules and in particular the long-awaited new Party Programme, designed for the period of 'full-scale communist construction' and the purported transformation of the Soviet Union into an 'all-people's state' or 'state of the whole people'. If plans for constitutional reform had advanced since the preceding Congress this clearly was the occasion on which a progress report could be expected. Instead, Khrushchev once again referred briefly to the great changes which the USSR had undergone since 1936 and noted that these would be taken into account in 'the new constitution of the USSR which we are now beginning to draft'. It was the first public acknowledgement that the original intention to introduce 'certain amendments and additions' to the 1936 constitution had escalated into the promulgation of an entirely new constitution.

Presumably, as Khrushchev implied, some work on the drafting of a new constitution had already begun. If so, however, the task had not been entrusted to a public and duly authorized constitutional commission, as on the previous three occasions of Soviet constitution-making. It was only one year later, on 25 April 1962, that a formal proposal for constitutional reform was presented by Khrushchev to the Supreme Soviet, the only organ constitutionally competent to authorize such reform. This time Khrushchev explicitly argued the need for an entirely new constitution:

> The constitution of a socialist state must change with the transition of society from one historical stage to another . . . The constitution adopted in 1936 conformed to the period of the consolidation of

socialism . . . Naturally, the chief provisions of this constitution are now obsolete.

As to the contents of the proposed new constitution, Khrushchev was deliberately vague – 'at the present time it would be premature to determine in detail what the constitution ought to be like'. The basic objective would be to register the internal progress of the USSR toward 'full-scale communist construction', including the consequent transition from the dictatorship of the proletariat to the 'all-people's state' (Khrushchev ignored Stalin's fine distinction between 'proletariat' and 'working class' – see p. 81), as well as its enhanced international status at the centre of a world system of socialist states. It followed that the constitution should reflect firstly, the further development of 'socialist democracy to a higher level' – from 'proletarian democracy' to 'democracy of the whole people' leading eventually to 'communist self-government' – and also the further strengthening of legal guarantees so as to ensure the 'strict observance of socialist legality'. Secondly, as Khrushchev put it somewhat tentatively, 'the new constitution should probably include formulations of the basic principles' of Soviet foreign policy, especially as 'the question of the peaceful co-existence of countries with different social systems' had assumed 'enormous significance'.

The Supreme Soviet naturally adopted Khrushchev's proposals and on the following day established a constitutional commission under his chairmanship. It was an unprecedentedly large commission with ninety-seven members, including among others the entire membership of the party Presidium (now Politburo) and Secretariat, representatives from each of the union republics, and several legal experts (the Chairman of the USSR Supreme Court, the Procurator General and two academics). For the next two years occasional references to the work of the commission appeared in the Soviet press. On 16 June 1962 the commission heard a brief statement by Khrushchev on its 'basic tasks' and organized itself into nine sub-commissions. In contrast to 1935 neither the composition of the sub-commissions nor the identity of their chairmen were revealed.

Two years later, a second announcement reported a meeting of the constitutional commission of 16 July 1964, one day after the Supreme Soviet had elected Mikoyan as Chairman of its Presidium in place of Brezhnev. Apart from Khrushchev who, after reporting on the commission's recent work, made some 'preliminary remarks concerning the principles on which the draft . . . should be based', seven other members reported on the work of various sub-commissions.[2] A discussion ensued (its contents were not disclosed) and the sub-commissions were instructed to report back to the main commission. It was to be the last reported meeting of a constitutional commission until May 1977.

In October 1964 Khrushchev was ousted from the Soviet leadership and at the Supreme Soviet session in December of that year he was formally replaced as chairman of the constitutional commission by Brezhnev, his successor as First (later General) Secretary of the CPSU. For the next year and a half no further reference to the new constitution was made by any Soviet leader, until Brezhnev, in a pre-election speech to his constituents in Moscow on 10 June 1966, suddenly announced that the new constitution would be completed in time for the 50th anniversary of the revolution in the following year:

> The experience we have accumulated during the years of Soviet rule opens broad opportunities for the further improvement of Soviet democracy. All the best things that the practice of state construction in our country has offered should be crystallized in the new USSR constitution which will crown the magnificent, half-century path of our country – the first genuine people's state in the history of mankind.

What was remarkable about Brezhnev's announcement was not only that it was entirely unexpected but that, as in the case of Khrushchev, seven years earlier, it was not echoed by any of the other Soviet leaders who were similarly engaged at the time in addressing their constituents in the course of their election 'campaigns'.

That Brezhnev was determined to proceed with what, under the circumstances, can only be regarded as a new initiative by a new party leader was confirmed at the end of the year. On 5 December 1966 the customary *Pravda* editorial for Constitution Day referred to the constitution that was 'now' being prepared, repeating Brezhnev's earlier promise that it would 'crown' the 50th anniversary of the revolution. Later in the month the Supreme Soviet elected thirty–three new members to the constitutional commission to replace those who had 'left' since 1962 or who were 'not at present deputies of the USSR Supreme Soviet'. It seemed like a clear attempt to revive a body that had been allowed to atrophy. Six of the original members had died since 1962 and twenty-six others were dropped (in addition to Khrushchev, removed two years earlier). The election of thirty-three new members thus brought the commission back to its original strength of ninety-seven members. The new restriction of membership to Supreme Soviet deputies may have been designed as a symbolic tribute to the standing of that body; it had no significant impact on the composition. (Only eight of the original members had not been Supreme Soviet deputies. The new restriction entailed the removal of the two academic lawyers, but these, and other experts, could presumably be expected to continue to serve the commission in an advisory capacity.)

Shortly after December 1966 the decision to enact a new constitution must have been abandoned or at least shelved. At any rate, the 50th anniversary in November 1967 was allowed to pass without a new constitution and for the next five years the subject vanished once more from all official pronouncements. Instead, the references to the constitution which appeared regularly in the Soviet press on such occasions as elections or Constitution Day, invariably paid tribute to the existing constitution as the perfect embodiment of Soviet democracy, without so much as the slightest hint that the revision of that constitution had ever been contemplated. As is often the practice in such cases, Brezhnev's own promise of constitutional reform of 10 June 1966 was deleted from the collection of his speeches and writings published in 1970.[3] There was every reason to believe that the project had been quietly laid to rest.

This is how matters stood until December 1972 when the subject once again emerged to the surface without prior warning of any kind. Once again it was Brezhnev who publicly associated himself with it and once again he promised what turned out to be an unrealistic target date for the completion of the project. In a speech commemorating the 50th anniversary of the treaty on the formation of the USSR he suddenly turned to the subject of the new constitution:

> We have spoken of this earlier, and the appropriate preparatory work is being carried on. Now, in the opinion of the Central Committee of the party, the Presidium of the Supreme Soviet and the Council of Ministers of the USSR, it is time to complete this work.

One can only speculate whether any significance is to be attached to Brezhnev's reference on this occasion to the 'opinion' of the three organs mentioned. Such references are often wholly meaningless formulae, ritual obeisances of the official Soviet communication code. Still, it is not inconceivable that in this case it signalled broad agreement for the project among Soviet leaders, or at least an attempt to commit the leadership as a whole to the project. In any event, Brezhnev apparently felt confident enough to declare that the draft of the proposed constitution would be submitted 'for nationwide discussion before the next party congress'.

Under the current Party Rules the next congress, the 25th, was due to be held in 1975, but it was delayed till 1976 without, alas, any apparent progress in the matter of the new constitution. It was, though, still on the agenda, as Brezhnev confirmed in his official Central Committee report to the Congress: 'This work is being carried out carefully and without haste so as to weigh as precisely as possible every problem that arises.' Another year was to pass before the subject surfaced once more, and this time events unfolded with extraordinary speed.

A decree of the Supreme Soviet Presidium of 29 April 1977 announced the 'election' of twenty-one new members to the constitutional commission in place of forty-three who had 'left' either because they were no longer Supreme Soviet deputies or because 'they cannot exercise their obligations for other reasons'. The reconstituted commission thus had only seventy-five members. Less than four weeks later, on 23 May 1977, the commission met to approve 'in the main' the draft of a new constitution and to recommend its submission for 'nationwide discussion'. On the following day, 24 May, a plenum of the party CC heard a report by Brezhnev (not published in full until 5 June) on the draft constitution, and after similarly approving it 'in the main' referred it to the Presidium of the Supreme Soviet with its own recommendations for public discussion.[4] On the same day the plenum, aside from approving a new version of the national anthem, also adopted certain so-called 'organizational measures', among them the dismissal from the party Politburo of N. Podgorny, Chairman of the Presidium of the Supreme Soviet since December 1965. (Podgorny's ousting was the prelude to his replacement as Chairman of the Supreme Soviet Presidium by Brezhnev three weeks later, on 17 June.) By decree of 27 May the Supreme Soviet Presidium, for its part, approved the draft constitution 'in the main' and ordered its publication for 'nationwide discussion' on 4 June; the decree also scheduled the draft for adoption by an extraordinary session of the Supreme Soviet in October. The 60th anniversary of the revolution was due one month later and this time the opportunity to 'crown' Soviet achievements with a new constitution was not to be missed. Henceforward the constitution-making machinery ticked over smoothly, each cog performing its assigned task with all the speed, facility and publicity familiar in earlier days.

The draft constitution was published, on schedule, on 4 June and the following day the press carried Brezhnev's speech at the CC plenum of 24 May. The reason for the delay in the release of Brezhnev's speech, a rather unusual procedure, can only be surmised. The release of the speech may have been designed to coincide with the inauguration of the 'nationwide discussion', but under Soviet conditions the possibility cannot be ruled out that the released version was especially prepared for public consumption.

The 'nationwide discussion' of the next four months was a repeat performance of the 1936 campaign, albeit on a much enlarged scale. When Brezhnev reported to the extraordinary session of the Supreme Soviet on 4 October 1977 he was able to announce that 'our country has never before known popular activeness of such sweep'. This time, according to the official tally, no less than 140 million people, i.e. over 80 per cent of the adult population, participated in the campaign. In countless newspaper articles, readers' letters and other comments forwarded to the constitutional commission, Soviet citizens proposed a total of 400,000 alterations of the draft. On the basis of what Brezhnev described as a 'careful study' of these proposals, the commission recommended that one article be added to the draft [article 102] and 110 others be subjected to various alterations. Since many articles were altered in several places, the total number of alterations in the draft presented in October, first to the CC of the party and then to the Supreme Soviet, was over 220.

The CC met on 3 October and approved the draft 'in the main', together with all alterations introduced 'as a result of the nationwide discussion'. It also elected two new candidate members to the party Politburo, one of whom was Deputy Foreign Minister, V.V. Kuznetsov, who was scheduled to fill the post of First Deputy Chairman of the Supreme Soviet Presidium, an office created by the new constitution in order to relieve Brezhnev of some of the more onerous protocol duties of head of state. (Kuznetsov's elevation to the top policy-making organ of the party was clearly intended to underline the importance of Brezhnev's new office: if the General Secretary of the party was Chairman of the Supreme Soviet Presidium it was only fitting that his First Deputy should be a candidate member of the Politburo.) The Supreme Soviet met on the following day and, after hearing Brezhnev's report and electing an editorial commission of 163 members under his chairmanship, proceeded to 'debate' the draft constitution for three days in separate sittings of its two chambers. Altogether ninety-two deputies took the floor proposing a total of twelve further alterations, all of which were endorsed by Brezhnev in his winding-up speech.[5] Voting separately on the preamble and each of its nine parts, the Supreme Soviet adopted the final text of the constitution with traditional unanimity on 7 October. By law of the same date it also proclaimed 7 October as the new Constitution Day to be celebrated as an annual national holiday throughout the USSR.

While the alterations introduced into the final text as compared with the draft version published in June cannot here be analysed in detail, several broad categories should nevertheless be briefly identified. There were, first, the altogether laudable, if not always entirely successful, attempts to invest the wording of the constitution with greater clarity, precision and uniformity. Examples may be seen in the more consistent differentiation between 'law', 'decree' and other acts and decisions [e.g. articles 88, 114, 133 & 135]; the substitution of 'powers' for 'rights' [article 148], of 'or' for 'and' and 'must not' for 'cannot' [article 13], and of 'citizens' for 'toilers' and 'the Soviet person' [articles 9, 57 & 152; but, see paragraph 4 of the preamble and article 50]; the deletion of 'criminal' from 'criminal law' [article 160]; and the pairing of 'rights' with 'freedoms' [articles 4 & 131(3), but not 146].

Other alterations refer to the substantive contents of the constitution. The final text shows a rather more marked emphasis on popular participation – from the insertion of 'social communist self-administration' in the twelfth paragraph of the preamble to the new article on electoral mandates [article 102]. The extension of the referendum [articles 48, 108, 115 & 137], the upgrading of the role of labour collectives [article 8], the institutionalization of 'people's control' [article 126], the recall of judges and people's assessors [article 152], the strengthened right of constituents to information from their elected representatives [articles 94, 107 & 149] – all these point in the same direction.

In the realm of social policy, too, the final text goes somewhat beyond the benefits and services promised in the draft. The state now undertakes to provide public catering in rural localities [article 22] and trade and sport facilities for the population in general [article 24]; 'comfortable' housing is to be part of the construction programme with 'low charges for communal services' [article 44]; social security for the aged is not, as in the draft, limited to single persons [article 43]; education is to be 'improved' [article 25]; and stipends are no longer considered as 'benefits' [article 45]. While assistance to single mothers has been deleted from the final text, suitable work conditions for working mothers and a gradual reduction of work time for mothers of small children are promised [article 35; see also article 53]. The state is to concern itself with the 'protection' of labour [article 21], and undertakes to establish a legally binding minimum wage [article 40]; the 41-hour work week originally drafted as the norm is reformulated as the upper limit [article 46], and 'job placement' is added to vocational guidance as a state concern [article 40; cf. article 45].

Whereas the above were intended to strengthen the rights of the Soviet citizen another clearly identifiable set of alterations reinforced his constitutional duties. A notable addition to the draft is the generalized obligation 'to treat the people's wealth with proper care' [article 61], spelled out with regard to agricultural land [articles 12–13] and residential housing [article 44] and underscored with regard to historical monuments and cultural values [article 68]. The duty of children 'to be concerned about parents and assist them' may also be subsumed under this category [article 66], as may the addition of 'and other selfish ends' in the provision concerning the uses of 'socialist ownership' [article 10], the proscription of the 'evasion of socially useful work' [article 60], and the provision for state regulation of individual labour activity 'in the interests of society' [article 17].

The relationship between the Soviet Union and its constituent republics forms a further distinct category of alterations. Here comparison of the draft and final versions reveals a not altogether consistent but still notable tendency to shore up the 'federal' elements in the constitution. It is evident in the insertion of the reference to 'socialist federalism' [article 70] and of the traditional adjective 'sovereign' to describe the status of the union republics [article 76]. But the changes were not merely declaratory. The final text introduced substantive limitations on the powers of the union in regard to taxation and the direction of economic enterprises [articles 73(6) & (7)], and conversely expanded the powers of the republics to include 'integrated economic and social development' as well as a measure of control over enterprises of all-union subordination

THE USSR CONSTITUTION OF 1977

181

[article 77; see also article 83].

There were other interesting innovations which do not lend themselves to categorization. Some of these pertained to ideologically sensitive issues such as the mention of the 'dictatorship of the proletariat' and the 'all-people's state' in the first and twelfth paragraphs of the preamble, or the added reference to classes in the context of the growing social homogeneity of Soviet society in the seventh paragraph and in article 19 – thus rectifying what can only be regarded as a most curious omission from the draft of a Marxist-Leninist constitution. Others concerned more mundane matters of government: the raised minimum age (from 18 to 21 years) for deputies of the Supreme Soviet [article 96] (this after Brezhnev, in his speech at the May CC plenum, had described the lower age limit as 'vivid evidence of our society's concern for and confidence in young people'); the augmentation of the competencies of the Supreme Soviet Presidium to call new elections (another oversight of the draft?), to ensure the conformity of republican law with union law, and, particularly, to exercise unspecified 'other powers' under the laws and constitution of the USSR [article 121 (1), (4) & (18)]. Several of these will be taken up again in subsequent discussion and are only mentioned here to round off the picture of the changes made to the draft, subsequent to its publication.

It is impossible to try and trace the origins of the alterations; undoubtedly many of them were among the crop of 400,000 proposals yielded by the 'nationwide discussion'. But whatever their origin, the fact that the constitution makers found it necessary to introduce so many alterations into the draft at this late stage cannot but throw some doubt on the claim that it had been prepared, in Brezhnev's words, 'carefully and without haste so as to weigh as precisely as possible every problem that arises'. There were simply too many problems on which the Soviet leaders were persuaded to have second thoughts for such a claim to be entirely convincing.

The success of the mass discussion, in any case, must not be measured by the number of popular proposals that found their way into the final text of the constitution. The campaign was conceived as a vast legitimating exercise and as such it was eminently successful. As Brezhnev put it in his report of 4 October, 'the main political result' of the discussion was that the Soviet people affirmed: 'Yes, this is the Fundamental Law we looked forward to'. There were, of course, many proposals which were not adopted by the constitutional commission, and it is a reasonable inference that their authors had looked forward to a somewhat different constitution. In his report to the Supreme Soviet, Brezhnev mentioned several such proposals. There were those which, while 'correct in themselves', referred to matters that could best be dealt with by ordinary legislation, e.g. the frequency of sessions of local soviets, penalties for various offences, and measures designed to improve economic life, environmental protection, public transportation, etc. And there were others which the constitutional commission had found 'incorrect in substance'. Among these latter, Brezhnev listed proposals to equalize wages, abolish subsidiary smallholdings, restrict the rights of union republics and autonomous republics and even eliminate these state entities altogether (see also, p. 226 note 8), abolish the Council of Nationalities, extend the term of local soviets to five years, and to transfer state functions to the party.

There were other proposals which Brezhnev failed to mention. Amongst other things, they called for the strengthening of due process by constitutional provisions that stipulate the innocence of the accused until proved guilty and expressly protect the court from all outside interference; stricter safeguards for the right to lodge complaints against state and social organizations; constitutional status for the organs of popular law enforcement, the comrades' courts and people's volunteer guards, established under Khrushchev and hailed at the time as important milestones on the road to 'communist self-administration'; the formation of bi-cameral Supreme Soviets in multinational union republics; the redrawing of administrative-territorial boundaries in conformity with economic and geographic considerations; and expanded powers for republican organs as well as local soviets.

These and similar proposals were put forward by people from various strata of Soviet society – workers and collective farmers, students, army officers, scientists, government and party officials, economic managers and jurists. That Soviet citizens from all walks of life took the opportunity to formulate what were often detailed and reasoned proposals for constitutional reform must be taken as attesting, in some degree at least, not only to the importance which they attached to the constitution but also to the success of the campaign in eliciting extensive 'support input' from the population.[6]

The socio-political order

Passing now to an examination of the constitution itself and focusing on the main differences between it and the 1936 constitution, we note first that it is a much longer document, numbering 174 articles grouped in twenty-one chapters (and nine parts) as against 146 articles and thirteen chapters of the previous constitution; since many of its articles are also considerably more prolix, the document as a whole is nearly twice as long as its predecessor. Like the first two Soviet constitutions, but unlike the third, the new constitution contains a preamble and this together with the provisions of the first part ('Fundamentals of the Social Order and Policy of the USSR') reveal both its strong programmatic features and its character as a constitution of Soviet society as well as of the Soviet state.

Setting out the past accomplishments and future aspirations of Soviet society in language of deliberate pathos and explicitly 'preserving the continuity of the ideas and principles' of the first three Soviet constitutions, the preamble introduces three new concepts: the 'all-people's state', the 'developed socialist society', and the 'new historical community of people, the Soviet people'.

In adopting the concept of the 'all-people's state' (or 'state of the whole people') the constitution follows Khrushchev's original proposals. Not so, however, with regard to the 'developed socialist society', for under the periodization developed by Khrushchev the new constitution had been designed for the stage of 'full-scale construction of communism'. This notion, with its highly embarrassing time-table, was later quietly dropped in favour of that of the 'developed socialist society', which was Brezhnev's own contribution to the language of Soviet developmental dynamics. For a time the two stages cohabited uneasily, causing not a little confusion. Thus, for example, one Soviet jurist, writing in 1967, still argued the case for the new constitution in terms of 'the period of the construction of communism' while asserting that 'the period of developed socialist society found expression and consolidation in the existing constitutions of the Union of SSR and the union republics'.[7] But such lapses disappeared in the early 1970s once Brezhnev's innovation had become a firm part of official doctrine. The preamble now authoritatively affirms that 'a developed socialist society has been built in the USSR' and declares that society to be 'an objectively necessary stage on the path to communism'. Moreover, unlike the 'all-people's state', which the preamble merely mentions, (albeit three times), the principal features of 'a developed socialist society' are prominently adumbrated in a litany of five consecutive paragraphs, each of which opens with the words, 'This is a society of . . .'

The notion of 'a new historical community of people, the Soviet people' is mentioned in the second of these paragraphs as an integral element of the 'developed socialist society'. Formulated first by Khrushchev in his speech on the 1961 Party Programme, it was taken up by Brezhnev at the 24th Party Congress in 1971 and has since entered the body of Soviet nationality doctrine as another half-way house to communism. That its nationality connotation is here diluted by the simultaneous mention of classes and social strata must not be allowed to divert attention from the fact that the notion was devised, and continues to be generally applied, in the context of the 'drawing together' of nations and nationalities.[8] Nor can there be much doubt that its mention in the preamble – however moderated by the cliché, 'fraternal co-operation', added in the final version – signifies the regime's intention to legitimate the process by which the minority peoples in the Soviet 'family of nations' are expected to assimilate to their Russian 'elder brother'. Reference in the text to 'Soviet patriotism and socialist internationalism' [article 36] and, more concretely, the distribution of powers between the union and its constituent parts to be discussed shortly, testify further to this intention. It should be added, however, that in the Soviet lexicon 'drawing together' is a rather more moderate formulation for a process that has at times been described as 'merging'. That the former expression was chosen for the constitutional text may, therefore, be regarded as a concession to the sensibilities of the minority nationalities.

First among the principal aims of the constitution listed in the closing paragraph of the preamble (in its final version!) is the affirmation of 'the fundamentals of the social order and policy of the USSR', and this, as already noted, is also the heading of the first part of the text. That the first chapter of this part should be headed 'The Political System' may offend the Marxist purist, accustomed as he is to accord primacy to the economic 'base' rather than to the political 'superstructure'. But it must also be recognized as an accurate reflection of the dominance of the political system in Soviet society, the more so as the chapter contains in article 6 a singularly candid acknowledgement of the role of the Communist party.

The language of 'system', also applied in relative profusion in other chapters [chapters 2 and 12; the tenth paragraph of the preamble; and articles 24, 25, 30, 40, 126, & 131(1)], helps to impart a distinctly 'modern' hue to the constitution. 'Political system', by now a staple of political science in the west, is still only rarely found in Soviet writings. Its use in the constitution may well be explained by the need for a suitably vague, overarching concept capable of introducing the party into the constitution alongside state institutions, social organizations (trade unions, Komsomol, etc.), labour collectives, and citizens in their individual capacities – all treated in chapter 1 and therefore presumably regarded as jointly composing the Soviet political system. From the very first discussions in the early 1960s there had been clear indications that the party would receive greater prominence than in the 1936 constitution. Since it could not be easily accommodated in the chapters detailing the formal competencies of state organs a separate chapter under the heading 'The Political System' probably offered itself as an appropriate setting.

Be that as it may, the treatment of the party is certainly the single most important feature distinguishing the 1977 constitution from its predecessor. Whereas the latter had somewhat casually introduced the party in article 126 of chapter X (in the context of the right of association and alongside other social organizations), the 1977 constitution mentions it twice in its preamble, acknowledging its contribution to the October revolution and affirming that its 'leading role . . . has grown' [paragraphs 1 & 4], and then proceeds to give an elaborate definition of that role in a separate article [article 6] of the first chapter. Unlike article 126 of the 1936 constitution, article 6 of the 1977 text makes no reference either to the party's social composition or to its 'vanguard' status. (The standard designation of the party as a 'vanguard' – now of the 'entire people' – is confined to paragraph 4 of the preamble.) But in place of the single-clause definition of article 126 – 'the leading core of all organizations of the toilers, both social and state' – article 6 now specifies the party's role in two paragraphs. The party is defined, amongst other things, as 'the guiding and directing force of Soviet society' (as distinct from 'leading force', a description reserved for the working class [preamble, paragraph 4]) as well as the 'core of its political system and of state and social organizations', which determines both 'the general perspective' of the society and 'the lines of the internal and foreign policy of the USSR'.

Article 6 thus provides a far closer approximation to the real structure of power in the Soviet Union than that provided in any previous Soviet constitution. In so doing, of course, it also indicates rather obviously that the competencies of all state agencies, including those which the 1977 constitution continues to describe as 'the highest organs of state power and administration' [Part V], are circumscribed in important if unspecified ways. Beside the enhanced realism of the constitution, how-ever, the inevitable disparities between the relatively unadorned state-ment of the party's all-encompassing role in article 6 and the various traditional affirmations of Soviet constitutions, most notably that power resides in the people (formerly the 'toilers') and is exercised by their elected representatives [article 2] may perhaps be considered as minor blemishes.

The attempt to bring the party more fully within the purview of the constitution must not be interpreted as signalling a corresponding inten-tion to limit its freedom from constitutional restraints. In this regard, the provision requiring party organizations to 'operate within the framework of the Constitution', inserted in the final version of the text, emphasizes the self-evident without adding anything of substance; it also reiterates a norm that has been on the party's own 'statute book' since 1919 (see p. 22). Since the obligation of state and social organiza-tions to observe the constitution (and laws) of the country is stipulated in article 4, the addition of a similar provision in respect of party organiza-tion in article 6 merely serves to underline the party's distinctive status.

If the text of the constitution still left doubts as regards the party's eminence, they were entirely removed by Brezhnev's comments which emphatically asserted the party's indispensable contribution to Soviet achievements, past, present and future. In his speech to the May CC plenum, when listing the 'major changes of fundamental importance' which the USSR had undergone since 1936, Brezhnev noted:

> All these processes taking place in this country's life were led and
> continue to be led by the Communist party – the directing, organizing

and mobilizing force of our society from the time of October to the present. The problems it has to solve today have become more varied and complex. It now plays a still more important role in society and the guiding influence it exerts on the whole of the country's domestic life and foreign policy has grown.

In October he assured the Supreme Soviet that the party would not abuse its power at the same time as he reiterated its growing stature. The party, he said, 'conducts its policy on state matters above all through the Communists elected by the people . . . and those working in state organs'; the constitutional 'consolidation' of its role, far from granting any privileges to party members, 'imposes even greater duties upon them'. Criticism by the 'majority of bourgeois commentators' who asserted that the constitution proclaimed 'the dictatorship of the party', or 'the primacy of the party over the state', etc., were prompted by ill-will:

> What can one say on this score? The motives for this attack are clear enough. The Communist party is the vanguard of the Soviet people, their most conscious and advanced part, inseparably bound to the people as a whole. The party has no interests other than the interests of the people. To try to counterpose the party to the people . . . is tantamount to trying to counterpose, say, the heart to the rest of the human organism. Bourgeois critics . . . would like to weaken the role of the party in Soviet society, since in general they hope to weaken our country . . . As the Soviet people resolve the increasingly complex and responsible tasks of building communism, the role of the Communist party will continue to grow.

Altogether similar formulations had appeared on countless previous occasions. What was new and noteworthy about Brezhnev's statements was that they were made by the top Soviet leader in the context of the Soviet constitution. The party had 'arrived' on the constitutional scene, no longer by the side-door as in 1936, but through the main entrance. Indeed, the constitution itself was frankly acknowledged as the party's own creation: it was, Brezhnev stressed at the May plenum, *'based on the party's clear and concrete directives'* (emphasis in the original).

The rest of chapter 1 can be dealt with more briefly. Articles 1 and 2 parallel the first three articles of the 1936 constitution except that the USSR is no longer described as 'a state of workers and peasants' but as an 'all-people's state' and that, in line with this, the soviets are renamed 'soviets of people's deputies'. The other six articles of the chapter are entirely new. 'Democratic centralism' is given constitutional status in article 3, while article 4 enjoins 'socialist legality' upon the state and upon social organizations. Both of these principles have, of course, long been espoused as basic tenets of the theory and practice of Soviet government;

their added value, if any, as constitutional norms remains to be tested in practice and, on past record, must be judged as highly dubious. The same reservation applies to the principle of democracy which is in such pronounced evidence in the remaining articles of the chapter – from the 'nationwide discussion' and referendum for unspecified 'most important matters of state life' provided under article 5, to the other forms of popular participation set out in articles 7–9. In this connection, the greatly augmented article 8, which in its draft version (as article 16 of chapter 2) provided for the participation of labour collectives in the administration of economic enterprises only, deserves to be especially noted as a token of the constitution makers' desire to strengthen the political system's democratic credentials.

The subject matter of chapter 2, 'The Economic System', parallels that treated in articles 4–12 of the 1936 constitution under the heading 'The Social Structure'. Additional provisions relevant to the economic system are, as in the 1936 constitution, dispersed in other chapters, especially those dealing with the competencies of state organs and the fundamental rights of citizens.

Of the two pillars of the Soviet economic system, centralized planning and direction and socialist ownership, the constitution's treatment of the former is mainly noteworthy for three declaratory features. They are: the elaborate description of economic activity, listing not only its 'supreme goal' but also its principal methods [article 15]; the totalist definition of the economy as 'a single national economic complex embracing all links of social production, distribution, and exchange'; and the bland manner in which the constitution attempts to straddle the horns of the two perennial dilemmas of Soviet economic administration, namely, the contradiction between the territorial and branch principles, on the one hand, and that between centralized direction and enterprise autonomy, on the other [article 16].

The second pillar, socialist ownership, deserves closer scrutiny. There were two particular changes: first, the two forms of socialist ownership recognized in the 1936 constitution, state and collective farm-cooperative, are augmented by a third, namely 'the property of trade unions and other social organizations' [article 10]; and, second, state ownership is now declared as the 'basic' form of socialist ownership [article 11].

While the draft version of article 10 listed the three forms of socialist ownership consecutively without distinguishing between them in any way, the final version deals separately with the two older forms, calling them the 'foundation of the economic system of the USSR', and assigns the newcomer to a separate paragraph which declares it 'also' to be a form of socialist ownership. This, it appears, was a compromise formula adopted following the 'nationwide discussion' of the draft. That the property of social organizations would be taken as a form of socialist ownership was already heralded in the civil legislation of the 1960s. In the course of the discussion on the draft constitution, however, a number of objections were raised. There was no reason, it was argued, to breach the parallelism between the two traditional forms of socialist ownership and the two social classes of Soviet society, the working class and the collective farm peasantry, especially as the property of the social organizations differed in essence from the two older forms in that it did not consist predominantly of the means of production, and was, moreover, to a large extent derived from state subventions, e.g. for trade-union recreation facilities, sanatoria, and so on. These arguments, it would seem, convinced the constitution makers of the need to reformulate article 10 so as to draw some kind of distinction between state and collective farm-cooperative ownership, on the one hand, and the property of the social organizations, on the other.

More significant than the addition of a third form of socialist ownership or the compromise adopted in the final version of article 10 is the new emphasis on state ownership as the 'basic' form of socialist ownership in article 11. It should be taken together with the statement in the same article that the state owns the 'basic' means of production not only in industry and construction, but also in agriculture. The comparable article in the previous constitution [1936–article 6] merely stated that state ownership in agriculture consisted of 'large state-organized agricultural enterprises (state farms, machine-tractor stations, etc.)'. The exclusion, by implication, of the collective farms (which took over ownership of the machine-tractor stations in 1958) from the 'basic' means of production in agriculture is not attenuated by the provision requiring the state to 'promote the development of collective farm-cooperative ownership and its drawing together with state ownership' [article 12]. On the contrary, 'drawing together' is clearly designed as an asymmetrical process leading to the eventual transformation of collective farm ownership into state ownership, or, in more concrete terms, to the absorption of collective farms by state farms.

The 1961 Party Programme speaks in this connection of the 'gradual drawing together and, in the long run, also the merging of collective farm ownership with all-people's ownership into one communist ownership'. That 'communist ownership' is, in fact, synonymous with 'all-people's ownership' is evident from one of the opening sentences of the second part of the Programme itself in which communism is defined as, amongst other things, 'a classless social order with one form of all-people's ownership of the means of production'; and 'all-people's ownership', as in the 1977 constitution [article 10], or 'wealth of the whole people', as the 1936 constitution had it [1936–articles 5 & 6], refers, of course, to state ownership. Since the adoption of the Programme, the reduction in the number of collective farms, as a result of both amalgamation into larger units and transformation into state farms, has proceeded apace: the number of collective farms fell from 44,900 in 1960 to 27,900 in 1976, while the number of state farms rose in the same period from 7,400 to 19,600; the crop area of state farms, which was just over 50 per cent of that of the collective farms in 1960, exceeded the latter by nearly 15 per cent in 1976. Not least in the light of these figures – but, of course, also in the light of the oft-proclaimed ultimate goals of communist construction – the stipulation requiring the state to 'promote the development' of collective farms must be read 'dialectically', rather in the manner in which Stalin had once argued for 'the highest development of state power with the object of preparing the conditions for the withering away of state power' (see p. 276).

While the notion of the ultimate 'merging' of the two forms of socialist ownership has not been taken over from the Party Programme, it is worth noting that the land of collective farms is no longer, as in the 1936 constitution, allotted to them 'in perpetuity' [article 12; 1936–article 8] – obviously an intentional omission from an otherwise identically-worded provision.

The relative weakening of the position of the collective farms in 'socialist ownership' is paralleled by a comparable weakening of the position of individual collective farmers in 'personal ownership'. The 1936 constitution recognized the right of the 'collective farm household' to 'personal use' of a small plot of land and to 'personal ownership' of subsidiary husbandry, livestock, poultry, etc. [1936–article 7]. The 1977 constitution recognizes no specific ownership right for collective farmers; instead, omitting the concept of 'collective farm household' altogether, it treats the use of agricultural plots 'for subsidiary husbandry (including the keeping of livestock and poultry)' under the general 'personal ownership' provisions applicable to all Soviet citizens, workers and employees as well as collective farmers [article 13]. The net result of this change, which during the discussions of the draft was explained as an aspect of the eradication of differences between town and country, is that the role (and ownership right) of collective farmers in subsidiary farming is muted at the same time as that of the population as a whole is accorded broader constitutional legitimacy.

It is well known that subsidiary farming has filled large gaps in Soviet agricultural output, providing in some cases as much as half the total produce marketed. What is perhaps less well known is that the share of the urban population in the private agricultural sector has been steadily increasing, and, in both cultivated area and output, is now roughly equal to that of the collective farmers. The constitution acknowledges this development and, in a sentence added in the final version of article 13, even enjoins the state and the collective farms to assist in the running of subsidiary farming. It thus turns its back, at least for the time being, on the various attempts made under Khrushchev to reduce private farming and, incidentally, also ignores the forecast of the 1961 Programme that 'subsidiary individual farming will gradually become economically unnecessary'. As already intimated, Brezhnev, in his speech of 4 October 1977, expressly rejected proposals for the abolition of subsidiary smallholdings: this form of farming 'in which there is no exploitation, has a useful role to play in our economy at the present stage'; besides, those opposed to private smallholdings were 'clearly worried not so much by their existence as by their abuse for the purpose of profiteering', and this would be taken care of by the right of control granted to state agencies by the constitution.

Indeed, the proscription of the use of socialist ownership, in any of its forms, for 'personal gain and other selfish ends' [article 10], the requirement that collective farms as well as individual citizens must make effective or 'rational' use of the land [articles 12–13] and that property in personal ownership or use 'must not serve to derive unearned income or be used to the detriment' of society [article 13], are all notable innovations of the 1977 constitution; its Stalinist precursor imposed no such limitations in its ownership provisions. Even without these stipulations, however, the personal ownership rights of Soviet citizens appear somewhat more fragile in the new constitution. There has been no substantial change in the list of items recognized as comprising personal ownership; yet while article 10 of the 1936 constitution referred in this context to a 'right' protected by 'law', article 13 of the new constitution refers to items which 'may be' in personal ownership and vouchsafes their protection by the 'state' (note that the draft version had 'law').

Like its predecessor, the 1977 constitution sanctions what is now designated as 'individual labour activity' but was previously described rather more explicitly as 'small-scale private economy' [article 17; 1936–article 9]; unlike its predecessor, however, it affirms (in an addition of the final version) that such activity shall be subject to state regulation 'ensuring its use in the interests of society'. The mention of 'everyday services for the population', supplemented by the open-ended 'and also other forms of activity' – in addition to 'handicrafts and agriculture' (paralleled in the 1936 text by 'individual peasants and artisans') – reflects the contribution of the private sector to the servicing of consumer durables, and may be taken as a tacit admission that the state sector is unable to provide adequate repair and service facilities to meet the needs of the growing number of Soviet citizens who own cars, television sets, refrigerators and other mechanical appliances.

The duty to work, which was specified in article 12 of the 1936 constitution, is now appropriately listed together with the other duties of Soviet citizens [article 60]. But a chapter on the foundations of the economic system clearly could not forgo a declaration on the role of labour in Soviet society and such is to be found in article 14. While the motto 'From each according to his ability, to each according to his work', which also appeared in the 1936 text, still places the new constitution within the

time context of the lower, socialist, stage of communism, the concluding phrase of the article contains an obvious, future-oriented allusion to
Marx's vision of the higher stage of full communism.[9] It will also be noted
that the artlessly peremptory 'He who does not work, neither shall he
eat' (of pristine New Testament lineage) has been dropped; not, however, the underlying sentiment, which is merely couched in more pedes-
trian prose. In a way, it is precisely the matter-of-fact assertion of 'control
over the measure of labour and consumption' which brings the
plenitude of the state's powers *vis-à-vis* its citizens into full relief.

The programmatic features of the 1977 constitution are most pronounced in chapter 3, 'Social Development and Culture', which sketches
with an extremely broad brush the two principal goals of Soviet social
development. The first of these is the 'strengthening of the social
homogeneity of society': the eradication of class differences, of differences between town and country, and intellectual and physical labour,
and the 'drawing together' of all nationalities [article 19]. That this is
preceded, in the final version of the article, by a declaration of the
'indestructible alliance' of workers, peasants and intelligentsia, can
probably be ascribed to the desire to complement statements about the
political and economic 'foundation' of the USSR made respectively in
articles 2 and 10, by a similar statement on the country's 'social foundation'. The second goal is 'the all-round development of the individual',
its innate appeal being further enhanced by the famous epigram from the
Communist Manifesto [article 20][10]. The remaining seven articles elaborate in very general terms on the various ways in which the state is to
promote the above goals [articles 21–7]. They consist of vague, programmatic declarations on social and cultural policy – labour, rural life,
incomes, social services, education, science and culture – most of which
are reiterated in somewhat more specific form in the catalogue of socio-
economic rights under the heading, 'The Fundamental Rights, Freedoms
and Duties of Citizens of the USSR' contained in chapter 7.

Chapter 4 enunciates the principles of Soviet foreign policy in three
articles [28–30]. It had been clear from the original pronouncements of
the Soviet leaders, first Khrushchev and later Brezhnev, that the Soviet
Union's new status at the centre of the 'world socialist system' would
find expression in a constitutional statement of its foreign policy objectives. Declarations pertaining to matters of foreign policy, while absent
from the 1936 constitution, had already appeared in the 1918 and 1924
constitutions; the 1977 text may therefore be said to have reverted to a
tradition established in the early years of Soviet rule. However, unlike
the first two Soviet constitutions, which placed their foreign policy
declarations mainly in their preambles and framed them in the rhetoric
of revolution ('capitalist encirclement', 'complete victory of the international workers' revolt against the yoke of capitalism', 'union of the toilers
of all countries into one World Socialist Republic', etc.), the 1977 con-

stitution gives the subject a separate chapter and treats it in terms that are almost entirely devoid of ideological overtones and clearly designed to demonstrate the USSR's adherence to universal norms of international conduct. Chapter 4 reflects not the revolutionary credo of an embattled bastion of socialism but the sober, self-confident assertion of a world power conscious of its place in the community of nations.

Students of Soviet international behaviour may well attribute significance to the formulations adopted for the various foreign policy objectives in article 28 as well as to the order in which they are set out. For our purposes it will be sufficient to take note of three points. First, the list of objectives is broad enough to cover every conceivable policy alternative (in terms compatible with international law). This, of course, is only to be expected: the USSR, like any other state, is hardly likely to foreclose its foreign policy options by provisions in its domestic law. Second, the insertion – in the final version – of the defence of 'the state interests of the Soviet Union' as the second objective seems perilously close to an admission that these interests need not in all circumstances coincide with either the building of communism in the USSR (the first objective) or the strengthening of world socialism (the third objective). Third, and more important, the article raises the vague and controversial principle of peaceful coexistence to the status of a constitutional norm. Even the current revisionist interpretation that peaceful coexistence among states of 'different' – or as they are sometimes called, 'opposing' – social systems does not preclude 'peaceful competition'. Nor is it incompatible, as article 28 itself makes clear, with Soviet support for movements of 'national liberation and social progress'. (Note that the prevention of war refers to 'aggressive wars', as distinct, presumably, from wars of 'national liberation'.) Least of all, does it signify the abatement of ideological conflict. It is, as Soviet spokesmen have been at pains to emphasize time and again, merely 'a specific form of the class struggle', one that is conducted in the economic, political and ideological spheres and not in the military sphere.

Whether peaceful coexistence may rightly be regarded as part of the 'Leninist policy of peace' under which all the foreign policy goals listed in article 28 are subsumed, must remain a moot point; the question was contested within the post-Stalin leadership in the latter 1950s and early 1960s (when Molotov in particular argued the contrary), and also became a major issue in the Sino-Soviet ideological disputes. The invocation of Lenin's name belongs to the ritual of legitimation for any Soviet policy and must not be taken too literally. Presumably a case can be made out for the proposition that Lenin, who generally regarded violent conflict with capitalism as inevitable, would have revised his view in the light of nuclear realities; though it is only right to add that it was Stalin who first declared in 1927 that 'our relations with the capitalist countries are based on the assumption that the coexistence of the two opposite systems is possible',[11] and that it was Stalin's Commissar of Foreign Affairs, Litvinov, who in September 1934 described USSR entry into the League of Nations as 'the final acknowledgement of the principle of peaceful coexistence'.

Article 29 affirms the principles which are to guide the Soviet Union in the pursuit of the objectives set out in the preceding article. The new constitutional stance of the USSR as a solid pillar of the world community is here most clearly in evidence, for the ten principles listed in the article are all recognized norms of international law. In fact, they appear to have been taken almost verbatim from the headings of the relevant sections of the Final Act of the 1975 Helsinki Conference on Security and Cooperation in Europe. (The reversal of the first two principles in the final version of article 29 brought them into line with the order in which they are listed in the Helsinki accords.) The only significant divergence between the Helsinki list and that of article 29 of the constitution relates to what the former describes as the 'self-determination of peoples' and the latter renders as 'the right of peoples to decide their own destiny'. No ready explanation for this deviation from the language of Helsinki offers itself other than that it reflects a new sensitiveness to centrifugal tendencies within the Soviet bloc; it is, of course, all the more remarkable for the fact that the right to self-determination is firmly enshrined in Leninist doctrine and has generally – though not at Helsinki – been consistently argued by Soviet spokesmen at international forums. But whatever the reason for the substitution of a 'softer' formulation in regard to self-determination, the Soviet Union, by including the Helsinki catalogue in its constitution, has become the first state to have transformed such an impressive catalogue of international norms into its domestic fundamental law. This may not increase the likelihood that the Soviet leadership will actually observe all or any of these norms in its relations with foreign states, but it is a measure of its concern for international respectability.

The last article of this chapter, article 30, refers to intra-bloc relations. It pledges the Soviet Union to develop 'friendship, cooperation, and comradely mutual assistance' in accordance with the principle of 'socialist internationalism' and also to participate in 'economic integration'[12] and the 'international socialist division of labour'. The failure to qualify 'economic integration' by reference to the socialist countries is puzzling, unless it is intended to leave the door open for broader integration outside the framework of the Soviet-dominated Council for Mutual Economic Assistance (better known under the acronym COMECON). 'Comradely mutual assistance' and especially 'internationalism' – whether 'socialist', as in the constitution, or 'proletarian', as in the 1961 Party Programme – have in the past been used to justify Soviet intervention in Eastern Europe, including – under the guise of the so-called 'Brezhnev doctrine' – the 1968 invasion of Czechoslovakia. But it must be added that these and similar formulations appear also in the constitutions of other East European states, including those most likely to feel threatened by Soviet armed intervention – Romania, Yugoslavia and Albania. (The Albanian constitution of 1976 still adheres to the now defunct 'proletarian internationalism'.)

Chapter 5, 'The Defence of the Socialist Fatherland', which concludes the first part, is also entirely new. Its two articles are primarily notable for the declaration that defence is 'among the most important functions of the state' [article 31] and the assurance that the Soviet armed forces will be equipped 'with everything necessary' [article 32]. Both of these statements reflect the importance which the military establishment has assumed in the Soviet power structure under Brezhnev.

The rights and duties of the individual

The constitution's treatment of individual rights and duties has understandably attracted a great deal of attention both inside and outside the Soviet Union: if the new constitution portended any significant changes they could be expected to be reflected above all in the provisions establishing the relationship between the state and the individual citizen. In assessing these provisions, the background against which they were formulated should be borne in mind. It was one in which preoccupation with human rights had become a major international concern – not least owing to the activities of the dissident movement in the USSR itself. It was also one in which the Soviet Union had become a party to formal international commitments, most notably the two 1966 UN Covenants on Economic, Social and Cultural Rights and on Civil and Political Rights (ratified by the USSR in 1973) and the 1975 Helsinki Final Act. More important, the post-Stalin leadership of the USSR greatly expanded both the material welfare and the legal security of Soviet citizens. In regard to both socio-economic rights and civil liberties, therefore, the new constitution was able to incorporate changes already accomplished and in large part embodied in ordinary legislation; even where these changes did not lead to new constitutional rights, it must be recognized that the provisions bore a closer link with socio-political reality than had any of their predecessors.

On a purely external plane, the prominence accorded to the individual in the 1977 constitution is immediately evident. Whereas the 1936 constitution treated fundamental rights and duties in sixteen articles and relegated them to one of the last chapters, the new constitution devotes thirty-seven articles to the subject and places them well to the fore of the text under a heading which juxtaposes 'the State' with 'the Individual'. Of the sixteen articles in the 1936 constitution, three dealt with the equality of Soviet citizens and the right of asylum of foreigners [articles 122, 123 & 129]. Together with a provision on Soviet citizenship [1936–article 21] and a new provision on the rights of foreign citizens and stateless persons they are now grouped in a separate chapter of Part II.

The citizenship clause [article 33; 1936–article 21] remains practically unchanged except that it is augmented by a stipulation extending the protection of the USSR to its citizens abroad. The right of asylum for foreigners is also formulated in very similar, though somewhat more elaborate, terms [article 38; 1936–article 129]: it now also covers persons persecuted for defending 'the cause of peace' (and not only 'the interests of the toilers'), for participating in the 'revolutionary' (and not only the 'national liberation') movement, and for conducting 'progressive socio-political, scientific, or other creative activity' (and not only 'scientific activities'). Article 37 grants foreign citizens and stateless persons resident in the USSR 'the rights and freedoms provided by law' (mentioning expressly protection by the courts and other state agencies of 'personal, property, family and other rights') and obliges them to respect the constitution and laws of the country; it thus provides a constitutional framework for rights which the previous constitution left to all-union legislation [1936–article 14(v)].

The removal of the equality clauses from the bill of rights is in keeping with recent Soviet legal thinking which has tended to regard non-discrimination not as a right but as a general 'democratic principle' underlying all rights and freedoms. Of the three relevant clauses [articles 34–6], two deal with equality of the sexes [article 35], and of races and nationalities [article 36], both of which had also figured in the previous constitution [1936–articles 122 & 123]. The former equality is now some-what more detailed, but otherwise unremarkable. The latter is no longer 'an undefeasible right', and is supplemented by a paragraph which specifies the conditions for the equality of races and nationalities but – except for a reference to 'the possibility to use the native language' – reads like a prescription for the 'new historical community, the Soviet people'. An innovation of the 1977 text is that the above articles are preceded by a general clause [article 34] stipulating equality before the law irrespective not only of race, nationality and sex, but also of 'social and property position', education, language, occupation, domicile and 'other circums-tances'. The article appears to have been formulated in correspondence with the 1966 Convenant on Civil and Political Rights; still, it is some cause for surprise that in the constitution of 'developed socialist society' it should still be thought necessary to guarantee non-discrimination on grounds of social and especially property status, just as it is altogether unsurprising that non-discrimination on grounds of 'political and other opinion' was not taken over from the UN Covenant.

Comparison of the rights listed under the heading, 'The Fundamental Rights, Freedoms and Duties of the Citizens of the USSR', in chapter 7, with those of the 1936 constitution reveals that previous rights were amplified and a number of new rights added, and this, too, it would seem, with a view to bringing the constitutional bill of rights as far as possible into conformity with the two 1966 UN Covenants. Several omissions are nevertheless immediately noticeable: the freedoms of movement and of religious education and the right to strike – particularly conspicuous by its absence because all other rights of the Covenant on Economic, Social and Cultural Rights are mentioned.

All the socio-economic rights of the 1936 constitution reappear in the new constitution, albeit in somewhat more extended formulations: the right to work, again first in the list and now supplemented by the right to choice of profession and occupation [article 40], the right to rest and leisure [article 41], the right to material security [article 43], and the right to education [article 45]. Entirely new socio-economic rights concern health protection [article 42], housing – ensured, amongst other things, by the promotion of 'individual housing construction' [article 44], the use of cultural achievements [article 46], and 'freedom of scientific, technical and artistic creativity' [article 47]. A new article providing for the protection of the family by the state [article 53] may also be included in this category even though it is not listed alongside the other socio-economic rights. In respect of all the above articles the Stalinist pattern of constitution making has been retained: a particular right is proclaimed in the first paragraph and then 'underwritten' by the appropriate 'material conditions' said to ensure its realization in practice. While the country's material progress over the past decades has undoubtedly enabled the state to improve these conditions considerably, with consequent benefits for its citizens, the mere fact of their assertion in the constitution does not, of course, transform them into reality, still less into guarantees of enforceable subjective rights. Though framed in the form of 'rights' they should therefore be seen as declarations of policy which do not differ in essence from the socio-economic objectives set out in chapter 3. Freedom of creativity, moreover, is accorded only 'in conformity with the aims of communist construction'; it is therefore considered entirely compatible with the state's powers to determine the 'basic directions of scientific and technical progress' [article 73(5)], though not apparently with the competence of the USSR Council of Ministers originally stated as the pursuit of 'a uniform policy' in science and technology but altered in the final version to 'the development of science and technology' [article 131(1)].

Of the political rights, the freedoms of speech, press, assembly and demonstration, now described as 'political freedoms', are formulated in a manner altogether similar to that of the 1936 constitution [article 50; 1936–article 125]. They are subjected to the proviso 'in conformity with the interests of the people and in order to strengthen and develop the socialist system . . .' and, like the socio-economic rights, they are again ensured by an array of material means which, in language identical to that of the 1936 constitution, 'are placed at the disposal of the toilers and their organizations'. That these means no longer include 'printing presses and stocks of paper' (listed by Stalin in 1936 among the resources without which 'all these liberties may be merely a hollow sound for the working class'), may perhaps be ascribed to the appearance of *samizdat*, i.e. dissident 'self-publishing'. The substitution of 'extensive dissemination of information' for 'means of communication' must have struck many a Soviet citizen as particularly ironical at a time when he first learned of the contents of the new constitution some ten days after CC approval of the draft and when the abrupt dismissal of the Soviet head of state merited no more than a laconic single-sentence notice in the Soviet press. The right of association, too, is preceded by the familiar caveat, though it now requires conformity with 'the aims of communist construction' rather than 'the interests of the toilers' [article 51; 1936–article 126] – surely a distinction without a difference. The new article is considerably shorter than its 1936 precursor, which, it will be recalled, specified the types of social organizations in which the toilers could unite and introduced the Communist party into the constitutional text. A welcome innovation is the recognition that the role of social organizations includes not only 'the development of political activity and initiative' – a formula almost identical with that of the 1936 constitution – but also 'the satisfaction of their diverse interests'; it is the first constitutional acknowledgement of the existence of different societal interests with a legitimate claim to satisfaction.

Two entirely new provisions relate to political participation. Article 48 emphasizes the citizen's right to participate in the 'administration of state and social affairs' and should be seen in the context of articles 7 and 8, since it is mainly through the social organizations and labour collectives that this right can be exercised. The participatory activities and arenas listed in the second paragraph of the article, from voting to meetings at places of residence, have always served the regime to mobilize the population in support of official policies. Nevertheless, this first constitutional elaboration of participatory rights deserves to be noted, especially as it is not hedged in by the stipulations of conformity with 'the interests of the toilers' or 'the aims of communist construction'. The same is true of article 49 which guarantees the citizen's right to submit proposals, including criticisms, to state agencies and social organizations. Once again, the right as such is not new; Soviet citizens have always been urged to make constructive proposals for policy implementation and to expose bureaucratic shortcomings at the local level. Certainly neither of the two new constitutional provisions can be interpreted as sanctioning autonomous participation in the input processes of policy making or untrammelled feedback from the grassroots of Soviet society.

The civil liberties, too, are generally framed in traditional terms. But they also include some minor innovations. Freedom of conscience is now 'guaranteed', and not simply 'recognized', and the separation of church and state and church and school is stated as a fact rather than as a condition ensuring freedom of conscience [article 52; 1936–article 124]. The new article provides not only for the right 'to perform religious worship' but also for the right 'to profess' any religion (or none). The asymmetrical right to conduct 'atheist propaganda' (previously 'anti-religious propaganda') – and not, as in the 1918 constitution, both 'religious and anti-religious propaganda' [1918–article 13] – has been retained and a clause prohibiting incitement to hostility 'in connection with religious beliefs' has been added. (The latter presumably in line with the International Covenant on Civil and Political Rights which prohibits among others the advocacy of 'religious hatred'.) The personal inviolability clause has remained substantially unchanged [article 54; 1936–article 127]. Inviolability of the home and secrecy of correspondence are now treated in two separate articles [articles 55–6; 1936–article 128]; the former has been somewhat strengthened by the express proscription of unauthorized entry, and the latter has been expanded to cover 'private life' in general, as well as telephone and telegraph communications.

The value of these guarantees depends, of course, primarily on the legal protection accorded them in practice. The new constitution, aside from incorporating some of the legislation of the post-Stalin period in the provisions on the legal system (Part VII), contains in its bill of rights two pertinent new articles. Article 57 guarantees protection of citizens' rights *by* the state: it declares it the duty of all state and social organizations and their officials to respect the individual and to protect his rights, and also recognizes the right of citizens to 'judicial protection against attempts on their honour and dignity, life and health, and personal freedom and property'. More important, at least at first sight, seem the guarantees of protection *against* the state contained in article 58. The three paragraphs which make up this article acknowledge the rights of Soviet citizens to lodge complaints against state officials and organs, to appeal administrative decisions to a court, and to claim compensation for damages. None of these rights is new though each makes its first appearance in a Soviet constitution.[13] Potentially the most significant, perhaps, is the elevation of judicial review of administrative acts to a constitutional principle. But it will be noted that this provision is qualified by the words 'in the procedure established by law', and, though Soviet jurists have denied that this refers to substantive law, it will be wise to suspend judgment on the actual scope of judicial control envisaged. The third paragraph of article 58, which relates to the liability of state and social agencies for damages, is not – in the final version of the text – similarly circumscribed by reference to subsidiary law. But on 12 December 1977 the Presidium of the Supreme Soviet drew up a legislative programme for the next few years and this provided among others for the adoption of 'legislative acts' (not 'laws') covering both matters. It therefore remains to be seen whether the courts will be granted the general supervision over administrative actions that Soviet jurists have been demanding for some years and whether the existing limitations on the right to recover damages in tort will be removed.[14]

Two entirely new important qualifications 'frame' the constitutional bill of rights in its opening and closing articles. Because they naturally attracted much critical attention outside the Soviet Union, Brezhnev went out of his way to defend them in his speech to the Supreme Soviet of October. With the scathing hyperbole which Soviet leaders reserve for such occasions he attributed to foreign critics the views that 'the exercise of civil rights in the USSR must consist in violations of the law!' or that Soviet citizens should have the 'one and only "right" . . . to fight against the Soviet state, against the socialist system, so as to gladden the hearts of the imperialists'.

The first of the qualifications is contained in article 39 which, after declaring that Soviet citizens shall enjoy 'in full' the various rights specified in the constitution and laws of the country and that the 'socialist system' shall ensure the continuous expansion of these rights, then proceeds to add the following condition: 'The exercise by citizens of rights and freedoms must not harm the interests of society and the state or the rights of other citizens.' The priority of the general interest over the private interest of the individual has always been an integral part of Soviet constitutional doctrine expressed among others in the provisos attached to particular rights in both the 1936 and 1977 texts. The novelty of article 39 lies in the explicit assertion of this doctrine in the form of an omnibus clause covering all constitutional rights. To be sure, most states find it necessary to qualify their constitutional guarantees of fundamental rights and freedoms. If government is to be effective, if the rights of other citizens are to be protected, if public order is to be maintained and the prevailing community standards of morality respected, then few constitutional rights can be framed in absolute terms. What is so disturbing though about article 39, particularly in the light of the Soviet Union's dismal record in questions of human rights, is the vague and all-encompassing nature of the qualificatory formula. That the exercise of rights must not infringe the rights of others seems self-evident; it is entailed in the principle of equal rights and is, moreover, restated in article 65 which lists respect for the rights of other persons among the constitutional duties of the Soviet citizen. The 'interests of society and the state', however, are a different matter altogether, not least because it is the Communist party which, by virtue of article 6, is now constitutionally acknowledged as the ultimate arbiter of such interests. Article 39, in fact, places the entire array of constitutional rights and freedoms at the mercy of the party's – more precisely – the party leadership's interpretation of the public interest.

The second qualification appears in article 59 which bridges the transition from the list of rights to the list of duties and links enjoyment of the former to fulfilment of the latter: 'The exercise of rights and freedoms shall be inseparable from the performance by a citizen of his duties.' Since 'inseparable from' in this context can presumably only mean 'contingent upon', the clause would seem to provide blanket constitutional sanction for the deprivation of any right on grounds of alleged dereliction of duty. Here again, however, it must be stressed that the doctrine of the unity of rights and duties is not new, and while its elevation to the rank of a constitutional norm may possibly enhance the legitimacy of prosecutions brought against, say, political dissidents or religious believers, its primary importance must be seen in the spirit of intolerance of non-conformity which it imparts to the constitution, a spirit, it may be added, that is hardly compatible with that of a society in which 'the free development of each is the condition for the free development of all'.

The list of duties is formidable enough, spanning eleven articles as against five in the previous constitution. Two of the older articles are again singled out: the protection of socialist ownership is no longer marked by the notorious 'enemies of the people' clause, but it is equipped with a provision specifically making offences punishable 'according to the law' [article 61; 1936–article 131]; and defence of the USSR is still described as a 'sacred duty', while treason, no longer 'punishable with all the severity of the law', is still the 'gravest' crime [article 62; 1936–article 133]. None of the other articles in the catalogue of duties is similarly reinforced by the threat of criminal sanctions for non-compliance. Indeed, the catalogue is principally remarkable for the fact that it includes a number of broadly defined behavioural norms designed to spell out moral precepts, rather than legal obligations, for Soviet citizens. The virtuous citizen is one who 'bears with dignity the lofty title of citizen of the USSR' [article 59], who works conscientiously in his chosen 'socially useful' field of activity [article 60] and raises his children to become 'worthy members of socialist society' [article 66], who preserves the riches of nature [article 67] and culture [article 68], and helps to promote friendship, cooperation and peace among nations [article 69]. Above all he is an active citizen, now required by the constitution not only 'to treat the people's wealth with proper care' but also 'to struggle against theft and waste' [article 61]; not only 'to respect the national dignity of other citizens' but also 'to strengthen the friendship of nations and nationalities of the Soviet multinational state' [article 64]; not only 'to respect the rights and legitimate interests of other persons', but also 'to be intolerant of anti-social acts and to promote the protection of public order in every way' [article 65].

These are hardly precise, legally enforceable rules; they are exhortations of the kind to be found in 'the moral code of the builder of communism' of the 1961 Party Programme. Aside from providing the authorities – via the link of rights and duties of article 59 – with diffuse 'legal' grounds for the denial of constitutional rights, their incorporation into the fundamental law of the land is an emphatic affirmation of the extensive claims which the contemporary Soviet state makes upon its citizens. The preamble of the constitution describes 'developed socialist society' as, amongst other things, one possessed of 'a high degree of organization, ideological commitment and consciousness' and proclaims that 'rearing the man of communist society' is among the state's 'principal tasks' [paragraphs 8 & 12]. The catalogue of duties of chapter 7 spells out the implications of these ambitious notions.

The structure of the Union

In place of the single chapter II of the 1936 constitution, the 1977 text treats the structure of the union in four separate chapters which, in altogether 18 articles (as compared with 17 in 1936), cover not only the USSR and the union republics [chapters 8 & 9] but also the subordinate national units: the autonomous republics [chapter 10] as well as the autonomous regions and autonomous (previously: national) areas [chapter 11].

'Experience has shown that the basic elements of the federal structure of the USSR have fully justified themselves', declared Brezhnev at the May CC plenum, 'There is therefore no need to introduce any major changes in the forms of the Soviet socialist federation.' Certainly the relevant articles of the new constitution contain few 'major changes'; here as elsewhere a basic continuity with the 1936 constitution has been maintained. And yet, careful reading of the text reveals a pronounced centralist trend, the true import of which will be appreciated if it is remembered, both that nationality policy is one of the most sensitive and potentially disruptive problem areas of the Soviet system, and that previous constitutional arrangements, backed up by the all-powerful centralized party apparatus, have hitherto proved entirely adequate to preserve Moscow's hegemony. If the present Soviet leaders nevertheless thought it appropriate to build further centralist elements into formal constitutional law it must be taken as testimony of their determination to press ahead, albeit guardedly and gradually, with the creation of an institutional infrastructure capable of facilitating the much-vaunted 'drawing together of nations'. This much was intimated by Brezhnev when he said at the May plenum that 'the further drawing together of nations and nationalities of the USSR has made it necessary to consolidate the union principles of the state'. And in October, when he rejected suggestions for the dismantling of the federal structure (see p. 182), he did so not because he disavowed the long-term objective of full integration but because 'we would be taking a dangerous path if we were artificially to step up the objective process of the drawing together of nations'.

The assimilationist hue of the constitution is evident in a number of entirely new formulations. Aside from references, in various parts of the text, to 'the Soviet people' [preamble, paragraph 7; articles 6, 11 & 31], to 'Soviet patriotism and internationalism' [article 36] and 'the drawing together of nations and nationalities' [articles 19 & 36], the constitution contains a definition of the USSR as 'a single union multinational state' amplified by the statement that it embodies the 'state unity of the Soviet people' [article 70], as well as affirmations to the effect that the territory of the USSR is a 'single entity' and that the 'sovereignty of the USSR shall extend throughout its territory' [article 75].

The practice of enumerating the powers of the union and leaving those of the republics in residual form has been retained. It is interesting, however, that, while article 76 (in its final version) restored the adjective 'sovereign' to the definition of the union republics, it failed to restore another statement included in both the previous union constitutions, namely, that the 'sovereignty of the union republics shall be restricted only within the limits' of the jurisdiction assigned to the union [1924–article 3; 1936–article 15]. This was presumably because such a statement was difficult to reconcile with the claim of USSR sovereignty over the entire territory of the country.

Matters falling within the jurisdiction of all-union organs are specified in article 73. It is a much more compact article than the corresponding article 14 of the 1936 constitution (with only twelve as against twenty-three sections) and at the same time also more comprehensive. By far the most notable of the new powers assigned to the union is that of 'deciding other questions of all-union significance' which concludes the list of enumerated powers [article 73(12)]. By writing this kind of 'blank cheque' to the benefit of the union, the constitution empties the preceding elaborate listing of powers of all but illustrative meaning. Only the 1918 constitution of the RSFSR which, of course, hardly made any pretence of providing a federal or even a quasi-federal framework, contained a similar clause [1918–article 50]. Less sweeping, but still interesting, new union competencies are granted in sections 3, 4 and 5 of article 73. The first of these empowers the union to establish 'general principles' for both the organization and the activity of republic and local organs. The second provides for a general union competence to determine 'the fundamentals of legislation'; hitherto this competence was limited to specific subject areas enumerated in the constitution. (The 'unity of legislative regulation' entrusted to the union in the first part of this section was formerly anchored in articles 19 and 20 of the 1936 constitution. In the present text the relevant provisions – that union laws apply with equal force in all union republics and prevail over union republic

laws in cases of divergence between them – are combined in article 74.)
The third strengthens the role of the union in the realms of socio-economic life; in particular, the 'determination of the basic directions of scientific and technical progress' is expressly assigned to the jurisdiction of the USSR and the implementation of 'policy' as well as the planning of 'development' now extend, not only to economic, but also to social matters. (Note that the draft also provided for union competence in the development of culture.)

One of the more irrelevant provisions of the 1936 constitution, the 1944 amendment empowering union republics to maintain their own military formations, has been dropped from the new text. Its 'twin', which provided for the foreign relations of the union republics, has been modified: the union republics are now expressly entitled to participate in international organizations – in any case their principal international activity – but only enjoy the right to enter into 'relations' – and not, as formerly, into 'direct relations' – with foreign states. In line with this, the power of the union now includes explicitly the 'coordination' of the foreign relations of the union republics, in addition to the establishment of 'general procedures' [article 73(10); 1936–article 14(a)].

All of these new powers have always been exercised by the union at will. In codifying these powers the new constitution merely brings the country's 'fundamental law' into conformity with long-established practices. By the same token, of course, the constitution also legalizes these practices, and while the removal of the old constitutional fiction, as such, can only be welcomed, the creation of the new constitutional reality must also be recognized for what it is, namely an attempt to consolidate the centralist pillars of the Soviet state structure.

To be sure, some of the former 'federal' features have been preserved. The traditional right to secession, in particular, is reiterated in identical language [article 72]. Never very meaningful in practical terms, its theoretical status as the principal touchstone of union republic 'sovereignty' is now further eroded by the new constitution's emphasis on the 'unity' of the Soviet state and people. Still, its retention is all the more remarkable for the fact that it has provided legal argument for separatist aspirations in recent years. The new constitution also continues to guarantee that the territory of a union republic may not be altered without its consent [article 78; 1936–article 18], and to place its 'sovereign rights' under the protection of the USSR [article 81; 1936–article 15]. Union republic constitutions are still required to conform to the USSR constitution but the demand for 'full' conformity has been dropped [article 76; 1936–article 16].

Several provisions which at first sight appear to grant new powers to the union republics are included in article 77. There is, first, the right of union republics to participate in deciding all-union matters in the USSR Supreme Soviet, its Presidium, the Council of Ministers and 'other organs of the USSR'. This right has not been explicitly formulated in Soviet constitutional law before but in so far as the three named institutions are concerned, it has, of course, been implicit in the representation of the union republics in these institutions. As for the unnamed 'other organs of the USSR', it is difficult to see how the participatory rights of the union republics are to be ensured in practice – except, that is, in the case of the USSR Supreme Court where the *ex officio* membership of the chairmen of union republic supreme courts has been constitutionally provided for since 1957 [1936–article 105]. Indeed, it is very likely that the entire provision was introduced to compensate somewhat for the arrogation of article 73(12). The power to 'ensure integrated economic and social development in its territory', assigned to the union republic in the final version of the second paragraph of article 77, must be set against both the union's own increased competence in this field [article 73(5)] and the new stipulation, included in the same paragraph, requiring the union republics to 'further the exercise of the powers of the USSR . . . and implement the decisions of the highest organs of state power and administration', which articulates the function of republican organs as agents of the central government. Finally, the third paragraph of article 77, also inserted in the final version, empowers the union republic 'to coordinate and control' all-union enterprises, institutions and organizations 'in matters that come within its jurisdiction'. Since the jurisdiction of the union republic is, in fact, severely restricted, this power remains but operationally trivial.

As regards the autonomous territorial entities within the union republics, the fact that they are now allotted separate chapters may be taken as enhancing the 'dignified' features of their constitutional status. The above-mentioned provisions of article 77 are extended (with appropriate modifications) to the autonomous republics and are, here, still less meaningful [article 83]. One unambiguous new provision, previously found only in the constitutions of the autonomous republics themselves, requires the consent of an autonomous republic to any modification of its territory [article 84]. For the rest, the two brief chapters contain little that is both new and notable.

The framework of government

The post-Stalin years have seen a consistent trend to upgrade the 'representative' institutions of Soviet government. The new constitution reflects this trend and in some respects carries it further. One indication of this may already be found in chapter 1 which, like its 1936 precursor, defines the soviets as 'the political foundation of the USSR', but stipulates in addition that all other state organs are 'under the control of and accountable to the soviets' [article 2; 1936–article 2]. Other indications are to be found in Part IV which, under the heading 'Soviets of People's Deputies and the Procedure for their Election', precedes the constitution's detailed treatment of the institutions of government and is clearly designed both to accentuate the status of the soviets as the 'political foundation' of the state and to convey the notion that all soviets are in principal equal, irrespective of their position in the administrative-territorial hierarchy.

The opening article in this part establishes that the soviets constitute 'a single system of organs of state power' [article 89]. This perspective is adhered to throughout. With two exceptions (articles 90 & 96), the provisions apply uniformly to soviets at all levels – from the Supreme Soviet of the USSR to the lowliest village soviet. By thus focusing on the elective – as distinct from the executive – organs, the constitution seeks to emphasize the character of the Soviet state as a state of the soviets, and in this respect, at least, may be seen as an attempt to support the notion of 'social communist self-administration' which – in the final version of the preamble [paragraph 12] – forms part of the constitutional definition of 'the highest goal of the Soviet state'.

Chapter 12, 'The System and Principles of Activity of Soviets of People's Deputies', is almost entirely new. Five of its six articles contain general declarations that are reiterated in more concrete form in subsequent chapters. Thus, for example, article 91 provides that, amongst other things, the soviets shall decide the 'most important matters' within their jurisdictions; what these matters are, however, is spelled out in the articles that define the competencies of the soviets at the national, republic and local levels [articles 108, 137, 143, 146 & 147]. Only article 90 contains operative clauses, and significantly this is also the only article of the chapter in which a distinction between the various levels of soviets is drawn. The article raises the terms of supreme soviets (all-union, union republic and autonomous republic) from four to five years and those of local soviets from two to two-and-a-half years, and stipulates that elections are to be held not later than two months before the expiry of the term of the respective soviets.

Chapter 14, 'The People's Deputy', is also for the most part new. Only the deputy's duty to report on his own work and that of his soviet and the right of recall were provided under the previous constitution; a minor innovation is the extension – in the final version of the 1977 text – of the deputy's duty to report not only to the electorate but also to the collectives that nominated him as candidate [article 107; 1936–article 142]. The other articles of the chapter incorporate the main provisions of the Law on the Status of Deputies of 20 September 1972 and thus invest them with the authority of constitutional norms. Though drawn in very broad terms they undoubtedly amount to a considerable enhancement of the deputy's formal status.

'The Electoral System', chapter 13, parallels the identically headed chapter XI of the 1936 constitution but contains several new provisions. One is the lowering of the age limit for deputies to the USSR Supreme Soviet from 23 to 21 [article 96]. It is of some minor interest that the constitutional draft followed the original text of the 1936 constitution in setting a uniform age limit of 18 years for deputies to all soviets. Just as the 1936 limit was later raised to 23 by an amendment of 1946, so the makers of the 1977 constitution were persuaded to raise their original limit to 21 in their final version of the text. For obvious reasons, the practical importance of these changes was and remains wholly negligible; that they were nevertheless introduced in both cases can only be ascribed to a belated recognition that a higher age limit befits the special status of the USSR Supreme Soviet. Another innovation is the specific guarantee of free election campaigns, granted as an additional fundamental right, as it were, in the second paragraph of article 100; other provisions of this article that go beyond the comparable article 141 of the 1936 constitution – the extension of the right to nominate candidates to labour collectives and meetings of military servicemen, and the provision for state financing of elections – were taken over from existing electoral law. Also new is the clause added in the final version of article 101 that stipulates that citizens may not 'as a rule' serve concurrently in more than two soviets. This, Brezhnev explained in October, would 'facilitate the influx of fresh forces into state bodies and help to increase the number of people taking part in the administration of the affairs of state'.

Finally, mention must be made of article 102 on electoral mandates. None of the previous constitutions mentioned electoral mandates, but they have been widely practised[15] and Soviet commentators have always regarded them as binding or 'imperative mandates' implicitly sanctioned in the long-established constitutional right of recall. The makers of the 1977 constitution were obviously concerned to accord electoral mandates considerable prominence. Not content with having introduced them into constitutional law in article 103, they allocated a separate article to them in the final version of the text – the only entirely new article added to the draft. Yet while the notion of the deputy mandated by his voters to carry out their will is conspicuously displayed, the precise nature of the mandate is carefully obscured. On the one hand, the soviets 'organize the fulfilment of the mandates and inform citizens about their realization', and this certainly reads like a binding injunction, while, on the other hand, the very same article stipulates that the soviets 'consider' the mandates and 'take them into account' when drawing up budgets and development plans [article 102], which would seem to leave them with a great deal of discretion. Similarly, article 103 refers to deputies as 'authorized' representatives who are guided by the 'interests of the state as a whole', although they also 'take account' of the needs of their electors and 'endeavour' to implement their mandates. The reason for this ambiguous language is not far to seek: a binding mandate, apart from being impracticable, would obviously be difficult to reconcile with either the principle of 'democratic centralism' [article 3] or the claim of the Communist party to constitute 'the guiding and directing force of Soviet society' [article 6].

The powers and functions of state institutions still occupy the bulk of the new constitutional text, taking up forty-three articles (as compared with seventy-one in the shorter 1936 constitution), grouped in two Parts (V and VI) and five chapters (15–19). Many of the articles were reformulated and in some cases this led to greater clarity and precision. But although several comparatively minor shifts in competencies can be observed the basic structure of Soviet government has remained unaffected. If the Soviet leadership at any time contemplated using the constitution as the occasion for major institutional reform, as had been speculated by some western observers, the text itself shows no evidence of it.

The fiction of the Supreme Soviet as 'the highest organ of state power of the USSR' is maintained [article 108] and even somewhat elaborated, in keeping with the constitution's emphasis on the 'representative' organs generally. Yet some of the effort expanded on the new formulations can only be described as tinkering with the constitution's more obvious irrelevancies. Thus, extraordinary sessions of the Supreme Soviet can now also be convened on the proposal of one-third of the deputies of one of the chambers [article 112; 1936–article 46], and sessions of the two chambers are no longer required to begin and end simultaneously [article 112; 1936–article 41]. Whereas the 1936 constitution was content to stipulate a simple majority of votes in both chambers of the Supreme Soviet for the adoption of laws, the new constitution requires an absolute majority and – in the final version – differentiates between laws and other acts [article 114; 1936–article 39]. The provisions for the improbable case of disagreement between the two chambers have also been modified: if the conciliation procedure fails, it will no longer be necessary to dissolve the Supreme Soviet call new elections; instead, a clause added in the final version provides that the matter shall be carried over to the next session or submitted to referendum [article 115; 1936–article 47]. Finally, the legal equality of the two chambers is now also expressed in their numerical equality [article 110]. This, it will be recalled, was one of the few alterations to the 1936 draft endorsed by Stalin but not carried into effect (see p. 96); forty years later his successors accomplished this quite marginal piece of electoral engineering. The 1977 constitution replaces the fixed electoral norm for the Council of the Union (one deputy per 300,000 of population) by 'electoral districts of equal size'; since representation in the Council of Nationalities remains unchanged each chamber henceforth numbers 750 deputies.[16]

Legislative initiative, which under the previous constitution was recognized only for the two chambers, is greatly enlarged in the new constitution [article 113; 1936–article 38]. In so far as such initiative is now granted to the Presidium of the Supreme Soviet and the Council of Ministers, it brings the constitution into line with the bulk of actual legislative practice. But Soviet commentators have long claimed this right for most of the other new bearers of legislative initiative as well. For some of these – the Supreme Court, under the 1957 Statute on the Supreme Court of the USSR, and individual deputies, under the 1972 Law on the Status of Deputies – it was anchored in ordinary legislation. Of the 'social organizations', mentioned separately in the second paragraph of the article, the right to initiate legislation was acknowledged for the Central Council of Trade Unions in the 1970 Fundamentals of Labour Legislation. The new provisions concerning the standing commissions of the Supreme Soviet [articles 113 & 125] similarly incorporate previous legislation – in this case the 1967 Statute on Standing Commissions of the Council of the Union and the Council of Nationalities of the USSR. Although not mentioned in the previous constitution, standing commissions appeared soon after its adoption, and their number and legislative role greatly expanded from the mid-1960s onward (see p. 98). This development is now given constitutional expression.

The Supreme Soviet's right of control, hitherto implicit in its position at the pinnacle of the state structure, is explicitly stated in article 126, which also empowers the Supreme Soviet to form the People's Control Committee. Specific control organs have functioned in the Soviet Union from the earliest days under various designations. The People's Control Committee was formed in December 1965 and, according to the Statute of People's Control Organs of 19 December 1968, operated as a union-republic agency 'under the direction of the party and the government'. In the new Law on People's Control of 30 November 1979, enacted under the mandate of article 126 of the constitution, all references to direction by the party have been dropped; instead, people's control organs at all levels are required to 'report regularly to the soviets and labour collectives', to work 'in cooperation' with the soviets and to maintain 'ties with appropriate state organs'. The People's Control Committee deploys an army of nearly ten million volunteer 'citizen inspectors', whose main task is to check on the fulfilment of directives and economic plans.[17] That it is now formed by the Supreme Soviet rather than, as hitherto, by the Council of Ministers does not mean that it has been turned into a control agency of the Supreme Soviet and its Presidium, functioning independently of the 'executive branch' of Soviet government. The Chairman of the People's Control Committee continues to serve as a member of the Council of Ministers (now by virtue of his office) and the Council continues to 'direct' the Committee's work.

From a purely legal-technical point of view, probably the most interesting innovation among the provisions relating to the Supreme Soviet is the attempt to delineate its powers in article 108, both by enumerating the matters that fall within its exclusive jurisdiction and by clarifying its legislative competence. The 1936 constitution did not provide an exhaustive list of the Supreme Soviet's powers. Instead, it vested in the Supreme Soviet all rights belonging to the union with the exception of those assigned by the constitution to the Presidium of the Supreme Soviet, the Council of Ministers and individual Ministries [1936–article 31]. The new constitution proceeds by a different route. Article 108 first claims for the Supreme Soviet all powers which under the constitution belong to the USSR, without qualification, and then enumerates the powers that are to be exclusively exercised by the Supreme Soviet. Whereas article 32 of the 1936 constitution vested 'the legislative power of the USSR' in the Supreme Soviet, article 108 assigns the adoption of 'laws of the USSR' to the Supreme Soviet's competence. Leaving aside the provision for referenda, added in the final version, this is a far more realistic statement of actual practice, for 'the legislative power of the USSR' has always been shared by other all-union organs, most conspicuously the Supreme Soviet Presidium in the form of edicts.

A clear, if not exactly momentous, increase in the power of the Supreme Soviet Presidium, which now has thirty-nine rather than thirty-seven members and includes the new post of First Deputy Chairman [article 120], is one of the more tangible institutional changes of the new constitution. The constitution of 1936, unlike that of 1924, did not contain a definition of the Presidium's role; it listed the Presidium's powers in great detail but otherwise confined itself to a statement of its composition and its accountability to the Supreme Soviet [1936–article 48; cf. 1924–article 29]. The 1977 constitution is less reticent about the Presidium's place in the Soviet structure, describing it as 'the permanently functioning organ of the Supreme Soviet' which – in an addition to the final version – exercises the functions of 'the highest organ of state power' in the intervals between Supreme Soviet sessions [article 119].

The constitution also equips the Presidium with several new powers, but above all it achieves a clearer delimitation of its authority from that of the Supreme Soviet by separating its 'independent' powers from those exercised by it subject to approval by the Supreme Soviet. The latter are listed in article 122 and comprise the amendment of existing 'legislative acts', the approval of boundary changes of union republics, the formation and abolition of all-union ministries and state committees (on the proposal of the Council of Ministers), and the appointment and dismissal of individual members of the Council of Ministers (on the recommendation of the Council's Chairman). With one exception – the formation of state committees – all of these were performed by the Presidium until now (with subsequent approval by the Supreme Soviet), but only the appointment and dismissal of members of the Council of Ministers was explicitly sanctioned under the terms of the constitution [1936–article 49(f)].

The 'legalization' of the Presidium's legislative power is particularly noteworthy and should be seen in connection with the reformulation of the legislative power of the Supreme Soviet in article 108. If nothing else, it may be expected to put to rest some of the legal argument (and linguistic hairsplitting) which engaged Soviet scholars in the post-Stalin years over whether or not the Presidium was acting within its constitutional authority when it issued edicts that went beyond the mere 'interpretation' or 'concretization' of Supreme Soviet enactments.[18] Note, however, that while the authority granted in article 122(1) to 'amend, when necessary, the legislative acts of the USSR currently in force', clearly covers 'laws' of the Supreme Soviet, it does not sanction the enactment of entirely new legislation by the Presidium. Whether this power may be derived from article 123 which authorizes the Presidium to 'issue edicts and adopt decrees' (without requiring Supreme Soviet approval) seems highly doubtful.

The Presidium's 'independent' powers are enumerated in article 121. The list is very similar to that of article 49 in the 1936 constitution, but contains several new powers. Two of these, the coordination of the standing commissions of the Supreme Soviet chambers [section 3] and matters of citizenship and asylum [section 10], were already exercised by the Presidium. Another, the control of constitutionality [section 4], harks back to a similar provision in the 1924 constitution, except that the latter allowed for judicial participation [1924–articles 30 & 43(c)]. It is an improvement on the 1936 constitution, which simply assigned this power to the jurisdiction of all-union organs, those of 'state administration' as well as 'state power', without specifically charging any one of them with its exercise [1936–article 14(d)]. Article 121 further authorizes the Presidium not only to 'establish' military and diplomatic ranks, as under the former article 49(k), but also to 'confer the highest military ranks [and] diplomatic ranks' [section 8]. Especially in respect of the former, this may well be a new power, in fact as well as in law, depending on how 'the highest military ranks' will be defined in practice; hitherto the Presidium conferred only the ranks of Marshal and Army General, while lower generals' ranks were conferred by the Council of Ministers. A more significant mark of the Presidium's enhanced position is the power to form the Defence Council of the USSR and approve its membership [section 14]. Very little is known about this, the highest military leadership organ in the Soviet Union, other than that it is headed by Brezhnev who with the rank of Marshal now also holds the post of Commander-in-Chief of the Armed Forces; indeed, the very existence of the Defence Council was only confirmed in May 1976. Attention must finally be drawn to the open-ended clause added in the final version of article 121: by declaring that the Presidium may exercise 'other powers established by the Constitution and laws of the USSR' [section 18], it creates a wide opening through which the powers of the Presidium can be augmented at will.

More important by far than any of the new legal provisions is the new political fact that the post of Chairman of the Presidium is now occupied by the General Secretary of the CPSU. For the first time in Soviet history the Presidium is headed by the top leader of the party and this itself adds greatly to the authority of that body, regardless of its formal constitutional competencies. One may reasonably assume that some of the new constitutional provisions are not unconnected with Brezhnev's accession to the chairmanship; probably the clearest indication of this is the newly created post of First Deputy Chairman. Yet it should be pointed out that while this and other provisions may have been tailored to the requirements of the General Secretary, the constitution nowhere confers any powers whatever on the office of Chairman of the Presidium. Instead, it has remained faithful to the collegial principle, refusing to follow the example of either the 'Presidential' or the 'state council' constitutions of other Soviet-type states in which the positions of party leader and head of state have come to be held by the same person, e.g. the GDR, Romania, Yugoslavia, Cuba or North Korea.

The constitution's treatment of the USSR Council of Ministers similarly contains only comparatively minor changes of substance. The enumeration of individual ministries and other government agencies, and the distribution of the former as between union and union republic ministries, which occupied three amendment-ridden articles in the previous constitution [1936–articles 70, 77 & 78], has been abandoned.[19] Article 129, which now specifies the composition of the all-union Council of Ministers in very general terms, introduces two innovations. One is the rather loosely drawn clause referring to the possibility of membership in the Council of 'the heads of other organs and organizations of the USSR', a formulation that is broad enough to include the leaders of non-governmental, social organizations, the Chairman of the Central Council of Trade Unions, for example, or the First Secretary of the Communist Youth League (Komsomol). The other, added in the final version of the article, requires the resignation of the Council of Ministers at the first session of a newly elected Supreme Soviet and is no more than the constitutional regulation of a time-honoured formality. It is also the only provision relating to the resignation of the Soviet government.

Like its predecessor, the 1977 constitution both affirms that the government is responsible and accountable to the Supreme Soviet and its Presidium [article 130; 1936–article 65] and fails to provide for the government's dismissal in the admittedly remote event that it no longer enjoys the confidence of these 'highest organs of state power'. The new clause of article 130 that requires the government to 'report regularly on its work' to the Supreme Soviet (but not its Presidium) is hardly likely to compensate for the absence of a sanction that is generally regarded as an essential, if ultimate, safeguard of 'legislative supremacy'.

The Presidium of the Council of Ministers, which has officially been in existence since 1953, but has not apparently functioned continuously since then, is now given its first legal recognition. Article 132 defines it as 'a permanent organ' of the Council of Ministers and charges it with responsibility for the direction of the national economy and other matters of state administration'. The article also stipulates that it should be made up by the Chairman, the First Deputy Chairman and the Deputy Chairmen of the Council. Both from the designation of its functions and from its composition it is clear that the Presidium, often described in Western literature as a kind of 'inner cabinet', is now in fact primarily concerned with the direction of economic affairs. (It does not, for example, include such key figures as the Defence and Foreign Ministers or the Chairman of the State Security Committee, the KGB – all three, incidentally, members of the present party Politburo.) The Council of Ministers formed on 19 April 1979, following the last elections to the Supreme Soviet, had 109 members altogether, of whom fourteen qualified for membership in the Presidium: the Chairman of the Council, A.N. Kosygin, the First Deputy Chairman, N.A. Tikhonov, and twelve Deputy Chairmen. The constitution does not prescribe the frequency of meetings for either the Council or its Presidium, but this is now regulated by the Law on the USSR Council of Ministers of 6 July 1978, which stipulates that meetings of the full Council are to be held at least once every three months, while meetings of the Presidium are to be held 'regularly (when the need arises)'.

The competencies of the Council of Ministers are formulated rather more elaborately than in the 1936 constitution [article 131; 1936–article 68]. They remain substantially unchanged except that the right to form state committees, granted to the Council by a 1963 constitutional amendment, has now been transferred to the Presidium of the Supreme Soviet [article 122(3); cf. article 131(7) and 1936–article 68 (f)]. The greater weight given the Presidium is also evident in two other new provisions. Article 66 of the old constitution empowered the Council of Ministers to issue its normative acts on the basis of existing 'laws', while the parallel article 133 in the new constitution provides that the Council shall issue such acts not only on the basis of laws but also of Presidium edicts or (in the language of the final version) of 'other decisions' of the Supreme Soviet and its Presidium. In the same vein is the clause, added in the final version of article 135, empowering the Presidium of the Supreme Soviet to determine the procedure for the transfer of economic enterprises and associations from republic and local subordination to all-union subordination. By edict of 8 June 1978 the Presidium reserved for itself the right to carry out such transfers 'on the recommendation of the Chairman of the Council of Ministers'.

The state committees set up in the wake of Khrushchev's administrative reforms did not figure in the former constitution, except in article 68(f) and in two articles [70 & 83] which specified the composition of the union and republic governments; all other articles mentioned only 'ministries' or 'ministers' [1936–articles 71–8 & 84–8]. The new constitution corrects this anomaly by bracketing the state committees together with the ministries [articles 134–6 & 142; also article 164]. In so doing, however, it also indicates that the distinctive character of the state committees has been fundamentally altered, if not altogether obliterated. Originally, it will be recalled, the difference between the ministries and the majority of state committees was that the former administered the agencies and enterprises in their jurisdictions while the latter functioned primarily as planning and coordinating bodies without executive responsibilities. The draft version of the new constitution ignored this or any other distinction between the two when it declared that both ministries and state committees 'shall direct branches of administration entrusted to them', 'directly administer enterprises and associations', and exercise 'responsibility for the state and development of branches of administration entrusted to them' [articles 135 & 142]. It is only in the final version of the constitution that a distinction between ministries and state committees is intimated by the insertion of the words 'or carry out interbranch administration' and the substitution of 'spheres' for 'branches'. That these alterations were made with a view to taking into account the specific character of the state committees, now held to be that of organs of 'functional' rather than 'branch' administration has since been confirmed by the 1978 Law on the USSR Council of Ministers. The definition of ministries and state committees given in articles 21 and 22 of that law are identical: both are 'central organs of administration'. But whereas the former 'shall exercise direction over *branches* of administration entrusted to them and shall be responsible for the state and development of these branches', the latter 'shall carry out *interbranch* administration and shall be responsible for the state and development of the *spheres* of administration entrusted to them' (emphasis added).

This is the sum total of the constitutional innovations at the centre of the state structure. The two brief chapters that treat jointly the organs of 'state power and administration' of the union republics and autonomous republics (chapters 17 and 18) cover the same ground much more swiftly, leaving most of the details for their own constitutions.

The next chapter, 'The Local Organs of State Power and Administration' (chapter 19) reveals substantial changes when compared with the parallel chapter VIII in the 1936 constitution. Most of the new provisions, reflecting the considerable expansion in the competencies of the local soviets over the past two decades, were, however, already embodied in all-union or union republic legislation pertaining to various levels of local government (see p. 111). They are now generalized and anchored in the constitution. Two provisions, not found in previous legislation, were added in the final version of the text. In line with the constitution's emphasis on mass participation, publicity and accountability, article 149 requires executive committees to report at least once a year not only to their respective soviets but also to meetings of labour collectives and residents; and article 146 reinforces centralist control by explicitly introducing the right of superior soviets to 'direct the activity of lower-ranking soviets'. Since this latter clause may appear to be at variance with the constitutional grant of increased competencies for local organs, it should be stressed that local autonomy is no more part of the new constitution than it was of the old. The local soviets are still 'organs of state power' in the localities rather than organs of local self-government, and their powers, though greatly enlarged, are still exercised subject to control and direction from above. The strict 'dual subordination' of the executive organs of local soviets, reaffirmed in the new constitution in terms practically identical to those of its predecessor, leaves little doubt on this score [article 150; 1936–article 101].

The legal system

The seventh part, 'Justice, Arbitration and Procuracy', probably makes fewer changes in the material law of the USSR than any other part of the constitution. Nearly all its new provisions incorporate norms hitherto contained in ordinary legislation. Since many of the latter, in turn, originated in the important legal reforms of the late 1950s and early 1960s, the two chapters that make up this part differ favourably from the parallel chapter ix in the 1936 constitutions.

The opening article of chapter 20, 'The Courts and Arbitration', precedes its enumeration of Soviet courts (which now specifically include the military tribunals) with the affirmation: 'Justice in the USSR shall be administered solely by a court' [article 151]. The previous constitution lacked a similar statement of judicial monopoly over the administration of justice (it was, however, included in post-Stalin civil and criminal procedural law); nor could it be inferred from its enumeration of Soviet courts, for this enumeration included 'special courts of the USSR created by decree of the Supreme Soviet' and therefore remained open-ended [1936–article 102]. To be sure, aside from the crucial question of the independence of Soviet courts, reservations about the extent of the courts' monopoly are still appropriate. There is, first, the matter of 'administrative justice': article 4 of the 1961 Fundamentals of Civil Procedure allows 'disputes arising from civil, family labour and collective farm legal relations' to be assigned by law to the jurisdiction of 'administrative and other organs'; in criminal law, the practice of dealing with minor offences by administrative procedures has been greatly expanded in recent years – partly with a view to relieving the caseload of the ordinary courts. There is, second, the 'comradely justice' meted out by the comrades' courts which are not acknowledged in article 151 among the 'courts functioning in the USSR'. There is, third, the constitutional power of the Supreme Soviet Presidium to 'interpret the laws of the USSR' [article 121(5)]; the distinction between this power and that granted to supreme courts under ordinary legislation to 'issue guiding explanations' concerning the 'application of legislation' remains tenuous. And there is, fourth, some question whether 'special courts' have altogether disappeared; they are known to have operated in the first half of the 1970s (for employees of secret institutions and enterprises)[20] even though, from 1958 onward, they were no longer sanctioned under ordinary legislation on court organization.

Guarantees of due process, again in line with existing substantive and procedural law, are constitutionally strengthened in several ways. The principle of equality, already asserted in three separate articles of chapter 6, is specifically reaffirmed with regard to the 'equality of citizens before the court and the law' [article 156]. Open trials and the right of the accused to a defence, which in the 1936 constitution were included in a single article, are now separated and the clause covering exceptions to open trials is formulated rather more stringently, stipulating 'observance of all the rules of procedure' rather than merely the right to a defence [article 157-8; 1936–article 111]. The provision concerning the language of court proceedings has been extended to allow the language of the autonomous area or the majority of the local population to be used; while the right to an interpreter has been widened to cover full participation in the court proceedings [article 159; 1936–article 110]. More important, the constitution articulates a basic principle of the rule of law in article 160: 'No one may be deemed guilty of committing a crime and subjected to criminal punishment other than by the judgment of a court and in accordance with the law.' By requiring a court judgment to be in accordance with the 'law' (in the draft too restrictively: 'criminal law'), this article tightens corresponding provisions in the existing law on court organization (which has instead, 'legislation') and on criminal procedure (which is content with 'judgment of a court' without further qualification).

The constitution also clarifies the position of the people's assessors. It is now established that they 'enjoy all the rights of judges' [article 154] and like them are 'independent and subordinate only to the law' [article 155; cf. 1936–article 112]; that they participate in the hearing of civil and criminal cases in all courts of first instance, and not 'in all courts except in instances provided' by law [article 154; 1936–article 103]; that assessors of all courts are elected and that those of people's courts are elected (by meetings of citizens) in open elections [article 152; cf.

1936–article 109]. An inconsequential innovation which actually alters the material law is the extension of the tenure of people's assessors of people's courts and military tribunals – two-and-a-half years instead of two years [article 152].

Two elements of 'democratic' participation are adopted from existing legislation. One is the responsibility and accountability of judges and people's assessors to their electors (or the organs which elected them), backed up – in an addition to the final version – by the right of recall [article 152]; to the extent that this strengthens 'popular' influence over the courts it renders their formal independence still more fragile. The other allows for the participation of 'representatives of social organizations and labour collectives' in civil and criminal cases [article 162]; this is a broader formulation than that provided under ordinary all-union law for the participation, subject to a court ruling, of so-called 'social accusers' and 'social defenders'.

A rather unusual provision – unusual, also, among constitutions in other Soviet-type states – introduces the Soviet bar [article 161]. Only in recent decades has the role of the bar in the proper functioning of a legal system come to be recognized in the Soviet Union. The new constitution does little more than acknowledge its existence as well as the possibility of free legal aid in cases so provided for by legislation. In so doing, however, it 'promotes' the Soviet advocate from the relative obscurity of ordinary legislation to the prominence of the country's fundamental law and at the same time 'reinforces' the right-to-defence clause of article 158.

Another long-established institution of the Soviet legal system that makes its first appearance in a Soviet constitution is state arbitration [article 163]. As presently constituted, state arbitration tribunals operate under the executive organs of soviets at three levels: city or region, union republic and all-union. They deal with economic disputes between public corporations, in cases involving breaches of 'supply contracts' when, say, damages are claimed for defective goods or for failure to deliver contracted goods within the agreed time limit, but also with 'pre-contract disputes', when enterprises obliged under the directives of the economic plan to conclude a contract are unable to agree on its terms. Because they partake of the nature of both courts and administrative agencies, the arbitration tribunals may, perhaps, be properly described as quasi-judicial organs. They do not, as the name suggests, provide voluntary conciliation procedures that are freely submitted to by the parties to a dispute, but have compulsory jurisdiction and, unlike courts, may themselves take the initiative in directing cases to be brought before them.

The procuracy [articles 164–8] now receives a separate chapter (chapter 21) and enhances its standing as an independent component of the Soviet legal system. Its supervisory jurisdiction is stated far more comprehensively than in the old constitution [article 164; 1936–article 113], but was already formulated in very similar terms in the 1955 Statute on Procuracy Supervision. The tenure of the Procurator General has been reduced from seven to five years and is now the same as that of lower-ranking procurators [article 167]. This should not, however, be taken as intimating a diminution in his status, for the constitution preserves the strict hierarchical structure of the procuracy and leaves the powers of the Procurator General, *vis-à-vis* subordinate procurators, unchanged. Rather, it was probably designed to remove an anomalous, if long-standing, asymmetry between the constitutional terms of office of the Procurator General and the USSR Supreme Court. (Procurator General R.A. Rudenko occupied this office uninterruptedly from 1953 onward; he was reappointed in April 1979 and held the post until his death in January 1981.) Similarly, the new provision concerning the responsibility and accountability of the Procurator General to the Supreme Soviet and the Presidium, already stipulated under the 1955 Statute, merely fills an obvious lacuna in constitutional law [article 165].

With few and relatively insubstantial exceptions neither of the above chapters on the legal system create new law. Their importance, such as it is, lies rather in the fact that they constitutionalize antecedent legal norms many of which bear the marks of the post-Stalin reforms. They may therefore be taken as attesting to the Soviet leadership's concern for the stability of the 'legal culture' that has evolved over the past two decades.

Absent from this as from all earlier Soviet constitutions is a provision for the judicial review of constitutionality. The absence is now particularly conspicuous because the 1977 constitution, unlike its predecessors, affirms in article 173 the principle of constitutional supremacy over all other law: 'The Constitution of the USSR shall have supreme legal force. All laws and other acts of state organs shall be issued on the basis of and in conformity with the Constitution'. In the light of this unequivocal assertion the question of the control of constitutionality naturally presents itself: which organ shall determine whether a particular act is in conflict with the constitution? The constitution, as we have seen above, replies that it is the Presidium of the Supreme Soviet of the USSR [article 121(4)]. But this is, of course, a political and not a judicial organ. Moreover, it is clear – and entirely logical, given that the Presidium is the 'permanently functioning organ' of the USSR Supreme Soviet – that its 'control over the observance of the USSR constitution' does not extend to acts of the Supreme Soviet itself. The latter is 'the highest organ of state power of the USSR', and as such its acts cannot be subject to review; nor, if such review were to be acknowledged in principle, would it make any sense at all to assign it – other than in the form of a consultative power – to the competence of an organ accountable to the Supreme Soviet.

It is of some interest in this connection that the subject has occasionally been raised in Soviet legal literature. Thus, for example, a proposal for independent, not necessarily judicial, review was recently framed in the following terms:

> Subjectivism and voluntarism in their very nature are enemies of constitutional legality. Therefore it would be expedient to establish in the USSR, and also in each of the union republics, a constitutional council as an organ of supreme supervision over all, even including the supreme, legislative agencies to maintain adherence to the Constitution.[21]

Judicial review has operated in Yugoslavia since 1963 and is also provided for, but not implemented, under the Czechoslovak constitution of 1968. The makers of the new Soviet constitution chose to ignore these proposals and precedents. The constitution proclaims its supremacy over all other laws but fails to provide any means by which that supremacy can be enforced in respect of 'the highest organs of state power of the USSR'.

Retrospect and postscript

At this point it may be useful to return briefly to the strange course of the constitution's genesis. Now that the reader has familiarized himself with the principal innovations of the document, he may well feel that they contain little if anything that could be regarded as sufficiently controversial to explain the long delay in the preparation of the constitution. But this need not mean that there were no controversies. Since we do not know the contents of the early draft or drafts the possibility cannot be precluded that it was precisely because the controversies could only be resolved by compromise that the document took so long to emerge into the light of day and then bore few scars of antecedent conflict. The constitutions of other states, too, are more often than not the result of compromise, because only compromise can achieve the broad consensus necessary to ensure the legitimacy and stability of fundamental law. In the Soviet Union, because of the nature of its political system, the conflicts that precede such compromises would necessarily be confined to a small group of political leaders and would be fought out in comparative secrecy. If this is indeed what happened in the case of the constitution it would itself be a matter of some significance. A document over which politicians quarrel is a document which they regard as important. If the Soviet leaders quarrelled over the new constitution it would mean that they regarded it as an instrument at least potentially capable of affecting actual power relationships.

But did they quarrel over the constitution? And if they did, what issue or issues was the quarrel about? That there was at different times formidable opposition to constitutional reform, first under Khrushchev and then under Brezhnev, is strongly indicated not only by the extraordinary long duration but also by the jerky, 'stop-go' character of the process by which the constitution came into being. There is probably no precedent in Soviet history of a case in which a project prominently endorsed by a top party leader – in this case, two top party leaders – was held up so obviously and for so long a time. But to what extent, if at all, did this opposition turn on the contents of the constitution? Perhaps it was simply prompted by the reluctance of other members of the CPSU Presidium/Politburo to tolerate the prestige gain that could be expected to accrue to Khrushchev and later to Brezhnev from the promulgation of a 'Khrushchev constitution' or a 'Brezhnev constitution'? The fact that these two men were virtually alone among the Soviet leadership in publicly endorsing constitutional reform would certainly seem to support such a view.

Let us acknowledge that we cannot account for either the circumstances that held up constitutional reform from 1959 or those that permitted the final breakthrough in 1977. The sporadic public pronouncements on the subject were so laconic, indeed the entire operation was conducted in such a curious and clandestine fashion that any such attempt could only be based on speculation unwarranted by the evidence. What we propose to do instead is to try and trace the contours of a possible constitutional conflict through the writings of Soviet legal scholars. The reader should be warned, however, that this too is an exercise with very definite limitations. It is only right that these should be stated at the outset.

First, although some of the jurists who went into print on the question of the proposed new constitution were closely associated with the project at various times, the assumption that their opinions reflected those of the political leaders, while perhaps plausible, is no more than an assumption. There were cases, particularly in more recent years, when the writings of Soviet jurists could be interpreted as being aimed at influencing rather than reflecting the views of the Soviet leadership.[22]

Secondly, the directly pertinent literature is extremely sparse. It was only after the draft of the 1977 text was published and particularly after its adoption that Soviet legal journals began to print lengthy – and uniformly laudatory – comments on the new constitution.[23]

Thirdly, the writings of jurists on the constitution were often framed in vacuous generalities. An example of such writing is an article by A. Denisov published at the end of 1966. As one of the two prominent academic lawyers who served on Khrushchev's constitutional commission Denisov could be expected to be familiar with the proposals under discussion. Yet, without so much as a single allusion to the substance of these proposals, he chose to deliver himself of such commonplaces as:

'The constitution will undoubtedly rest upon the ideological heritage of V.I. Lenin . . . . There is every reason to assume that the new constitution will be characterized by exceptionally rich content . . . . It may be boldly asserted that the democracy of the new USSR constitution will be even broader.'[24]

Fourthly, even when legal scholars ventured to tackle the specifics of constitutional reform they often concentrated on matters of little consequence. Thus, for example, it was proposed – on the lines eventually adopted – that legislative initiative in the Supreme Soviet of the USSR should be extended, or that extraordinary sessions of the Supreme Soviet should also be convened at the demand of one-third of the deputies of one of the chambers. Whatever importance their authors might have attached to these proposals – and it surely could not have been very great – they are not likely to have exercised the political leaders of the Soviet Union.

Bearing in mind these reservations, our first task will be to set out those features of the new constitution which already figured in the legal literature under Khrushchev. Basing ourselves on writings of the late 1950s and early 1960s, including an account of a scholarly conference held in 1959 and two articles by P.S. Romashkin, the other academic lawyer on Khrushchev's constitutional commission,[25] we find that the following were among items already envisaged in early discussions: the character of the constitution as a document combining programmatic with 'confirmatory' elements and pertaining to Soviet society as well as to the Soviet state; the disposition of its various parts: fundamental rights and duties to be moved to the beginning of the text, the electoral system to precede the organs of government, a separate chapter on the procuracy; acknowledgement of the status of the Communist party more in keeping with its real role in the Soviet system; the socio-economic rights to health protection and housing; the right to submit complaints to state agencies; the duty of parents to bring up their children 'in the spirit of Communist morality and consciousness of civic duties'; the strengthening of 'socialist legality' by the guarantee that no one will be deemed guilty of a crime and subjected to criminal punishment except by the sentence of a court based on the law; the renaming of the soviets as 'soviets of people's deputies' and greater emphasis on their contribution to Soviet democracy; public discussion of the most important draft laws; definition of the exclusive legislative competence of the Supreme Soviet; references to the Soviet Union's role in the international system and its relations with 'fraternal' states; the inclusion of the property of social organizations among the forms of socialist ownership alongside state and cooperative-collective farm ownership, duly noting the 'drawing together' of the two latter forms.

The above list does not cover all the new constitutional provisions; rather it identifies some of the likely areas of agreement between the

Khrushchev and Brezhnev drafts. Perhaps it even permits the conclusion that the two were not radically different documents.

Let us now turn to the unsuccessful proposals, i.e. proposals that were raised in the literature at different times under both Khrushchev and Brezhnev but were not incorporated into the constitution. They divide broadly into two groups: proposals of a primarily declarative nature affecting the ideological complexion of the constitution, and those with direct bearing on the constitution's operative clauses.

The first group includes proposals for statements that Soviet foreign policy was directed against 'imperialist aggressors and warmongers', that national economic planning was no longer confined to the Soviet Union but coordinated with planning 'in all the other countries of the world socialist system', and that cooperation with 'fraternal socialist countries' was reflected 'particularly in implementing economic integration' (see p. 193). Most of the proposals in this group were intended to translate the precepts of the 'full-scale construction of communism' into the language of the constitution. Thus it was suggested that 'it would be desirable to add . . . a formulation to the effect that, with time, the process of transfer of a number of functions of state organs to social organizations will develop to an even greater extent', that the soviets are not only state organs but also social organizations, that the mass social organizations should be mentioned alongside the soviets as the 'political foundation' of the USSR, that the abolition of taxes (promised by Khrushchev for 1965) should be constitutionally affirmed, and that the 'growing role' of the communist principle of distribution should be expressed by noting the 'prospect of transition' from the socialist principle 'From each according to his ability, to each according to his work' to the communist principle 'From each according to his ability, to each according to his needs'. Since Khrushchev's successors generally muted the more utopian themes of the transition to communism, it comes as no surprise that these declarations did not find their way into the constitutional text.

The second group of unsuccessful proposals focused on two issues. One of these concerned the enhancement of the 'democratic' attributes of the Soviet polity. Probably the most far-reaching and potentially controversial proposal was for the introduction of multi-candidate elections; it was raised with proper caution, but it appeared to have substantial backing in academic circles.[26] Others suggested that the present system of nominating candidates by labour collectives at places of work should be applied to the elections themselves (the 'production principle') or called for the establishment of a system of congresses of soviets which would be composed of deputies to soviets at different levels and would periodically discuss matters of state and social life. The need to extend the sessions of the USSR Supreme Soviet so as to enable it to perform its legislative functions more effectively was noted in several contributions. On the troublesome question of the legislative powers of the Presidium of the Supreme Soviet legal opinion was divided, with some authors, probably a majority, in favour of giving the Presidium authority to enact laws, and others insisting that all the Presidium's legislative acts, without exception, should have provisional legal force only and be subject to ratification by the Supreme Soviet. Lastly, the literature echoed proposals of the 1961 Party Programme which envisaged the introduction of rotation procedures to ensure regular renewal of all soviets and their elected organs.

The other issue was that of Soviet federalism. While there was some dispute over the proposals mentioned above in the literature, federalism was the only area in which a genuine and protracted debate developed. It went beyond the confines of the legal community, involving historians, writers on nationality questions and professional ideologists, and – in a manner characteristic of many Soviet-style debates – relied a great deal on textual exegesis of Lenin's writings.[27] It was of some significance that the views expressed were sharply polarized. On one side were the 'pro-federalists', who called for an unequivocal affirmation of 'the principle of self-determination' and accordingly sought to limit the powers of the central organs *vis-à-vis* those of the constituent republics. The 'anti-federalists', on the other side, more or less openly implied that the federal structure had outlived its usefulness and should be replaced by more rational territorial divisions based on the 'economic principle'.[28] If one had to choose a single issue to account for substantive constitutional conflicts among Soviet leaders that of federalism would probably be the most likely candidate.

It will be clear from the aforesaid that if the promulgation of the constitution was delayed by conflict among the Soviet leaders regarding its contents, then the writings of the legal scholars offer only the most tentative clues to the nature of that conflict. We cannot even claim to have isolated the main issues. If it can be argued that the conflicting views of the Soviet leaders are refracted in the scholarly literature, it cannot be argued that the refracted image is true to the original. Some of the issues may have been distorted or even totally obscured. It is quite possible that the agenda of constitutional debate precluded or at least moderated precisely those issues on which the Soviet leaders were known or suspected to be most sharply divided. It would not be the first time that Soviet scholars have exercised such self-restraint.

But even if it has only served to convey something of the flavour of Soviet constitutional debate this highly speculative excursus may not have been entirely in vain. If the fact that the project of the new constitution took so long to come to fruition may be taken to mark the extent of the change since the days of Stalin (when such matters were decided by fiat of one man and executed with due dispatch) then the fact that the public evidence on the real issues at stake is still so slender may also be taken to mark the limits of that change. That so much of the preparation of the country's 'fundamental law' was conducted behind the scenes, that neither the political decision-makers nor the legal experts (not to mention other interested parties) were able to argue their views fully and publicly, probably says as much about the nature of the Soviet system as do all the 174 articles of its formal constitutional text.

Developments subsequent to the promulgation of the constitution were by and large unremarkable. Not surprisingly, the reaction of legal scholars, once the document had been enacted, was one of unreserved approval. But echoes of long-standing legal controversies were still audible and the echo of one such controversy, that concerning the applicability of constitutional provisions, was particularly resonant. The draftsmen of the Soviet text did not follow the example of their colleagues in the GDR who in all their constitutions since 1949 had included a clause declaring constitutional provisions to be directly binding law. And Brezhnev's own reference, in his speech of October 1977, to 'basic, fundamental provisions which, while having direct force, are expressed and spelled out in other legislative acts', was hardly calculated to provide much in the way of clarification. Some legal commentators attempted to cope with the problem by distinguishing several categories of constitutional provisions, such as norms directly regulating specific areas of social life, 'general–regulatory norms' requiring implementing legislation, 'norm–principles' defining the activities of state and social organizations, and 'norm-aims' setting forth overall programmatic objectives.[29] The issue came into sharp focus in mid-1979 when the country's leading law journal published side-by-side two artices that argued diametrically opposed views. According to one, all constitutional provisions were directly enforceable law, unless otherwise stipulated in the constitution, and the fact that a particular constitutional norm had not been 'concretized' in subsidiary legislation did not mean that the courts were not required to be guided by it in deciding concrete cases that came before them.[30] According to the other, 'no matter how progressive the point of view might seem that all constitutional provisions have direct legal force . . . it nevertheless cannot be accepted, for it fails to correspond to reality and to the very character of the Fundamental Law'.[31] The authors naturally supported their views with detailed arguments, but in our context these are less interesting than the fact that such basic controversies concerning the legal significance of constitutional provisions have remained unresolved to this day.

The new constitutions of the union republics, adopted in 1978, followed the text of the USSR constitution, as required under article 76 of the latter, with only minor variations, reflecting, in the main, differences in administrative–territorial arrangements.[32] One variation of a declarative character that should be mentioned is the inclusion in the preambles of the RSFSR, Ukrainian and Azerbaidzhani constitutions of a statement affirming that their peoples considered themselves 'an inalienable part of the whole Soviet people'. Why these declarations, which clearly place a further question mark behind the notional right of secession, were not included in the constitutions of the other twelve union republics is not known. Another variation concerns the provision for an official language in the constitutions of the three Transcaucasian republics – Georgia, Armenia and Azerbaidzhan. These were the only republics which in their previous constitutions had provisions designating the national language of each as the 'state language' of the republic. With a view to abolishing, or at least reducing, this positive discrimination, the draft constitutions of the three republics omitted this provision, replacing it, in the case of the Georgian and Armenian constitutions, with a clause guaranteeing the use of the national language in public institutions and promising 'state concern for its all-round development'. In Georgia and Armenia attachment to the national cultural heritage has always been particularly strong and the authorities apparently felt that, for these two republics, but not for Azerbaidzhan, some compensatory formula was called for. Even so, the proposed change gave rise to sharp protests in the two republics, including, in at least one instance, a public demonstration in the Georgian capital. Quite evidently in response to this the final texts of all three constitutions restored their respective national languages to their former status. Such open retreat in the face of public opposition was quite unprecedented in the annals of Soviet constitution-making and deserves to be noted for that reason no less than for the light which it throws on the continued sensitivity of the nationality question in Soviet politics.

Finally, it should be added that the 1977 constitution has had no discernible effect on the political practices of the Soviet regime or the status of its citizens. It is not necessary to revise anything said in chapter 3 about the actual working of the constitution, for the system continues to function in all its essentials very much as it did in the years preceding the adoption of the 1977 constitution. To mention only a few points: the 1979 elections to the Supreme Soviet, conducted under the new constitution and the new electoral law, produced the same massive majority as all previous elections;[33] the proceedings of the newly elected 10th Supreme Soviet have proved as predictable as those of its nine predecessors; the practice of legislating by joint party-government decrees has continued unchanged; and, most important, the liberties of the individual have remained as fragile under the new constitution as they were under the old.[34] In sum, whatever the long-run effects of the 1977 constitution may turn out to be, its immediate impact, on present evidence at least, can be dismissed as wholly negligible.

Notes

1 Quoted in G. Ginsburgs, 'A Khrushchev Constitution for the Soviet Union: Projects and Prospects', *Osteuropa – Recht*, 1962, no. 3, p. 192.

2 From the names of the speakers the identities of the chairmen of seven out of the nine sub-commissions could be inferred. They included, apart from Khrushchev, five other members of the party Presidium (Politburo): L.I. Brezhnev (sub-commission on state administration, activity of soviets and social organizations), G.I. Voronov (social and state structure), A.N. Kosygin (national economy), N.M. Shvernik (people's control and socialist legality), A.I. Mikoyan (nationality matters), CC Secretary B.N. Ponomarev (foreign policy), and Minister for Higher and Specialized Secondary Education, V.P. Yelyutin (science, culture, education and health). Khrushchev himself presumably headed the editorial sub-commission as well as the sub-commission on general political and theoretical questions.

3 Only the first sentence of the passage quoted on p. 176 above was allowed to stand. (L.I. Brezhnev, *Leninskim kursom*, 2 vols, Moscow, 1970, I. 434.)

4 It will be recalled that the last reported meeting of the constitutional commission took place in July 1964. There can be no doubt that the latest replenishment of the commission, less than four weeks before it was due to approve the new draft constitution, was little more than an attempt to put the gloss of procedural legitimacy on a largely finished product.

It may also be noted that in contrast to previous occasions this latest reorganization of the commission was authorized by the Presidium of the Supreme Soviet, rather than by the Supreme Soviet itself which merely confirmed the election by decree of 17 June. Moreover, the re-organization was not, as on previous occasions, announced in the press, but only in the official gazette of the Supreme Soviet. The general public learned of the commission's renewed existence on 24 May when the meeting of the previous day approving the draft constitution was announced.

A further sidelight on the lack of publicity, not to say secretiveness, with which such matters are handled in the Soviet Union, is shed by the fact that only a few days before the approval of the draft constitution was made public, *Pravda* carried two long articles on related themes neither of which made any mention of the new constitution. The first (on 13 May), by two legal scholars, contrasted 'bourgeois rights' with Soviet rights. The second (on 20 May), by USSR Minister of Justice, V. Terebilov (himself a newly-elected member of the constitutional commission), opened with the statement that the 'improvement of Soviet legislation has great socio-political significance in the life of our country' and devoted itself to showing that 'the creation of a reliable legal foundation for the society of mature socialism proceeds step by step'.

All quotations from Brezhnev's two reports on the constitution, to the May CC plenum and the October session of the Supreme Soviet, are, respectively, from the translated texts issued in booklet form by Novosti Press Agency: L.I. Brezhnev, *On the Draft Constitution of the Union of Soviet Socialist Republics*, Moscow, 1977, and L.I. Brezhnev, *On the Draft Constitution (Fundamental Law) of the Union of Soviet Socialist Republics and the Results of the Nationwide Discussion of the Draft*, Moscow, 1977.

5 The alterations referred to articles 12–16, 27, 35, 42, 46–7, 94 and 125. There can

be no doubt that they were prepared in advance as part of the 'script' for the Supreme Soviet proceedings.

6 To place the above in correct perspective two points should be briefly noted. First, as in other mass campaigns, much of this participation is most unlikely to have been entirely spontaneous. The Soviet regime disposes over many instrumentalities to induce and direct popular reaction to official policies and there is no reason to assume that they were not used in this case. Second, the above selection of proposals must not be taken as a representative sample. Many proposals published in the Soviet press were unreservedly laudatory; others sought stricter constitutional sanctions to combat various forms of social and political 'deviation', or pleaded for special interests – from car owners to inventors. For fuller, though necessarily still impressionistic, summaries of the proposals, readers may wish to consult *Radio Liberty Research Bulletin*, 1977, nos 185, 190, 208, 211, 226; R. Sharlet, 'The New Soviet Constitution', *Problems of Communism*, 1977, no. 5, pp. 1–24; E. Schneider, 'The Discussion of the New All-Union Constitution in the USSR', *Soviet Studies*, 1979, no. 4, pp. 523–41. Some findings of a Soviet survey of 'public opinion' on the draft constitution were published in D.A. Kerimov and Zh.T. Toshchenko, 'Konstitutsiya SSSR i razvitie sotsial'no-politicheskoi aktivnosti trudyashchikhsya', *Sotsiologicheskie issledovaniya*, 1978, no. 1, pp. 12–18.

7 F.I. Kalinychev, 'Osnovnye osobennosti sovetskoi sotsialisticheskoi Konstitutsii', *Sovetskoe gosudarstvo i pravo*, 1967, no. 11, p. 42.

8 The nationality context was acknowledged among others by Brezhnev in his speech to the Supreme Soviet of 4 October 1977:

As we know, a new higher community, the Soviet people, has taken shape in the USSR. Some comrades – it is true that they are not many – have drawn incorrect conclusions from this. They propose introducing the concept of a single Soviet *nation*, liquidating the union and autonomous republics or drastically restricting the sovereignty of the union republics, depriving them of the right to secede from the USSR and to have external relations (emphasis in the original).

9 The transformation of labour from 'a means of life' to 'life's prime want' constitutes one of Marx's best-known pronouncements on communist society. (K. Marx and F. Engels, *Selected Works*, 2 vols, Moscow, 1951, II, 23.)

10 The relevant passage from the Manifesto reads: 'In place of the old bourgeois society, with its classes and class antagonisms, we shall have an association, in which the free development of each is the condition for the free development of all.' (ibid., I, 54.)

11 J.V. Stalin, *Works*, 13 vols, Moscow, 1952–5, vol. 10, p. 296.

12 In an unwarranted departure from the Russian original the official English version of the final text, published by the Novosti Press Agency, rendered this as '*socialist* economic integration'. (*Constitution (Fundamental Law) of the Union of Soviet Socialist Republics*, Moscow, 1977.) The translation of the draft version put out by Tass was faithful to the original. (*The Times*, 6 June 1977.)

13 The right to lodge complaints is now regulated by the edict of the Supreme Soviet Presidium of 12 April 1968 'On the Procedure for Considering Proposals, Applications and Appeals of Citizens'; a revised version of this edict was issued on 4 March 1980. As to the courts' jurisdiction over administrative

decisions, see p. 122. State liability in tort was greatly expanded as part of the post-Stalin reforms of the civil law.

14 One such limitation is the exclusion of the CPSU from tort liability. (See D. Barry, 'Governmental Tort Liability in the Soviet Union', *Law in Eastern Europe*, vol. 17, 1970, esp. pp. 29–31, 74–6.) Special legislation regulating the liability of state organs of enquiry and preliminary investigation, as well as of the courts and the procuracy, was already envisaged by the 1961 Fundamentals of Civil Legislation, but has not yet been brought in.

With regard to the question of legal protection against administrative acts, it may be noted that article 58, paragraph 2 (and the corresponding mandate for further legislative regulation) served to revive discussion of this important subject in Soviet legal circles and with it the demand for improved and even general court supervision. English translations of some contributions to the discussion will be found in *Soviet Law and Government*, 1979, no. 1, pp. 28–60.

15 In his speech to the Supreme Soviet in October, Brezhnev claimed that over 700,000 electoral mandates had been implemented in the preceding two years. According to a report in *Izvestiya* of 2 March 1979, of 800,000 mandates to local soviets adopted in 1977, some 270,000 had been implemented by the end of 1978.

16 The first elections to the Supreme Soviet of the USSR under the new constitution and the electoral law of July 1978 were held on 4 March 1979.

17 A detailed study of the history and mode of operation of people's control in the USSR is J. S. Adams, *Citizen Inspectors in the Soviet Union*, New York, 1977.

18 For a most instructive account of some of the conflicting legal interpretations see D. Richard Little, 'Legislative Authority in the Soviet Political System' *Slavic Review*, 1971, no. 1, pp. 57–73.

19 The Council's composition is still fixed by law, however; it is now included in the law on the USSR Council of Ministers of July 1978. (An English translation will be found in *Current Digest of the Soviet Press*, 1978, no. 27, pp. 20–4, 27.)

20 See the account by a former Soviet lawyer, Y. Luryi, 'The Right to Counsel in Ordinary Criminal Cases in the USSR', in D.D. Barry, G. Ginsburgs and F.B. Maggs, eds., *Soviet Law after Stalin* (Part I: The Citizen and the State in Contemporary Soviet Law), Alphen aan den Rijn, 1977, pp. 106–7.

21 Translated from S.I. Rusinova and V.A. Rianzhin, eds., *Sovetskoe konstitut-sionnoe pravo*, Leningrad, 1975, pp. 60–1, in J.N. Hazard, W.E. Butler and P.B. Maggs, eds., *The Soviet Legal System*, 3rd edn, Dobbs Ferry, N.Y., 1977, p.54.

22 See, e.g., D.D. Barry, 'The Specialist in Soviet Policy-Making: The Adoption of a Law', *Soviet Studies*, 1964, no. 3, pp. 152–65; D.D. Barry and H.J. Berman, 'The Jurists', in H. Gordon Skilling and F. Griffiths, eds., *Interest Groups in Soviet Politics*, Princeton, 1971, pp. 291–333; P.H. Solomon, *Soviet Criminologists and Criminal Policy*, New York, 1978, passim.

23 Soviet jurists naturally participated very extensively in the 'nationwide discussion' during the summer of 1977. Our purpose here, however, requires us to confine ourselves to comments published prior to the release of the draft constitution, even though some of the subsequent comments offered interesting insights into Soviet legal thinking and may well have echoed antecedent controversies.

24 A. Denisov, 'Some Theoretical Problems of the Constitutional Structure of the Soviet State', translated in *Soviet Law and Government*, 1967, no. 4, pp. 20–5.

25 Romashkin's articles appeared in 1960 and 1961. A translation of the first article is in *Current Digest of the Soviet Press*, 1960, no. 40, pp. 3–7.

26 See R.J. Hill, 'Soviet Literature on Electoral Reform: A Review Article', *Government and Opposition*, 1976, no. 4, pp. 481–95. Typical of the way in which Soviet authors tackled this sensitive issue is the following passage from an article by A.I. Lepeshkin, a well-known legal scholar:

> The CPSU Programme states that the party considers it necessary to develop the democratic principles of the Soviet electoral system. With this as background, we should think about a certain improvement in present electoral practices that would enable voters to exercise their will better and more fully . . . . As is known, Soviet legislation on elections does not limit the number of candidates who can be nominated as deputies to the soviets. Nevertheless, the practice of elections to the soviets at all levels has evolved in such a way that the ballots for deputies list only one candidate. . . . Numerous articles and proposals . . . have raised the question of the advisability of allowing on the ballot not one but several candidates. . . . It goes without saying that the democratism of any electoral system is not measured solely by how many candidates are listed on the ballot, one or two; nevertheless, this question is not a secondary one.

27 See G. Hodnett, 'The Debate over Soviet Federalism', *Soviet Studies*, 1967, no. 2, pp. 458–81.

28 A recent Soviet emigrant, who was a member of Soviet legal research institutes involved in the drafting of the constitution in the early 1960s, reports that the right to secession was not included in the drafts circulated at the time. (A. Shtromas, 'The Legal Position of Soviet Nationalities and their Territorial Units According to the 1977 Constitution of the USSR', *Russian Review*, 1978, no. 3, p. 267.)

29 Yu. A. Tikhomirov, 'Problemy teorii sotsialisticheskoi Konstitutsii', *Sovetskoe gosudarstvo i pravo*, 1978, no. 2, pp. 3–11; for another such classificatory attempt see V.S. Osnovin, 'Osobennosti konstitutsionnykh norm', ibid., 1979, no. 4, pp. 12–19.

30 V.A. Perttsik and L.P. Shmailova, 'Realizatsiya konstitutsionnykh norm', ibid., no. 5, pp. 3–10.

31 N.S. Malein, 'Grazhdansko-pravovaya okhrana lichnosti v svete Konstitutsii SSSR', ibid., pp. 11–17.

32 The translated texts of the republican constitutions will be found in F.J.M. Feldbrugge, ed., *The Constitutions of the USSR and the Union Republics*, Aalphen an den Rijn, 1979.

33 For an analysis of the 1978 Law on Elections to the Supreme Soviet in the light of the new constitutional prescriptions see Ger P. van den Berg, 'A New Electoral Law in the Soviet Union', *Review of Socialist Law*, 1978, no. 4, pp. 353–62. The author's prediction that electoral practices under the new law would be similar to those under the old was fully borne out by the 1979 elections. Indeed, if the official returns are accepted at face value, the Soviet electorate edged even closer to total unanimity: the percentage of eligible voters who voted 'yes' for candidates to the Council of the Union rose to 99.89 and the absolute number of those who voted 'no' dropped to 185,522 (cf. p. 113).

34 The illegal exile of Academician A.D. Sakharov from Moscow to the 'closed'

city of Gorky in January 1980 attracted world-wide attention because of the victim's reputation as a scientist and Nobel Peace Prize laureate, but it was only one instance of the continuing repression of all forms of dissent in the Soviet Union.

The USSR Constitution of 1977

Constitution (Fundamental Law) of the Union of Soviet Socialist Republics

[Adopted at the Extraordinary Seventh Session of the Supreme Soviet on 7 October 1977][1]

The Great October socialist revolution carried out by the workers and peasants of Russia under the leadership of the Communist Party headed by V.I. Lenin, overthrew the power of the capitalists and landowners, broke the fetters of oppression, *established the dictatorship of the proletariat* and created the Soviet state – a new type of state and the basic instrument for the defence of the gains of the revolution and the construction of socialism and communism. *The world-historic turn of mankind from capitalism to socialism began*.

Having achieved victory in the civil war and having repulsed imperialist intervention, Soviet power carried out the most profound social and economic transformations, and put an end for ever to the exploitation of man by man, to class antagonisms and national enmity. *The unification of the Soviet republics in the Union of SSR multiplied the forces and potentialities of the peoples of the country in the construction of socialism*. Social ownership of the means of production and genuine democracy for the toiling masses were established. For the first time in the history of mankind a socialist society was created.

The unfading exploit of the Soviet people and their Armed Forces in achieving the historic victory of the Great Patriotic War was a vivid demonstration of the strength of socialism. This victory strengthened the *authority and* international position of the USSR and opened up new favourable possibilities for the growth of the forces of socialism, national liberation, democracy and peace in the entire world.

Continuing their creative activity, the *toilers of the Soviet Union*[2] have ensured the country's rapid and all-round development and the improvement of the socialist order. The alliance of the working class, the collective farm peasantry and the people's intelligentsia and the friendship of the nations and nationalities of the USSR have been consolidated. The socio-political *and ideological* unity of Soviet society, of which the working class is the leading force, has been attained. Having fulfilled the tasks of the dictatorship of the proletariat, the Soviet state has become an all-people's state. The leading role of the Communist Party, the vanguard of the entire people, has grown.

A developed socialist society has been built in the USSR. At this stage, when socialism is [already] developing on its own foundation, the creative forces of the new order and the advantages of the socialist way of life are revealing themselves ever more fully and the toilers are ever more widely enjoying the fruits of their great revolutionary gains.

This is a society in which mighty productive forces and an advanced science and culture have been created, in which the well-being of the people is constantly growing and ever more favourable conditions for the all-round development of the individual are taking shape.

This is a society of mature socialist social relations, in which a new historical community of people, the Soviet people, has been formed on the basis of the drawing together of all *classes and* social strata and the legal and actual equality of all nations and nationalities *and their fraternal cooperation*.

This is a society with a high degree of organization, ideological commitment and consciousness of the toilers – of patriots and internationalists.

This is a society in which the concern of all for the welfare of each and the concern of each for the welfare of all is the law of life.

This is a society of genuine democracy, the political system of which ensures the effective administration of all public affairs, the ever more active participation of the toilers in the life of the state and the combination of real *citizens' rights and freedoms with their duties and responsibility to society*.[3]

The developed socialist society is an objectively necessary stage on the path to communism.

The highest goal of the Soviet state is the building of a classless communist society *in which social communist self-administration will be developed*. The principal tasks of the *socialist all-people's* state are: creating the material and technical base of communism, improving socialist social relations and transforming them into communist relations, rearing the man of communist society, raising the material and cultural standard of life of the toilers, ensuring the security of the country, and furthering the consolidation of peace and the development of international cooperation.

The Soviet people,

guided by the ideas of scientific communism and remaining true to their revolutionary traditions,

relying on the great socio-economic and political gains of socialism,

striving toward the further development of socialist democracy,

taking into account the international position of the USSR as an integral part of the world system of socialism, and conscious of their international responsibility, preserving the continuity of the ideas and principles of the *first Soviet constitution of 1918*,[4] the 1924 Constitution of the USSR and the 1936 Constitution of the USSR,

affirm the fundamentals of the social order and policy of the USSR, establish the rights, freedoms and duties of citizens and the principles of organization and aims of the socialist all-people's state and proclaim them in this Constitution.[5]

I Fundamentals of the Social Order and Policy of the USSR[6]

Chapter 1 The Political System

Article 1 The Union of Soviet Socialist Republics is a socialist all-people's state, expressing the will and interests of the *workers, peasants*[7] and intelligentsia, *the toilers* of all the nations and nationalities of the country.

Article 2 All power in the USSR shall belong to the people.

The people shall exercise state power through soviets of people's deputies, which shall constitute the political foundation of the USSR.

All other state organs shall be under the control of and accountable to the soviets *of people's deputies*.

Article 3 The organization and activity of the Soviet state shall be constructed in conformity with the principle of democratic centralism: the electivity of all organs of state power from top to bottom, their accountability to the people, and the binding nature of decisions of higher-ranking organs for lower-ranking ones. Democratic centralism shall combine unified direction with local initiative and creative activism and the responsibility of each state organ and official for the business entrusted to them.

Article 4 The Soviet state and all its organs shall operate on the basis of socialist legality and ensure the protection of the legal order, and the rights *and freedoms* of citizens.

State [institutions] and social organizations and officials shall be obliged to observe the Constitution of the USSR and Soviet laws.

Article 5 The most important matters of state life shall be submitted for nationwide discussion and also to a nationwide vote (referendum).

Article 6 The Communist Party of the Soviet Union shall be the guiding and directing force of Soviet society, the core of its political system and of [all] state and social organizations. The CPSU shall exist for the people and shall serve the people.

Armed with the Marxist-Leninist teaching, the Communist Party shall determine the general perspective of the development of society and the lines of the internal and foreign policy of the USSR, direct the great creative activity of the Soviet people, and impart a planned, scientifically-founded character to its struggle for the victory of communism.[8]

All party organizations shall operate within the framework of the Constitution of the USSR.

Article 7   Trade unions, the All-Union Leninist Communist Youth League, cooperative, and other [mass] social organizations shall, in accordance with the tasks set out in their charters, take part in the administration of state and social affairs and in deciding political, economic, and socio-cultural questions.

Article 8   *Labour collectives shall participate in the discussion and deciding of state and social affairs, in the planning of production and social development, in the training and placing of personnel, and in the discussion and deciding of questions of the administration of enterprises and institutions, the improvement of working and living conditions, the use of funds earmarked for the development of production, and also for socio-cultural measures and material incentives.*

Labour collectives shall develop socialist competition, further the dissemination of progressive work methods and the strengthening of labour discipline, rear their members in the spirit of communist morality, and concern themselves with raising their political consciousness, culture, and professional qualifications.[9]

Article 9   The further unfolding of socialist democracy shall be the basic direction of the development of the political system of Soviet society: ever broader participation of *citizens*[10] in the administration of the affairs of *the state and society,*[11] improvement of the state apparatus, increasing the activity of social organizations, intensifying people's control, strengthening the legal basis of state and social life, expanding publicity and constant consideration for public opinion.

Chapter 2 The Economic System

Article 10   Socialist ownership of the means of production *in the form of state (all-people's) and collective farm-cooperative ownership* shall constitute the foundation of the economic system of the USSR.

The property of trade unions and other social organizations needed by them to carry out the tasks set out in their charters shall also be in socialist ownership.[12]

The state shall protect socialist ownership and create the conditions for its increase.

No one shall have the right to use socialist ownership for the purpose of personal gain *and other selfish ends.*

Article 11   State ownership, the common wealth of the entire Soviet people, shall be the basic form of socialist ownership.

There shall be in the exclusive ownership of the state: the land, its minerals, the waters and forests. The basic means of production *in industry, construction, and agriculture*, means of transport and communication, banks, *the property of trade, municipal, and other enterprises organized by the state*, the bulk of urban housing, *and also other property needed to carry out the state's tasks*, shall belong to the state.[13]

Article 12 The property of collective farms and other cooperative organizations, and their associations, shall comprise the means of production and other property *needed by them*[14] to carry out the tasks set out in their charters.

The land occupied by collective farms shall be allotted to them free of charge for use for an unlimited time.[15]

The state shall promote the development of collective farm-cooperative ownership and its drawing together with state ownership.

The collective farms, like other land users, shall be obliged to use the land effectively, to treat it carefully, and to increase its fertility.[16]

Article 13 *Earned income shall constitute the basis of personal ownership of citizens of the USSR. Articles of everyday use, personal consumption and convenience, subsidiary household husbandry, a dwelling house, and earned savings may be in personal ownership. The personal property of citizens and the right to inherit it shall be protected by the state.*[17]

Citizens may have the use of plots of land granted [by the state or by the collective farms] in a procedure established by law for subsidiary husbandry (including the keeping of livestock and poultry), gardening, and vegetable growing, and also for individual housing construction. *Citizens shall be obliged to make rational use of the land plots granted to them. The state and the collective farms shall render assistance to citizens in the running of subsidiary husbandry.*

Property in the personal ownership *or*[18] use of citizens *must not*[19] serve to derive unearned income or be used *to the detriment of the interests of society.*[20]

Article 14 The [free] labour of the Soviet people, *free from exploitation*, shall be the source of the growth of social wealth and of the well-being of the people and every Soviet person.

In accordance with the principle *of socialism*: 'From each according to his ability, to each according to his work', the state shall exercise control over the measure of labour and consumption. It shall determine the amount of tax on incomes *subject to taxation.*[21]

Socially useful labour and its results shall determine a person's position in society. The state shall, by combining material and moral incentives, *encouraging innovation and a creative attitude toward work*, promote the transformation of labour into the primary vital need of every Soviet person.

Article 15   The supreme goal of social production under socialism shall be the fullest satisfaction of the growing material and spiritual needs of the people.

Relying on the creative activity of the toilers, socialist competition, and the achievements of scientific-technical progress, *and improving the forms and methods of the direction of the economy*, the state shall ensure the growth of labour productivity, the increase in production efficiency and work quality, and the dynamic, *planned*, and proportional development of the national economy.

Article 16   The economy of the USSR shall constitute a single national economic complex embracing all links of social production, distribution, and exchange in the territory of the country.

The direction of the economy shall be carried out on the basis of state plans for *economic and social development*,[22] taking into account branch and territorial principles and combining centralized *administration*[23] with the economic independence and initiative of enterprises, associations, and other organizations, and active use being made of economic accountability, profit, cost *and other economic levers and incentives*.

Article 17   In the USSR individual labour activity shall be permitted in accordance with the law in the sphere of handicrafts, agriculture, everyday services for the population, and also other forms of [labour] activity based exclusively on the personal labour of citizens and members of their families. *The state shall regulate individual labour activity, ensuring its use in the interests of society*.

Article 18   In the interests of present and future generations, necessary measures shall be taken in the USSR for the protection, and the scientifically-founded, rational utilization of the land and its minerals, *water resources*, flora and fauna, for the preservation of the purity of air and water, for ensuring the reproduction of natural wealth, and the improvement of man's environment.

Chapter 3 Social Development and Culture

Article 19   *The indestructible alliance of workers, peasants, and intelligentsia shall constitute the social foundation of the USSR*.

The [Soviet] state shall further the strengthening of the social homogeneity of society: the eradication *of class differences and* of substantial differences between town and country and intellectual and physical labour, and the *all-round*[24] development and drawing together of all nations and nationalities of the USSR.

Article 20   In accordance with the communist ideal, 'The free development of each is the condition for the free development of all', the [Soviet] state shall have as its aim the expansion of the real possibilities for the [development and] application by citizens of their creative forces, abilities, and talents, for the all-round development of the individual.

Article 21 The state shall concern itself with the improvement of conditions *and protection* of labour, and *its scientific organization*, and with the reduction and, eventually, the complete abolition of arduous *physical*[25] labour on the basis of the complex mechanization and automation of production *processes in all branches of the national economy*.

Article 22 The USSR shall consistently implement a programme for transforming agricultural labour into a variety of industrial labour; expanding the network of institutions in rural localities for public education, culture, public health, trade *and public catering*, everyday services, and municipal economy; and the transformation of hamlets and villages into well-appointed settlements.

Article 23 *On the basis of*[26] the growth of labour productivity, the state shall steadfastly pursue the policy of raising the level of payment for labour and the real incomes of the toilers.

Social consumption funds shall be created with a view to the more complete satisfaction of the requirements of *the Soviet people*.[27] With the broad participation of social organizations and labour collectives, the state shall ensure the growth and just distribution of these funds.

Article 24 State systems of public health, social security, *trade and* public catering, everyday services and municipal economy shall operate and be developed in the USSR.

The state shall encourage the activity of cooperative and other social organizations in *all spheres*[28] of services for the population. *It shall promote the development of mass physical culture and sport*.

Article 25 In the USSR a uniform system of *public* education shall exist *and be improved*; it shall *provide general education and professional training for citizens*, serve communist upbringing, the spiritual and physical development of youth, and *prepare them*[29] for labour and social activity. [Education in the USSR shall be free.]

Article 26 In conformity with the requirements of society, the state shall ensure the planned development of science and the training of scientific personnel, and organize the introduction of the results of scientific research into the national economy and into other spheres of life.

Article 27 The state shall concern itself with the protection, increase and extensive utilization of spiritual values [of society] for *the moral and aesthetic upbringing and* the raising of the cultural level of the Soviet people.

The development of professional art and the artistic creativity of the people shall be encouraged in the USSR in every way.

Chapter 4 Foreign Policy

Article 28 *The USSR shall steadfastly*[30] pursue the Leninist policy of peace and stand for the consolidation of the security of peoples and broad international cooperation.

The foreign policy of the USSR shall be aimed at ensuring favourable international conditions for the building of communism in the USSR, *defending the state interests of the Soviet Union*, strengthening the position of world socialism, supporting the struggle of peoples for national liberation and social progress, preventing aggressive wars, *achieving general and complete disarmament*, and consistently implementing the principle of peaceful coexistence of states with different social systems.

War propaganda shall be prohibited in the USSR [by law].

Article 29 Relations of the USSR with other states shall be built on the basis of the observance of the principles of *sovereign equality; mutual renunciation of the use of force or threat of force;*[31] inviolability of frontiers; territorial integrity of states; peaceful settlement of disputes; noninterference in internal affairs; respect for human rights and fundamental freedoms; equality and the right of peoples to decide their own destiny; cooperation among states; fulfilment in good faith of obligations arising from generally recognized principles and norms of international law and from international treaties concluded by the USSR.

Article 30 The USSR, as an integral part of the world system of socialism and the socialist community, shall develop and strengthen friendship, cooperation and comradely mutual assistance with the countries of socialism on the basis *of the principle* of socialist internationalism and shall participate actively in economic integration and in the international socialist division of labour.

Chapter 5 Defence of the Socialist Fatherland

Article 31 Defence of the socialist fatherland *shall be among the most important functions*[32] of the state *and shall be* the cause of the whole people.

For the purpose of defending socialist gains, the peaceful labour of the Soviet people, and the sovereignty and territorial integrity of the state, the *Armed Forces of the USSR have been created*[33] and military service established.

The duty of the Armed Forces of the USSR to the people shall be to provide reliable defence of the socialist fatherland, to be in constant combat readiness, guaranteeing an immediate rebuff to any aggressor.

Article 32 The state shall ensure the security and defence capability of the country and equip the Armed Forces of the USSR with everything necessary.

The duties of state organs, social organizations, officials, and citizens in ensuring the security of the country and strengthening its defence capability shall be determined by *legislation of the Union of SSR*.[34]

II The State and the Individual

Chapter 6 Citizenship of the USSR – Equality of Citizens

Article 33   *A single union citizenship has been established in the USSR*.[35] Every citizen of a union republic shall be a citizen of the USSR.

The grounds and procedure for the acquisition and loss of Soviet citizenship shall be *determined by the Law on Citizenship of the USSR*.[36]

Citizens of the USSR abroad shall enjoy the defence and protection of the Soviet state.

Article 34   Citizens of the USSR shall be equal before the law irrespective of origin, social and property position, racial and national affiliation, sex, education, language, attitude to religion, type and nature of occupation, place of residence, and other circumstances.

The equality of rights of citizens of the USSR shall be ensured in all fields of economic, political, social, and cultural life.

Article 35   *Women and men shall have equal rights in the USSR*.[37]

The exercise of these rights shall be ensured by granting women equal opportunities *with men* for education and professional training, employment, remuneration and promotion, socio-political and cultural activity, and also by special labour and health protection measures for women; *by the creation of conditions allowing women to combine work with motherhood*; by legal protection and material and moral support for mothers and children, including the granting of paid vacations and other benefits for pregnant women and mothers, [state assistance to single mothers] *and a gradual reduction of working time for women with small children*.

Article 36   USSR citizens of different races and nationalities shall have equal rights.

The exercise of these rights shall be ensured by the policy for the all-round development and drawing together of all nations and nationalities of the USSR, the bringing up of citizens in the spirit of Soviet patriotism and socialist internationalism, and the possibility to use the native language and the languages of other peoples of the USSR.

Any direct or indirect restriction of rights or the establishment of direct or indirect privileges for citizens on grounds of race or nationality, and equally any advocacy of racial or national exclusiveness, hostility or contempt, shall be punished by law.

Article 37   Foreign citizens and stateless persons in the USSR shall be guaranteed the rights and freedoms provided by law, including the right to turn to a court and to other state organs in order to defend personal, property, family, and other rights belonging to them [by law].

Foreign citizens and stateless persons on the territory of the USSR shall be obliged to respect the Constitution of the USSR and to observe Soviet laws.

Article 38   The USSR shall grant the right of asylum to foreigners perse-cuted for defending the interests of the toilers and the cause of peace, for participating in the revolutionary and national liberation movement, and for progressive socio-political, scientific, or other creative activity.

Chapter 7 The Fundamental Rights, Freedoms and Duties of Citizens of the USSR

Article 39   Citizens of the USSR shall possess in full the socio-economic, political, and personal rights and freedoms proclaimed and guaranteed by the Constitution of the USSR and Soviet laws. The socialist system shall ensure the expansion of rights and freedoms, the uninterrupted improvement in the conditions of life of citizens in step with the fulfil-ment of programmes for socio-economic and cultural development.

The exercise by citizens of rights and freedoms must not harm the interests of society and the state or the rights of other citizens.

Article 40   Citizens of the USSR shall have the right to work, that is, to guaranteed employment with payment for work in conformity with its quantity and quality *and not below the minimum established by the state*, including the right to choose a profession, type of occupation and work in accordance with their vocation, abilities, professional training and education, taking account of social requirements.

This right shall be ensured by the socialist economic system, the steady growth of the productive forces [of society], free vocational train-ing, the improvement of work skills, the training in new specialities, *and the development of systems of vocational guidance and job placement*.

Article 41   Citizens of the USSR shall have the right to rest and leisure.

This right shall be ensured *by the establishment for workers and employees of a work week not exceeding forty-one hours*,[38] a reduced work day for a number of professions and production sectors and shorter hours for night work; by granting annual paid vacations, weekly days of rest, and also expanding the network of cultural-enlightenment and health-care institutions, the development of mass sport, physical culture, and tour-ism; the creation of favourable possibilities for rest and leisure at places of residence and other conditions for the rational utilization of free time.

The duration of work time and of rest and leisure for collective farmers shall be regulated by the [charters of] collective farms.

Article 42   Citizens of the USSR shall have the right to health protection.

This right shall be ensured by free professional medical care rendered by state health institutions; by the expansion of the network of institutions providing medical treatment and improving the health of citizens; by the development and improvement of safety techniques and production sanitation; by the implementation of extensive prophylactic measures; by measures for improving the environment; by special concern for the health of the growing generation, including the prohibition of child labour *not connected with study and labour upbringing*; by the development of scientific research directed at preventing and reducing the incidence of disease and ensuring a long active life for citizens.

Article 43   Citizens of the USSR shall have the right to material security in old age, in the event of illness, and also in the event of complete or partial loss of the capacity to work or loss of the breadwinner.

This right shall be guaranteed by social insurance for workers, employees and collective farmers, *and by temporary disability allowances; by payment by the state and collective farms of old-age and invalid pensions and pensions for loss of breadwinner;*[39] by job placement for partially disabled citizens; by care for [single] elderly citizens and invalids; *and by other forms of social security.*

Article 44   Citizens of the USSR shall have the right to housing.

This right shall be ensured by the development and protection of state and social housing, the promotion of cooperative and individual housing construction, the just distribution, under social control, of housing space allocated in step with the implementation of the construction programme for *comfortable* dwellings, and also by low rents *and low charges for communal services. Citizens of the USSR must take good care of the housing allocated to them.*

Article 45   Citizens of the USSR shall have the right to education.

This right shall be ensured by free education of all types, the implementation of universal compulsory secondary education for the young, the extensive development of vocational-technical, secondary specialized, and higher education on the basis of linking study with life and production; by the development of correspondence and evening education; by the granting of state stipends and [other] benefits to pupils and students; by the issue of school textbooks free of charge; by the possibility of school instruction in the native language, [and the development of a system of vocational guidance] and the creation of conditions for [the toilers'] self-education.

Article 46   Citizens of the USSR shall have the right to benefit from the achievements of culture.

This right shall be ensured through popular access to the values of Soviet and world culture in state and social collections; by the development and equitable geographic distribution of cultural-enlightenment institutions in the territory of the country; *by the development of television and radio, book publishing and the periodical press, and a network of free libraries;* and by the expansion of cultural exchange with foreign states.

Article 47   Citizens of the USSR shall, in conformity with the aims of communist construction, be guaranteed freedom of scientific, technical, and artistic creativity. This freedom shall be ensured by the extensive development of scientific research, invention and rationalization activity, and the development of *literature and* art. The state shall create the necessary material conditions and render support to voluntary societies and unions of creative artists, *and organize the introduction of inventions and rationalization proposals into the national economy and into other spheres of life*.

The rights of authors, inventors, and rationalizers shall be protected by *the state*.[40]

Article 48   Citizens of the USSR shall have the right to participate in the administration of state and social affairs *and in the discussion and adoption of laws and decisions of all-state and local significance*.

This right shall be ensured by the opportunity to elect and to be elected to soviets of people's deputies and other elective state organs, to take part in nationwide discussions and voting, in people's control, in the work of state organs, social organizations, and public initiative organs, and in meetings of labour collectives and meetings at places of residence.[41]

Article 49   Every citizen of the USSR shall have the right to submit proposals to state organs and social organizations concerning the improvement of their activity and to criticize shortcomings in their work.

Officials shall be obliged, within *established time limits*,[42] to consider proposals and applications of citizens, to reply to them, and to take the necessary measures.

Persecution for criticism shall be prohibited. *Persons who persecute for criticism shall be called to account*.

Article 50   In conformity with the interests of the *people*[43] and in order to strengthen *and develop* the socialist system, citizens of the USSR shall be guaranteed freedom of speech, press, assembly, meetings, street processions, and demonstrations.

The exercise of these political freedoms shall be ensured by placing public buildings, streets and squares at the disposal of the toilers and their organizations, and by the extensive dissemination of information, and the opportunity to use the press, television and radio.

Article 51   In conformity with the aims of communist construction, citizens of the USSR shall have the right to unite in social organizations which further the development of political activity and initiative and the satisfaction of their diverse interests.

Social organizations shall be guaranteed conditions for the successful fulfilment of the tasks set forth in their charters.

Article 52 *Citizens of the USSR shall be guaranteed freedom of conscience*,[44] that is, the right to profess any religion or none, to perform religious worship, or to conduct atheist propaganda. Incitement to hostility and hatred in connection with religious beliefs shall be prohibited.

The church in the USSR shall be separated from the state, and the school from the church.

Article 53 The family shall be under the protection of the state.

Marriage shall be *based upon*[45] the voluntary consent of the woman and the man; the spouses shall be completely equal in family relations.

The state shall *display concern for*[46] the family through the creation and development of an extensive network of children's institutions, the organization and improvement of everyday and public catering services, the payment of an allowance for the birth of a child, the provision of allowances and benefits to families with many children, *and also other types of allowances and assistance to the family*.

Article 54 Citizens of the USSR shall be guaranteed inviolability of the person. No one may be subjected to arrest except *on the basis of a court decision*[47] or with the sanction of a procurator.

Article 55 Citizens of the USSR shall be guaranteed inviolability of the home. No one shall have the right to enter a home without legal grounds against the will of the persons residing therein.

Article 56 The private life of citizens, and the secrecy of correspondence, telephone conversations and telegraph communications shall be protected by law.

Article 57 Respect for the individual and the protection of the rights and freedoms of *citizens*[48] shall be the duty of all state organs, social organizations and officials.

Citizens of the USSR shall have the right to judicial protection against attempts on their *honour and dignity, life and health, and personal freedom and property*.[49]

Article 58 Citizens of the USSR shall have the right to lodge complaints against the actions of officials *and state and social organs*.[50] The complaints must be considered in the procedure and within the time limits established by law.

The actions of officials that violate the law or exceed their powers, and infringe the rights of citizens may be appealed to a court in the procedure established by law.

Citizens of the USSR shall have the right to compensation for damage caused by the illegal actions of state [institutions] and social organizations, or officials in the performance of their duties [in the procedure and within the limits established by law].

Article 59   The exercise of rights and freedoms shall be inseparable from the performance by a citizen of his duties.

A citizen of the USSR shall be obliged to observe the USSR Constitution and Soviet laws, respect the rules of socialist community life, and bear with dignity the lofty title of citizen of the USSR.

Article 60   Conscientious work in one's chosen field of socially useful activity and the [strict] observance of labour [and production] discipline shall be the duty of, and a matter of honour for, every able-bodied Soviet citizen. *The evasion of socially useful work is incompatible with the principles of socialist society*.

Article 61   A citizen of the USSR shall be obliged to preserve and strengthen socialist ownership. The duty of a citizen of the USSR shall be to struggle against theft and waste of state and social property *and to treat the people's wealth with proper care*.

Persons encroaching on socialist ownership shall be punished according to the law.

Article 62   A citizen of the USSR shall be obliged to safeguard the interests of the Soviet state and to further the strengthening of its might and authority.

Defence of the socialist fatherland shall be the sacred duty of every citizen of the USSR.

Treason to the motherland shall be the gravest crime against the people.

Article 63   Military service in the ranks of the USSR Armed Forces shall be the honourable duty of Soviet citizens.

Article 64   It shall be the duty of every citizen of the USSR to respect the national dignity of other citizens and to strengthen the friendship of the nations and nationalities of the Soviet multinational state.

Article 65   A citizen of the USSR shall be obliged to respect the rights and lawful interests of other persons, to be intolerant of anti-social acts and to promote the protection of public order in every way.

Article 66   Citizens of the USSR shall be obliged to be concerned about the upbringing of children, to prepare them for socially useful labour, and to raise worthy members of socialist society. *Children shall be obliged to be concerned about parents and to assist them*.

Article 67   Citizens of the USSR shall be obliged to conserve nature and to protect its riches.

Article 68   Concern for the preservation of historical monuments and other cultural values shall be a duty *and obligation* of citizens of the USSR.[51]

Article 69 The internationalist duty of a citizen of the USSR shall be to promote the development of friendship and cooperation with the peoples of other countries and the maintenance and strengthening of world peace.

III   The National-State Structure of the USSR

Chapter 8 The USSR – A Union State

Article 70 The Union of Soviet Socialist Republics shall be a single union multinational state formed *on the basis of the principle of socialist federalism* as a result of the free self-determination of nations and the voluntary association of equal Soviet socialist republics.

The USSR shall embody the state unity of the Soviet people and unite all nations and nationalities for the purpose of the joint construction of communism.

Article 71 There shall be associated in the Union of Soviet Socialist Republics:

the Russian Soviet Federated Socialist Republic,
the Ukrainian Soviet Socialist Republic,
the Belorussian Soviet Socialist Republic,
the Uzbek Soviet Socialist Republic,
the Kazakh Soviet Socialist Republic,
the Georgian Soviet Socialist Republic,
the Azerbaidzhan Soviet Socialist Republic,
the Lithuanian Soviet Socialist Republic,
the Moldavian Soviet Socialist Republic,
the Latvian Soviet Socialist Republic,
the Kirghiz Soviet Socialist Republic,
the Tadzhik Soviet Socialist Republic,
the Armenian Soviet Socialist Republic,
the Turkmen Soviet Socialist Republic,
the Estonian Soviet Socialist Republic.

Article 72 Every union republic shall retain the right of free secession from the USSR.

Article 73 The jurisdiction of the Union of Soviet Socialist Republics as embodied in its highest organs of state power and administration shall include:

(1) admission of new republics into the USSR; approval of the

formation of new autonomous republics and autonomous regions within union republics;

(2) determination of the state frontier of the USSR and approval of modifications of boundaries between union republics;

(3) establishment of general principles for the organization and activity of republic and local organs of state power and administration;

(4) ensuring the unity of legislative regulation throughout the territory of the USSR, the establishment of the fundamentals of legislation of the Union of SSR and the union republics;

(5) implementation of a uniform socio-economic policy and direction of the economy of the country; determination of the basic directions of scientific and technical progress *and general measures for the rational utilization and protection of natural resources*; the working out and approval of *state plans for the economic and social development*[52] of the USSR and the approval of reports on their fulfilment;

(6) working out and approval of a single state budget for the USSR and approval of the report on its execution; direction of a single monetary and credit system; establishment of taxes and revenues which go to form the *USSR state budget*;[53] determination of policy in the field of prices and wages;

(7) direction of the branches of the national economy, associations and enterprises of union subordination; general direction of branches, [associations and enterprises] of union-republic subordination;

(8) questions of peace and war, defence of sovereignty, protection of the state frontiers and territory of the USSR, organization of defence and direction of the Armed Forces *of the USSR*;

(9) ensuring state security;

(10) representation of the USSR in international relations; links of the USSR with foreign states and international organizations; establishment of the general procedure for, and coordination of, the relations of union republics with foreign states and international organizations; foreign trade *and other types of external economic activity* on the basis of state monopoly;

(11) control over the observance of the USSR Constitution and ensuring the conformity of the union republic constitutions to the Constitution of the USSR;

(12) deciding other questions of all-union significance.

Article 74 The laws of the USSR shall have the same force on the territory of all union republics. In the event of a divergence between a union republic law and an all-union law, the law of the USSR shall prevail.

Article 75 The territory of the Union of Soviet Socialist Republics shall be a single entity and shall include the territories of the union republics. The sovereignty of the USSR shall extend throughout its territory.

Chapter 9 The Soviet Socialist Union Republic

Article 76 The union republic shall be a *sovereign* Soviet socialist state which has united with other Soviet republics in the Union of Soviet Socialist Republics.

Outside the limits specified in article 73 of the Constitution of the USSR, a union republic shall exercise state power independently in its territory.

A union republic shall have its own constitution conforming to the Constitution of the USSR and taking into account the specific features of the republic.

Article 77 A union republic shall participate in the Supreme Soviet of the USSR, the Presidium of the Supreme Soviet of the USSR, the Government of the USSR, and other organs of the USSR, in deciding matters that come within the jurisdiction of the USSR.

A union republic shall *ensure integrated economic and social development in its territory*, further the exercise of the powers of the USSR in *this*[54] territory, and implement the decisions of the *highest* organs of state power and administration of the USSR.

In matters that come within its jurisdiction, a union republic shall coordinate and control the activity of enterprises, institutions, and organizations of union subordination.

Article 78 The territory of a union republic may not be modified without its consent. The boundaries between union republics may be modified by mutual agreement of the respective republics, subject to approval by the USSR.

Article 79 A union republic shall determine its division into territories, regions, areas and districts and decide other questions of administrative and territorial structure.

Article 80 A union republic shall have the right to enter into relations with foreign states, conclude treaties with them and exchange diplomatic and consular representatives, and to participate in the activity of international organizations.

Article 81 The sovereign rights of the union republics shall be protected by the USSR.

Chapter 10 The Autonomous Soviet Socialist Republic

Article 82 An autonomous republic shall be a part of a union republic.

Outside the limits of the rights of the USSR and the union republic, an autonomous republic shall independently decide matters that come within its jurisdiction.

An autonomous republic shall have its own Constitution conforming to the Constitution of the USSR and the union republic Constitution and taking into account the specific features of the autonomous republic.

Article 83 An autonomous republic shall participate in deciding matters that come within the jurisdiction of the USSR and the union republic through the highest organs of state power and administration of the USSR and union republic, respectively.

An autonomous republic shall *ensure integrated economic and social development in its territory*, further the exercise of the powers of the USSR and union republic in *this*[55] territory, and implement the decisions of the *highest* organs of state power and administration of the USSR and the union republic.

In matters that come within its jurisdiction, an autonomous republic shall coordinate and control the activity of enterprises, institutions, and organizations of all-union and republic (union republic) subordination.

Article 84 The territory of an autonomous republic may not be modified without its consent.

Article 85 The Russian Soviet Federated Socialist Republic shall include the Bashkir, Buryat, Daghestan, Kabardino-Balkar, Kalmyk, Karelian, Komi, Mari, Mordovian, North Ossetian, Tatar, Tuva, Udmurt, Chechen-Ingush, Chuvash and Yakut autonomous soviet socialist republics.

The Uzbek Soviet Socialist Republic shall include the Kara-Kalpak Autonomous Soviet Socialist Republic.

The Georgian Soviet Socialist Republic shall include the Abkhaz and Adzhar autonomous soviet socialist republics.

The Azerbaidzhan Soviet Socialist Republic shall include the Nakhichevan Autonomous Soviet Socialist Republic.

Chapter 11 The Autonomous Region and Autonomous Area

Article 86 An autonomous region shall be a part of a union republic *or territory*. A law on an autonomous region shall be adopted by the Supreme Soviet of the union republic upon the recommendation of the soviet of people's deputies of the autonomous region.

Article 87 The Russian Soviet Federated Socialist Republic shall include the Adygei, Gorno-Altai, Jewish, Karachai-Cherkess and Khakass autonomous regions.

The Georgian Soviet Socialist Republic shall include the South Ossetian autonomous region.

The Azerbaidzhan Soviet Socialist Republic shall include the Nagorno-Karabakh autonomous region.

The Tadzhik Soviet Socialist Republic shall include the Gorno-Badakhshan autonomous region.

Article 88   An autonomous area shall be a part of a territory or region. A *law*[56] on autonomous areas shall be *adopted*[57] by the Supreme Soviet of the union republic.

IV   Soviets of People's Deputies and the Procedure for Their Election

Chapter 12 The System and Principles of Activity of Soviets of People's Deputies

Article 89   Soviet's of people's deputies – the Supreme Soviet of the USSR, the Supreme Soviets of union republics, the Supreme Soviets of autonomous republics, territory and regional soviets of people's deputies, autonomous region and autonomous area soviets of people's deputies, district, town, borough, settlement, and rural soviets of people's deputies – shall constitute a single system of organs of state power.

Article 90   The term of the Supreme Soviet of the USSR and the Supreme Soviets of union republics and autonomous republics shall be five years.

The term of *local soviets of people's deputies*[58] shall be two-and-a-half years.

Elections to soviets of people's deputies shall be called not later than two months before the expiry of the term of the respective soviets.

Article 91   The most important matters that come within the jurisdiction of the respective soviets of people's deputies shall be considered and decided at their sessions.

Soviets of people's deputies shall elect standing commissions and create executive and administrative and also other organs accountable to them.

Article 92   Soviets of people's deputies shall form people's control organs, combining state control with social control of the toilers at enterprises, collective farms, institutions and organizations.

The people's control organs shall supervise the fulfilment of state plans and tasks, combat violations of state discipline, manifestations of localism, a departmental approach to matters, mismanagement, wastefulness, red tape, and bureaucratism, and promote the improvement of the work of the state apparatus.

[The procedure for the organization and activity of the people's control organs shall be determined by law.]

Article 93 Soviets of people's deputies shall, directly and through organs created by them, direct all branches of state, economic and socio-cultural construction, adopt decisions, ensure their execution, and exercise control over the implementation of decisions.

Article 94 The activity of soviets of people's deputies shall be built on the basis of collective, free, and business-like discussion and resolution of questions, publicity, and regular accountability of executive and administrative organs, and other organs created by soviets, to the soviets and to the population, and on the extensive involvement of citizens in their work.

Soviets of people's deputies and organs created by them shall systematically inform the population about their work and the decisions adopted.

Chapter 13 The Electoral System

Article 95 Deputies to all soviets of people's deputies shall be elected on the basis of universal, equal, and direct suffrage by secret ballot.

Article 96 Elections of deputies shall be universal: all citizens of the USSR who have reached the age of eighteen shall have the right to elect and to be elected, with the exception of persons certified as insane in the procedure established by law.

A citizen of the USSR who has reached the age of twenty-one may be elected a deputy of the Supreme Soviet of the USSR.

Article 97 Elections of deputies shall be equal: every elector shall have one vote; all electors shall participate in elections on an equal basis.

Article 98 Elections of deputies shall be direct: deputies of all soviets of people's deputies shall be elected by citizens directly.

Article 99 Voting in elections of deputies shall be secret: control over the expression of the will of electors shall be *inadmissible*.[59]

Article 100 The right to nominate candidates for deputy shall belong to organizations of the Communist Party of the Soviet Union, trade unions, the All-Union Leninist Communist Youth League, cooperative and other social organizations, labour collectives, *and also meetings of servicemen in military units*.

Citizens of the USSR and social organizations shall be guaranteed free and comprehensive discussion of the political, professional, and personal qualities of candidates for deputy, and also the right of agitation at meetings, in the press, and on television and radio.

Expenses connected with the conduct of elections to soviets of people's deputies shall be defrayed by the state.

Article 101   Elections of deputies to soviets of people's deputies shall be conducted on the basis of electoral districts.

A citizen of the USSR may not, as a rule, be elected to more than two soviets of people's deputies.

The conduct of elections to soviets shall be ensured by electoral commissions, formed from representatives of social organizations, labour collectives, *and meetings of servicemen in military units.*

The procedure for holding elections to soviets of people's deputies shall be determined by *laws of the USSR and union and autonomous republics.*[60]

Article 102   *The electors shall give mandates to their deputies.*

The respective soviets of people's deputies shall consider the mandates of electors, take them into account when working out the plans for economic and social development and when drawing up the budget, organize the fulfilment of the mandates, and inform citizens about their realization.

Chapter 14 The People's Deputy

Article 103   Deputies shall be the authorized representatives of the people in the soviets of people's deputies.

In participating in the work of the soviets, deputies shall decide matters of state, economic, and socio-cultural construction, organize the implementation of decisions of the soviets, and exercise control over the work of state organs, enterprises, institutions, and organizations.

A deputy shall be guided in his activity by the interests of the state as a whole, shall take account of the needs of the population of the electoral district and shall endeavour to implement the electors' mandate.

Article 104   A deputy shall exercise the functions of his office without discontinuing his production or service activity.

During the sessions of the soviet, and also in order to exercise the functions of a deputy in other instances provided by law, a deputy shall be relieved from performing production or service duties, while retaining his average earnings at his place of permanent employment.

Article 105   A deputy shall have the right to address an inquiry to the appropriate state organs and officials, who shall be obliged to reply to the inquiry at a session of the soviet.

A deputy shall have the right to turn to all state and social organs, enterprises, institutions and organizations on matters arising from his activity as deputy and to take part in the consideration of such matters. The heads of the respective state and social organs, enterprises, institutions and organizations shall be obliged to receive the deputy without delay and to consider his proposals within the *established time limits.*[61]

Article 106   A deputy shall be provided with conditions for the unhindered and effective exercise of his rights and duties.

The immunity of deputies, and also other guarantees of deputy activity, shall be established by the Law on the Status of Deputies and other *legislative acts*[62] of the USSR and the union and autonomous republics.

Article 107   A deputy shall be obliged to report on his work and the work of the soviet to the electors, *and also to collectives and social organizations that nominated him as a candidate for deputy*.

A deputy who has not justified the trust of the electors may be recalled at any time by decision of the majority of electors in the procedure established by law.

V   The Highest Organs of State Power and Administration of the USSR

Chapter 15 The Supreme Soviet of the USSR

Article 108   The Supreme Soviet of the USSR shall be the highest organ of state power of the USSR.

The Supreme Soviet of the USSR shall be empowered to decide all matters which, under the present Constitution, fall within the jurisdiction of the USSR.

The adoption of the Constitution of the USSR and its amendment; the admission of new republics to the USSR and the approval of the formation of new autonomous republics and autonomous regions; the approval of state plans for the *economic and social development*[63] of the USSR, of the USSR state budget, and reports on their fulfilment; and the formation of USSR organs accountable to it, shall be carried out exclusively by the Supreme Soviet of the USSR.

Laws of the USSR shall be adopted [solely] by the Supreme Soviet of the USSR *or by a nationwide vote (referendum) held by decision of the Supreme Soviet of the USSR*.

Article 109   The Supreme Soviet of the USSR shall consist of two chambers: the Council of the Union and the Council of Nationalities.

The chambers of the Supreme Soviet of the USSR shall have equal rights.

Article 110   The Council of the Union and the Council of Nationalities shall consist of an equal number of deputies.

The Council of the Union shall be elected by electoral districts of equal population size.

The Council of Nationalities shall be elected on the basis of thirty-two deputies from each union republic, eleven deputies from each autonomous republic, five deputies from each autonomous region, and one deputy from each autonomous area.

The Council of the Union and the Council of Nationalities shall, upon the recommendation of credentials commissions elected by them, adopt a decision recognizing the credentials of deputies and, in the event of a violation of election legislation, declaring the elections of individual deputies null and void.

Article 111 Each chamber of the Supreme Soviet of the USSR shall elect a Chairman of the chamber and four Deputy Chairmen.

The Chairmen of the Council of the Union and of the Council of Nationalities shall direct the sittings of the respective chambers and have charge of their internal proceedings.

Joint [plenary] sittings of the chambers of the Supreme Soviet of the USSR shall be conducted alternately by the Chairmen of the Council of the Union and the Council of Nationalities.

Article 112 Sessions of the Supreme Soviet of the USSR shall be convened twice a year.

Extraordinary sessions shall be convened by the Presidium of the Supreme Soviet of the USSR at its initiative, *and also upon the proposal of a union republic or not less than one-third of the deputies of one of the chambers*.[64]

A session of the Supreme Soviet of the USSR shall consist of separate and joint [plenary] sittings of the chambers, and also of sittings of the standing commissions of the chambers or of the commissions of the Supreme Soviet of the USSR held *in the interim between sittings of the chambers*.[65] The sessions shall be opened and closed at *separate or joint* [plenary] sittings of the chambers.

[Sessions of the Council of the Union and the Council of Nationalities shall begin and terminate simultaneously.]

Article 113 The *right of* legislative initiative in the Supreme Soviet of the USSR shall belong to the Council of the Union, [and] the Council of Nationalities, the Presidium of the Supreme Soviet of the USSR, the Council of Ministers of the USSR; the union republics through their supreme organs of state power, the commissions of the Supreme Soviet of the USSR and the standing commissions of its chambers, deputies of the Supreme Soviet of the USSR, the Supreme Court of the USSR, and the Procurator General of the USSR.

The right of legislative initiative shall also be enjoyed by [mass] social organizations through their all-union organs.

Article 114 *Draft laws and other matters submitted for the consideration of the Supreme Soviet of the USSR shall be discussed by the chambers at their separate or joint sittings. If necessary, a draft law or other matter may be referred for preliminary or additional consideration to one or several commissions*.[66]

A law of the USSR shall be considered adopted if a majority of the total number of deputies of a chamber have voted for it in each of the chambers of the Supreme Soviet of the USSR.[67] *Decrees and other acts of the Supreme Soviet of the USSR shall be adopted by a majority of the total number of deputies of the Supreme Soviet of the USSR.*

Draft laws [of the USSR] *and other most important matters of state* may be submitted for nationwide discussion [and also for nationwide vote (referendum)] by decision of the Supreme Soviet of the USSR or the Presidium of the Supreme Soviet of the USSR, adopted at their initiative or upon the proposal of a union republic.

Article 115   In the event of disagreement between the Council of the Union and the Council of Nationalities, the matter shall be referred for settlement to a conciliation commission formed by the chambers on a parity basis, after which the matter shall be considered for a second time by the Council of the Union and the Council of Nationalities at a joint sitting. *If, in this case, agreement is still not reached, the matter shall be held over for discussion at the next session of the Supreme Soviet of the USSR or submitted to a nationwide vote (referendum).*

Article 116   Laws of the USSR, decrees, and other acts of the Supreme Soviet of the USSR shall be published in the languages of the union republics over the signatures of the Chairman and Secretary of the Presidium of the Supreme Soviet of the USSR.

Article 117   A deputy of the Supreme Soviet of the USSR shall have the right to address an inquiry to the Council of Ministers of the USSR and to ministers and heads of other organs formed by the Supreme Soviet of the USSR. The Council of Ministers of the USSR or the official to whom the inquiry is addressed shall be obliged to make an oral or written reply at the *current* session of the Supreme Soviet of the USSR within not more than three days.

Article 118   A deputy of the Supreme Soviet of the USSR may not be brought to criminal responsibility, arrested, or subjected to measures of administrative sanction imposed in a judicial proceeding, without the consent of the Supreme Soviet of the USSR and, in the interim between its sessions, without the consent of the Presidium of the Supreme Soviet of the USSR.

Article 119   The Supreme Soviet of the USSR, at a joint sitting of the chambers, shall elect the Presidium of the Supreme Soviet of the USSR, the permanently functioning organ of the Supreme Soviet of the USSR, accountable to it for all its activity, *and exercising the functions of the highest organ of state power of the USSR in the interim between its sessions, within the limits prescribed by the Constitution.*

Article 120   The Presidium of the Supreme Soviet of the USSR shall be elected from among the deputies and shall consist of the Chairman of the

Presidium of the Supreme Soviet, the First Deputy Chairman, fifteen Deputy Chairmen – one from each union republic, the Secretary of the Presidium, and twenty-one members of the Presidium of the Supreme Soviet of the USSR.

Article 121 The Presidium of the Supreme Soviet of the USSR shall:

(1) *call elections to the Supreme Soviet of the USSR*;

(2) convene sessions of the Supreme Soviet of the USSR;

(3) coordinate the activity of the standing commissions of the chambers of the Supreme Soviet of the USSR;

(4) exercise control over the observance of the USSR Constitution and ensure the conformity of the union republic constitutions *and laws* to the USSR Constitution *and laws*;

(5) interpret the laws of the USSR;

(6) ratify and abrogate international treaties of the USSR;

(7) annul decrees and regulations of the Council of Ministers of the USSR and the Councils of Ministers of the union republics in the event that they do not conform to the law;

(8) establish military ranks, diplomatic ranks, and other special titles; confer the highest military ranks, diplomatic ranks, and other special titles;

(9) institute orders and medals of the USSR; establish honorary titles of the USSR; award orders and medals of the USSR; confer honorary titles of the USSR;

(10) admit to citizenship of the USSR, decide questions of renunciation of USSR citizenship and deprivation of USSR citizenship, and of granting asylum;

(11) issue all-union acts concerning amnesty and grant pardons;

(12) appoint and recall *diplomatic*[68] representatives of the USSR to foreign states and international organizations;

(13) accept the credentials and letters of recall of diplomatic representatives of foreign states accredited to it;

(14) form the Defence Council of the USSR and approve its membership, and appoint and remove the high command of the Armed Forces of the USSR;

(15) proclaim martial law in individual localities or throughout the country in the interests of the defence of the USSR;

(16) proclaim general or partial mobilization;

(17) in the interim between sessions of the Supreme Soviet of the USSR, proclaim a state of war in the event of an armed attack on the USSR or in the event of the need to fulfill international treaty obligations on mutual defence against aggression.

(18) *exercise other powers established by the Constitution and laws of the USSR*.

Article 122 The Presidium of the Supreme Soviet of the USSR, in the interim between sessions of the Supreme Soviet and with subsequent submission for its approval at a regular session, shall:

(1) amend, when necessary, the *legislative acts*[69] of the USSR currently in force;

(2) approve modifications of boundaries between union republics;

(3) form and abolish ministries of the USSR and state committees of the USSR upon the proposal of the Council of Ministers of the USSR;

(4) dismiss and appoint individual *persons to membership*[70] of the Council of Ministers of the USSR upon the recommendation of the Chairman of the Council of Ministers of the USSR.

Article 123   The Presidium of the Supreme Soviet of the USSR shall issue edicts and adopt decrees.

Article 124   Upon expiry of the term of the Supreme Soviet of the USSR, the Presidium of the Supreme Soviet of the USSR shall retain its powers until the formation of the newly elected Presidium by the newly elected Supreme Soviet of the USSR.

The newly elected Supreme Soviet of the USSR shall be convened by the outgoing Presidium of the Supreme Soviet of the USSR not later than two months after the elections.

Article 125   The Council of the Union and the Council of Nationalities shall elect standing commissions from among the deputies for the preliminary consideration and preparation of matters which come within the jurisdiction of the Supreme Soviet of the USSR, and also for furthering the implementation of laws of the USSR and other decisions of the Supreme Soviet of the USSR and its Presidium, and for control over the activity of state organs and organizations. The chambers of the USSR Supreme Soviet may *also* create joint commissions on a parity basis.[71]

The Supreme Soviet of the USSR, when it considers it necessary, shall create commissions of investigation and inspection, and other commissions on any matter.

All *state and social organs, organizations*[72] and officials shall be obliged to comply with the demands of *the commissions of the Supreme Soviet of the USSR and the commissions of its chambers*[73] and to submit to them the necessary materials and documents.[74]

The recommendations of the commissions shall be subject to obligatory consideration by state and social organs, institutions and organizations. The results of the consideration or of the measures taken must be notified to the commissions within the established time limits.

Article 126   The Supreme Soviet of the USSR shall exercise control over the activity of all state organs accountable to it.

The Supreme Soviet of the USSR shall form the People's Control Committee of the USSR heading the system of people's control organs.

The organization and procedure of the activity of the people's control organs shall be determined by the Law on People's Control of the USSR.

Article 127   The procedure for the activity of the Supreme Soviet of the USSR and its organs shall be determined by the standing orders of the Supreme Soviet of the USSR[75] and *other* laws of the USSR issued on the basis of the Constitution of the USSR.

Chapter 16 The Council of Ministers of the USSR

Article 128   The Council of Ministers of the USSR – the Government of the USSR – shall be the highest executive and administrative organ of state power of the USSR.

Article 129   The Council of Ministers of the USSR shall be formed by the Supreme Soviet of the USSR at a joint sitting of the Council of the Union and the Council of Nationalities and shall consist of the Chairman of the Council of Ministers of the USSR, the First Deputy Chairmen and the Deputy Chairmen, ministers of the USSR, and chairmen of the state committees of the USSR.

The chairmen of the union republic Councils of Ministers shall be ex officio members of the Council of Ministers of the USSR.

Upon the recommendation of the Chairman of the Council of Ministers of the USSR, the Supreme Soviet of the USSR may include in the Government of the USSR the heads of other organs and organizations of the USSR.

The Council of Ministers of the USSR shall tender its resignation to a newly elected Supreme Soviet of the USSR at its first session.

Article 130   The Council of Ministers of the USSR shall be responsible and accountable to the Supreme Soviet of the USSR and, in the interim between sessions of the Supreme Soviet of the USSR, to the Presidium of the Supreme Soviet of the USSR.

The Council of Ministers of the USSR shall report regularly on its work to the Supreme Soviet of the USSR.

Article 131   The Council of Ministers of the USSR shall be empowered to decide all matters of state administration that come within the jurisdiction of the USSR in so far as they are not, *according to*[76] the Constitution, within the competence of the Supreme Soviet of the USSR and the Presidium of the Supreme Soviet of the USSR.

Within the limits of its powers, the Council of Ministers of the USSR shall:

(1) ensure the direction of the national economy and socio-cultural construction [and pursue a uniform policy in the field of science and technology]; work out and implement measures ensuring the growth of the well-being and culture of the people, *the development of science*

and technology, the utilization and protection of natural resources, the strengthening of the monetary and credit system, and the pursuit of a uniform policy of prices, wages and social security,[77] the organization of state insurance and of a uniform system of accounting and statistics; organize the administration of industrial, construction and agricultural enterprises and associations, transport and communications enterprises, banks, as well as other organizations and institutions of union subordination;

(2) work out and submit to the Supreme Soviet of the USSR current and long-term state plans for the *economic and social development*[78] of the USSR and the state budget for the USSR; take measures for the implementation of the state *plans*[79] and the budget; submit reports on the fulfilment of the plans and the budget to the Supreme Soviet of the USSR;

(3) implement measures to defend the interests of the state, protect socialist ownership and public order, and ensure and protect the rights *and freedoms* of citizens;

(4) take measures to ensure state security;

(5) exercise general direction over the construction of the Armed Forces of the USSR and determine the annual contingent of citizens subject to call-up for active military service;

(6) exercise general direction in the field of relations with foreign states, foreign trade, and economic, scientific-technical, and cultural cooperation of the USSR with foreign countries; take measures to ensure the fulfilment of international treaties of the USSR; ratify and abrogate international intergovernmental treaties;

(7) form, when necessary, committees, chief administrations, and other departments, attached to the Council of Ministers of the USSR for matters of economic, socio-cultural, and defence construction.[80]

Article 132 The Presidium of the Council of Ministers of the USSR, consisting of the Chairman of the Council of Ministers of the USSR, the First Deputy Chairmen and the Deputy Chairmen, shall function as a permanent organ of the Council of Ministers of the USSR and shall decide matters connected with ensuring the direction of the national economy and other matters of state administration.

Article 133 The Council of Ministers of the USSR shall, on the basis and in execution of laws of the USSR and *other decisions of the Supreme Soviet of the USSR and its Presidium*,[81] issue decrees and regulations and verify their execution. Decrees and regulations of the Council of Ministers of the USSR shall be binding throughout the territory of the USSR.

Article 134 The Council of Ministers of the USSR shall have the right to suspend *the execution of* decrees and regulations of the Council of Ministers of union republics on matters that come within the juristiction of the

USSR, and also to annul acts of USSR ministries, USSR state committees, and other organs under its jurisdiction.

Article 135   The Council of Ministers of the USSR shall coordinate and direct the work of all-union and union-republic ministries and state committees of the USSR and other organs under its jurisdiction.

All-union ministries and state committees of the USSR shall direct branches of administration entrusted to them *or carry out interbranch administration* throughout the territory of the USSR, directly or through organs created by them.

Union-republic ministries and state committees of the USSR shall direct branches of administration entrusted to them *or carry out interbranch administration*, as a rule, through the respective ministries, state committees *and other organs* of union republics, and directly administer enterprises and associations *of union subordination. The procedure for the transfer of enterprises and associations from republic and local subordination to that of the union shall be determined by the Presidium of the Supreme Soviet of the USSR.*[82]

USSR ministries and state committees shall bear responsibility for the state and development of *spheres*[83] of administration entrusted to them; within the limits of their competence they shall issue acts on the basis and in execution of laws of the USSR, of *other decisions of the USSR Supreme Soviet and its Presidium,*[84] and of decrees and regulations of the Council of Ministers of the USSR; and organize and verify their execution.

Article 136   The competence of the Council of Ministers of the USSR and its Presidium, the procedure for their activity, relations of the Council of Ministers with *other state organs,*[85] and also a list of all-union and union-republic ministries and state committees of the USSR shall be determined *on the basis of the Constitution* by the Law on the Council of Ministers of the USSR.[86]

VI Fundamentals of the Structure of Organs of State Power and Administration in the Union Republics

Chapter 17 The Highest Organs of State Power and Administration of the Union Republic

Article 137   The Supreme Soviet of a union republic shall be the highest organ of state power of the union republic.

The Supreme Soviet of a union republic shall be empowered to decide all matters assigned to union republic jurisdiction by the Constitution of the USSR and the union republic Constitution.

The adoption of a union republic Constitution and its amendment; the approval of state plans for *economic and social development*[87] and of the union republic state budget *and reports on their fulfilment;* and the formation of organs accountable to it, shall be carried out exclusively by the Supreme Soviet of the union republic.

Union republic laws shall be adopted [solely] by the Supreme Soviet of the union republic *or by a popular vote (referendum) held by decision of the Supreme Soviet of the union republic.*

Article 138 The Supreme Soviet of a union republic shall elect the Presidium of the Supreme Soviet, the permanently functioning organ of the Supreme Soviet of the union republic, accountable to it for all its activity. The composition and powers of the Presidium of the Supreme Soviet of a union republic shall be determined by the Constitution of the union republic.

Article 139 The Supreme Soviet of a union republic shall form the Council of Ministers of the union republic – the Government of the union republic – which shall be the highest executive and administrative organ of state power of the union republic.

The Council of Ministers of a union republic shall be responsible and accountable to the Supreme Soviet of the union republic and, in the interim between sessions of the Supreme Soviet, to the Presidium of the Supreme Soviet of the union republic.

Article 140 The Council of Ministers of a union republic shall issue decrees and regulations on the basis and in execution of *legislative acts*[88] of the USSR and the union republic and of decrees and regulations of the Council of Ministers of the USSR, and shall organize and verify their execution.

Article 141 The Council of Ministers of a union republic shall have the right to suspend *the execution of* decrees and regulations of the Councils of Ministers of autonomous republics and to annul decisions and regulations of executive committees of territory, regional, town (towns of republic subordination) soviets of people's deputies, autonomous region soviets of people's deputies, and, in union republics not divided into regions, of executive committees of district and corresponding town soviets of people's deputies.

Article 142 The Council of Ministers of a union republic shall coordinate and direct the work of union-republic and republic ministries, union republic state committees, *and other organs under its jurisdiction.*

Union-republic ministries and state committees of a union republic shall direct the branches of administration entrusted to them *or carry out interbranch administration*, being subordinate both to the Council of Ministers of the union republic and to the corresponding union-republic ministry of the USSR or state committee of the USSR.

Republic ministries and state committees shall direct branches of administration entrusted to them *or carry out interbranch administration*, being subordinate to the Council of Ministers of the union republic.

Chapter 18 The Highest Organs of State Power and Administration of the Autonomous Republic

Article 143 The Supreme Soviet of an autonomous republic shall be the highest organ of state power of the autonomous republic.

The adoption of an autonomous republic Constitution and its amendment; the approval of state plans for *economic and social development*[89] and also the autonomous republic state budget; and the formation of organs accountable to it shall be carried out exclusively by the Supreme Soviet of the autonomous republic.

Laws of an autonomous republic shall be adopted [solely] by the Supreme Soviet of the autonomous republic.

Article 144 The Supreme Soviet of an autonomous republic shall elect the Presidium of the Supreme Soviet of the autonomous republic and shall form the Council of Ministers of the autonomous republic – the Government of the autonomous republic.

Chapter 19 The Local Organs of State Power and Administration

Article 145 The organs of state power in territories, regions, autonomous regions, autonomous areas, districts, towns, boroughs, settlements, and rural communities shall be the corresponding soviets of people's deputies.

Article 146 The local soviets of people's deputies shall decide all matters of local significance, proceeding from the interests of the state as a whole and the interests of citizens residing in the territory of the soviet, implement decisions of higher-ranking state organs, *direct the activity of lower-ranking soviets of people's deputies*, participate in the discussion of matters of republic and all-union significance and submit their proposals in regard to such matters.

The *local* soviets of people's deputies shall direct state, economic, and socio-cultural construction in their territory; approve plans for economic and *social*[90] development, and the local budget; exercise direction over state organs, enterprises, institutions, and organizations subordinate to them; ensure the observance of laws and the protection of state and public order and of the rights of citizens; and promote the strengthening of the defence capability of the country.

Article 147 Within the limits of their powers, the local soviets of people's deputies shall *ensure the integrated economic and social development of their territory;* exercise control over the observance of legislation by enterprises, institutions, and organizations of superior subordination which are located in *this*[91] territory; coordinate and control their activity in the field of land utilization, nature conservation, construction, *utilization of labour resources,* production of consumer goods, and socio-cultural, domestic, everyday services and other services to the population.

Article 148   The local soviets of people's deputies shall adopt decisions within the limits of the *powers*[92] granted them by *legislation*[93] of the USSR and union and autonomous republics. Decisions of local soviets shall be binding for all enterprises, institutions, and organizations located in the territory of the soviet, and also for officials and citizens.

Article 149   The executive committees elected from among the deputies shall be the executive and administrative organs of the local soviets of people's deputies.

The executive committees shall report at least once a year to the soviets which elected them, *and also to meetings of labour collectives and at the place of residence of citizens.*

Article 150   The executive committees of local soviets of people's deputies shall be directly accountable to both the soviet which elected them and to the superior executive and administrative organ.

VII   Justice, Arbitration and Procuracy Supervision

Chapter 20 The Court and Arbitration

Article 151   Justice in the USSR shall be administered solely by a court.

The courts functioning in the USSR shall be the Supreme Court of the USSR, the Supreme Courts of union republics, the Supreme Courts of autonomous republics, territory, regional, and city courts, courts of autonomous regions, courts of autonomous areas, district (or town) people's courts, and also military tribunals in the Armed Forces.

Article 152   All courts in the USSR shall be formed on the principle of the electivity of judges and people's assessors.

People's judges of district (or town) people's courts shall be elected by the citizens of the district (or town) on the basis of universal, equal and direct suffrage by secret ballot for a term of five years. People's assessors of district (or town) people's courts shall be elected at meetings of *citizens*[94] at their place of work or residence by open ballot for a term of two-and-a-half years.

Superior courts shall be elected by the corresponding soviets of people's deputies for a term of five years.

Judges of military tribunals shall be elected by the Presidium of the Supreme Soviet of the USSR for a term of five years, and people's assessors, by meetings of servicemen, for a term of two-and-a-half years.

Judges and people's assessors shall be responsible to the electors or to the organs which elected them and shall *account*[95] to them, *and may be recalled by them in the procedure established by law.*

Article 153   The Supreme Court of the USSR shall be the highest judicial organ of the USSR and shall exercise supervision over the judicial activity of the courts of the USSR, and also of union republic courts, within the limits established by law.

The Supreme Court of the USSR shall be elected [for a term of five years] by the Supreme Soviet of the USSR and shall consist of a chairman, his deputies, members, and people's assessors. The chairmen of the union republic Supreme Courts shall be ex officio members of the Supreme Court of the USSR.

The organization and procedure of the activity[96] of the Supreme Court of the USSR shall be determined by the Law on the Supreme Court of the USSR.[97]

Article 154   The hearing of civil and criminal cases in all courts shall be carried out collegially and, in a court of first instance, with the participation of people's assessors. In administering justice people's assessors shall enjoy all the rights of judges.

Article 155   Judges and people's assessors shall be independent and subordinate only to the law.

Article 156   Justice in the USSR shall be administered on the principle of equality of citizens before the law and the court.

Article 157   Examination of cases in all courts shall be open. The hearing of cases in a closed session of a court shall be permitted only in instances established by law and with observance of all the rules of procedure.

Article 158   An accused shall be ensured the right of defence.

Article 159   Court proceedings shall be conducted in the language of the union or autonomous republic, autonomous region, autonomous area, or in the language of the majority of the population of the given locality. Persons participating in a case who do not know the language in which the court proceeding is conducted shall be ensured the right to familiarize themselves fully with the materials of the case, to participate in the proceedings through an interpreter, and to speak in their native language in court.

Article 160   No one may be deemed guilty of committing a crime and subjected to criminal punishment other than by the judgment of a court and in accordance with the [criminal] law.

Article 161   Colleges of advocates shall be available to render legal assistance to citizens and organizations. In the instances provided for by *legislation*[98] legal assistance shall be rendered to citizens free of charge.

   The organization and procedure of the activity of the bar shall be determined by USSR and union republic legislation.[99]

Article 162   The participation of representatives of social organizations and labour collectives shall be permitted in court proceedings in civil and criminal cases.

Article 163   The settlement of economic disputes between enterprises, institutions and organizations shall be carried out by state arbitration organs *within the limits of their competence.*

   The organization and procedure of the activity[100] of state arbitration organs shall be determined by *the Law on State Arbitration in the USSR.*[101]

   [The direction and supervision of all arbitration organs shall be exercised by the State Arbitration of the USSR. The Chief Arbitrator of the State Arbitration of the USSR shall be appointed by the Supreme Soviet of the USSR for a term of five years.]

Chapter 21 The Procuracy

Article 164   Supreme supervision over the strict and uniform execution of the laws by all ministries, state committees and departments, enterprises, institutions, and organizations, executive and administrative organs of local soviets of people's deputies, collective farms, cooperative and other social organizations, officials, and also citizens, shall be vested in the Procurator General of the USSR and in procurators subordinate to him.

Article 165   The Procurator General of the USSR shall be appointed by the Supreme Soviet of the USSR and shall be reponsible and accountable to it and, in the interim between sessions of the Supreme Soviet, to the Presidium of the Supreme Soviet of the USSR.

Article 166   Procurators of union republics, autonomous republics, territories, regions, and autonomous regions shall be appointed by the Procurator General of the USSR. Procurators of autonomous areas, and procurators of districts and towns, shall be appointed by procurators of union republics and confirmed by the Procurator General of the USSR.

Article 167   The term of office of the Procurator General of the USSR and of all lower-ranking procurators shall be five years.

Article 168 The organs of the procuracy shall exercise their powers independently of any local organs whatsoever, being subordinate solely to the Procurator General of the USSR.

The organization and procedure of the activity of procuracy organs shall be determined by the Law on the Procuracy of the USSR.[102]

VIII   Arms, Flag, Anthem and Capital of the USSR

Article 169 The state arms of the Union of Soviet Socialist Republics shall depict a sickle and hammer against the background of a globe in the rays of the sun and framed by ears of grain, with the inscription in the languages of the union republics: 'Proletarians of All Countries, Unite!' *In the upper portion*[103] of the arms shall be a five-pointed star.

Article 170 The state flag of the Union of Soviet Socialist Republics shall be a red rectangular cloth with a golden sickle and hammer depicted in the upper corner near the staff and a five-pointed red star bordered in gold above them. The ratio of the width of the flag to its length shall be 1.2.

Article 171 The state anthem of the Union of Soviet Socialist Republics shall be approved by the Presidium of the Supreme Soviet of the USSR.

Article 172 The city of Moscow shall be the capital of the Union of Soviet Socialist Republics.

IX   The Legal Force of the Constitution of the USSR and the Amending Procedure[104]

Article 173 The Constitution of the USSR shall have supreme legal force. All laws and other acts of state organs shall be issued on the basis of and in conformity with the Constitution of the USSR.

[The Constitution of the USSR shall be effective from the time of its adoption.]

Article 174 The Constitution of the USSR shall be amended by decision of the Supreme Soviet of the USSR, adopted by a majority of not less than two-thirds of the total number of deputies of each of its chambers.

Notes

1 The text and notes below indicate changes introduced in the final version of the constitution, as compared with the draft published on 4 June 1977. Additions to, and deletions from, the draft are noted in the text – the former by italics, the latter by square brackets. In the case of new wording, the

changes in the final version are placed in italics in the text and the original version of the draft is given in the notes. Minor stylistic changes – narrowly defined – are ignored. For the translation of the designations of official enactments, see p. 159, no. 1.

2 Draft: 'Soviet people'.

3 Draft: 'human rights and freedoms with civic responsibility'.

4 Draft: '1918 Constitution of the RSFSR'.

5 Draft: 'proclaim the aims and principles and establish the bases of the organization of the all-people's socialist state and affirm them in this Constitution'.

6 Draft: Fundamentals of the Socio-Political and Economic Order.

7 Draft: 'working class, the peasantry'.

8 Several of the above formulations were almost literally taken over from the preamble of the 1961 Party Rules.

9 This article is an expanded version of article 16 of the draft. The original version read:

Article 16 [Draft] Collectives of toilers and social organizations shall participate in the administration of enterprises and associations and in deciding questions of the organization of work and everyday life and the use of funds earmarked for the development of production, and also for socio-cultural needs and material incentives.

10 Draft: 'toilers'.

11 Draft: 'society and the state'.

12 The draft version of the first two paragraphs of this article read [draft article 9]:

Socialist ownership of the means of production shall constitute the foundation of the economic system of the USSR. Socialist ownership shall include: state (all-people's) ownership; ownership of collective farms and other cooperative organizations (collective farm-cooperative); ownership of trade unions and other social organizations.

13 The draft version of the second paragraph of this article read [draft article 10]:

There shall be in the exclusive ownership of the state: the land, its minerals, the waters and forests. The basic means of production shall belong to the state – industrial, construction and agricultural enterprises, means of transport and communication, and also banks, trade enterprises and community services and the bulk of urban housing.

14 Draft: 'which serves them'.

15 In the draft this was not a separate paragraph.

16 Draft: 'The trade unions and other social organizations shall have ownership of property needed by them to carry out the tasks set out in their charters'. (Cf. article 10 paragraph 2 of the final text.)

17 The draft version of the first paragraph of this article read [draft article 12]:

Earned income and savings, a dwelling house and subsidiary husbandry, and articles of everyday use and of personal consumption and convenience, may be in the personal ownership of citizens. The right of citizens to personal property, and also the right to inherit it shall be protected by law.

18 Draft: 'and'.

19 Draft: 'cannot'.

20 Draft: 'to harm society'.

21 Draft: 'and establish the level of wages exempted from taxation'.

22 Draft: 'the development of the national economy and socio-cultural construction'.
23 Draft: 'direction'.
24 Draft: 'further'.
25 Draft: 'manual'.
26 Draft: 'In conformity with'.
27 Draft: 'members of society'.
28 Draft: 'the field'.
29 Draft: 'their preparation'.
30 Draft: 'The Soviet state shall consistently'.
31 In the draft the order of these two principles was reversed: 'mutual renunciation of the use of force or threat of force; sovereign equality'.
32 Draft: 'shall be a most important function'.
33 Draft: 'Armed Forces have been created in the USSR'.
34 Draft: 'law'.
35 Draft: There shall be a single Soviet citizenship for the entire USSR'.
36 Draft: 'established by a law of the USSR'. A Law on Citizenship of the USSR was adopted by the Supreme Soviet on 1 December 1978.
37 Draft: 'Women in the USSR shall have equal rights with men'.
38 Draft: 'by a forty-one-hour work week for workers and employees'.
39 Draft: 'by old-age and invalid pensions and pensions for loss of breadwinner; by temporary disability allowances'.
40 Draft: 'law'.
41 The draft version of the second paragraph of this article read:
Citizens of the USSR shall elect and may be elected to the soviets of people's deputies, and shall participate in the discussion and elaboration of draft laws and decisions of all-state and local significance, in the work of state organs, cooperative and other social organizations, in the control of their activity, in the management of production and the affairs of labour collectives, and in meetings at places of residence.
42 Draft: 'time limits established by law'.
43 Draft: 'toilers'.
44 Draft: 'Freedom of conscience shall be recognized for citizens of the USSR'.
45 Draft: 'entered into with'.
46 Draft: 'aid'.
47 Draft: 'by court decree'.
48 Draft: 'the Soviet person'.
49 Draft: 'life and health, property and personal freedom, and on their honour and dignity'.
50 Draft: 'with state organs and social organizations'.
51 In the draft, article 68 formed the second paragraph of article 67.
52 Draft: 'plans for the development of the national economy and socio-cultural construction'.
53 Draft: 'union, republican and local budgets'.
54 Draft: 'its'.
55 Draft: 'its'.
56 Draft: 'statute'.
57 Draft: 'approved'.
58 Draft: 'territorial and regional soviets of people's deputies, soviets of people's

deputies of autonomous regions and autonomous areas, town, district, borough, settlement and village soviets of people's deputies'.

59 Draft: 'excluded'.
60 Draft: 'law'. A Law on Elections to the USSR Supreme Soviet, superseding the Statute on Elections to the USSR Supreme Soviet of 9 January 1950, was enacted on 7 July 1978.
61 Draft: 'time limits established by law'.
62 Draft: 'legislation'.
63 Draft: 'development of the national economy and socio-cultural construction'.
64 Draft: 'or on the proposal of not less than one-third of the deputies of one of the chambers, and also upon the demand of one of the union republics'.
65 Draft: 'held during the session'.
66 The draft version of the first two paragraphs of this article read:
After discussion of a draft law at sittings of the chambers, it may be referred for consideration to one of several commissions. The chambers shall also have the right to discuss and vote on a draft law without referring it to a commission.
   Laws of the USSR, decrees and other acts of the Supreme Soviet of the USSR shall be adopted at separate or joint sittings of the chambers.
67 This sentence constituted paragraph 3 in the draft.
68 Draft: 'plenipotentiary'.
69 Draft: 'legislation'.
70 Draft: 'members'.
71 The last sentence of this paragraph constituted a separate second paragraph of the corresponding article in the draft [article 123].
72 Draft: 'state organs, institutions'.
73 Draft: 'these commissions'.
74 The second and third paragraphs of this article constituted respectively the first and second sentences of article 125 of the draft.
75 Standing orders were adopted by the Supreme Soviet on 19 April 1979.
76 Draft: 'by force of'.
77 Draft: 'the strengthening of a uniform monetary and credit system, the pursuit of a uniform price policy'.
78 Draft: 'the development of the national economy and socio-cultural construction'.
79 Draft: 'plan'.
80 In the draft, section 7 formed the second paragraph of the succeeding article.
81 Draft: 'edicts of the Presidium of the Supreme Soviet of the USSR'.
82 Draft: 'according to a list approved by the Presidium of the Supreme Soviet of the USSR'.
83 Draft: 'branches'.
84 Draft: 'edicts of the Presidium of the Supreme Soviet of the USSR'.
85 Draft: 'ministries of the USSR and state committees of the USSR'.
86 The Law on the Council of Ministers of the USSR was adopted by the Supreme Soviet on 6 July 1978.
87 Draft: 'the development of the national economy and socio-cultural construction'.
88 Draft: 'laws'.

89 Draft: 'the development of the national economy and socio-cultural construction'.

90 Draft: 'socio-cultural'.

91 Draft: 'their'.

92 Draft: 'rights'.

93 Draft: 'laws'.

94 Draft: 'toilers'.

95 Draft: 'be accountable'.

96 Draft: 'The procedure for the organization and activity'.

97 The Law of the Supreme Court of the USSR was adopted by the Supreme
Soviet on 30 November 1979.

98 Draft: 'law'.

99 A Law on the Bar in the USSR was adopted by the Supreme Soviet on 30
November 1979.

100 Draft: 'The procedure for the organization and activity'.

101 Draft: 'law'. In the draft version this sentence was part of the first paragraph
of the corresponding article [article 162]. The Law on State Arbitration in the
USSR was adopted by the Supreme Soviet on 30 November 1979. It is worth
noting that the law provides for the appointment of the Chief Arbitrator by
the Council of Ministers and not, as originally envisaged by the draft of the
constitutional article, by the Supreme Soviet.

102 Draft: 'The procedure for the organization and activity of the procuracy
organs of the USSR shall be determined by the Law on Procuracy Supervision in the USSR.' The Law on the Procuracy of the USSR was adopted by the
Supreme Soviet on 30 November 1979.

103 Draft: 'At the top'.

104 In the draft this heading read:
The Procedure for the Force and Amendment of the Constitution.

5
Conclusion

Constitutional Development in Review

The latest Soviet constitution proclaims in its preamble adherence to the 'ideas and principles' of the three previous constitutions. And Brezhnev, in introducing the draft text to the May Central Committee plenum, emphasized: 'In preparing the draft *we stood firmly on the ground of continuity.*' That continuity has been a hallmark of Soviet constitutional development will be readily apparent if we recall briefly some of main elements common to all four constitutions.

There is, first, the ideological dimension. Marxism, or Marxism-Leninism, has been the official ideology of the state from the moment of its birth and this is clearly reflected in the declarative provisions of all its constitutions. The 1918, 1924 and 1977 constitutions reflect it primarily, but not exclusively, in their respective preambles. The 1936 constitution lacks a preamble but the ideological orientation is unmistakable in many of its provisions, above all those of chapter I.

Secondly, all constitutions have espoused the principle of popular sovereignty. Power, such has been the official theory throughout, flows from the people (or the 'toilers') and is exercised by their democratically elected representatives. Until 1936 the 'people' did not include 'former people', but this restriction of political rights was merely one aspect of the recognition of continuing class struggle, just as the granting of the universal franchise in 1936 merely signalled recognition of a new social reality in which class exploitation and antagonisms had allegedly been abolished and 'toilers', 'people' and 'citizens' could be taken to mean the same thing.

Thirdly, all of the constitutions have repudiated the separation of powers. Marxism-Leninism regards the separation of powers between the three traditional branches of government as nothing but a façade concealing the exploitative essence of 'bourgeois' states. In a socialist state each branch derives its authority from the will of the people as institutionally embodied in the highest popularly-elected assembly. While a measure of functional division has increasingly been introduced, the official doctrine remains that the exercise of state power is ultimately one and indivisible.

Fourthly, and entirely in keeping with the notions of popular sovereignty and the unity of state authority, is the absence of meaningful protection of constitutional norms. The 1918 constitution ignored the problem altogether; the three subsequent constitutions assigned the control of constitutionality to the central political organs of the state. None of the constitutions provided for review of the acts of the all-union legislature in any form whatsoever.

Fifthly, the federal framework, though subjected to centralist stress, has remained basically unchanged. The 1918 constitution contained no operative provisions in this regard, but the actual arrangements that were to govern relations between the several republics that eventually made up the union were established under its aegis, and, having been formalized in the 1924 constitution, have remained in force ever since. That the federation is a voluntary union of 'sovereign' republics, that the borders of the republics cannot be changed without their consent, that each republic retains the right of secession, that the powers not specifically assigned to the union government are reserved for the governments of the republics – these have been the pillars of the federal structure from the moment of its inception.

Finally, coming to the 'heart' of constitutionalism, at least in the Western sense of the term, the bill of rights, though considerably expanded over the years, has always rested on two propositions: that the interests of the individual are subordinate to those of society and in particular to the collective enterprise of building socialism (or communism); and that the rights of the individual are inseparably linked to his duties. The first proposition was unadornedly enunciated in the 1918 constitution when it arrogated to the state the power to deprive individuals and groups of rights used to the detriment of the socialist revolution [article 23]. It subsequently provided the rationale for the limiting provisos attached to the rights of expression, assembly and association, and is now explicitly articulated in the 1977 constitution, albeit in a more moderate version [1936 – articles 125–6; 1977 – articles 39 & 50–1]. The second proposition was not spelled out in a constitutional text until 1977 [article 59]. But it was always part of Soviet constitutional doctrine, expressed succinctly in earlier texts by the formula 'He who does not work, neither shall he eat' [1918 – article 18; 1936 – article 12]. Underlying these propositions is the premise that all legal rights of the individual emanate from the state and are enumerated in positive law. There are no natural or inalienable rights of man. Rights are granted by the state for the attainment of certain precise societal objectives and they are restricted to citizens who identify with these objectives and contribute to their fulfilment.

If these are the contours of constitutional continuity, which are the landmarks of change? The 1918 constitution, apart from marking the break with the past order, was also an 'original constitution' in the sense that it advanced 'a new, truly creative, and, hence, "original", functional principle for the process of political power and the formation of the will of the state'.[1] The 1924 constitution had the limited and comparatively mundane objective of establishing the formal structure of federal union. But what of the 1936 and 1977 constitutions, both of which were occasioned – such at least was the official claim in both cases – by major developments in Soviet society's progress towards communism?

The 1936 constitution undoubtedly introduced many changes. It provided an elaborate bill of rights, recognized the existence of the Communist party, reformed the electoral system and dismantled the pyramidal structure of the soviets, establishing institutions which with minor modifications continue to survive to the present. But these and other innovations, already noted in the preceding pages, were merely the specific expressions of a more general change in the basic assumptions concerning the nature of the Soviet state and law. More than any other single act the 1936 constitution both signalled and symbolized this change.

Critical observers of Soviet politics have often pointed out that the fundamental thesis of economic determinism, from which the official teaching of the state derived, was disregarded by the Bolsheviks in their initial decision to make the proletarian revolution in Russia, despite the fact that by Marxist criteria the economic base had not yet sufficiently matured. It was later implicitly repudiated in the introduction of NEP, which envisaged a proletarian government presiding over a semi-capitalist economic system, and soon found its complete anthithesis in Stalin's 'revolution from above', in which the state deliberately set out to create that economic base which could alone legitimate its existence. Under the circumstances, it was inevitable and possibly quite in accord with the Marxist teaching that the state, far from 'withering away', continued to expand and entrench itself. Yet throughout the 1920s the original concepts of the nature and destiny of the state remained part of official doctrine: the Soviet state, like any other state, was an instrument of class suppression, though it differed from other states in its proletarian class content and it was a transient phenomenon destined to disappear in proportion as the need for class suppression subsided.[2]

In 1927 Stalin took the first step towards bridging the gap between avowed theory and manifest reality when he warned delegates to the 15th Party Congress:

> To carry the struggle against bureaucracy in the state apparatus to the point of destroying the state apparatus, of discreding the state apparatus . . . means forgetting that our apparatus is a Soviet apparatus, which is a state apparatus of a higher type then any other state apparatus in the world.[3]

Even more far-reaching in its implication than the idea of the Soviet state as 'a higher type of state apparatus', was the interpretation which Stalin offered at the next Party Congress in 1930:

We stand for the withering away of the state. At the same time we stand for the strengthening of the dictatorship of the proletariat, which is the mightiest and strongest state power that has ever existed. The highest development of state power with the object of preparing the conditions for the withering away of state power – such is the Marxist formula. Is this 'contradictory'? Yes, it is 'contradictory'. But this contradiction is bound up with life and it fully reflects Marx's dialectics.[4]

This thesis followed naturally from that of the intensification of the class struggle which Stalin had begun to expound a year before in his polemics with Bukharin's 'right deviation'. Just as, in dialectical fashion, the abolition of the state was accomplished by way of 'the highest development of state power', so the abolition of classes could, according to Stalin, be accomplished 'only by means of a stubborn class struggle, which under the dictatorship of the proletariat becomes ever fiercer'.[5] Thus, if the class struggle grew 'ever fiercer' in the period of the proletarian dictatorship, a powerful state – in fact, nothing less than 'the mightiest and strongest state power that has ever existed' – would be required to conduct that struggle on behalf of the proletariat.

During the next few years Stalin made a number of similar pronouncements. In 1933 he linked the intensification of the class struggle to the issue of 'capitalist encirclement' which was subsequently to become a main argument for the retention of the state even under communism:

The abolition of classes is not achieved by the subsiding of the class struggle, but by its intensification. The state will wither away, not as a result of a relaxation of the state power, but as a result of its utmost consolidation, which is necessary for the purpose of finally crushing the remnants of the dying classes and of organizing defence against the capitalist encirclement, which is far from being done away with as yet, and will not soon be done away with.[6]

The most significant change, however, came in 1936, on the occasion of the adoption of the new constitution. It will be recalled that in his speech on the draft constitution Stalin claimed three major accomplishments for Soviet society: first, the successful establishment of socialism – 'for the USSR socialism is something already achieved and won'; second, the abolition of the class struggle – Soviet society now consisted of 'two friendly classes', the workers and peasants, and one 'stratum', the intelligentsia; and third, the transformation of the dictatorship into a system of 'state guidance of society'.[7] The 1918 constitution had defined its objective as 'establishing socialism, under which there will be no division into classes and no state power' [article 9]. Stalin now pronounced the establishment of socialism with both classes (albeit non-antagonistic ones) and the state. In this novel perspective the state was no longer a class-repressive organ, 'a special machine of suppression', a 'cudgel' with which to beat down the resistance of the 'dying classes', but became instead a universal and constructive category, an essential instrument for the 'guidance' of a class-harmonious society.

It was a corollary of this conception of the state that the prospect of its extinction could be postponed into the distant and indeterminate future. Since the state was no longer linked to the class struggle it would not become redundant simply because the class struggle had ended. Already three years later, at the 18th Party Congress in 1939, Stalin affirmed that the state would be needed even under full communism, for as long, in fact, as 'capitalist encirclement' persisted.[8] In subsequent years the case for the preservation of the state was further elaborated by Stalin, most significantly in his last two theoretical writings, especially his 1950 essay on linguistics, which virtually reversed the Marxist teaching on the relationship between base and superstructure.[9] The point to be noted here is that the rehabilitation of the socialist state as a class-conciliatory and – for all practical purposes – permanent institution of Soviet society was inaugurated with the adoption of the 1936 constitution.

Together with the rehabilitation of the Soviet state came the rehabilitation of Soviet law. Stalin's affirmation, at the Eighth Congress of Soviets which adopted the 1936 constitution, of the 'principle that laws should be stable . . . we need stability of laws now more than ever', almost instantly became the signal for a veritable revolution in the official approach to the role of law in Soviet society.

The dominant legal doctrine of the preceding two decades had adhered strictly to orthodox Marxist conceptions: law, like the state, was a product of class society ('a command of the ruling class') and would wither away as classes were abolished and the society advanced on the road to communism. Soon after taking power the regime was compelled to modify its early millenarian aspirations for a system of 'revolutionary justice' based on little more than the 'revolutionary legal consciousness' of the new proletarian ruling class. Particularly during the period of NEP, between 1921 and 1928, the partial restoration of private enterprise in the economy brought with it a corresponding restoration of formal law. In December 1921 the 11th Party Conference called for the introduction of 'strict principles of revolutionary legality', including 'increased guarantees of the citizen's person and property'. And in the years that followed an extensive codification programme, which drew both on pre-revolutionary Russian and on several Western codes, was undertaken. But this return to law was, like NEP itself, viewed as a temporary 'retreat'; it would delay, but could not divert, progress toward the ideological objective – the creation of a society without law. Certainly it was not envisaged, at least not by the Marxist jurists who made up the Soviet legal 'establishment', that the new codes would form the building blocks of what later came to be called 'socialist law'. The very idea of 'socialist law' was anathema. Law was an essential component of the superstructure of class society; it could not develop further under social- ism, it could only wither away. 'Communism', wrote P.I. Stuchka, the first Chairman of the USSR Supreme Court, in a much-quoted passage, 'means not the victory of socialist law, but the victory of socialism over any law, since with the abolition of classes, with their antagonistic interests, law will die out altogether'.[10]

The law temporarily restored under NEP was regarded frankly as 'bourgeois' law, a temporary concession made necessary by the restora- tion of capitalist forms in the economy. E.B. Pashukanis, who was probably the best-known Soviet legal theorist of the time, developed the so-called 'exchange commodity theory of law' which sought to account for the essence of all law not merely as an instrument of class domination but as a reflection of the contractual relationships involved in commercial exchange. It was for this reason that law, according to Pashukanis, attained its highest development under capitalism. 'In bourgeois- capitalist society', he declared in 1930,

> the legal superstructure should have maximum immobility – maximum stability – because it represents a firm framework for the movement of the economic forces whose bearers are capitalist entrepreneurs. . . Among us it is different. We require that our legislation possess max- imum elasticity. We cannot fetter ourselves by any sort of system . . . We have a system of proletarian politics, but we have no need for any sort of juridical system of proletarian law . . . Revolutionary legality is for us a problem which is ninety-nine per cent political.

'Maximum elasticity' for proletarian legislation, proletarian politics in place of proletarian law, 'no need for any sort of juridical system' – it is not necessary to emphasize the extent of the shift implied by Stalin's affirmation, six years later, of 'the principle that laws should be stable'. Pashukanis, in the manner of the time, paid for his views with his life, and two decades of Marxist legal thinking were promptly denounced as legal 'nihilism' and displaced by a new orthodoxy, which exalted 'social- ist law' as an active, creative instrument in the construction of commun- ist society. In the words of Vyshinsky, who became the chief theoretician of 'socialist law', it was not under capitalism that law achieved full development – capitalism led to 'the decay of law and legality' – but precisely under socialism: 'History demonstrates that under socialism, on the contrary, law is raised to the highest level of development.'

That the rehabilitation of the Soviet state and Soviet law went hand in hand will seem natural to a Western reader. But in the Soviet Union of the 1930s this was by no means self-evident. In the perspective of Bolshevik doctrine a strong state did not imply a firm legal order, 'a living body of effective rules', in Sir Ernest Barker's telling phrase.[11] Long before Stalin, Lenin had also affirmed that the victorious proletariat needed a strong state; it would wither away because it would be adminis- tered directly by the broad mass of the people, but while it lasted it would be strong – and it would be based on violence. 'But when the state will be a proletarian state', he wrote on the eve of the revolution, 'when it will be an instrument of violence exercised by the proletariat against the bourgeoisie, we shall be fully and unreservedly in favour of a strong state power and of centralism.'[12] Thus, when Stalin advanced his thesis of the further strengthening of the state, the 'nihilist' Marxist jurists did not interpret this as necessarily requiring a corresponding strengthening of the law, for they did not view law as the sole or even the principal instrument of state control and regulation of social life. 'Revolutionary legality', to recall Pashukanis, was a problem that was 'ninety-nine per cent political'. Now, to note this is not, of course, to suggest that the repudiation of 'nihilism' in theory led directly to the abolition of lawlessness in practice. Judging by the course of events, the immediate consequences were, if anything, the opposite. Yet, it would also be true to say that such repudiation was an essential step if any 'space', however modest, was to be carved out for a functioning legal order.

The carving out of such a 'space' began immediately in the wake of the promulgation of the 1936 constitution, even as the purges ravaged Soviet society with unprecedented ferocity. The constitution itself contained a mandate for the enactment of all-union legal codes to replace the separate codes of the individual union republics, but of the legislation authorized under article 14(u) only the 1938 Law on Court Organization was enacted. The comprehensive re-codification of substantive and procedural law – in the form of republican codes based on all-union 'Fundamentals', in accordance with the amended article 14(u) – was not implemented until some twenty years later. But the new direction in legal policy was soon evident in theoretical works, in law text books, in university syllabuses, and increasingly, too, in court rulings. All of these displayed a new recognition of the crucial importance of order and discipline in civil life, of regularity and knowability, and therefore of law. N.V. Krylenko, then USSR Commissar of Justice, who in an earlier 'nihilist' stage had equated the courts with the secret police, now argued that the projected criminal code 'must be firmly based on the exact definition [of crime]'.[13] Similar emphasis on a positivist jurisprudence marked other legal writings on criminal and civil law. Perhaps the rationale of 'socialist law' was best expressed by Vyshinsky. 'Dictatorship of the proletariat', he wrote in 1938,

> does not signify anarchy and disorder but, on the contrary, strict and firm authority which operates upon strict principles, set out in the fundamental law of the proletarian state – the Soviet Constitution . . . The special character of social relationships during the transitional period makes it inconceivable to suppose that it is possible to solve the problems of restraint merely by administrative repression with the aid of extraordinary and exceptional measures and methods. The proletarian dictatorship acts also by legal means with the aid of

courts, of procedural rules and orders . . . Court and law are necessary to the proletariat, as are the criminal code, the civil code, and
codes of procedure.[14]

The burden of Vyshinsky's message, it will be noted, was not that
'exceptional measures' were no longer needed, but that they no longer
sufficed, that the dictatorship was required to act *'also* by legal means'.
Law would not replace 'administrative repression' but take its place
alongside it: law and force would jointly constitute the social regulation
mechanism of Soviet society. The idea of 'strict and firm authority'
operating on 'strict principles' set out in the 'fundamental law' was
clearly not to be interpreted too strictly. Nevertheless, there was also to
be room for law. Legal 'nihilism' might have been appropriate for
Lenin's dictatorship as 'rule based directly upon force and unrestricted
by any laws'; Stalin's version of the dictatorship as 'state guidance of
society' would be based on the 'principle that laws should be stable'.

The importance of the 1936 constitution in Soviet constitutional
development lay in this dual restoration of the state and the law. It was
not the specific contents of the constitutional provisions which signified
change. The new institutions established by the constitution did not
involve any substantive reforms in governmental practice, the introduction of direct, universal and secret elections did not alter the 'inputs' of
Soviet citizens into the political system, nor did the superficially impressive catalogue of fundamental rights affect the limits of individual freedom. In adopting a new 'fundamental law' for what was officially
declared a 'socialist' society, the regime acknowledged that such a society, like any other, required a state and that a state required law.

The 1977 constitution re-affirms this commitment and strengthens it
further. Not only are the salient features of the previous constitutional
structure preserved, but many of the new provisions constitutionalize
norms of subsidiary law enacted for the most part during the preceding
two decades. At the May CC plenum Brezhnev confirmed the conservative thrust of the 1977 text, when he declared that it retained 'many of the
basic provisions' of the 1936 constitution, 'for these continue to correspond to the essence of our system and to the pattern of our development', while various legislative acts of the past years formed 'the building blocks, as it were, of many articles of the constitution'.

The extent to which the 1977 constitution incorporates antecedent
constitutional and other legislative norms has already been noted in our
detailed discussion of the text. What has not been noted, and therefore
deserves examining briefly, is the extent to which it incorporates recent
innovations of other communist constitutions. For the 1977 constitution
is not only a conservative but also, in many respects, a derivative document. From 1960 onward all other communist states adopted new con-

stitutions or enacted far-reaching revisions of existing ones; and, as Brezhnev acknowledged at the May plenum, the Soviet text 'took account' of this recent constitutional experience of 'fraternal socialist countries'.[15] An exhaustive inventory of comparable provisions would lead far beyond the confines of the present study. But even a cursory review of some of the new provisions introduced in the post-Stalin constitutions will show that they anticipated many of the innovations of the 1977 Soviet constitution. Perhaps it may not even be too fanciful to suggest that in the opinion of some Soviet leaders, at least, a general revision of the 1936 constitution was warranted for no other reason than the need to keep in step with constitutional developments in the communist world.[16]

The single most striking innovation of the 1977 constitution, the explicit and prominent affirmation of the role of the Communist party, will be found in the constitutions of Yugoslavia [Introduction Part VIII], Czechoslovakia [article 4], Mongolia [preamble], Romania [articles 3 & 26], Bulgaria [article 1], Hungary [article 3], Cuba [article 5] and Albania [article 3]. A particularly conspicuous expression of the party's role is contained in both the Chinese constitutions of 1975 and 1978; apart from referring to the party several times in their respective preambles and asserting its status as 'the leading core of the whole Chinese people' in the second article of each text, both constitutions stipulate that the armed forces are subordinate to the party, that the head of the government is appointed on the recommendation of the party Central Committee and that it is the duty of Chinese citizens to support the party leadership [1975 – preamble paragraphs 1, 2, 4 & 7; articles 2, 13, 15, 16, 17 & 26; 1978 – preamble paragraphs 1, 2 & 4; articles 2, 19, 22 & 56]. (A notable change in the 1978 Chinese text is the omission of a reference to the party's leadership of the national legislature; also the recommendation of the party Central Committee is now only needed for the appointment of the Prime Minister and no longer for other members of the government [cf. 1975 – articles 16–17; 1978 – articles 20 & 22].) In sharp contrast to the general trend of recent communist constitutions, particularly both recent constitutions of its large neighbour, the North Korean constitution makes only a passing, and almost indirect, reference to the party [article 4].

The provisions relating to the mass social organizations, too, have precedents in other post-Stalin constitutions. The property of the social organizations is constitutionally recognized as part of socialist ownership (alongside state and cooperative property) in the constitutions of the GDR [article 10(1)] and Bulgaria [articles 14 & 20], and the latter – again in a manner similar to that of the Soviet constitution – affirms the priority of state ownership as 'a supreme form of socialist ownership' as well as the eventual drawing together of all forms of ownership 'into a unified ownership of all the people' [article 15]. The participation of social organizations, work collectives and individual citizens in the affairs of state and society is similarly acknowledged, not only in the Yugoslav constitutions which have been built around an explicit doctrine of social 'self-management', but also in several others. The constitutions of Czechoslovakia [article 5], Cuba [article 7] and Bulgaria [article 10(2)] even allude to the transfer of state functions to social organizations – a subject conspicuously avoided in the Soviet constitution. Moreover, whereas the latter refers somewhat vaguely to the function of social organizations in satisfying 'the diverse interests' of their members, the constitutions of Bulgaria [article 10(1)] and Cuba [article 7] declare explicitly that these organizations 'express and defend' or 'represent' the 'specific interests' of their members, while the constitutions of the GDR [article 44(1)], Hungary [article 4(3)] and Poland [article 85] confine similar formulations to the trade unions. For the participation of individual citizens, provisions are made in the constitutions of the GDR [articles 19(1), 21 & 42(1)], Hungary [article 68], Bulgaria [article 24] and Poland [article 86(1)].

Individual rights are generally given greater prominence in the post-Stalin constitutions. When the Soviet draftsmen decided to place the chapter on rights and duties in the forefront of the text they merely followed well-established precedent; only the new constitutions of Mongolia and China and the revised constitutions of Poland and Hungary still adhere to the Stalinist scheme and place the relevant chapters towards the end of their texts. For each of the novel rights granted in the 1977 Soviet constitution a parallel can be found in other communist constitutions. Thus the right to choice of profession is granted in the constitutions of Yugoslavia [article 160], Albania [article 44], the GDR [article 24(1)], Bulgaria [article 40(2)] and North Korea [article 56]; provisions for the protection of health and the family are included in the constitutions of Yugoslavia [articles 162 & 190], Albania [articles 47 & 49], the GDR [articles 35 & 38], Bulgaria [articles 38 & 47], Czechoslovakia [articles 23 & 26], Poland [articles 70 & 79] and North Korea [articles 58 & 63]; the right to housing is contained in the constitutions of Yugoslavia [article 164], and the GDR [article 37], and the right to the use of cultural facilities is vouchsafed in the constitutions of Poland [article 73] and the GDR [article 18]; freedom of scientific and artistic activity is granted in the constitutions of Yugoslavia [article 169], Hungary [article 60], Albania [article 51], China [article 52], Cuba [article 38], North Korea [article 60] and North Vietnam [article 34]; respect for and protection of the freedom and dignity of the individual are extended in the constitutions of the GDR [articles 19(2) & 30] and Bulgaria [article 50]; the right of citizens to submit proposals and complaints to official agencies is recognized in the constitutions of Mongolia [article 85], North Korea [article 55], North Vietnam [article 29], Cuba [article 62], China [article 55], Albania [article 59], and Romania [article 34], among others; judicial review of administrative acts is provided in the constitutions of Yugoslavia [article 216], Romania [articles 35 & 103] and Bulgaria [article 125(3)]; and the right to recover damages in tort from official agencies is extended in the constitutions of Yugoslavia [article 199], Romania [article 35], Bulgaria [article 56] and the GDR [article 104], but no longer in the constitution of North Korea [cf. article 55 and 1948 – article 25].

It will add perspective to the 1977 Soviet bill of rights if we note that several communist constitutions are rather more generous in their grant of individual rights than the latest Soviet constitution. Particularly interesting is the right to strike in the Chinese constitution [article 45] – also contained in the first GDR constitution of 1949 [article 14], but since withdrawn – and the rights to freedom of movement and domicile in the constitutions of Yugoslavia [article 183] and North Vietnam [article 28]. In some cases, too, the old-established political rights of expression, assembly and association are extended without the restriction, familiar from Soviet constitutions, requiring conformity with 'the interests of the toilers' or 'the aims of communist construction' [GDR – articles 27–9, Bulgaria – article 54, China – article 45, Poland – article 83, North Vietnam – article 25, North Korea – article 53]. Some of these constitutions, and also several others, include an omnibus clause, such as that introduced in the 1977 Soviet constitution [article 39], stipulating that rights and freedoms may not be exercised to the detriment of the public interest [Bulgaria – article 9(2), North Vietnam – article 38, Cuba – article 61, Hungary – article 54(2), Albania – article 39]. A notable exception is the Yugoslav constitution; not only is its bill of rights by far the most liberal of any communist constitution, but it is prefaced by a general clause declaring that the rights and freedoms granted therein are restricted by the interests of the community only insofar as the latter are constitutionally specified [article 153].

A further limitation on the exercise of individual rights, namely that arising from the link between rights and duties as formulated in article 59 of the Soviet constitution, is also found in the constitutions of Albania [article 39] and Hungary [article 54(2)]. While most of the communist constitutions confine themselves to the relatively modest range of individual duties already listed in the 1936 Soviet constitution, some anticipate several of the new duties introduced in the 1977 Soviet text. The protection of the natural environment is made the responsibility of the state, as well as of 'every citizen', in the constitutions of the GDR [article 15(2)] and Cuba [article 27], and the protection of both natural and cultural treasures is among the duties of citizens in the constitutions of Bulgaria [article 31], Hungary [article 69] and Yugoslavia [article 193]. The Cuban constitution includes the duty of parents to prepare their children for life in socialist society and the duty of children 'to respect and help their parents' [article 37]; the Bulgarian constitution obliges citizens to strengthen the country's 'political, economic and defensive might' and also to promote peace [articles 60 & 63(1)]; the Albanian constitution lists the preservation and strengthening of the socialist order among the duties of its citizens [article 60]; the North Korean constitution requires citizens to treat public property 'with care' [article 70]; and the Mongolian constitution establishes the duties of combatting 'anti-social' manifestations, educating children in the values of socialist society and furthering international friendship [article 89]. Indeed, the Mongolian constitution adds a few unique duties of its own, obliging the citizen to devote 'all his efforts and knowledge to the building of social-ism', 'to ensure the unity of personal and social interests and give priority to social and state interests', and to fulfill 'impeccably' not only his own civic duties but also to 'demand the same of others' [article 89]. The North Korean constitution for its part expects citizens to 'display a high degree of collectivist spirit' and also 'heighten their revolutionary vigilance against the manoeuvres of the imperialists' [articles 68 & 71]. But these, together with the clause of the Chinese constitution which, as mentioned above, requires citizens to support the party leadership, are the only instances in which other communist constitutions 'outbid' the formidable catalogue of duties of the 1977 Soviet text.

Another innovation of the latest Soviet constitution, at least when compared to its immediate predecessor, is the inclusion of foreign policy principles and objectives. This, too, is anticipated in all other constitu-tions except that of North Vietnam. Some proclaim their adherence to 'socialist internationalism' [Yugoslavia – Introduction Part VII; Bulgaria – article 5; Romania – article 14], others to 'proletarian internationalism' [North Korea – article 16, Albania – article 15, Mongolia – preamble, China – preamble], and one, the Cuban constitution, to both [preamble and article 12]. The Albanian and Chinese constitutions, in a transpar-ent, if indirect, reference to the Soviet Union, affirm their opposition to 'hegemony' or 'hegemonism' [Albania – article 15; China – preamble]. Other constitutions, with the notable exception of Romania, emphasize their special allegiance to the Soviet Union [GDR – article 6(2), Bulgaria – preamble, Poland – article 6(2), Czechoslovakia – preamble and article 14 (2), Hungary – preamble, Cuba – preamble and article 12(f)]. With varying emphasis the principles of peaceful coexistence, respect for the sovereignty of other nations, and friendship and cooperation with other 'socialist' states are affirmed in most of the constitutions. Support for movements of national liberation is declared in the constitutions of the GDR [article 6(3)], North Korea [article 16], Albania [article 15], Bulgaria [preamble] and Cuba [article 12(c)]; the Yugoslav constitution affirms the 'right to wage a liberation war' [Introduction Part VII], and the Cuban constitution 'recognizes the legitimacy of wars of national liberation' [article 12(c)].

The provisions relating to the structure and powers of the formal organs of government naturally differ somewhat. But it is worth pointing out

that several of the innovations introduced by the post-Stalin constitutions antedate those of the 1977 Soviet text. Thus, for example, the
concept of political system appears in the Czechoslovak constitution
[article 2(1) of Law No. 143], the Bulgarian constitution [article 5] and the
revised Polish constitution [chapter 1]; and democratic centralism is
specified as the basic principle of governmental organization in the
constitutions of the GDR [article 47], Czechoslovakia [article 18], Bulgaria [article 5], China [article 3] and North Korea [article 9]. The functioning of a Presidium of the Council of Ministers (or Government) is
recognized in the constitutions of the GDR [article 80(2)] and Czechoslovakia [article 137 (2) of Law No. 143], and that of a Defence Council (or
similar body) is recognized in the constitution of the GDR [articles 50 &
73], Bulgaria [article 93(10), Hungary [article 31(1)], Albania [article 89]
and Romania [article 77(8)]. (In Poland, Czechoslovakia and Yugoslavia
defence councils were created by legislative acts in 1967, 1969 and 1973
respectively.) The extension of the term of the central legislature to five
years is a feature of the constitutions of the GDR [article 54], Bulgaria
[article 6], Czechoslovakia [article 30(3) of Law No. 143], Romania [article
45], China [article 21] and Cuba [article 70]; and the functioning of
legislative commissions, if not always their right to legislative initiative,
is acknowledged in all communist constitutions except that of China
[GDR – article 61, Romania – article 52, Albania – article 71, Bulgaria –
article 76, Poland – articles 23(4) & 26, Hungary – article 25(1), Yugoslavia
– article 297, Czechoslovakia – article 45(1) of Law No. 143, North
Vietnam – article 57, Mongolia – article 28, North Korea – article 83, and
Cuba – articles 73(n) and 86 (ch)].

The above are but some of the new provisions of the 1977 Soviet constitution which may be said to have been modelled upon, or at least influ-
enced by, similar provisions in the recent constitutions of other communist states. There were others which the Soviet draftsmen did not
choose to incorporate in their own text. Some of these have already been
noted above. Others that might be mentioned are: the eventual abolition
of both the state and the constitution [Mongolia – article 94]; the
requirement that state officials 'serve the people' and also take part in
'productive' labour [China – article 16; Albania – article 9 ('in order to
prevent the creation of a privileged stratum')]; and the provision for a vote
of confidence in the government by the legislature [Yugoslavia –
article 360; Czechoslovakia – article 43 of Law No. 143]. It should also be
noted that the Soviet draftsmen, unlike their colleagues in some of the
other communist countries, were most careful to maintain the separation
of party and state: the 1977 text contains no provisions in its organizational sections reserving particular state functions to the top party
leader, such as can be found in the constitutions of Yugoslavia [article
321], China [article 19] and Albania [article 89]. Nor did they follow the
example of the Romanian and North Korean constitutions and replace

the collegial head of state by a single (presidential) executive, or that of
the GDR and Bulgarian constitutions which created a new plural ('council of state') executive but reserved specific powers for its chairman [GDR
– articles 52, 69, 71(1) & 75; Bulgaria – article 96]. (In all these cases
constitutional change was associated, as in the Soviet Union, with the
assumption of the post of head of state by the top leader of the party.)
But, we should stress once more, we have not here attempted anything
like a comprehensive comparison of communist constitutions; our purpose has been to draw attention to the imitative aspects of the latest
Soviet text and with this in view we have naturally focused on
similarities rather than on differences.

One basic and wholly original feature that distinguishes the 1977
constitution both from its 1936 predecessor and from all other communist constitutions is its ideological underpinning, as expressed in the
notions of 'developed socialist society' and its corresponding state form,
the 'all-people's state'. The periodization of the society's progress
towards full communism has at various times caused much controversy,
confusion and re-interpretation in the communist world. But until 1960,
when the second wave of communist constitution-making began, one
point at least was clear: the Soviet Union was the only country which had
officially completed the construction of 'socialism'. Accordingly, it was
also the only country which defined itself constitutionally as a 'socialist
state'. All others were denied the title 'socialist' and were generally
known as 'people's democracies'.[17] Their constitutional designations
differed somewhat: the most common was 'people's republic', but some
– China, North Korea and Czechoslovakia – inserted the adjective
'democratic', while the GDR – for reasons connected with the question of
German re-unification – identified itself simply as a 'democratic
republic'.

Beginning with the promulgation of the new Mongolian and Czechoslovak constitutions in July 1960, however, all communist countries
assumed the constitutional designation of 'socialist state' or 'socialist
republic', though only four – Czechoslovakia, Yugoslavia, Romania and
Albania – actually adopted the word 'socialist' in their official titles. The
result of this 'promotion' was to challenge the position of the Soviet
Union as the senior and 'most advanced' member of what now became
an increasingly uniform 'socialist' community.[18] If Soviet primacy was to
be preserved a new formula was clearly needed for its own constitutional
text. Presumably if the Soviet constitution had been enacted under
Khrushchev, the formula chosen would have reflected the claim that
Soviet society had embarked upon the stage of 'full-scale construction of
communism'. As it was, Khrushchev's successors prudently and tacitly
abandoned this particular stage and substituted that of 'developed
socialist society'. Apart from anything else, the 'full-scale construction of
communism' as elaborated in the 1961 Party Programme was tied to

some obviously unrealistic and uncomfortably specific target dates: amongst other things, it was envisaged that the USSR would surpass the US in per capita production by 1970 and complete the construction of communism 'in the main' by 1980.

The concept of 'developed socialist society' made its first appearance in the Declaration of the Moscow Meeting of Eighty-One Communist Parties in 1960, which acknowledged the unique status of the Soviet Union, as the only country 'successfully implementing the full-scale construction of communist society', and then went on: 'Other countries of the socialist camp are successfully laying the foundations of socialism, and some of them have already entered the period of the construction of developed socialist society.' The first intimation that Soviet doctrine was about to adopt the stage of 'developed socialist society' in place of the 'full-scale construction of communism' came some six years later in an article by a prominent scholar, F. M. Burlatskii, published in *Pravda* of 21 December 1966 under the title 'On the Construction of Developed Socialist Society'. In the following year, on the occasion of the 50th anniversary of the October revolution, Brezhnev referred to 'the developed socialist society that has been built in our country'. From then on the concept, in this or a slightly modified version ('mature' or 'advanced socialist society') was increasingly applied to the Soviet Union in ideological writings, though it was only after the 24th Party Congress in 1971 that it entered Soviet doctrine as a fully-fledged, 'objectively necessary' stage on the road to communism. Whether 'developed socialist society' would lead directly into communism or pass through a further self-contained stage of 'the direct construction of communism' (or 'the construction of the foundations of communism') remains a matter of scholastic dispute among Soviet ideologues. In either view, the injection of the stage of 'developed socialist society' served the purpose of covering the retreat from the utopian goals of the 1961 Programme and at the same time re-establishing the necessary distance between the Soviet Union and other communist countries. All the latter were 'socialist', some had begun to build the 'developed socialist society', but only the Soviet Union had completed the process, only Soviet society *was* a 'developed socialist society'. The point, as we have seen, is emphatically made in the preamble of the 1977 constitution.[19]

These concerns may seem trivial to a Western student of constitutions. But Soviet leaders have always used solemn declarations of all kinds, including constitutions, to communicate a spirit of accomplishment, of stages passed and targets reached, of inexorable progress along a pre-ordained path. Such documents determine the ideological dimension of the proper 'pecking order' in the communist world and are therefore possessed of considerable political significance. Certainly, Soviet spokesmen lost no time in pointing out that theirs was the constitution of 'the world's first state of developed socialism'.

The draftsmen of the 1977 constitution opted for Khrushchev's 'all-people's state' as being appropriate to a society of 'developed socialism'. Again, the objective was to make a clear distinction between the Soviet Union and other communist states. The latter, in Soviet doctrine at least, were still 'dictatorships of the proletariat', though only some of them declared themselves as such in their constitutions – China [article 1], Albania [article 2], North Korea [article 10] and, surprisingly enough in this company, Yugoslavia [Introduction Part IV].[20] Again, the adoption of the concept was also attended by considerable vacillation and not a little confusion. For one thing, there were signs, soon after Khrushchev's dismissal, that the concept was being discarded in the Soviet Union.[21] For another, several other communist states – Czechoslovakia, the GDR and Bulgaria – began to lay claim to it. But these uncertainties were definitively resolved by 1971 when the Soviet party's chief ideologue, M.A. Suslov, authoritatively established the 'all-people's state' as the 'political superstructure' corresponding to 'developed socialist society'.[22] Once it thus became clear that Soviet doctrine had decided to appropriate the concept for the Soviet Union the spokesmen of other communist countries backtracked on their own claims to it.[23]

As already noted, the 'all-people's state' was a Khrushchevian legacy. It was officially introduced into Soviet doctrine by the 1961 Party Programme and was then widely hailed as an important addition to the Marxist teaching. In fact, of course, it was an entirely un-Marxist construct, as was quickly pointed out by Chinese and other critics from the 'left'.[24] Nor was it as innovative as Soviet spokesmen liked to make out. The advent of the state of friendly classes had, after all, been announced by Stalin as long ago as 1936 and it is difficult to accept the 'all-people's state' as more than a verbal amplification of that notion. The 1961 Programme affirmed that the 'all-people's state' – like most other states in modern times – regarded itself as 'an organ expressing the interests and will of the people as a whole'. This is essentially what Stalin had asserted for his own class-friendly state – 'democracy for the working people, i.e., democracy for all'.[25]

Such novelty as could justly be claimed for the 'all-people's state' derived entirely from its association with the stage of 'full-scale construction of communism'. The 'all-people's state' was the political superstructure of a society that had started on the last stage of the process of building communism, and the withering away of that superstructure, envisaged as the progressive transfer of state functions to social organizations, was a built-in component of that process. In the words of the 1961 Party Programme: 'As socialist democracy develops, the organs of state power will gradually be transformed into organs of social self-government.' True, this prognosis was hedged in by various caveats: the state would not disappear before the advent of full communism, nor would it be weakened while shedding its functions. Nevertheless, the mere revival of the withering-away theme constituted a major break with previous orthodoxy.[26] Just how far Khrushchev intended to proceed with his initiative – among others the organs of popular law enforcement (notably comrades' courts and 'anti-parasite' assemblies) were set up at this time – remains an open question. The point of interest for our purposes is that the 'all-people's state' originated in Soviet doctrine as a transitional category: the appearance of the concept was firmly linked to the prospective disappearance of its empirical referent.

This, most decidedly, is not how the concept is applied in the 1977 constitution. There is no hint in the constitution of the state's eventual disappearance, and only a single reference – added almost as an afterthought in the final version of the twelfth paragraph of the preamble – to the development of 'social communist self-administration' in the context of the *future* classless society. It is surely no accident that the comprehensive list of tasks set for the 'all-people's state' in the same paragraph makes no mention of the transfer of state functions to social organizations. Nor, of course, is this omission unconnected with the fact that the 'all-people's state' has been separated from the society of the 'full-scale construction of communism' and attached to that of 'developed socialism'. The insertion of the latter into the developmental sequence signifies not only that the launching of 'full-scale construction of communism' had been premature but also that Soviet society has now reached a relatively stable plateau in its progress towards communism. Soviet commentators generally, including Brezhnev in his speech on the constitution in October 1977, carefully point out that 'developed socialist society' is 'a relatively long stage in the development from capitalism to communism'. One may perhaps argue that it makes more sense to enact a new constitution for a state spanning 'a relatively long stage of development' rather than, as Khrushchev had apparently intended, for one engaged in its own self-effacement in the course of the 'full-scale construction of communism'. The fact remains, however, that in adopting the 'all-people's state' for their new constitution, the present leaders of the Soviet Union have shorn the concept of the one feature that had originally distinguished it from the class-friendly state of the 1936 constitution.[27]

Indeed, the Soviet state's rehabilitation as 'a new type of state', with an essential role in the construction of both socialism and communism, is now solemnly affirmed in the opening paragraph of the preamble – the first such affirmation in a Soviet constitution and therefore something of a high point in the tortuous history of the state's doctrinal vindication. Other writings of the Brezhnev era, too, bear a remarkable resemblance to those of late Stalinism. Now, as then, the state is described as 'the main instrument in the transformation and perfection of social relations', as a 'creative force', whose role will expand rather than diminish as the society marches into the future.[28] Moreover, a very distinctive feature of contemporary Soviet theorizing about the state is its concern with the 'scientific management' of society, with the so-called 'scientific–technical revolution' and its implications for information processing and rational decision-making. The complex problems of administering the advanced economy and society of 'developed socialism', it is argued, can only be solved by a professional state apparatus equipped with an appropriate organizational and technological capacity for centralized planning and control.[29] 'Developed socialist society', in other words, requires a highly developed socialist state. The 1977 constitution was not only designed for the 'all-people's state'. What is equally obvious – and rather more to the point – is that it was designed for what might more appropriately be termed the 'all-embracing state'.[30]

In his speech on the constitution at the October session of the Supreme Soviet, Brezhnev referred to the challenge facing all socialist states as that of 'mastering the difficult art of organizing the entire life of society along socialist lines'. If there is a single theme running through the text of the 1977 constitution it is that of 'organizing the entire life of society'. On the same occasion Brezhnev identified the new constitution as 'the law of life of developed socialist society', and 'The Law of Our Lives', was also the heading under which *Pravda* published its daily page of readers' contributions to the 'nationwide discussion' of the draft constitution. These phrases are more than rhetorical flourishes. They express a view of the constitution as that 'of a society which has to deal with *all-embracing* creative tasks'.[31]

Indeed, it is only a slight exaggeration to say that the 1977 constitution encompasses the whole of social life. The specificity and concreteness with which individual areas of life are regulated in the text varies but virtually no area goes unmentioned. We need not recapitulate the individual provisions testifying to the breadth of the state's concerns. It will suffice to recall that they range from 'control over the measure of labour and consumption' to 'moral and aesthetic upbringing'. Such a breadth of state concerns naturally devolves a corresponding burden of obligations upon the state's citizens. This, too, is spelled out in the constitution, though again with varying specificity and concreteness, and now includes the duty of citizens 'to make rational use' of the garden plots 'granted' them, as well as the duty of parents 'to raise worthy members of socialist society'.

Soviet jurists used to debate whether the constitution was the 'fundamental law' of the state alone or of society as a whole. If there was room for argument on this score in the past, the matter is clearly no longer debatable. And this not only because the character of the 1977 constitution as 'the law of life of developed socialist society' has been authoritatively established by Brezhnev himself, but because the issue has become irrelevant. It assumed a distinction between state and society that is manifestly repudiated by the present text. The all-embracing state recognizes no boundaries; state and society are indistinguishable.

In an article published abroad, a Ukrainian dissident described the 1977 draft constitution as 'from beginning to end . . . a lie'.[32] Similar, if less pungent, judgements were pronounced by other dissidents and also in Western press comments. The assertion that the constitution is nothing but a lie was obviously not intended to be taken literally – Moscow *is* the capital of the USSR [article 172]; on the other hand, to assert that it is nothing but the truth would be equally exaggerated – all power does *not* belong to the people [article 2]. Probably, if one were to balance the 'weight' of arguably true and false statements contained in the constitution, the scales would come down heavily on the side of the latter. But this also applies to earlier Soviet constitutions. If the 1977 constitution is compared to its predecessors, and especially to its immediate predecessor, it stands out as a much more truthful document – more truthful, because it acknowledges the extent of the state's usurpation of society.

This does not mean that the actual extent of this usurpation has increased over the years. It is Stalinist Russia that is generally taken as paradigmatic of modern totalitarian rule, and it is no part of the above argument that public power under Brezhnev is in some sense 'more all-embracing' or 'more total' than it was under Stalin.[33] Apart from being semantically awkward, such an argument would have to be based on other evidence than can validly be adduced from a comparison of constitutional texts alone. Rather, the argument is that the scope of public power has been brought more fully within the purview of the 1977 constitution, and that, as a result, the latter reflects the reality of the all-embracing state more accurately than did earlier texts.

The significance of this, in Soviet conditions, is symbolic rather than real. It testifies to the Soviet leadership's intent to invest the aspirations and practices of the all-embracing state with the dignity of the constitution, and thereby with legitimacy and stability. By the same token, it records the belief of the Soviet leadership that these aspirations and practices have been sufficiently tested to be made permanent and sufficiently accepted to be embodied in public law.

In a way, of course, the expansion of the ambit of the constitution may also be taken as signifying the expansion of law in Soviet society – but not in some Western 'rule of law' or *Rechtsstaat* sense. The nearest that Soviet law comes to Western tradition is to the law of the Prussian *Polizeistaat*, i.e. the law of a state which seeks to provide orderly and predictable government and, to that end, imposes an elaborate system of rules upon officials and citizens alike; but also one which postulates an identity of interests between the state and its citizens, which grants the citizen no inherent rights against the state, which leaves the arbitrary conduct of its officials unsanctioned whenever such conduct conforms to 'reasons of state' and, above all, one which places no restraints whatever upon the state's supreme rulers.[34]

Some observers in the West have interpreted the last clause of article 6, which requires all party organizations to operate 'within the framework of the constitution', as an attempt to subordinate the party to the constitution.[35] If correct, this would indeed portend a very profound change. For this reason precisely it seems exceedingly doubtful that this single clause, added only in the final version of the text, can bear the weight of such interpretation. It is much more likely, as another commentator has suggested, that it was inserted in response to Western criticisms of article 6 in its draft form.[36] If the article is read as a whole it illustrates the point made above: it constitutionalizes the party's prerogative and in so doing removes the façade behind which its leaders exercise their hegemony over Soviet society.

Neither this nor any other provision of the constitution, nor any of the many official and semi-official commentaries, nor, more importantly, Soviet practice since the enactment of the constitution, gives ground for the belief that the country's leaders are ready to submit themselves to the authority of the constitution. Soviet government remains a government of men and not of laws, even though it is a government of men who have come to appreciate the value of positive law in 'mastering the difficult art of organizing the entire life of society'. The basic difference between Western constitutionalism, which regards the constitution as the legal embodiment of a mechanism enabling society to control its power holders, and Soviet 'constitutionalism', which regards the constitution as the legal embodiment of a mechanism enabling the power holders to control their society, is as valid today as it was at the beginning of Soviet statehood.

Notes

1 K. Loewenstein, *Political Power and the Governmental Process*, Chicago, 1957, p. 140.
2 After the Bolshevik revolution Lenin became extremely non-committal in regard to the timing of the state's withering away. In March 1918 he rejected Bukharin's attempt to include a provision regarding the future course of the proletarian state in the Party Programme because it would 'distort the historical perspective'. (V.I. Lenin, *Collected Works*, 45 vols, Moscow, 1960–70, vol. 27, p.148.) In July 1919 he said in a lecture devoted to the subject of the state that it would only disappear 'when the possibility of exploitation no longer exists anywhere in the world'. (ibid., vol. 29, p. 488).
3 J.V. Stalin, *Works*, 13 vols, Moscow, 1952–5, vol. 10, p. 327.
4 ibid., vol. 12, p. 381.
5 J.V. Stalin, *Problems of Leninism*, Moscow 1954, p. 313. On the same occasion Stalin also revived an old dispute between Lenin and Bukharin on the need for a state machine after the proletarian revolution.

6 ibid., p. 538.
7 It may be added that two years earlier Stalin had still identified socialism with the abolition of classes and not merely the abolition of class antagonisms: The Seventeenth Party Conference [in 1932] declared that we are heading for the formation of a classless society. It goes without saying that a classless society cannot come of itself, spontaneously, as it were. It has to be achieved and built by the efforts of all the working people, by strengthening the organs of the dictatorship of the proletariat, by intensifying the class struggle, by abolishing classes, by eliminating the remnants of the capitalist classes, and in battles both internal and external.
   The point is clear, one would think. (ibid., p.631).
8 ibid., p. 797.
9 J.V. Stalin, *Marxism and Problems of Linguistics*, Moscow, 1952, and *Economic Problems of Socialism in the USSR*, Moscow, 1952.
10 This and the succeeding two quotations are taken from H.J. Berman, *Justice in the USSR*, Cambridge, Mass., rev. edn, 1966, pp. 26, 42 & 54.
11 E. Barker, *Principles of Social and Political Theory*, London, 1963, p. 89.
12 'Can the Bolsheviks Retain State Power', in V.I. Lenin, *On the State Apparatus*, Moscow, 1969, p. 76.
13 Quoted in R. Sharlet, 'Stalinism and Soviet Legal Culture', in R.C. Tucker, ed., *Stalinism: Essays in Historical Analysis*, New York, 1977, p. 172. In a work published in 1934 Krylenko had written: 'To a certain extent the courts must be like the *Cheka*, an instrument of terrorism. The courts and the *Cheka*, being agencies of the government authority, perform the same tasks.' (Quoted in V. Gsovski and K. Grzybowski, eds., *Government, Law and Courts in the Soviet Union and Eastern Europe*, 2 vols, London, 1959, vol. 2, p. 923.) Krylenko was purged in 1938 for his earlier 'nihilist' views and shot in 1940.
14 A.Y. Vyshinsky, ed., *The Law of the Soviet State*, New York, 1948, pp. 48 & 50.
15 Brezhnev's acknowledgement was, in fact, somewhat ambivalent. Having introduced constitutional developments in the communist world as 'another factor of great importance', he then went on to mention the recent constitutions of Bulgaria, Cuba, the GDR 'and a number of other socialist countries', and ended with the low-key declaration: 'A number of provisions in these constitutions are of interest to us and have not been ignored.'
16 Of the communist states, China and Albania clearly do not fall under Brezhnev's category of 'fraternal socialist countries'; nevertheless, for the sake of completeness – and if only because their constitutions might be expected to have served as negative models for the Soviet draftsmen – they will be considered below. The following communist constitutions were enacted, or substantially revised, from 1960 onward: Vietnam – the first constitution (of North Vietnam) was adopted on 1 January 1960 (following the unification of the country a constitutional commission was formed in 1976 to draft a new constitution and on 15 August 1979 a draft text was made public); Mongolia – a third constitution was adopted on 6 July 1960; Czechoslovakia – a second constitution was adopted on 11 July 1960, but following the Prague Spring of 1968 many of its provisions were replaced by a series of constitutional laws, most notably Law No. 143 of 27 October 1968; Yugoslavia – a third constitution was adopted on 7 April 1963 and replaced by a fourth constitution on 21 February 1974; Romania – a third constitution was adopted on 20 August 1965 and revised on 8 April 1974; GDR – a second constitution was adopted on 6

April 1968 and revised on 7 October 1974; Bulgaria – a second constitution was adopted on 16 May 1971; Hungary – the original 1949 constitution was completely revised on 19 April 1972; North Korea – a second constitution was adopted on 27 December 1972; China – a second constitution was adopted on 17 January 1975 and replaced by a third constitution on 5 March 1978; Cuba – a constitution, replacing the Fundamental Law of 1959, was adopted on 15 February 1976; Poland – the second (1952) constitution was revised on 16 February 1976; Albania – a second constitution was adopted on 28 December 1976. English texts of most of the constitutions are in A.P. Blaustein and G.H. Flanz, eds., *Constitutions of the Countries of the World,* Dobbs Ferry, N.Y., 1971–; translations of the 1976 Albanian and 1978 Chinese constitutions will be found, respectively, in *Review of Socialist Law,* 1977, no. 3, pp. 227–68 and *Peking Review,* 1978, no.11, pp. 5–14. For some of the earlier constitutional texts see J.F. Triska, ed., *Constitutions of the Communist Party-States,* Stanford, Calif., 1968.

17 The Soviet Union, of course, had adopted the title 'socialist' from the outset.

18 To date, the constitution of North Vietnam alone still identifies the country as 'a people's democratic state' [article 2].

19 Typical of the manner in which this topic has been treated in Soviet writings is the following reference to 'the experience of the Soviet Union, where we have already built a developed socialist society, and that of a number of fraternal countries, which have laid (or are laying) the foundations of socialism and have gone over (or are going over) to building developed socialism'. (P. Demichev, 'Developed Socialism – A Stage on the Way to Communism', *World Marxist Review,* 1973, no. 1, p. 6. The article, by a candidate member of the Politburo and then secretary of the Central Committee of the CPSU, was the first of a series on 'developed socialism' by representative authors from various communist countries published in this journal during 1973.)

20 The final version of the Yugoslav constitution unexpectedly introduces a statement defining its 'socialist self-management democracy' as 'a special form of the dictatorship of the proletariat'.

21 See R.E. Kanet, 'The Rise and Fall of the "All-People's State": Recent Changes in the Soviet Theory of the State', *Soviet Studies,* 1968, no. 1, pp. 81–93.

22 'KPSS – Partiya tvorcheskogo marksizma', *Kommunist,* 1971, no. 14, p. 19.

23 The Czechoslovak constitution of 1960 still contains in Part I of its preamble a statement to the effect that the state 'has become a people's organization in the truest sense of the word – a socialist state'. Similarly, the 1971 Programme of the Bulgarian party claims that the state 'grows more and more into a political organization of the whole people'. But the country's new constitution, enacted in the same year, remains that of a proletarian dictatorship; see the article by the Bulgarian legal scholar, B. Spasov, 'Konstitutsiya pobedivshego sotsializma', *Sovetskoe gosudarstvo i pravo,* 1972, no. 1, p. 126.

24 The task of Marxist critics was made all the easier by the fact that the founding fathers had explicitly recorded their disapproval of the term 'people's state' in their polemics with the German social democrats. In a famous passage of his *Critique of the Gotha Programme,* Marx wrote:

The question then arises: what transformation will the state undergo in communist society? In other words, what social functions will remain in existence that are analogous to present functions of the state? This question can only be answered scientifically, and one does not get a flea-hop nearer to the problem by a thousandfold combination of the word people with the word state.

Between capitalist and communist society lies the period of the revolutionary transformation of the one into the other. There corresponds to this also a political transition period in which the state can be nothing but *the revolutionary dictatorship of the proletariat.*

And Engels, in a letter to A. Bebel, added the following comment:

As, therefore, the state is only a transitional institution which is used in the struggle, in the revolution, in order to hold down one's adversaries by force, it is pure nonsense to talk of a free people's state: so long as the proletariat still *uses* the state, it does not use it in the interests of freedom but in order to hold down its adversaries, and as soon it becomes possible to speak of freedom the state as such ceases to exist. (K. Marx/F. Engels, *Selected Works*, 2 vols, Moscow, 1951, II, 30 and 39; emphases in the original.)

25 Stalin, *Problems of Leninism*, p. 700. Nor did the 1961 Programme affect the 'leading role' of the working class: 'Since the working class is the foremost and best organized force of Soviet society, it plays a leading role also in the period of the full-scale construction of communism.'

26 The first signs that Khrushchev intended to revive the theme of the state's withering away appeared in early 1958 in two interviews with Western correspondents (*The Times*, 1 February 1958 and *Le Figaro*, 19 March 1958). In April of that year Khrushchev took up the subject in his speech to the 13th Komsomol Congress and at the 21st Party Congress, in 1959, he elaborated on it in some detail.

27 It is customary for Soviet leaders to seek support for their ideological formulae in Lenin's voluminous writings and Brezhnev followed this tradition in regard to 'developed socialism'. At the 24th Party Congress he referred to 'the developed socialist society of which Lenin spoke in 1918 as the future of our country', and he made a similarly vague allusion to Lenin in his speech on the constitution in October 1977. What Brezhnev did not mention was that Lenin had identified 'developed' socialism with communism and the abolition of the state. Opposing some of Bukharin's proposals for the Party Programme (see p. 292, note 2), Lenin spoke in 1918 of 'socialist society in its developed form, i.e. communism . . . where the state will cease to exist'. (Lenin, *Coll. Works*, vol. 27, p. 147.)

28 A. Kositsyn, 'Gosudarstvo razvitogo sotsialisticheskogo obshchestva', *Kommunist*, 1973, no. 6, p. 63; see also the same author's article in *Pravda*, 26 September 1975. These had been standard descriptions of the state in the last years of Stalin's rule and even for some time thereafter. See, e.g., Ts. Stepanyan, 'Sovetskoe gosudarstvo – glavnoe orudye postroeniya kommunizma v SSSR', *Bolshevik*, 1949, no. 14, pp. 10–26; A.S. Fedoseyev, *Tvorcheskaya rol' sovetskogo gosudarstva i prava v postroienii sotsialisticheskogo i kommunisticheskogo obshchestva*, Moscow, 1951, esp. pp. 45–8; A.I. Sobolev, 'Velikaya sozidatel'naya rol' Sovetskogo gosudarstva, *Voprosy filosofii*, 1954, no. 5, pp. 28–42.

29 See also A.B. Evans, 'Developed Socialism in Soviet Ideology', *Soviet Studies*, 1977, no. 3, pp. 409–28; and R.F. Laird, ' "Developed" Socialist Society and the Dialectics of Development and Legitimation in the Soviet Union', *Soviet Union*, 1977, no. 1, pp. 130–49.

30 See also P. O'Brien, 'Constitutional Totalitarianism', *Survey*, 1978, no. 3, pp. 70–80.

31 B. Ponomarev, 'International Significance of the New Constitution of the USSR', *World Marxist Review*, 1978, no. 2, p. 3 (emphasis added). The author is a candidate member of the CPSU Politburo and secretary of its Central Committee.

32 *Le Monde*, 7 July 1977; *Die Welt*, 19 July 1977.

33 The concept of totalitarianism has in recent years become controversial, but if there is a common thread running through most definitions it is the notion of totality, which forms the root of the word 'totalitarianism', i.e. of the unlimited expansion of public power. There is by now a vast literature on the subject. I have stated my own view in *The Totalitarian Party: Party and People in Nazi Germany and Soviet Russia*, Cambridge, 1974, pp. 1–5 and 263–71.

34 See B. Chapman, *Police State*, London, 1970, esp. pp. 17–19.

35 J.N. Hazard, 'A Constitution for "Developed Socialism" ', in Barry *et al.*, *Soviet Law After Stalin*, Part II, p. 14; also V. Chalidze, 'Human Rights in the New Soviet Constitution', in ibid. p. 71.

36 Yu. Luryi, 'The New Constitution of the USSR, From Draft to Law: An Analysis of the Changes Adopted', in ibid. p. 39.

Select Bibliography

Barry, D.D., Ginsburgs, G. and Maggs, P.B., eds, *Soviet Law after Stalin* (Part II: Social Engineering through Law), Aalphen aan den Rijn, 1978.

Berg, G.P. van den, 'Elements of Continuity in Soviet Constitutional Law', in W.E. Butler, ed., *Russian Law: Historical and Political Perspectives*, Leyden, 1977.

Brunner, G., 'The Functions of Communist Constitutions: An Analysis of Recent Constitutional Developments', *Review of Socialist Law*, 1977, no. 3, pp. 121–53.

Dobrin, S., 'The New Soviet Constitution', *Transactions of the Grotius Society*, 1962, vol. 22, pp. 99–116.

Feldbrugge, F.J.M., ed., *The Constitutions of the USSR and the Union Republics*, Aalphen aan den Rijn, 1979.

Gilison, J., 'Khrushchev, Brezhnev and Constitutional Reform', *Problems of Communism*, 1972, no. 5, pp. 69–78.

Ginsburgs, G., 'A Khrushchev Constitution for the Soviet Union: Projects and Prospects', *Osteuropa – Recht*, 1962, no. 3, pp. 191–214.

Kovacs, I., *New Elements in the Evolution of Socialist Constitutions*, Budapest, 1968.

Lapenna, I., 'Marxism and the Soviet Constitutions', *Conflict Studies*, April 1979, no. 106.

Nove, A., 'Some Aspects of Soviet Constitutional Theory', *Modern Law Review*, 1949, no. 1, pp. 12–38.

O'Brien, P., 'Constitutional Totalitarianism', *Survey*, 1978, no. 3, pp. 70–80.

Osakwe, C., 'The Common Law of Constitutions of the Communist-Party States', *Review of Socialist Law*, 1972, no. 3, pp. 155–217.

'The Theories and Realities of Modern Soviet Constitutional Law: An Analysis of the 1977 Constitution', *University of Pennsylvania Law Review*, 1979, no. 5, pp. 1350–437.

Schneider, E., 'The Discussion of the New All-Union Soviet Constitution in the USSR', *Soviet Studies*, 1979, no. 4, pp. 523–41.

Sharlet, R., *The New Soviet Constitution of 1977: Analysis and Text*, Brunswick, Ohio, 1978.

Shtromas, A., 'The Legal Position of Soviet Nationalities and their Territorial Units according to the 1977 Constitution of the USSR', *Russian Review*, 1978, no. 3, pp. 265–72.

Starr, J.R., 'New Constitution of the Soviet Union', *American Political Science Review*, 1936, no. 4, pp. 1143–52.

Triska, J.F., ed., *Constitutions of the Communist Party-States*, Stanford, Calif., 1968.

Uibopuu, H.-J., 'Soviet Federalism under the New Soviet Constitution', *Review of Socialist Law*, 1979, no. 2, pp. 171–85.

Name Index

The main state institutions, together with the Communist party, are to be found in the subject index. Each has a cross-reference from the name index.

Subject Index

administration: citizen's right of participation in, 197, 243; illegalities of, 123, 127–8, 244; judicial review of, 122–3, 198, 292–3; public, 56

agriculture, 140–1, 188–90; Ministry of, 109; state ownership in, 140, 188–9, 236

all-people's state, 3, 84, 174, 175, 181, 183, 233, 234, 286, 288–9, 290

All-Russian Congress of Soviets, *see* Congress of Soviets, All-Russian

All-Union Congress of Soviets, *see* Congress of Soviets, All-Union

amendment of, and amendments to, constitutions, *see* constitutions

amnesty, right of granting, 33, 62, 72, 148

analogy, doctrine of, 128–9

anti-parasite legislation, 131, 289

anti-religious (atheist) propaganda, freedom of, 13, 28, 116, 119, 156

anti-semitism, 120

arbitration tribunals, state, 216, 265

areas, national (autonomous), *see* national areas *and* autonomous areas

army: Red, 26, 45, 90, 157, 158; Soviet, 90, 239

assembly, freedom of, 13, 28, 116, 119, 120, 156, 196, 243, 274, 283

assessors, people's, 124, 154, 215–16, 263–4

association, freedom of, 13, 28, 116, 117, 120, 156, 197, 243, 274, 283

asylum, right of, 13, 29, 116, 157, 195, 241

'autonomization' plan, 48

autonomous (*previously* national) areas, 201, 249–50, 254, 262, 263, 265; *see also* nationalities, minority

'autonomous regional unions' (of RSFSR), 19, 28

autonomous regions, 55, 91, 153–4, 201, 249–50, 262; formation of, 89; judicial institutions of, 153–4, 263–5; representation on Council of Nationalities, 50, 53, 63, 144–5, 254; of RSFSR, 45; Statute on the, 91; *see also* nationalities, minority

autonomous republics (ASSR), 55, 91–2, 152–4, 201, 204, 248–9, 262; constitutions of, 91, 148, 152, 249, 262; formation of, 88–9, 142; judicial institutions of, 124, 153–4, 263–5; organs of government, 94, 152, 205, 250, 261, 262; representation on Council of Nationalities, 50, 53, 63, 144–5, 253–4; in RSFSR, 45, 50; *see also* nationalities, minority

bar, the, 216, 265

Bolshevik party, 2, 16, 18–19, 20, 22, 52, 275; doctrine of state and law, 4, 18, 275; nationality policy, 45–9, 54–5; and 1918 constitution, 9–11; Programme (1903), 14, 46, 123; and soviets, 15, 22; *see also* Communist party

'bourgeois parliamentarism', 94, 95

budgetary law, 38–9, 61

capitalism, 59, 82, 192, 232, 278, 295 n. 24

'capitalist encirclement', 60, 191, 276, 277

capital punishment, 102, 131–2

CC, *see* Central Committee

CEC, *see* Central Executive Committee

Central Committee (CC), 4, 21, 22, 105, 106, 107, 178–9; decrees on soviets, 110, 111; and 1918 constitution, 9, 10; and 1936 constitution, 79, 80, 85; and 1977 constitution, 177, 178–9, 273

Central Executive Committee (CEC), All-Russian, 9–10, 15, 17–18, 20,